Playing with Fire

Playing with Fire

The Looming War with China over Taiwan

JOHN F. COPPER

PRAEGER SECURITY INTERNATIONAL
Westport, Connecticut • London

Library of Congress Cataloging-in-Publication Data

Copper, John Franklin.
  Playing with fire : the looming war with China over Taiwan / John F. Copper.
    p. cm.
  Includes bibliographical references and index.
  ISBN 0-275-98888-0 (alk. paper)
  1. United States—Foreign relations—China.   2. China—Foreign relations—
United States.   3. United States—Foreign relations—Taiwan.   4. Taiwan—
Foreign relations—United States.   5. China—Foreign relations—Taiwan.
6. Taiwan—Foreign relations—China.   I. Title.
  E183.8.C5C66 2006
    327.73051—dc22   2006009798

British Library Cataloguing in Publication Data is available.

Library of Congress Catalog Card Number: 2006009798
ISBN: 0-275-98888-0
First published in 2006

Praeger Security International, 88 Post Road West, Westport, CT 06881
An imprint of Greenwood Publishing Group, Inc.
www.praeger.com

Printed in the United States of America

The paper used in this book complies with the
Permanent Paper Standard issued by the National
Information Standards Organization (Z39.48-1984).

10 9 8 7 6 5 4 3 2 1

Contents

Preface

In the spring of 1996, the Chinese People's Liberation Army fired missiles with live warheads at targets close to Taiwan's shores during a presidential election campaign. Chinese leaders charged that the election was "foreign inspired to separate Taiwan from China."

The United States reacted quickly; President Clinton ordered two aircraft carrier battle groups clad with nuclear weapons to the scene. The consequence was a face-off between the world's only superpower and the world's preeminent rising power. Observers feared war.

Though the crisis subsided, Washington-Beijing relations were permanently scarred. The triangular Washington-Taipei-Beijing relationship became hypersensitive; small matters created tension, and observers talked of the inevitability of war between the United States and China over Taiwan.

This situation had a background. After the Tiananmen massacre in 1989, the United States no longer held China in high esteem. With the subsequent collapse of the Soviet bloc, Washington no longer needed Beijing; good relations with China had been built upon a common enemy.

Meanwhile Congress gained influence in the making of China policy. Heretofore this responsibility had belonged to a select few individuals, so Congress knew little about the constraints upon decision makers in Beijing and strongly favored democratic Taiwan over authoritarian China.

In China, a virulent nationalism enveloped the country, and the military gained political influence. As a result, officials in Beijing could not be moderate regarding the "Taiwan issue."

Leaders in Taiwan perceived that democratization entitled them to choose their own destiny, and that meant independence. They assumed the United States would protect them if they provoked China, which they did.

The United States had a conundrum on its hands: China pledged that it would use military force to stop secession; Taiwan thumbed its nose at China.

The events of 1996, as well as prior and subsequent crises, made it seem highly possible that there would be a worse U.S.-China conflict, one that might spin out of control.

John F. Copper

PART I

INTRODUCTION

1

Beijing Intimidates Taiwan with Missile Tests, Creates Rift in U.S.-China Relations

March 1996 was a fateful month. Washington and Beijing squared off. It was a red-alert situation. The cause: the Chinese People's Liberation Army (PLA) fired a bevy of missiles at targets very near Taiwan's shores. Beijing then ordered military maneuvers that seemed to be preparations for an invasion of the island.

The United States responded. President William Jefferson Clinton dispatched two aircraft carriers with a flotilla of ships accompanying each to the waters separating Taiwan from China, the Taiwan Strait. The pilots on the aircraft carriers were ready for war.

The crisis passed, but the face-off transformed the Strait into the world's number one flash point.

The backdrop to this explosive situation was an historic election in Taiwan, its first direct presidential election. Americans felt Taiwan's electorate had a right to choose its leaders. To Chinese leaders, Taiwan was not a nation but "lost territory." Furthermore, China believed that foreign forces (particularly the United States) were jealous of China's rise and were bent on keeping China split by supporting Taiwan's independence; these forces' support of democracy in Taiwan was a ruse. Washington was thus dangerously at odds with Beijing over what appeared to be a nonnegotiable issue: Taiwan's right as a democratic country to decide its future and remain separate from China if it wished.

Taiwan held the election. In a campaign mode, politicians were more critical than ever of China's dictatorial government, its poor human rights record, and its coveting of Taiwan. This provoked Beijing even more. In the aftermath, it was clear that Washington-Beijing relations would never again be the same.

—✤—

On March 5, 1996, China jolted the world when the government-controlled media in Beijing announced that in three days, during the run-up to Taiwan's presidential election, Chinese military forces would conduct missile tests very near Taiwan's shores.

On March 8, special units of the PLA aimed and fired three M-9 surface-to-surface missiles. Two hit targets in the waters west of Kaohsiung, Taiwan's largest port and its second largest city; one hit west of Keelung, a port near Taipei.[1] Taiwan was "bracketed"; the PLA could now strike targets in between at will.

The missiles themselves were scary and portentous. They were Chinese-built, patterned after Russian SCUD missiles, infamous for their use during the Gulf War. They were mobile, solid-fuel missiles with a range of 350 miles, capable of carrying nuclear warheads as well as chemical and biological weapons. Taiwan had little or no defense against any missile attack, but these missiles were especially ominous.

The next day, in an unveiled effort to heighten the intimidation and escalate the crisis, Beijing announced that it would conduct live ammunition missile tests fifty-five kilometers (about thirty-three miles) from Taiwan's Pescadore Islands. The PLA warned ships not to enter the nearby waters from March 12 to March 20.[2] Chinese military leaders made other bellicose statements.

A day later the PLA ratcheted up the tension further when it announced that it would conduct a large military exercise not far from Taiwan during the period from March 21 to March 23. Taiwan's presidential and National Assembly elections were scheduled for March 23. This exercise, said a PLA official, would involve 150,000 troops, three hundred planes, five guided-missile destroyers and frigates, four submarines, and a number of Sukhoi-27 fighters (the top-of-the-line Russian planes that China had recently purchased). General Zhang Wannian, vice chairman of the Chinese Communist Party's Central Military Commission and director of the Headquarters for Operations Against Taiwan, which had been set up in 1995, was in command.

Leading up to the crisis the military labeled the Taiwan Strait the "Nanjing War Zone." Communist Party–controlled newspapers also used this term. Taiwan, for all intents and purposes, was, as one China-watcher put it, "80 percent quarantined." Some observers made a comparison with President John Kennedy's actions against Cuba that created a nuclear scare in 1962.

Giving the PLA's actions greater shock value, the missiles landed in vital sea-lanes in the Taiwan Strait. This was a frontal challenge to the United States, a strong advocate (and enforcer) of freedom of the seas, to do something.

Japan's oil lifeline to the Persian Gulf, the pathway for nearly two-thirds of its energy, was temporarily severed. That Tokyo was America's ally by treaty meant the situation created a vital strategic concern in Washington for another reason. The same obtained for South Korea.

China's PLA coordinated the military exercises and the missile tests to look like a softening-up action before an all-out attack on Taiwan. PLA officials even said so. In fact, there were reports suggesting that the PLA planned to lay siege to one of Taiwan's offshore islands—islands the Nationalist Chinese have held since 1949, when the Communists won control of mainland China. The PLA had assaulted Quemoy and Matsu twice in the 1950s, causing a global crisis each time. Both brought the United States into the fray. An assault and landing on one of these islands was not a difficult matter and seemed highly possible. Beijing also repeated an earlier threat to nuke American cities if Washington intervened.[3] This quickly grabbed the attention of Americans.

When the missile tests began, China's defense minister, Chi Haotien, declared that Lee Teng-hui was trying to create two Chinas. This, he charged, justified the missile tests and maybe more. Subsequently, in what some interpreted as a fit of rage, Chi quoted from one of the founders of the Red Army, who had declared that "Chinese would suffer humiliation until Taiwan [was] liberated." The PLA's mouthpiece, Liberation Daily, asserted, "We will never permit a single inch of China's territory to be split from our motherland." This statement was subsequently repeated in China's international news magazine, Beijing Review.[4] This seemed proof that officials in China would not hesitate to transform the feud with Taiwan into a global crisis.

The president and secretary-general of the Chinese Communist Party, Jiang Zemin, chimed in with a spate of vitriolic statements and accusations, though it seemed he was reluctant to do so. As a matter of fact, Jiang had little choice, lest the military take action without him and thus undermine his authority, reducing his hopes for becoming Deng Xiaoping's successor. Even though he was formally China's head of state (president) and head of the ruling Communist Party, Jiang was still only an heir apparent. He declared that the People's Republic of China "would not halt the struggle against an independent Taiwan until Taiwan gives up."

While the missile firings were going on, Foreign Minister and Vice Premier Qian Qichen stated that it was "futile for the Taiwan authorities to don the legal cloak on themselves by using a new form of choosing leaders in Taiwan."[5] He, like Jiang, did not dare challenge the military. Some PLA officers openly doubted whether Qian really wanted to anyway. Top military brass opined that he "wouldn't last a minute" if he did.

As the crisis continued, it became obvious that military leaders were calling the shots. Some said the generals were "in control and wanted to invade Taiwan."

—⁓—

For China, the crisis had a background that gave it resonance. PLA leaders harbored an uncontrollable hatred toward Taiwan, especially Lee Teng-hui and others alleged to be supporting independence and "splitting Chinese territory." Patriotic feelings had been running high. There had been talk coming from the Chinese military of "defending China's sovereignty with blood and lives." Taiwan was considered China's property. The "Taiwan issue" also connected intimately to the Chinese nationalism that the government had been cultivating for a decade or more; some thought this nationalism was now out of control.

To nationalist-minded Chinese leaders, especially military brass, Taiwan's "phony bourgeois democracy" was the product of "foreign elements" promoting Taiwan's independence. They asserted Taiwan was not a country; it was part of China. So how could it be democratic? Chinese officials were aware of and had often discussed the fact that in five thousand years, no leader who had allowed China to lose territory was treated well by later historians. China's heroes were expanders and unifiers.

This was clearly on the minds of leaders in Beijing in early 1996.

It is also worthy of note that China had in recent years been quite successful in propagating the view that Taiwan did not possess sovereignty. Taiwan was isolated and its "diplomatic space" shrunk after 1971, when China was accepted into the United Nations and Taiwan was expelled, and it became even more isolated after the United States broke diplomatic relations with Taipei in 1979. Recently, however, Taiwan's successful and widely acclaimed democratization had helped it break out of this diplomatic isolation, and it appeared time was not on China's side.

China was also experiencing a leadership crisis. Deng Xiaoping was old and in the final stage of transferring political power to Jiang Zemin. But Jiang lacked Deng's stature, especially with the military. Jiang Zemin was clearly unable to resist the rabid nationalists. He couldn't refute the military's contention that Taiwan's "secessionism," which the presidential election underscored, required military action.

There was yet another factor behind the military's tough stance: the PLA had enjoyed vastly larger budgets for several years and wanted to keep the money flowing. A conflict would do this.

Military leaders were also feeling confident about China's rapidly growing military power and influence. Chinese aircraft, boasted officials in Beijing at this time, possessed capabilities that surpassed planes in Taiwan's arsenal, including the F-16s Taipei had recently purchased from the United States and the Mirage 2000-5 it had bought from France.

The PLA's most recent "job," some said, made its officers arrogant. In 1995, the Chinese navy seized an island in the South China Sea claimed by the Philippines. It was an easy take. The military also talked about Japan's alleged designs on Taiwan. "Why not put the Japanese in their place," mused some Chinese military leaders. Japan was afraid of China. Chinese military leaders knew this. "Let's keep it that way," one top PLA officer said.

"And the United States is a paper tiger," bleated some military officers when a reporter asked a pointed question suggesting that China wasn't prepared to deal with America's strong military.

Talk abounded among Chinese leaders about Clinton's ineptitude in making foreign policy, some said replicating and even outdoing President Jimmy Carter's "dumb" performance.

U.S. policies on Taiwan were addressed in the context of a "failed Clinton foreign policy" and America's declining image abroad. Some Chinese leaders connected Clinton's mishandling of foreign affairs to his women scandals. Chinese Communist Party higher-ups used these to explain why the Republicans won an election victory in 1994.

Others said President Clinton was beholden to Beijing. Clinton, who was at first seen as sympathetic toward Taiwan (having made four trips there as governor of Arkansas to promote his state's products) suddenly changed his views about China and Taiwan. China engineered that, or so said Chinese leaders in private.

Clinton put business before U.S. security, they explained. Alternatively he wanted to build a legacy, which he could do by improving relations with China (as Nixon had done).

Clinton was taking money from China for his fall reelection campaign. The PLA contributed generously. Some Chinese officers even referred to Clinton as a "puppet on a PLA string."

Chinese officials assumed the U.S. Department of State was in their corner. Before the United States established diplomatic relations with China, the State Department lobbied for it, wanting more consulates. Taiwan was too small to care about, so State Department officers wanted the authority to negotiate important issues with Beijing.

The State Department was unabashedly on China's side regarding Taiwan, according to ready evidence held by officials in Beijing. In April 1995, a State Department report on democracy in Asia did not mention Taiwan, even though a host of scholars said Taiwan had democratized faster than any nation in the world and was a model of democratization in East Asia. The U.S. Department of State, Beijing calculated, thought China was too important economically and too powerful militarily to challenge on the trivial "Taiwan matter." Beijing officials felt this about Americans generally. They had been telling themselves and the Chinese population that Congress would not act. Big business had too much influence on members of Congress, and the White House could always trump Congress on U.S. foreign policy matters.

Chinese leaders also cited recent public opinion polls in the United States that indicated that the American public did not want to shed blood over Taiwan. And they noted that Washington had not shown much mettle elsewhere. In October 1993, the United States allowed demonstrators in Port-Au-Prince, Haiti, to turn around an American warship at sea. The United States was driven from Somalia by eighteen military casualties in early 1994. U.S. actions in Bosnia likewise showed a lack of willpower.

There was more evidence. In mid-1995, China conducted missile tests in the Taiwan Strait to intimidate Taiwan after President Lee Teng-hui paid a visit to the United States. In response the White House ordered the carrier *U.S.S. Nimitz* to the Taiwan Strait—but only after the missile tests were finished. Later there was speculation about whether President Clinton himself had ordered the *Nimitz* into the Taiwan Strait or whether the directive came from CINCPAC (U.S. Navy headquarters for the Pacific, located in Honolulu).[6] Thus, in the face of a military threat, it was assumed that Taipei would knuckle under without U.S. help, which would not be forthcoming.

Even if the United States called its military into action, PLA leaders were certain that "China could handle it." When U.S. aircraft carriers arrived, Chinese generals threatened a "head-on blow" if the United States intervened.[7]

—⚅—

When President Clinton was told of Beijing's announcement that the PLA was going to conduct threatening missile tests off Taiwan's coast in three days, his response was, "Goddamn![8] Clinton was surprised. He hadn't been paying attention to China or Taiwan.

Clinton quickly summoned his closest foreign policy experts to a meeting. His military advisors took center stage, notably the chairman of the Joint Chiefs of Staff, General John Shalikashvili, who had distinguished himself as a "soldier's soldier" during the Gulf War. It was an awkward situation. Shalikashvili and a large number of other top-ranking military officers were known around Washington to have little respect for the president.

Shalikashvili presented his case. He called for a quick and decisive military response. He also declared soberly that the risk of accidental war was high. Clinton seemed incredulous. He did not want to act. But even his civilian advisors told him that he had to do something. Otherwise, they said, Congress would. If Congress took the initiative, it would drastically weaken his presidency. Even if Congress didn't and the president failed to meet the challenge, the United States would have no credibility left in East Asia—or for that matter anywhere in the world.

"Clinton was caught between a rock and a hard place," said one of his aides later. The president's inclination was to wait, to demur, but he couldn't. So he turned over decision-making authority to his aides.

The day the missile tests began, U.S. Secretary of Defense William Perry, who had been assigned to lead the White House crisis team (some say because Clinton could not deal with the generals) was in command.[9] He called repeated meetings, some without the president present. He formulated a plan and promptly put it into operation. He announced his moves.

Perry sought to send some clear signals to China. He called Beijing's actions "reckless" and what they did an "action of coercion" against Taiwan. The secretary then announced to the press that a battle group, including the aircraft carrier *U.S.S. Independence*, which was docked in Manila when the missile tests were announced, had been dispatched to the Taiwan area to "deal with the situation."

Anyone with a smattering of knowledge of U.S. military capabilities knew the carrier's nuclear weapons and a vast array of missiles and planes could do horrendous damage to both military and civilian targets in China. The carrier's planes could also defend the skies around Taiwan.

It was subsequently disclosed in the media that the battle group included the *U.S.S. O'Brien*, a guided missile destroyer, and the *U.S.S. Bunker Hill*, a guided missile cruiser. U.S. Air Force RC-135 reconnaissance aircraft were also in the area.

Two days later, President Clinton, upon Perry's and others' advice, ordered a second aircraft carrier, the *U.S.S. Nimitz*, to the Taiwan Strait. The *Nimitz* took with it a number of accompanying ships, including replenishment ships and at least one submarine. According to the Pentagon, this action was taken to "make sure there was no miscalculation" on the part of the Chinese "as to our interest in the area" and to "reassure our friends that the United States will maintain peace and stability in that region."

The sending of the second aircraft carrier to the crisis area was much more significant and provocative than sending the first. The *U.S.S. Independence* operated out of Japan, and its moving to the vicinity of the Taiwan Strait could be explained simply as the "repositioning of vessels." Sending the *U.S.S. Nimitz*, however, signaled the United States was preparing for a fight, possibly for war. The *Nimitz* came from the Mediterranean area. Going to the Taiwan Strait represented not just moving American navy ships around, which the Pentagon does routinely, but also a calculated massing of U.S. military power.[10] In marked contrast to the visit of the *Nimitz* to the area three months earlier in response to Beijing's 1995 missile tests, this time much ado was made about America's military presence.

American news reporters were flown to the *Independence*. One reporter wrote of U.S. fighter pilots using models to engage in dogfights with China's recently purchased Sukhoi-27 fighters. Helicopter pilots spoke of pursuing and destroying Chinese submarines.[11] It was a formidable buildup of American forces, the largest in the Far East since the Vietnam War. It gave the impression of a high likelihood of conflict. Secretary of Defense Perry said to reporters, "America has the best damned navy in the world, and no one should forget that."

The secretary followed up, "Beijing should know, and this U.S. fleet will remind them, that the premier military power in the Western Pacific is the United States."[12]

Admiral Joseph Preuher, who commanded U.S. Pacific forces from Honolulu, Hawaii, readied an arsenal in case the crisis escalated into a full-scale war. There was talk of U.S. troops being sent to Taiwan, evoking questions about when they would leave and what kind of precedent this would create.[13]

During the crisis, the Pentagon and the U.S. Pacific Command, the decision-making center for military action in the area, reportedly examined war plans that had not been looked at for more than two decades, dating back to before the Washington-Beijing rapprochement engineered by President Nixon. As part of this new appraisal of China as an enemy, the Pentagon placed targets in China back into its nuclear war plans.[14] It seemed the clock had been turned back to a time when the United States and China were archenemies.

—⁂—

President Clinton was obviously very shaken by what happened. It was an election year, and this crisis was going to hurt if not handled well. Fighting in

Somalia during Clinton's first year in office had turned into a public relations disaster. The president had no military credentials and this Taiwan situation was not likely to be one where he could acquire them.[15] But there was more to it than that.

Why President Clinton was so surprised by China's actions is telling. Chinese leaders disclosed well in advance, in fact, a number of times, what they would do. The U.S. media reported it. U.S. intelligence agencies had described the buildup of Chinese troops in the area adjacent to Taiwan in detail well in advance.

Despite these indicators, Clinton apparently thought that negotiations going on with China ensured there would be no missile crisis over Taiwan. The *U.S.S. Fort McHenry* had made a port call in Shanghai just a month before. The Department of State had just resolved a flap over Taiwan's Vice-President Li Yuan-zu's making a transit stop in the United States. U.S.-China trade was booming; many thought China would not dare disrupt that because it would set back China's economic development and enlarge unemployment, which would engender social and even political instability.[16] Clinton thought that reformists in the Chinese Communist Party and the government were completely in charge.

President Clinton obviously put too much faith in China's civilian leaders. He looked at opinion polls daily; they told him little or nothing about the crisis in the Taiwan Strait. He didn't have close contact with the intelligence community or the military. He was also busy with other matters. He was the "domestic president" and delegated authority on foreign matters. According to an aide, "Clinton wasn't watching his rear."

Congress, which usually stays on the sidelines or supports the president when a war situation breaks out, quickly engaged. Individual members of Congress made statements in public. On January 31, 1996, a "sense of the Congress" resolution was passed that called on the president to condemn Beijing's military intimidation of Taiwan and report to the Congress on how the United States could defend Taiwan against a Chinese missile attack. Congress implied that the United States should provide Taiwan with missile defenses and more arms.

Subsequently, the Republican Policy Committee in the House of Representatives issued a report that was harshly critical of the administration's China policy. It cited Clinton's "ambiguous posture" and charged that the president had encouraged Beijing to intimidate Taiwan.

Before the missile tests had begun the Subcommittee on East Asian and Pacific Affairs of the Senate Foreign Relations Committee called hearings for February 7. Representative Douglas Bereuter, chairman of the committee, posited several questions to witnesses. The main queries concerned the seriousness of the threat to Taiwan posed by missile tests and whether the U.S. policy of strategic ambiguity was a wise one. Their answers indicated that the missile tests and military exercises planned by the PLA constituted a genuine peril to Taiwan and that they constituted an effort to disrupt Taiwan's democratization at a very critical juncture.

Just days before the missile tests were announced, Senator Frank Murkowski from Alaska, who was visiting Taiwan at the time, declared publicly, "If the security of Taiwan is at risk, the President has the obligation to report to Congress, and I think Taiwan has many friends in Congress. We would be compelled to take appropriate action.[17]

Senator Robert Dole, who had the Republican Party's presidential nomination, declared that he would tell China the United States was "committed to help Taiwan."

Speaker of the House Newt Gingrich, whose political influence in Washington had grown such that many speculated it eclipsed Clinton's, called the missile tests an "act of terror."

Congressional leaders were obviously poised to do something if Clinton did not, thus exerting pressure on the White House to act with resolve to aid Taiwan. A number of Republicans and even some Democrats were eager to attack Clinton's China policy and come to Taiwan's rescue.[18]

Former Director of the Central Intelligence Agency James Woolsey, when called to testify before the House Committee on National Security after the crisis started, said that the PLA's tests and military exercises constituted a "de facto, partial, temporary blockade" of Taiwan. Woolsey went on to say that the "deliberate purpose" of the missile tests was to influence Taiwan's election and Taiwan's relations with other countries. He compared the situation to Saddam Hussein's use of SCUD missiles against Israel during the Gulf War.[19] Secretary of Defense Perry said, almost as an afterthought, that threatening Taiwan would be "of grave concern" to the United States. Perry acknowledged that Beijing's conducting the missile tests would influence the election in Taiwan.[20]

In the midst of Beijing's threatening missile tests and military exercises, Congress passed a nonbinding resolution calling for U.S. intervention in support of Taiwan if Chinese forces invaded the island. Members of Congress became a cheering section for "democratic Taiwan," said one observer, implying that China was a bully run by evil dictators.

Even the notoriously pro-Beijing Department of State reluctantly joined the chorus. After the PLA's announcement that it would conduct military exercises, Secretary of State Warren Christopher, appearing on the television program *Meet the Press*, stated meekly that Beijing "had an obligation" to try not to resolve the issue with force. China's actions, Christopher asserted, created this state of affairs. He charged that Beijing's acts were "risky." He went on to say that the United States had "real interests" in Taiwan and that the situation was a "grave matter" for the United States.

All of this created such momentum in favor of Taiwan that both President Clinton and the Department of State, said one observer, had to show their spines or lose control of the situation.

—⁄⁄⁄—

Taipei's response made the crisis worse. What Taiwan's leaders said angered Beijing and fanned the flames of Washington-Beijing tensions that were already serious. In anticipation of the tests, defense officials in Taipei put the military on high-alert status, creating an atmosphere of war in and around Taiwan. When the missile tests started, Defense Minister Chiang Chung-ling declared that Taiwan was "prepared for Beijing's aggression" and "could and would defend the island." The defense minister then shocked listeners by asserting that the country's armed forces "would be compelled to counterattack" if any missiles fell within the Republic of China's territorial waters (which the tests near Keelung might do, according to Beijing's announcement about the test area)"This would mean an expanded conflict," he declared. A few days later, the Ministry of National Defense revealed that military spending would increase 3.8 percent the coming year, suggesting an arms race.

The government meanwhile issued instructions that sea and air lanes going into and out of Keelung and Kaohsiung were closed. They warned of the precedent, of the shock to international commerce and freedom of the seas. Officials in Taiwan knew the White House, the Pentagon, and Congress were listening.

The PLA had closed sea-lanes to international traffic. This challenged the United States on an important principle: the United States was absolutely committed to open sea-lanes. Freedom of the seas and the effectiveness of the U.S. Navy depended on this.

Beijing also challenged international free trade, so officials in Taipei made much of this in order to influence the United States.

Taipei also sent warnings it might escalate the conflict. Taiwan could not be ignored.

When the tests started, the defense minister immediately announced that Taipei was opening a new missile base on the Pescadore Islands ahead of schedule. He also said Taiwan had weapons the press didn't know about. The implication was that Taiwan had deterrence; its offensive weapons served as the trip wire that would compel the United States to act much as the French nuclear force during the Cold War guaranteed that the United States could not write off France in the event of a nuclear confrontation with Moscow. According to some insiders, Taipei let certain people in both Beijing and Washington think that Taiwan had nuclear weapons.

Taiwan had, in fact, launched a nuclear weapons program a couple of decades earlier, and though it had been put on hold due to American pressure, Taipei had developed the know-how to build atomic bombs and might, some suggested, do so quickly if it felt the United States would abandon it.[21] There was also mention of a presumed promise Washington had made to Taiwan when it halted the nuclear weapons program: that the United States, as a quid pro quo for Taiwan ending its atomic bomb project, pledged military help if Taiwan was attacked by China. Others cited the Nuclear Non-Proliferation Treaty signed by the United States in 1968. In that agreement Washington pledged to protect nonnuclear countries from the intimidation of nuclear ones.[22]

Officials in Taiwan meanwhile released information that Chinese Communist agents were spreading rumors that the United States was preparing to evacuate Americans from Taiwan, that rice supplies were depleted, and that Taiwan's NT dollar was about to plunge. Also they said, "Mainland Chinese agents" had hired gangs to disrupt the elections and even to assassinate candidates. Stories were broadcast hourly by Taiwan's television stations, giving the impression that Taiwan was under siege. The stock market dropped 120 points during the two days prior to the tests. There was capital flight. During the crisis foreign exchange reserves dropped by US$300 to US$500 million a day.[23]

To keep America's attention, top officials in Taiwan mentioned that U.S. investments in Taiwan were considerable. The press repeated this. Some U.S. businesses responded by expressing apprehension to Washington. The U.S. computer industry became very concerned: most of the computers and peripherals sold in the United States were made in Taiwan. In fact, Taiwan supplied more than half of the world's market in computer ingredients.

Hospitals were soon inundated with demands for physical examinations required for applying for visas to the United States. Would the United States, wondered government officials and the press, provide safe haven to a million or more people from Taiwan fleeing from the PLA?

Stories circulated, many reported in the press, about the human rights horrors that could ensue if China invaded. Might there be massive genocide? How else could Beijing control the island? What about the flight of refugees to nearby countries, especially to the United States? Many of the stories seemed to have been planted by government officials. But they were believable.

In any event, officials in Taipei wanted to send the message that Washington could not fail Taiwan. Leaders in Taipei were quick to make the case that the "situation" involved authoritarian China against democratic Taiwan, that Beijing did not like Taiwan's democratization and ignored the fact that democracy was the wave of the future. Leaders in Beijing were portrayed as living in the fourteenth century and hanging on to communism after it was dead and buried elsewhere. Taiwan also portrayed itself as the victim: it did not have the largest army in the world or nuclear weapons; China did.

Some officials spoke of the missile tests as a surprise, a decision made secretly by the military in China. Analogies were made with Pearl Harbor. This, of course, was not true but the situation made it appear plausible.

President Lee Teng-hui declared that the missile tests were the product of a power struggle in Beijing and that China had no system for picking a leader, insinuating that it was a communist dictatorship. That was true. Lee asserted that Beijing feared Taiwan's democratization because Taiwan's example might cause the people of China to rise up against the government. The main opposition party's candidate, Peng Ming-min, was even more provocative than Lee. He called for an immediate cessation of cooperation with China and said the government should consider holding its own war games off the coast of Shanghai or Guangdong Province. Peng advised that if Taiwan were to proclaim independence, Beijing could no longer claim that the "Taiwan issue" was a domestic matter; China's actions would constitute an invasion of one country by another and would be condemned under international law.

When the first U.S. aircraft carriers arrived, Peng's party, the opposition Democratic Progressive Party, issued a formal statement of welcome and sent a message of thanks to the Taipei office of the American Institute in Taiwan (the United States' unofficial diplomatic representative office in Taiwan). Opposition politicians declared loudly that the United States would protect Taiwan's democratization, which they said meant independence. Government of Taiwan by the people, one person said, "would have nothing to do with China." One opposition activist, whom reporters called a "Taiwanese nationalist," remarked that it was appropriate that Washington dispatched the aircraft carrier *U.S.S. Independence* to protect Taiwan. "It stands for Taiwan's independence and will help us get it," he proclaimed.

President Lee Teng-hui chimed in. In strong terms he lauded Taiwan's democratization and underscored it as the reason for the crisis. He said the process was unstoppable, that it was the wave of the future. Lee depicted Beijing's leaders as "vile dictators" and said the United States and the rest of the world supported democracy and favored Taiwan. Lee even mentioned sarcastically that Beijing should be grateful to Taiwan for stabilizing cross-strait trade and for investing so much money in China. He was suggesting that Beijing's leaders had become irrational.

Taipei's statements, especially those of President Lee, had a lasting effect. Lee's words were burned into the minds of Chinese leaders in Beijing, who recalled them with rage years later.

—⁂—

The wartime atmosphere faded quickly after Beijing's missile tests were completed. It was like a typhoon had passed, one observer noted. Yet the problems that led to the crisis had not been resolved. The crisis itself was over, but the near-confrontation created a situation of permanent standoff between Washington and Beijing and between Taipei and Beijing.

The fact that Washington, Beijing, and Taipei all interpreted the crisis very differently (almost in diametrically opposed ways) suggested that more blowups could be expected, and the next ones might be worse.

The U.S. view of the crisis was that a show of American military power caused the Chinese military to back down. American aircraft carriers were a formidable force and everyone knew this. They could destroy everything in sight. China understood. The world took notice. The PLA, said a U.S. military officer, was "a barking dog with no bite" and had been humiliated by what had transpired. "Civilian leaders in China would now put the military in its place," he said. U.S. military brass also said that Beijing realized the inferiority of its forces and that an American demonstration of its military prowess and its resolve saved the day.

Secretary of State Christopher declared after the crisis that America's one-China policy was predicated on a peaceful resolution of the "Taiwan issue" and that stating this in the context of the crisis had forced the PLA to retreat again.

In other words, the United States won the face-off.

Washington also took pride in the fact that other countries in East Asia supported the United States. The South Korean government approved of the U.S. naval deployment, including the sending of aircraft carriers, referring to them as playing a "balancing" or "equalizing" role. The Philippine government allowed U.S. ships to refuel at Subic Bay. U.S.-Philippine military exercises were held the month following the crisis. The Japanese government stated clearly that its position was not neutral, and this led directly to closer military ties between Washington and Tokyo. In April, a month after the crisis, President Clinton and Japan's Prime Minister Ryutaro Hashimoto signed a new version of the U.S.-Japan security alliance. U.S.-Japan military cooperation had been compromised after U.S. soldiers stationed on Okinawa viciously raped a schoolgirl, prompting calls for an end to or at least a reduction of America's military presence in Japan. The Taiwan Strait missile crisis had diverted attention from this incident, becoming the only serious topic of discussions between the two sides when they met.[2]

It was as if the United States had gathered its allies in a war effort. China was isolated and cowed. Beijing would not intimidate Taiwan again. One had to wonder, however, if U.S. power were so formidable, why it would matter whether other Asian countries supported Washington. That American officials mentioned this could have been a sign of weakness.

While the United States pictured the Chinese military in retreat at the close of the crisis, this was not at all the view in Beijing. PLA brass said that after China's entrance into the Korean War, the United States took China seriously. After this crisis it did so again. A PLA spokesmen said proudly that China's "successful" confrontation with the United States increased China's status as a military power. Moreover, said Chinese analysts, it was only logical that the United States could not react to protect Taiwan on each and every occasion that Beijing might choose to do more tests in the future—perhaps weekly.

Chinese strategists pointed out that the missile tests had been conducted with both their military and political results attained. The missiles hit where they were supposed to and Taiwan was traumatized. They proclaimed also that China had made significant progress in its missile accuracy since 1995. More missiles would be built and put online. Most important, Beijing could conduct future tests at any time and there was little Taiwan could do. Chinese leaders also observed that Taiwan's stock market plummeted, there was a run on Taiwanese currency, and people fled the country. The missile tests had a broad effect, they said, as expected.

Chinese leaders wrote off America's decisive actions as an anomaly. "Congress," said one official, "forced Clinton to act but it would not do it whenever needed as it cannot stay focused." Beijing also asserted that the United States succumbed to China's military resolve: Washington had promised during the heat of the crisis not to support independence for Taiwan or its membership in the United Nations. Wasn't this proof, a military spokesman in Beijing asked, of the U.S. bending? An academic analyst of U.S. policy in Beijing noted that before the missile tests there was talk in Congress about formal diplomatic recognition of Taiwan. Since the missile crisis this has gone away.[25]

President Jiang Zemin boasted to Japanese politicians in April, a month after the crisis, that he had ordered the missile tests to continue after the U.S. armadas had moved into the area of the Taiwan Strait. He said he was undaunted by the U.S. carriers. Then he questioned Washington's purposes and legitimacy in responding to China's missile tests and military exercises. Jiang asked pointedly, "Why were foreign aircraft carriers dispatched in response to military drills within our own territory?"[26] It was as if Jiang wanted to pull Washington's tail, in view of the fact that the United States regards the Taiwan Strait as an international waterway and freedom of unrestricted passage something the United States has always made plain it will fight for.

Further demonstrating that the PLA was not chastened by Clinton's sending aircraft carriers to the Taiwan Strait, the media in China reprinted, a number of times, the statements made by Chinese generals about dealing U.S. aircraft carriers a "head-on blow." China, it was reported, had been developing antiaircraft carrier missiles.

Officials in Beijing also claimed that China's actions had quieted calls for independence in Taiwan, scaring those advocating separation. The results of the Taiwanese election, in which the opposition Democratic Progressive Party's performance was not good, had proved that, they said.

In August, Beijing issued a startling proclamation: its arms negotiator at the United Nations declared that China's no-first-use of nuclear weapons policy does not apply to Taiwan—a "blood-curdling warning," said one observer.[27] At the end of the year, China's defense minister, Chi Haotien, visited the United States and, in a public address in Washington, compared Beijing's missile threat against Taiwan to President Abraham Lincoln's actions during the U.S. Civil War. He said he was confident that the American people "will understand the resolve and determination of the Chinese people to safeguard state unity." In early 1997, an article published in China's English-language newspaper, *China Daily*, followed up by suggesting that U.S. forces should leave East Asia.[28]

Taiwan also felt victorious. President Lee celebrated his election victory, saying that democracy had prevailed and that Beijing's missile tests had not intimidated Taiwan—that Beijing's bluff was just that. One official called Beijing's threats *pi* (breaking wind), a term that Mao Zedong used regarding Soviet threats against China during the 1970s. Taipei newspapers reported, in bold headlines, that the United States had proven dependable and caused the PLA to back down. Taiwan felt that with the United States as its protector, henceforth it could do what it wanted, including provoking Beijing more.

In November, President Lee deliberately insulted the Chinese leadership when he told *Newsweek* magazine that Jiang Zemin was "quite reasonable compared to others" but that the situation was difficult for Jiang "because he had no control over the military."[29] In later public statements Lee explained the crisis in terms of political factionalism in China, which, he said, was a fact of life in politics in Beijing. Communism was at fault, Lee insinuated. An evil government was responsible for the crisis, and only if that could be changed would the dispute would go away.

Some officials in Taiwan said that Beijing's objectives were limited from the start, to low level intimidation and "letting off steam." They said that civilian leaders in Beijing "allowed" the PLA to do the tests and "to prance a bit," knowing that military leaders would realize in the process that they would be foolish to start a conflict with the United States. Chinese leaders in Beijing, of course, took this as insulting.

Others in Taiwan, some time after the crisis was over, said that Washington and Beijing were indeed at the brink of war. Most in Taiwan, in particular top officials, perceived that the problems that led to the crisis were not resolved, that the Washington-Taipei-Beijing triangle was now more of a problem, and that worse was yet to come.

Top policy makers also perceived that the missile tests' causing panic in Taiwan was a good tactic, so they began working on plans to counteract it. Upgrades were planned to Taiwan's defenses, especially those against missiles.

One academic in Taipei remarked that Taiwan's spine had stiffened during the crisis and it was evident that Taiwan would resist Beijing's intimidation in the future. He compared Taiwan to Britain at the height of German bombing during World War II, which included missile bombing.

In short, the crisis was seen very differently in Washington, Beijing, and Taipei. None saw it as a defeat. All viewed the crisis as resulting in a blow or setback for its adversary. This was a recipe for future trouble.

PART II
PRELUDE TO THE MISSILE CRISIS

2

The Tiananmen Square Massacre Does Irreparable Damage to U.S.-China Relations

June 4, 1989 . . . the Chinese military, using machine guns, armored personnel carriers and tanks, brutally squashed a democratic gathering in Beijing" were the words in the lead story in a major Western newspaper. The next day an on-the-scene observer declared: "The cold-blooded killing of innocent people in Beijing became indelibly etched on the minds of people everywhere."

China was the focus of unprecedented press coverage, almost all negative. The massacre permanently changed world opinion of China. This was true of the United States more than other countries in the world. The public view of China in the United States, which had been very positive up to that time, shifted completely.

It was a defining event for another reason: the Soviet Union was in the midst of collapsing, meaning that the United States no longer needed China for strategic reasons, the raison d'être for close Washington-Beijing relations since 1969. So it was not just that China's government was evil: the United States no longer needed Beijing for leverage against the Kremlin.

The Tiananmen massacre had another effect: a small number of insiders in Washington could no longer make China policy. Congress was going to be much more influential in this process, and this would complicate U.S.-China relations.

Coinciding with the decision to extinguish the Democracy Movement in Tiananmen Square, the Chinese leadership in Beijing made a hard turn to the left politically. Hard-liners brooked no criticism from the West, especially from the United States.

Decision makers in Taiwan understood the importance of the event: the triangular relationship had been altered in Taipei's favor. Taiwan had promising new opportunities.

—ᴍ—

"June 4th is a day that will live in infamy," said the mother of a student who had been shot and killed in Tiananmen Square. "He was one of China's best and brightest," she sobbed.

"These were shots that will be heard around the world," asserted a news reporter on the scene that day.

Openly and brazenly the Chinese government ordered its military, the PLA, to use brute force to rid Tiananmen Square of "troublemakers" who had occupied the square to make known their ideas for reform and advocate democracy. The PLA did its job. Soldiers fired at Democracy Movement participants and onlookers, anyone in their line of sight. They shot not to frighten but to kill. In some places unarmed groups formed to express their defiance, only to be mowed down by machine gun bullets.

The soldiers had been carefully selected from among peasants who had joined China's vast army. Strongly influenced by their upbringing and rural culture, they resented city dwellers whose lifestyles were very different from their own. They were indoctrinated before they were ordered to assault Tiananmen Square. They were told there was a counterrevolutionary movement in progress that was instigated by "foreign elements," a movement that threatened China. They were instilled with fear. They were shown photos of their comrades who had been burned to death, lynched, and even castrated by the demonstrating students in the square.[1] They were deprived of sleep, and some say drugged, so they would obey orders to shoot and kill.

The soldiers had been provided with steel or steel-coated bullets, which shot through the bodies of several people and even penetrated the walls of buildings. This increased the number of casualties markedly. Those who led the soldiers wanted a high death toll to teach a lesson to those who challenged the government.

Western reporters later estimated the number killed to be between several hundred and seven thousand. Probably it was at least a thousand, maybe more.[2] It was unquestionably bloody by most counts and obviously brutal and callous, yet it is possible to put another twist on the event, to look at it in different terms.

One official, in an unusually candid statement for leaders of the Chinese Communist Party, declared that even if the highest casualty figure were true, this so-called massacre was small potatoes if compared to the millions of political prisoners who, according to Western human rights groups' estimates, were languishing in concentration camps.[3] Another official later pointed out that the Tiananmen massacre had received an unbelievable amount of attention given the fact that violence and mass killing occurred in a number of other places in China at the time; these other events were practically ignored. Young people and civilians were killed elsewhere in larger numbers, he said.[4]

Why indeed did the massacre focus world attention on Beijing and perpetuate concern about human rights in the People's Republic of China for months and years after? Wasn't June 4, as the two officials just quoted suggests, much less than an extraordinary event for China?

There are several explanations. First, the Western media was present en masse in Beijing at the time. Reporters had never been there before in such numbers for an occasion like this. Nor had they ever before proffered their interpretation of the events of the weeks and months leading up to the massacre to such a degree. For weeks prior to June 4 people throughout the world were fed steady information about the Democracy Movement via television cameras and vast numbers of written reports, and the Western media presented the movement as a defining moment in history—China was becoming democratic. Because China had the largest population of any country in the world, this would cause Asia and then the rest of the world to become democratic. China was, moreover, following the Western, particularly American, model of democracy. Students in the Democracy Movement were quoting Abraham Lincoln and had built their own Statue of Liberty.

Western culture, the media mused, would be preserved even though the West was in the process of being smothered by population growth among Third World countries. It had been uncertain whether developing countries would embrace democracy. But now, following China's lead, they would. The problem of the decline of the West and the consequent demise of democratic governance would be solved. Western ideals would become universal. Progress toward democracy in the Soviet Union was of minor importance in comparison, and in any case was questionable. After all, China was more than four times bigger and was booming economically; China was also the wave of the future.

China, some reporters noted in their background materials, would soon pass the United States to become the biggest economy in the world, according to World Bank and other studies on China's fast-growing economy. But this did not matter since China was in a reform mode, quickly becoming a democracy. Hope abounded.

This idealism was, in a most dastardly and cruel fashion, snuffed out. A horde of foreign reporters was there to observe the brutal killings. Many, in fact, were caught in the middle of the melee and feared for their lives. Some saw Chinese students shot right before their eyes. Others witnessed armored personnel carriers squash hapless onlookers like bugs. Several reporters later testified to seeing soldiers fire into crowds with machine guns. One reported seeing a four-year-old girl shot while clutching her mother's hand in fright. Some foreign reporters were beaten. Some were shot.[5]

These experiences would not soon be forgotten. They would influence many of the news commentators and writers who molded public opinion in the United States for a long time. Stories written about the "horrors" of Tiananmen abounded. They were vivid, some with personal touches, and mostly well written. Almost all expressed outrage at the Chinese leadership and China itself. The *Far Eastern Economic Review*, one of Asia's best and most influential magazines, printed on its cover five Chinese characters: *bei jing da tu sha*. Only one character was different from *nan jing ta tu sha*, the rape of Nanking (*beijing* means "northern capital," and *nanking* means "southern capital"). A comparison was being made with the Japanese atrocities committed against Chinese civilians in the Nanking area during World War II. One Chinese woman who saw the magazine cover reportedly fainted on the spot. A top Chinese official called for a ban on the sale of the *Far Eastern Economic Review* in China forever.

When the bedlam ended, the government decided on a rebuttal to counter what the Western media was saying and writing. A spokesman told a bald-faced lie: "No one had been killed." This statement was too blatantly false for words. Incredulous, said some. Stupid, said others. It made people even angrier with the government. It shattered respect for official Beijing, especially in the West. Months, even years, later Chinese leaders pooh-poohed the event, calling it "the turmoil" or the "counterrevolutionary rebellion." Jiang Zemin told Barbara Walters later that it was "much ado about nothing."

The statements made by government officials were belied by the multitude of personal accounts of the mass killing and by grisly photos, widely seen in Korea, Hong Kong, and other places in East Asia, of tanks running over demonstrators in their way.[6] Subsequent efforts to play down the event were equally unsuccessful because so many Western reporters had been present. In fact, efforts to do so just made the Western media write more, and more negatively, about the event and about China.

In meetings of foreign press people, not only in pressrooms but also at dinners and in bars years later, China's atrocities and the heroes and villains of Tiananmen were often the topic of conversation. Scores of foreign reporters, including those from the West's most important media organizations, had been put in a combat zone. Nothing like this had happened in recent history, even going back to the Vietnam War. Media people could name those responsible: Deng Xiaoping, Li Peng, Yang Shangkun, and the PLA. Deng had been praised in the West as a reformer, but no longer. In reporters' view, both China's leaders and China itself had devolved.

—⚏—

Those who knew China from the inside understood that there was more to what happened than merely the killing of students protesting for democracy in China.

A political struggle that preceded the massacre in large part explains what happened and why. Hard-liners—the orthodox Marxist-Leninists, or Maoists, the dyed-in-the-wool leftists in the Chinese Communist Party, the government, and the military, had long bristled at China's going capitalist and abandoning Maoist communism. They had interfered with the plans of China's new rightist reformists before, "redirecting," or sabotaging, student protest and democratic movements. They could do it again, and did.

In January 1987, Hu Yaobang, the general secretary of the Chinese Communist Party and Deng's right-hand man, a person many saw as Deng's heir apparent, was suddenly sacked. He was charged with having allowed students to demonstrate for democracy and against socialism. Hu was formally accused of not upholding China's once-rigorous ideological education of students. He was blamed for allowing intellectuals to spread "bourgeois ideals." Hu was demoted from the exalted position of chairman of the party and Deng's successor, yet kept his seat in the party's Central Committee. Deng had sacrificed Hu in order to stem the tide of leftist pressure. In this way, Deng and his rightist, capitalist reforms survived. This was a generally ignored chapter of China's recent history leading up to the Tiananmen massacre.

In April 1989 Hu died, just as Democracy Movement students were occupying Tiananmen Square. His death reportedly followed a vicious argument with leftist hard-liners in a party meeting that brought on a heart attack. The students made Hu a martyr. More important, his death became a rallying point for the movement and those that were a part of it. But in typical Chinese fashion, the student Democracy Movement was meanwhile infiltrated. Joining surreptitiously were Chinese Communist Party "operatives" working for a party left to radicalize the movement to sour public opinion on it or destroy it by turning the party, especially party elders, against it. At the same time, the Democracy Movement, which had been originally composed of students from Beijing's campuses, the country's elite universities, became largely manned by students from campuses elsewhere in the country, who didn't know Chinese politics very well, and workers (many ordered to join by their bosses). Student leaders were thrilled that their movement attracted supporters. They did not do background checks on those who joined them, which made it easy for thugs and hired guns to devolve the movement.

Hu's replacement as head of the party was Zhao Ziyang. Zhao realized what was happening, so he tried to get the protestors to limit their demands and not engage in violence. Some students listened; the infiltrators, of course, did not. For his failure, Zhao, like Hu before him, fell from grace.

The Western media did not see events unfolding this way. Foreign reporters did not give any credence to evidence that the student movement had been penetrated by hard-line orthodox communists, or Maoists, or hooligans hired by the Communist Party hierarchy and the government in order to radicalize and discredit democracy, to create a backlash that would justify smashing it. The press did not report that the actions of the infiltrators helped justify, especially to Communist Party leftists, the military's crushing the movement and killing or imprisoning those associated with it, or that most likely the pictures of soldiers that had been burned to death and disemboweled were real acts committed by the infiltrators but easily blamed on the students.[7]

The students made demands for change, for more democracy, and Deng Xiaoping and his rightist reformers wanted to give it to them. But Deng had to bend the other direction in the face of a sudden rise of leftist pressure. Weathering the leftist tide was critical. Survival was uppermost. Since there had been at least two major leftist backlashes since Deng had come to power, Deng and his supporters knew what to do. They knew how to compromise and live to fight another day. So either Deng gave the order to kill, or at least he did not try to stop hard-liners when they demanded draconian action.[8]

Deng survived. The reforms survived. China was in an advance and retreat mode of becoming capitalist. It was becoming a much freer place to live and work. The reforms were making China prosper, which was what a huge majority of China's population appreciated. Democracy may or may not have been needed; in any case it could wait. But the Western media, rather than carefully analyzing the situation, generalized and stereotyped. The press in the United States had always sympathized with the left. It was now in a peculiar dilemma. The left murdered students en masse, so the media simply attacked the Chinese leadership.

U.S. citizens, both liberal and conservative, but mostly the latter, felt the media attack against China was justified in view of the fact that the Chinese government had for so long been given the benefit of the doubt when it came to human rights abuses.[9] Such reports indeed had long been skewed when comparisons were made globally. If the abuse could be portrayed as part of white-black racial tensions, it was widely reported. Abuses in the Soviet Union, as a sort of concession to conservative critics, also got reported. Hardly anyone paid attention to human rights abuses in the People's Republic of China. To the fair minded, the distortion in reporting was nothing short of grotesque.[10] China was seldom taken to task for still another reason. It was a "progressive" (though admittedly repressive) regime. Mao's government was left of the Soviet Union, which he called revisionist and fascist, among other pejoratives. Mao built communes and strove for true egalitarianism. Finally, China did not allow foreign media people into China freely. When Beijing did permit reporters to cover China, it played favorites, welcoming "cooperative" reporters while refusing visas to others who reported on China's problems.

After the Tiananmen Square massacre, China was marked. The media reconstructed China as a nation of ogres, and this portrayal would not be likely to change soon. In fact, no subsequent news story on China got the attention the Tiananmen massacre received. Nearly half (forty-seven percent) of the American people watched the events on television. Only around ten percent saw Jiang Zemin's trip to the United States in 1997 or Bill Clinton's trip to China in 1998.[11] Tiananmen would profoundly affect U.S. policy toward China. Few in the United States would defend China anymore. Both the political left and the political right now disdained China.

—⚋—

Almost coinciding with the Tiananmen massacre was another event: the end of the Cold War. The Soviet Union at this time was in the process of imploding. This was fairly well known at the time of the massacre. To those who did not realize the Cold War was drawing to a close and that Soviet communism had lost, it was vividly apparent when the Berlin Wall fell just a few months later. Eastern Europe was breaking from its Kremlin fetters. This meant that the "China card," making a friend and even an ally of China to use as an instrument of pressure against the Soviet Union, as the United States had done for twenty years, was no longer necessary.

To understand the importance of this, one need only recall that after 1949 when China went communist and especially after the Korean War, when more than thirty thousand Americans were killed, many by Chinese troops, that China and the United States were archenemies. In those days, in fact for nearly two decades hence, China had been considered a worse communist country than the Soviet Union. The Soviet Union in America's eyes was prospering and was less anti–status quo than China. The Kremlin talked of peaceful coexistence. Mao condemned peace, saying that war was inevitable. He spoke of three hundred million Chinese dying in a nuclear war and China still defeating the imperialists. He said nuclear weapons were paper tigers.

Richard Nixon changed all of this in 1969, soon after he became president. He perceived that the United States, due to the terrible costs of the Vietnam War in terms of money, lives, and America's fallen image, had to get out of the war (preferably with honor, as his presidential campaign slogan said). American taxpayers, moreover, would not pay for more military spending. America hence could not continue the arms race against the Soviet Union. Washington had to seek allies.

China was the first candidate. Beijing had been seriously at odds with Moscow for some years, and their differences had steadily grown larger. The conflict had manifold aspects, including territorial disputes, economic matters, and personal animus between Mao and Kremlin leaders. In March 1969, the two countries engaged in a conflict on their border. Though it was not widely reported due to its isolated location and the consequent problem of media access, it was certainly a war in most respects. Soviet military brass clamored for orders from the Kremlin to take out China's nuclear weapons production plants and missile bases.

China had been a nuclear power since 1964. Most of its strategic weapons would be delivered by intermediate-range ballistic missile. Facilities for building and housing both its bombs and missiles were near the Sino-Soviet border. China possessed missiles that could hit targets all over the Soviet Union but did not have the range to strike cities in the mainland United States because the United States was not Mao's main target.

Nixon and Mao thus made a deal. It was justified to their supporters as a necessary strategic move. "My enemy's enemy is my friend," said both Nixon and Mao many times. The bargain worked; the United States and China became friends and, some said, allies. In 1979 when the United States lost its intelligence bases in Iran that collected information on the Soviet Union, Washington was in a bind. But it soon struck a deal to set up listening posts in China. This was proof positive of a new U.S.-China relationship. The United States subsequently helped China upgrade its military. A stronger China meant greater leverage to make the Kremlin behave. America became a market for Chinese products and the commercial relationship helped China prosper.

Nixon's rapprochement with China, which led to a strategic relationship cum alliance, was founded upon his balance-of-power view of global politics. Others described it as realpolitik or political realism. It translated into using

China to deal with the more threatening Soviet Union. This China card idea lasted through the Ford, Carter, and Reagan administrations and into the first Bush presidency.

In 1989, this strategic imperative in U.S. foreign policy was no more. Noted scholar Francis Fukuyama described the global situation as "the end of history." No longer was there a Cold War and bipolarity. Communism was dead. Neither ideology nor mutual assured destruction would any longer set the parameters for international politics.

It was also the end of an era in U.S.-China relations. For twenty years, from 1949 to 1969, the two countries had been hostile enemies. For the next twenty years, from 1969 to 1989, they had been friends, allies. Now their relationship would be a confused one, difficult to define and very difficult to manage. Perhaps they would become archenemies again.

President George H. W. Bush attempted to preserve the strategic rationale for U.S.-China relations. He tried to downplay China's human rights abuses and highlight its global importance. He tried to placate his critics by perfunctorily punishing China: He ended military sales to Beijing. He stopped high-level visits by U.S. military personnel and government officials above the rank of assistant secretary. He contacted international financial institutions and recommended they delay any further lending to China.

Bush acted under duress from Congress and public opinion, expressed through a host of human rights and other interest groups. Congress indeed reflected what the American people felt, anger at China. China policy at this juncture also became partisan. Democrats seized the opportunity to criticize Bush's foreign policy (even though Bush's conduct of foreign affairs was generally regarded as competent). Bush's predicament was something like Deng's. Bush certainly understood that his survival was paramount.

Congress was not satisfied with Bush's punitive actions, which they considered not stringent. Congress also wanted a bigger voice in making American foreign policy. Many in both the Senate and the House, especially Democrats, perceived that the American people were on their side; thus it was possible to make considerable mileage out of bashing China for its human rights violations (never mind that they had ignored them before).

Congress taking a direct interest in foreign policy making was largely without precedent; U.S. China policy up to this time had been made largely in secret, even more so starting with the U.S.-China rapprochement engineered by Nixon and Kissinger. How else could Nixon and Kissinger convert an archenemy into an ally so quickly? That was needed in 1969. It facilitated the remolding of U.S. policy toward China, as was required to deal with the Kremlin.

Even though Jimmy Carter had condemned such diplomacy, he soon became a practitioner. He didn't pay much attention to China during the first months of his presidency. Then, as his peace overtures to the Kremlin were rebuffed, his ideas about unilateral disarmament, and his friendly entreaties toward the Soviets were met with condescension and as other efforts to get

Moscow to convert failed, Carter's policy was exposed as foolishness. Then Carter used the China card to influence Soviet behavior, just as Nixon had. In 1978, President Carter said that had the Republicans known he was going to grant diplomatic recognition to Beijing, they would have blocked it and it might not have happened. Thus secret dealings were justified. Certainly Chinese leaders did not object; this was their way of making foreign policy.

Ronald Reagan also made China policy without consulting much with Congress. So too did George H. W. Bush—that is, before Tiananmen. The impact of including Congress in making China policy and the opportunities its members saw to play politics over "bad China," like the various interest groups that swarmed upon Congress at this time, changed the China policy equation.

According to some analysts, this caused President Bush to fail to win a second term as president.[12] It led to permanent, irreconcilable, and open disputes over China policy between the two branches of government. It gave Taipei an advantage because it, a democracy, understood this and could appeal to Congress (unlike Beijing, which perceived the U.S. government as dominated by the White House).

Thus, the Tiananmen massacre marked the end of an era. The United States now perceived China as bad. On this topic liberals and conservatives, the left and the right, agreed—though they disagreed on the details.

—␣␣—

Beijing reacted to the West's making it a pariah in a variety of ways. All of them alienated the West as much or even more than the Tiananmen killing had.

In the days and months following the massacre, Chinese leaders exhibited a profound lack of understanding about how the West now viewed China, how the West saw the Tiananmen massacre, and how disappointed in China it was. Chinese leaders initially denied that anything significant had occurred. As noted earlier, they declared that no one had been killed. But they soon realized that this was ridiculous and made China look foolish. Nevertheless, some top Chinese officials stuck to this line, even months later.

The Chinese government also responded with vengeance. Those thought to have been involved with the Democracy Movement, were arrested and jailed—1,800 within three weeks, according to Western sources. Forty thousand "criminals" reportedly turned themselves in during the next five months. Thousands were sent to labor camps. The Western media learned of twenty-seven executions, but there were, no doubt, many more.[13]

Rationalizing this, Chinese leaders took the position that the Democracy Movement was a "counterrevolutionary insurrection" fueled by foreign elements that sought to cause turmoil in China by undermining its communist system. Top members of the Politburo of the Chinese Communist Party, with the controlled media as their tool, charged that the United States had used the Voice of America broadcasts to "inspire traitors in China." They said that America "sought to cut China into pieces by first generating dissent against the government, then..." Parallels were made with America's sympathy with Tibetans in the 1950s and support found in the United States for Tibet today. America's relationship with Taiwan was also cited. Chinese leaders spoke of China's sovereign rights and the fact that no sane government would let enemies overthrow it or allow China to disintegrate. Abraham Lincoln's actions in preserving the Union were cited as an analogy, to the shock and disgust of many Americans.

This view prevailed for some time. In fact, when President Clinton visited China in 1998, Jiang Zemin told him, "Had the Chinese government not taken resolute measures, we could not enjoy the stability that we are enjoying today." This response was in accord with China's new nationalism and its xenophobia advanced by the hard-line left in China. It fit hand in glove with growing anti-Americanism in China.

The argument went thus: Washington sought to take advantage of trouble in China; otherwise, why would it constantly try to promote democracy and human rights in China? Bringing about reform in China "was not in America's national interest," explained Chinese hard-liners. "The U.S. must have ulterior motives."

Chinese leaders pointed to Washington's contacts with pro-Western leaders in the Communist Party and the government. One noted example was a former high official in the party, Fang Lizhi, who had joined the student demonstrators in early 1989. After the massacre, he took refuge in the American Embassy in Beijing. Fang became a centerpiece in the subsequent feud with the United States. He was finally allowed to leave China (purportedly for medical reasons) and move to the United States, but not before there was bitter rankling over his case.

The Chinese were told by their government that Washington planned to infiltrate the top ranks of political decision makers in China, that America was China's enemy. As a kind of delayed response, but one that was clearly well calculated and planned, Beijing attacked on the issue of human rights, publishing articles, especially in the *Beijing Review*, about homelessness, racism, crime, the elderly's fear to walk the streets, and so on, in the United States. Its sources of information were U.S. publications with household names; the spin was different, but the facts were well known. Chinese leaders even asserted that in many areas of human rights, China's record was superior to the United States. The state-controlled media published a number of newspaper and magazine articles that supported this.[14]

To an objective observer there might be some truth to these charges (especially about racism, homelessness, the number of people in jail in the United States). But China's charges did not impress many Americans, including news reporters. Later, Chinese spokespersons made the point that human rights conditions must be seen in the context of a nation's culture and history. In other words, human rights records are relative (in contrast to the dominant U.S. view that they are universal). Many Asian and Third World countries were sympathetic with China's view that historical and cultural factors must be taken into consideration. China subsequently won a battle on this issue when the Bangkok

Declaration (formalizing the results of a large international human rights conference) was passed, essentially concurring with Beijing's viewpoints. This only annoyed U.S. human rights activists against China even more. One reporter who had been in Beijing on June 4th remarked, "China's human rights whitewashing makes me want to vomit right on the head of one of those Chinese bastard leaders in Beijing."

Chinese leaders also off-handedly rejected President Bush's "new world order," wherein an expanding community of democratic and free market nations would rule the world. Instead Beijing's leaders regressed to a 1950s foreign policy mode. Beijing's media accordingly cited the Five Principles of Peaceful Coexistence (once promulgated by Mao) as the basis of China's foreign policy. One of these principles was mutual respect for each other's sovereignty and territorial integrity. Another was noninterference in each other's internal affairs.

China began to aggressively promote the so-called Westphalian view of the world, that international politics is fundamentally the interaction of sovereign nations states—clearly a Western idea but one that had faded in terms of the importance given to national sovereignty in order to allow for international law and global human rights standards.

Beijing argued the world was multipolar. Chinese leaders condemned the unipolar, "king of the mountain" view that American foreign policy officials espoused. China opposed "hegemonism." Chinese leaders also said that the United States did not have the willpower to fulfill Bush's idealist new order. This, of course, meant that the United States and China now held fundamental and seemingly irreconcilable differences in views not only about human rights but also about world politics.

—◊◊◊—

In Taiwan the perception of the Tiananmen Square massacre was very different from what many thought would be the case. So were Taipei's policies, or lack of them. Taipei did not try to take immediate advantage of Beijing's predicament. Why didn't it?

In 1979, when the United States jilted Taipei to establish formal diplomatic ties with Beijing, Chinese officials promptly made a spate of overtures to Taiwan, all intended to promote the process of unification. Taipei's initial response was a tough line summarized in its Three Noes Policy: No contact, no negotiations, no compromise. In response the Western media condemned Taiwan's "recalcitrance." So Taiwan toned down its objections. It instead said China was not democratic.

Later Taiwan changed its policy on economic ties with China. In October 1987, Taiwan's legislature passed a law allowing its citizens to visit the mainland. And visit they did—by 1989, nearly a million had gone to see relatives, which was the legitimate reason for the trip, but many just wanted to see China.

Trade and investment began to flourish as a result. In 1988 alone, Taiwan investors had set up over four hundred companies or subsidiaries in China at a cost of US$600 million. Beijing responded in kind. It needed Taiwan's investment money to build its economy. Deng and his capitalist, free-market reformists argued that economic integration would bring Taiwan back into the fold. Indeed, that seemed to be happening. Many Taiwan businesses, not to mention individuals, went to China to produce goods that Taiwan, because of high labor costs, could not make profitably. China was thus widely seen in Taiwan as a land of opportunity, a place to make money.

There were other reasons for Taiwan's "unique" view of events in China. In April, soon after the Democracy Movement had established its presence in Tiananmen, Taipei announced that Finance Minister Shirley Kuo, a member of the Standing Committee of the Nationalist Party, would lead a delegation to China. Although Kuo used neither title while on the trip, this was a breakthrough. She became the first high official from Taiwan to go to China on official business. Coinciding with the trip, the government lifted a ban on news media people from Taiwan visiting China. More than a hundred accompanied Kuo's delegation.

Taiwan, like the West, also espoused hope for China. For Taiwan, China's democratizing would be of even greater import. It would mean Taiwan would be free of the Beijing threat—or at least that threat would be diminished.

Taiwan's populace as well as its government sympathized with the students of the Democracy Movement in Beijing. Many perceived they were following the Taiwan model. On May 31, a hundred thousand students in Taiwan formed a human chain that extended from Keelung, a port city on Taiwan's northern coast, to Kaohsiung, Taiwan's major southern port, to express support for their brethren in China. Shortly afterward President Lee Teng-hui ordered government officials to support the cause of the students. President Lee disclosed at this time that the government was considering allowing government employees to visit China. (They were not included in the 1987 law allowing such visits.)

In early 1989, Taiwan was optimistic about China. Naturally Taiwan was dismayed when the Chinese government brutally turned against the student Democracy Movement and called on the military to suppress it. After the massacre, however, Taiwan's response to Beijing's bad deeds was very different from the West's response. Neither the government nor the people were as shocked as Americans or Europeans were, nor did they seek to punish China. Why?

Most people in Taiwan, like their government, had long (from 1949 to 1979 when the thaw occurred and to some degree after) viewed the regime in Beijing as vicious, ruthless and without shame. So for the Chinese government to massacre students and whoever else was present in Tiananmen Square simply fit the expectations of most people in Taiwan. In other words, the populace of Taiwan had been educated, or propagandized, by their government to believe the regime in Beijing was evil. The Western media now confirmed it.

In addition, there had been no really atmospheric expectations among the population in Taiwan (even though Taiwan had much to gain), not even among students, as there had been in the Western media. There was a host of reasons for this, most of which relate to Taiwan's understanding China better than the

West did. Newspapers, magazines, and television in Taiwan had for years carried more news about China by many times than their Western counterparts did. In the spring of 1989, the man on the street in Taiwan was aware that China had for several months experienced a crisis in its reform efforts and that it dovetailed with a succession problem as Deng had just abdicated the last of his official positions. This, Taiwan's population understood, was a recipe for trouble. Likewise, in-depth analyses of China's economic situation were reported daily in Taiwan. The thousands of visitors from Taiwan that came back from China weekly also provided informal assessments. Thus, even moderately educated citizens in Taiwan realized that there was widespread apprehension and unease about the decision made the previous year to end price controls and a host of subsidies that the population of China was addicted to and to move to a free market system.

People in China would see their food and housing costs multiply, in some cases manyfold, overnight. There was widespread unease about the future. In Taiwan, people know about this. Taiwan's politically aware citizens also grasped the importance of Politburo meetings to discuss the student demonstrations and realized that the leadership was fractured. In the past this situation was followed by setbacks to the reforms and crackdown policies. Even common people in Taiwan could easily identify the hard-line leftists and the reform rightists (who they were, their political backgrounds, etc.) and had some idea, even on a daily or weekly basis, which was in the ascendancy. Before the massacre, that events and personnel shifts clearly favored the left was widely reported in Taiwan as a situation that signaled trouble and a likely crackdown and repression. Most Western media people simply read background materials on China, almost always from Western sources, which did not provide them an understanding of China that equaled what the aware citizen in Taiwan knew.[15]

Another view of the Tiananmen event was in the minds of people (especially its top leaders) in Taiwan: the United States had reacted emotionally. As a consequence, it launched a moral crusade about human rights in China. But no one knew where this would go. It might end quickly, many in Taiwan thought, after which Taiwan would have made a mistake if it joined. Several government officials as well as people on the street opined at the time that Beijing would probably be forgiven after a short period of time.[16] In this respect, Taiwan's population, like Beijing's leaders, viewed America's human rights outrage as temporary. Human rights politics would soon be supplanted by power politics. When this happened Taiwan would be the loser.

Taiwan was also in a way sympathetic with Beijing's predicament. After all, Taiwan had been the target of the Western media for its "authoritarianism" and "vile human rights record" until only very recently. The Western media had never been fair to Taiwan, mainly because it had a right-wing government. Would the West's press be fair and continue to blast China's human rights record? Probably not, thought most people in Taiwan. Uppermost in the minds of those who had to make foreign policy in Taipei was the fact that they had been burned once before, when in the late 1960s they had made the assumption that China was isolated because of its insane internal politics and gross human rights violations, and would stay that way.

During the Great Proletarian Cultural Revolution launched by Mao in the mid-1960s, China became brutal and inward looking. Millions suffered. Torture and political murders abounded. Its external policies reflected the insanity of China's internal disorder. When it did conduct foreign relations, it alienated other countries. Taipei thus got a respite from a changing world that was otherwise evolving away from ideological polarization. Radicalism in China worked to Taipei's advantage.

After Mao's "revolution" ended, however, countries throughout the world quickly forgave China and adopted the view that it was too important to ignore, that Cold War rules needed to be revised to bring China into the community of nations, Taiwan be damned. So no sooner had Beijing ended its self-imposed isolationism and made an effort to play a legitimate, or at least more important, role in the global community than the welcome mats were put out. Beijing's leaders made an effort to gain membership in the United Nations. They succeeded, and Taiwan was booted out, an event political leaders in Taipei could never forget.

Still another factor to consider when trying to understand Taipei's perspective of Tiananmen was that Taiwan's decision-making hierarchy was, to a larger degree than most countries', dominated by economic thinking. To Taiwan, the world of 1989 was one evolving quickly from a bipolar world founded upon military power to one of economic might. It was dividing into giant trading blocs, and Taiwan was in the same bloc, the Pacific Basin bloc, with China. Thus, eschewing contact with China, if that were to mean commercial ties, was out of the question. Thus, when Beijing condemned "Taiwan authorities" for involvement in provoking the "counterrevolutionary revolt" and even arrested some of their own citizens for complicity in Taipei's efforts, Taipei ignored the accusations. Chinese leaders then forgave Taiwan and soon courted its businesspeople again. So the government, following its business community's lead and the views of its citizens about the situation, refused to launch any moral crusade against China or even get on the Western bandwagon to condemn China for human rights violations. Taipei certainly made no effort to make China a pariah or to bring about its isolation. It rather took a cautious, wait-and-see posture.

Yet Taipei saw future opportunities. Taiwan's government officials viewed the triangular relationship involving itself with Washington and Beijing as changed and more to its liking and its advantage. It understood that Washington-Beijing relations had deteriorated, perhaps with some permanence. Taipei likewise comprehended the shift in favor of Congress in making China policy and the growing importance of public opinion. According to several officials in Taipei, Taiwan had plenty of time to act based on these propositions.

It is also worthy of note that Taiwan had just embarked upon a new phase in its "flexible diplomacy." Early in the year, President Lee Teng-hui visited

Singapore as the President of Taiwan. He said upon his return to Taipei that he would visit again even after Singapore established formal diplomatic relations with Beijing, as was anticipated. Taipei also established diplomatic relations with Grenada that summer, even though Grenada had formal diplomatic relations with Beijing.

In other words, at this critical juncture Taipei dumped its policy of not allowing a nation to have diplomatic relations with Beijing before establishing formal ties. (Beijing naturally broke with Grenada, but Taipei sent a signal of its flexibility in any case.)

Chinese leaders in Beijing viewed both as efforts to make Taiwan independent, splitting Chinese territory, but they were in no position to do anything about it at this time. Beijing had too many other problems. Clearly Taiwan took advantage of this.

Finally, officials in Taipei understood better than ever before that Taiwan's democratization mattered. They noted comparisons made in the Western media, in Congress, and elsewhere between good, democratic Taiwan and bad, authoritarian and communist China. This they knew they could exploit. But they did not need to be in any hurry to do so.

In fact, one could argue that because Taiwan did not vent its anger and saw long-term advantages in Beijing's sullied image, it helped prolong the impact of the massacre and hostile U.S.-China relations.

The United States Sells F-16 Fighter Planes to Taipei: Strains Relations with China

In September 1992 President George H. W. Bush stunned China and the world when he announced the United States would sell 150 high-performance F-16 fighter aircraft to Taiwan. Since President Nixon visited China in 1972, U.S. weapons sales to Taiwan had been restrained. President Reagan had even agreed formally to reduce and finally end them. Cordial U.S.-China relations, it was argued, made the sales unnecessary. Was this no longer true?

The U.S. media reported that President Bush made the move to keep employees of General Dynamics Corporation in Dallas at work in order to increase his chances of carrying Texas in the November election. Military experts, however, said the decision had to do more with maintaining a balance of power in the Taiwan Strait and reducing the likelihood of conflict between Beijing and Taipei. China's recent massive military buildup, helped by huge defense budget increases after Tiananmen and purchases of Russian top-of-the-line weapons, had shifted the balance of forces in the area. Yet some said the U.S. decision was another means of punishing Beijing for the Tiananmen massacre and rewarding Taiwan for its democratic breakthrough in 1989. The decision was, in truth, based on all these factors.

In any case, the sale made the Washington-Taipei-Beijing triangle much more a military or strategic one, and a more dangerous one. It started an arms race and gave Taiwan confidence to resist Beijing's overtures and pressures to talk reunification.

—⚏—

U.S. arms sales to Taiwan had a long history. America sent weapons and volunteers to Chiang Kai-shek even before Pearl Harbor. Washington helped

Chiang fight Mao and the communists, sending military assistance to him for two decades after he fled to Taiwan.

This changed in 1969, when President Richard M. Nixon, "revolutionized" U.S. China policy and ended twenty years of U.S. official hostility toward China. Nixon desperately needed Beijing to help him get out of the Vietnam "mess." Obviously he had to make some concessions to get a deal. Taiwan was it, especially the United States providing arms to Taiwan. So, it became the stated policy of the U.S. government that better relations with Beijing meant that the danger of an attack by the Chinese PLA on Taiwan was reduced if not eliminated. Most observers, including the foreign policy elite and the media in the United States, accepted this theory.

Henry Kissinger also made a cogent argument that China was a very important nation and working relations with Beijing's leaders were vital to the interests of the United States and peace in Asia—including the Taiwan Strait.

The United States also had leverage. Sino-Soviet relations were very strained after their border war on the Ussuri River in March, and Chinese leaders thought Japan had an interest in Taiwan. At one point, to push the negotiations along, Nixon told Mao that if the United States pulled out of Taiwan too precipitously Japan could fill the void. Nixon even threatened to "let Japan go nuclear" if China bargained too hard on the Taiwan issue.[1]

But Nixon accompanied his stick with carrots. He promised to provide China with intelligence information on the Soviet Union, including satellite photos and data on troop deployments on the border, and to help China upgrade its military. U.S. assistance would make China stronger and better able to deal with the Soviet Union. American help also weaned the PLA off Mao's "People's War" doctrine and made it possible for China to upgrade its military technologically. In the process of professionalizing the military, after Mao's death Deng was able to turn it to the right politically and away from "Mao thought" and left-wing communism. He was able to dampen military leaders' criticism of the United States and their calls for recovering Taiwan by military means. All of this improved relations between Washington and Beijing during the 1970s and 1980s. As this happened, U.S. arms assistance to Taiwan diminished.

In 1974, Congress repealed the Formosa Resolution, which gave the president the authority to use American forces to defend Taiwan's offshore islands. In June 1975, the last U.S. combat aircraft stationed in Taiwan departed. Meanwhile, U.S. military personnel assigned to Taiwan were reduced in number from 8,500 in 1972 to 1,100 by mid-1977.[2]

But could China be trusted? Taiwan's supporters in the United States worried that China still threatened Taiwan. So Washington turned arms aid into sales. Taiwan's economy had been booming for some time, and Taipei could now afford to buy weapons and upgrade its military forces on its own. Sales would be private transactions, and China would have no cause to object it was thought. Taipei signed a contract with Northrop Corporation for coproduction of its mainstay fighter plane, the F-5E. Taipei also asked to buy ships, submarines, helicopters, and jet fighter aircraft from the United States.

When Beijing objected, Henry Kissinger assured Chinese leaders that the F-5E "could not be used against China" and that it was "for defense only." But he was compelled, or so he said, to declare that the "project" would not go beyond 1978. Other Chinese leaders did not dare challenge Mao on the matter. The issue of arms aid to Taiwan did not create an impasse in Sino-U.S. relations for another reason: the United States pledged to come to Beijing's rescue in the event of a Soviet attack on China.[3]

Nixon and Kissinger, continued to argue that Taiwan was safer than before because of close U.S.-China relations. Meanwhile, the duo was managing U.S. foreign relations deftly in dealing with the Soviet Union and other issues. Still, the sale of weapons to Taiwan remained a potentially sticky issue between Washington and Beijing, and for Taiwan a matter of life and death.

—⚏—

Arms sales to Taiwan, in fact, became problematic after Mao died in 1976. Over the next two years, Deng Xiaoping wrestled political power from Hua Guofeng, Mao's named successor. Opponents of Deng's policy of close relations with the United States, vexed him. Mao was trusted by party members not to sell out to the United States, as Nixon was trusted by the American people not to surrender to the communists in Beijing. Deng was neither Mao nor Nixon. If relations with the United States were so good, his opponents asked, why could not Deng persuade Washington to stop selling arms to Taiwan so that Beijing could get serious talks going with Taipei about reunification?

This was the milieu in which Deng Xiaoping and Jimmy Carter negotiated establishing formal diplomatic relations during the last half of 1978. Weapons sales to Taiwan threatened to derail the deal. In fact, hard-liners and top military leaders homed in on the matter while Deng was talking to American negotiators.

When talking to U.S. officials, Deng tried to make the point that if the United States continued to sell weapons to Taiwan, Taipei would not come to the negotiating table. Beijing would then have to employ military force. He also cited domestic problems, especially trouble with leftists that hated America.

But President Carter had his problems too. Congress was already suspicious of what Carter was doing, as witnessed by the fact that in the summer of 1978 the Senate passed a resolution proposed by Barry Goldwater, a good friend of Taiwan, declaring that the White House should not cancel a treaty without the concurrence of the Senate. (The Senate is empowered in the U.S. Constitution to approve treaties. The Constitution does not say whether the Senate must approve of the cancellation of a treaty.)

The point of reference was clear to almost everyone: the U.S.-Republic of China Defense Pact. Goldwater and others got wind that something was going on and feared Carter was planning behind the scenes to establish formal diplomatic relations with Beijing and end the defense pact with Taiwan, even though he, Carter, had loudly and publicly condemned Nixon and Kissinger's secret diplomacy.

Carter's advisors told him that he could not afford a fight with Congress after expending all of his chits in getting the Panama Canal Treaty approved and with the Strategic Arms Limitation Treaty pending. Their advice included the message that any agreement with Beijing had to include a provision that the United States would continue to provide for Taiwan's security, and that meant continued arms sales to Taipei.

At several points during the secret talks between American and their Chinese counterparts, the negotiations were about to break down over the issue. In fact, it was said that Deng became livid during some talks and screamed for a considerable time at the U.S. ambassador to China and those in his entourage about U.S. arms deliveries to Taiwan.[4] Deng relented only after the Carter administration agreed to a one-year moratorium on sales after recognition and a proposal for an official transition period wherein, assuming relations between Washington and Beijing improved, arms sales "could be resolved." The United States also made a concession in not demanding any formal Chinese statement on the arms sales to Taiwan, only its acquiescence.

Deng gave in because he desperately wanted to establish formal relations with Washington in order to protect his back against possible Soviet involvement when he went to war with Vietnam. Deng was going to teach Hanoi a lesson for killing and deporting large numbers of Chinese and for invading and occupying Cambodia. Deng planned to do that very soon.

In February 1979, he sent the PLA to war, essentially without help from the air force, save some ground support during the first few days of the war, which resulted in a sizeable number of Chinese aircraft being shot down by friendly fire. The navy likewise did not participate. The results were bad. The PLA was badly beaten (trampled on the ground, spit on, and defecated on, according to military brass in Hanoi) by Vietnamese army units comprised largely of irregulars. In fact, in just days the PLA lost as many soldiers as America had during three years of the Korean War—around thirty thousand (of the eighty-five thousand that were sent into battle).[5] Said one observer, "[Being] politicized with leftist Mao-thought and daily chanting People's War slogans had not made them combat ready. Thus they performed miserably. Deng wanted to make clear that they were incompetent, and he did."

Deng subsequently made another point: The military needed to be professionalized (which could be done only with outside, meaning U.S., help). Saber rattling over Taiwan was not helpful. But Deng could not control all the variables. In April, just after China's "Vietnam War" had ended, Congress passed the Taiwan Relations Act (TRA), which contained a provision promising U.S. arms to Taiwan. Carter signed the TRA into law rather than vetoing it, reckoning it would probably be passed over his veto.

Deng was bewildered. He beseeched the United States not to abet his enemies by selling more weapons to Taiwan. He had just gotten the military in China in line.

However, Deng did have another card up his sleeve. On January 1, 1979, the date official diplomatic relations between Washington and Beijing took effect, the Standing Committee of the National People's Congress published at Deng's behest a message to the people of Taiwan to "return to the embrace of the motherland at an early date so that we can work together for the great cause of national development." This was another prong of Deng's Taiwan policy: a "peaceful offensive." Deng signaled Taipei that it could not survive the loss of U.S. diplomatic relations and should make a deal. But for this to work for Deng he needed American cooperation in not further arming Taiwan.

Meanwhile, Jimmy Carter was under fire over his China policy. Conservatives, including Goldwater and Ronald Reagan, but also George H. W. Bush and others, assailed him for making a bad deal and selling out Taiwan. The U.S. media pointed out that Carter had once said that he "would not ass-kiss the Chinese," a comment that was picked up by the press without his knowledge. The media claimed he was now doing exactly that. Other critics pointed out that early in his administration Carter had labeled Nixon-Kissinger realism in foreign policy making immoral. Now Carter was doing it: he was using relations with China as a card (some said as a mace) against the Soviet Union while jilting Taiwan. Carter had also copied Nixon-Kissinger secret diplomacy, which he had pledged not to do, making him vulnerable to charges of hypocrisy from his critics.

Carter said that openness would give conservative Republicans such as Barry Goldwater an opportunity to derail talks leading to establishing formal diplomatic relations. He was doubtless right but that did not silence his critics. His secrecy was embarrassing in another way. The Carter administration gave Taiwan only two hours' warning before the announcement of establishing formal diplomatic relations with China, waking President Chiang Ching-kuo in the middle of the night to tell him. Chiang, reporters said, had cried upon hearing the news. President Carter's critics never forgot this.

Carter was also humiliated by China's dealing harshly with dissidents shortly after the diplomatic deal with Washington was made. A number of people were jailed; some were tortured. Observers said Deng was getting even with Carter. Jimmy Carter, who had declared upon becoming president that "human rights will be the soul of American foreign policy," had to grin and bear it.

So Carter did not make a concession to Deng and cut arms sales to Taiwan. Given the circumstances (his trouble with Congress, his bad image in foreign policy making, political problems in general, and the need to get ready for an election), he could not do otherwise.

After the one-year moratorium ended, U.S. weapons sales by the Carter administration to Taiwan resumed in large quantities. Deng was put in an awkward position, not only feeling let down by the United States, but with difficult domestic political problems and an energized opposition to deal with.

—m—

The matter of U.S. weapons deliveries to Taiwan did not, however, become a crisis after arms sales resumed in 1980. The crisis came in 1981, shortly after Ronald Reagan became president. Reagan had made a number of unabashedly pro-Taiwan statements during the campaign. He praised Taiwan, even using its official name, the Republic of China (which implied that it was the legitimate China). He condemned communism, including Chinese communism. He even mentioned reestablishing official ties of some kind with Taipei.

Deng and other Chinese leaders went berserk when they heard Reagan's proclamations. Deng's relationship with leftist hard-liners in the Communist Party and the government became much more tenuous. Would this derail U.S.-China relations? Some pundits said so. But after Reagan entered the White House, his close advisors, including Secretary of State Alexander Haig, Ed Meese, and others, persuaded him that his conservative base that wanted to sever relations with China and reestablish ties with Taiwan was neither very large nor very committed and that most conservatives were more worried about the Soviet Union. They pointed out that at least a working relationship with Beijing was needed to deal with the Soviet bear. China, as Nixon and Kissinger had proven, was a willing and useful ally against the Kremlin. In other words, U.S.-China relations constituted essential leverage for the United States to use against the Kremlin. Further, Reagan's advisors told him that he could not allow Sino-American relations to deteriorate; Beijing was too important for many other reasons, and the U.S. media would certainly ambush him if China policy suffered a setback. Haig and others thus pushed Ronald Reagan toward a friendlier stance toward Beijing.

Haig convinced Reagan that the Russians were racist and paranoid about China. Moscow, he argued, feared that China would do what the Mongols had done centuries ago—invade, occupy, and rule despotically. Coming from the Kissinger school, Haig believed in balancing power and thought that Sino-Soviet differences were so strained that Beijing would not oppose U.S. relations with Taiwan as long as Washington took a strong stance against Soviet hegemonism. This even included, Haig said, selling arms to Taiwan if American weapons were also sold to Beijing. So he soon put into operation a policy of granting Beijing the exemptions to buy not just dual-use or military technology but weapons from the United States and at the same time upgrading Taiwan's fighter planes, which he said were old and needed to be replaced.

Haig miscalculated badly. Deng was in the process of trying to parry leftist criticism that he was soft on Taiwan. Deng could not give the appearance he was making concessions because of U.S. pressure.

Deng took the initiative on Taiwan. In September 1981 Deng ordered Ye Jianying of the Standing Committee of the National People's Congress, an important government organ and one where some democratic decision making was going on, to issue a nine-point proposal to Taiwan. The proposal was in essence a restatement and formalization of Deng's offers after the sealing of China's diplomatic relations with the United States. Ye suggested talks between the Chinese Communist Party and Taiwan's ruling Nationalist Party; mail, shipping, and other ties between China and Taiwan; and an autonomous military for Taiwan. He said Taiwan would have a high degree of autonomy as a special administrative region after reunification.

Taipei's response was not positive. Officials in Taiwan said they had nothing to gain and everything to lose, including Taiwan's sovereignty, if they accepted. They recited Taiwan's stiff Three Noes Policy: No contact, no negotiations, no compromise. They also lampooned Beijing's offer of economic help. "It doesn't make sense for poverty-stricken China to aid rich Taiwan," they said sarcastically. "Aid should go the other way." Finally, political leaders as well as scholars in Taiwan asked, if Ye plans to give Taiwan's military autonomy, then why should Beijing object to U.S. arms sales to Taiwan? In a word, Taiwan was uncooperative.

Making matters worse, Deng was trying to purge many of the older members of the Communist Party, including many leftists and ideologues. He sought to get his own people into party and government positions to make his pragmatic, capitalist reforms work. This precipitated a backlash. Getting party elders, many his opponents, to retire or otherwise leave peacefully turned out to be a daunting task. Deng mentioned his predicament to American visitors. He hoped the White House and Congress would get the message that he was Washington's best hope for good U.S.-China relations and America should help him. Alternatively Deng was perpetrating a big ruse by exaggerating the strength of his opposition and the seriousness of his predicament, and he found Haig to be gullible.

Judging from several setbacks he had earlier experienced in both advancing his reformist policies and in keeping his people in positions of importance, Deng was truly on the hot seat. Deng, observers of Chinese politics said, had bent like a bamboo plant in supporting the Anti-Spiritual Pollution movement in 1983, which aimed to eradicate foreign, mostly American, influence in China. He expediently sided with his nemesis, the party left, that had launched the campaign. He had to save himself and his reforms. So, either because he had the Reagan administration's understanding or because his critics in China held him at bay, Deng objected strenuously, to the point of threatening to break off relations, rather than accept Haig's deal to allow the United States to sell arms to both China and Taiwan.

In June 1981, Chinese Foreign Minister Huang Hua told Haig that the United States would have to set a date ending all military sales to Taiwan. "One billion Chinese would not sacrifice their principles," he said. Huang even reminded Haig how angry President Lincoln had been during the U.S. Civil War about British arms sales to the Confederacy. American arms sales to Taiwan were regarded similarly, he said.[6] Deng followed up by talking about a "dark cloud" hanging over U.S.-China relations. Haig retorted saying that Taiwan had a "Soviet option" as well as the potential to build nuclear weapons. Deng and other Chinese leaders were not moved.

—〰—

Haig took a fallback position, ordering studies of the situation. The Defense Intelligence Agency launched one about Taiwan's need for a more advanced fighter plane. The Central Intelligence Agency undertook a study on Deng's predicament. The former concluded Taiwan did not need a better plane; the latter stated that Deng, America's good friend in the Chinese leadership, was in trouble and that powerful leftist opposition threatened Deng's continued leadership. It said that the sale of a new fighter plane to Taiwan could lead to a rupture in U.S.-China relations. If these reports were contrived or if they were contradicted by other analysis that said just the opposite, that did not come to light. In any case, in early 1982, Washington announced that the F-X fighter plane would not be sold to Taiwan.

But instead of expressing gratitude to the Reagan administration, China pushed to deny other weapons to Taiwan as well. Whether Deng was still genuinely afraid of an upsurge from the political left or whether he cleverly sought to use this to extract concessions from the United States is anyone's guess.

The Reagan administration not only wanted to help Deng, the global political milieu also influenced Washington. In contrast to the situation Carter faced in 1978 when he was negotiating diplomatic relations (Deng needed the United States to deal with Soviet pressure when he invaded Vietnam), Reagan faced a crisis in Poland and the possibility of Soviet intervention there. Reagan needed good relations with Beijing. In March 1982, Leonid Brezhnev made a conciliatory speech aimed at China, in effect canceling the Brezhnev Doctrine (which said that Moscow had the right to intervene in communist bloc countries to prevent the rise of capitalist forces inspired by foreign countries). China responded in kind, and began to send signals that it wanted better relations with the Soviet Union.

In this context, Haig orchestrated a major U.S. concession to China in the form of a communiqué that declared that the United States did not "seek to carry out a long-term policy of arms sales to Taiwan" and that sales would not "exceed, either in quantitative or qualitative terms, the level supplied in recent years" and, further, that the United States intended "to reduce gradually its sales of arms to Taiwan, leading over a period of time to a final resolution."

He presented the communiqué, later known as the August Communiqué or Shanghai II, to Reagan forcefully, knowing that Reagan would balk. Haig even said to Reagan that he would "lead the parade to publicly condemn the president" if the arms sales issue caused a crisis in U.S.-China relations and damaged U.S. foreign policy.

Haig got his communiqué.

Reagan got Haig's letter of resignation.

Deng lost his closest friend in the Reagan administration.

Subsequently, to put a good face on what otherwise seemed to be caving in to Beijing, President Reagan said the communiqué was concluded based on the assumption that Beijing had made a pledge for a peaceful solution only of the Taiwan issue. This got him off the hook, or so some said. Deng, however, replied he had not agreed to this. The communiqué was not subsequently signed. Later Department of State officials (even testifying before Congressional committees) said that it did not have standing in international law. The August Communiqué, nevertheless, didn't die—State Department personnel cited it as if it were law. It remained controversial, patently contradicting the Taiwan Relations Act.

Taipei expressed disappointment. Many Reagan supporters in Taiwan questioned the wisdom of the communiqué.

President Reagan was apparently convinced that Deng needed the United States and that he was a friend. Yet Reagan did not want to betray Taipei. He privately wrote a memo saying that the United States should restrict arms sales to Taiwan only as long as a cross-strait balance of power was preserved. The memo was placed in a National Security Council safe for future presidents to read.

The Reagan administration subsequently circumvented constraints imposed by the August Communiqué by saying that the United States could increase weapons sales to Taiwan while at the same time decreasing them, because of inflation affecting the values of the items being sold. Many found this humorous. Reagan also used US$835 million (a quite large figure), the value of the weapons that President Carter sold to Taiwan in his last year in office, as a starting point. Reducing sales by US$20 million yearly (in absolute dollars) became the guideline.

Meanwhile, the United States allowed Taiwan access to American military technology, which it claimed was not covered under the agreement. Taiwan subsequently sent weapons experts to the United States to learn how to build its own fighter plane. Many went to Dallas, where the F-16 was manufactured. U.S. engineers at General Dynamics Corporation, though not allowed to instruct them how to make a plane, were not restrained from telling them when they were making a mistake or going in the wrong direction. This was very helpful to Taiwan's engineers and technicians. Soon Taiwan had its own high-performance jet fighter plane, the IDF, or indigenous defense fighter, or the Ching Kuo for President Chiang Ching-kuo. The first IDF was completed in 1988; demonstration flights were conducted the next year. The first squadron of IDFs was commissioned in 1994.

Beijing was unhappy about this and said so. Chinese leaders charged that it was a violation of the August Communiqué. A deterioration in U.S.-China relations seemed to be in the cards anyway as George Schultz, Haig's replacement, gave Japan a higher priority in U.S. Asia policy and orchestrated a general shift to economic issues (as opposed to Haig's strategic emphasis). But Deng adjusted to the difficulties in U.S.-China relations caused by arms sales to Taiwan and growing leftist opposition to his pro-U.S. policies and his alleged abandoning the recovery of Taiwan. He adopted a new, "independent" foreign policy. He announced this new policy at the Twelfth Party Congress in September 1982. Deng's people called it an "equidistance policy" between Washington and Moscow, giving China a fulcrum role and greater leverage with both superpowers. This was further evidence of Deng's predicament but also of his ability to adjust. His new policy sounded tough and placated some of his critics, but kept relations with Washington on track.

In ensuing years China continued to support Reagan's anti-Soviet policies in Afghanistan and elsewhere. U.S. weapons and high-tech sales continued to flow to China. U.S.-China trade and other economic ties continued to grow. The Taiwan issue faded from view a bit.

—ᙡ—

The Tiananmen massacre caused a sea change in U.S.-China relations. It spelled the end of military cooperation between Washington and Beijing and was the starting point of a new policy of American weapons sales to Taiwan. It did not have an immediate impact though. On the arms sales, Bush claimed that he did not see "any holes" in Taiwan's military preparedness.

Meanwhile Taiwan experienced a democratic breakthrough that was to greatly impact its relations with the United States, America's stance toward China on arms sales to Taiwan, and much more. In December 1989, Taiwan held a legislative election. It was the fourth open and competitive national election beginning with the election contest in 1980. It was the second two-party election, after the 1986 contest following the formation of the Democratic Progressive Party (DPP).

In 1986, the DPP hadn't performed well. It was inexperienced and was seen as too radical, especially on the issue of Taiwan's independence—which it advocated openly. But 1989 was a different ball game—supporting Taiwan's separation from China was now seen in a very different atmosphere. In China the PLA killed those calling for democracy in Tiananmen Square. "Who would want to join a country like that, ruled by butchers," opposition candidates cried. "We would no longer have any human rights. Our progress toward democracy would not be respected; it would be destroyed." Thus the independence agenda of the DPP was no longer viewed as radical. Many viewed it as the only solution. That Taiwan could not become part of China as long as it was ruled by communists was a constant refrain. "Not for ten thousand years," one opposition candidate declared.

Events in Europe and elsewhere had a further impact on the electorate in Taiwan. The Berlin Wall fell. Romania's President Ceausescu was killed by citizens he had oppressed for years. Democracy was breaking out all over the world. Authoritarian regimes were falling. Kuomintang (KMT) or Nationalist Party rule in Taiwan seemed to many to be doomed; it was an authoritarian regime. Nationalist Party candidates stopped talking of one China or reunification. Instead they spoke of their success in making Taiwan's economic miracle, social stability, and other things.

The (heretofore radical) New Tide faction of the DPP called for writing a new constitution and declaring complete independence from China. Few thought these ideas were too much anymore. Opposition candidates cursed Deng Xiaoping and other Chinese leaders at campaign rallies. Many used foul language. DPP activists held regular public flag burnings—of Chinese flags. After they burned the flags they spit on them and some even urinated on them. Much of this was in front of television cameras. A few dared the PLA to attack Taiwan. When nothing happened they announced that Deng "had no balls."

Many opposition candidates spoke only in Taiwanese when campaigning. Mandarin Chinese, they said, was "the language of the enemy."

The DPP proclaimed that to have democracy in Taiwan the country had to have a two-party system. To support that voters needed to elect the DPP. This worked. Many DPP candidates, moreover, were not radical when it came to saying what they would do in office. A number had some experience in office. They had a quite reasonable mission, not a destabilizing one. Thus voters were no longer afraid to vote for them. DPP leaders said repeatedly that the United States wanted Taiwan to become a democracy and thus supported them. They also said that the United States would protect Taiwan in case China attacked. Members of the U.S. Congress confirmed these ideas.

When the votes were counted political pundits, the media, and even KMT leaders said the DPP had won the election. The opposition DPP had certainly performed better than in the previous election and well enough to generate speculation it might run the country in the near future.

But could the DPP really win control of the ship of state? Not as long as a majority of members of the elected bodies of government represented districts in China where they would not have to stand for election. Getting rid of them then became their battle cry. Progressives in the KMT agreed that the senior parliamentarians had to go. They tried to persuade them or coerce them to step down. The high court ruled that they had to go. Finally, they left office. In 1991, there was a plenary election for the National Assembly. There was another election, for the legislature, scheduled for late 1992, just before President Bush made his decisions on the sale of F-16s. These elections made it appear that Taiwan was no longer a part of China. There were token representatives of "Overseas Chinese." But the large majority of candidates running were representing Taiwan. One had to conclude that democracy was leading to a separate Taiwan. Furthermore, the United States supported Taiwan's democratization; thus it supported its independence. The weapons sale was, in this context, seen as America supporting Taiwan's succession with arms.

—⚹—

Meanwhile, after 1989 the status of China's military changed dramatically. Its political influence grew. It was treated very differently in budget discussions. Money began to flow its way. At this time Russian weapons also became more available for China to buy, and Beijing did buy. They were very useful to Beijing to shift the balance of power in the Taiwan Strait its way. More troubling yet for the United States, there began a major movement of weapons and troops from north China to areas near the Taiwan Strait. They were moved there because Sino-Soviet relations had improved and Beijing wanted to intimidate Taiwan. China's soft approach toward Taiwan had failed and the military (which hated Taiwan and saw advantages in a conflict with Taipei) exercised more clout; so Beijing adopted a more aggressive, threatening policy.

Because of all of this, on September 9, 1992, President George Bush announced that the United States would sell Taiwan 150 F-16 fighter planes. The deal was worth US$6 billion and included forty spare engines, nine hundred Sidewinder missiles, six hundred Sparrow missiles, other ammunition, and spare parts. The F-16, also called the Fighting Falcon, was America's top-of-the-line fighter plane. It could fly at Mach 2 plus, or more than 1,300 miles per hour, while carrying air-to-air missiles on its wing tips. The F-16 had a superb reputation. It had proven itself in various conflicts. Thus this was a landmark decision. The transaction would obviously alter the balance of power in the Taiwan Strait by giving Taiwan vastly improved air defense capabilities.[7] It was certain to cause Taipei to harden its stance vis-à-vis Beijing and parry its overtures to negotiate Taiwan's "return to the motherland."

The sale was justified at the time and after, according to most U.S. defense experts, because of a shift in the balance of power in the Taiwan Strait favoring Beijing. For a year prior to the F-16 decision, officials in Vice President Dan Quayle's office, the Central Intelligence Agency, the Department of Defense, and the National Security Council had met regularly to discuss the issue and had concluded Taiwan needed a better air defense fighter plane. Specifically, because of Beijing's purchase of Sukhoi-27s (Russia's top-of-the-line fighter) and Taiwan's deteriorating fleet of fighters (causing some to be labeled "widow makers" because of the many crashes that killed pilots), they had an argument to use against opponents who did not think U.S. policy of minimizing arms sales to Taiwan should change.

James Lilley, the assistant secretary of defense for international security affairs, argued for the sale. Lilley had been close to Bush for a long time and the president listened to him. Lilley also had the ear of Secretary of Defense Richard Cheney. In June, Cheney began to argue for the sale.[8] The deal required a thirty-day notification period and Congressional approval. But that was not a problem; many members of Congress were favorably disposed to approve the sale because it would be injurious to Beijing, or at least this was their rationalization.

Democrats had frequently made reference to the military's role in politics in China, as demonstrated by the PLA's increased clout after its Tiananmen "rescue" of the Communist Party and the government and its now increased involvement in politics. They also criticized China for not drawing down military spending after the end of the Cold War, noting that its defense budgets had increased when everyone else was cutting defense spending. Republicans had long advocated policies that called for more weapons sales to Taiwan so that Taipei could fend off a possible attack from China. They favored Taiwan over China and gave less credence to the argument that better U.S.-China relations made Taiwan more secure. Thus the sale had no problem getting Congressional approval.

On the other hand, it was campaign time, and Democrats were studiously looking for any issue they could use to criticize the Bush administration. They labeled Bush's action a cynical effort to win votes in Texas and carry an important state so that he could be reelected. The media said this. Many Americans believed it. Bush mentioned his predicament in talks with Chinese leaders. Some said he even asked for China's understanding, of the kind that Deng got from the Reagan administration in 1982 when the August Communiqué was signed, promising that the United States would cut arms sales to Taiwan.

Presidential candidate William Jefferson Clinton did not pounce on the issue as he might have. By this time he was confident of winning the election and did not really need another campaign issue, though some of his supporters, probably with his approval, continued to chide Bush for "playing dirty pool by selling weapons to win votes." Another reason for Clinton's personal silence was that his foreign policy team did not want to make their candidate out to be someone who did not understand the realities of international politics, which would have been Bush's reply to Clinton's opposition. Finally, being critical of the sale would have contradicted Clinton's harsh China policy. Clinton had launched a virulent crusade against appeasing China during the campaign. In his "Covenant with America," he declared that he would not "coddle dictators from Baghdad to Beijing." Clinton also agreed that because the balance of power in the Taiwan Strait had been affected by China's increasing its defense budgets and buying aircraft and other weapons from Russia, the sale was justified. Later the Clinton administration also pointed out that France would sell the Mirage to Taiwan if the United States did not sell F-16s, and American companies would lose the business.

Shortly after the sale was consummated, France, in fact, agreed to sell Taiwan sixty Mirage 2000-5 fighter planes, the top-of-the-line French-made aircraft. The Mirage was an all-weather, high-performance fighter similar to the F-16, but in some important ways it had quite different capabilities.

—⁂—

China's reaction to Bush's announcement appeared on the surface to be intense and threatening. The sale, Chinese leaders said, "broke fifteen years of U.S. promises" not to upgrade Taiwan's fighter planes and thereby not enhance Taipei's air defense capabilities. The Chinese foreign ministry summoned U.S. Ambassador Stapleton Roy and told him that the action "completely violates the Sino-U.S. Communiqué of August 17, 1982, grossly interferes in China's internal affairs, seriously jeopardizes Sino-U.S. relations, and obstructs and undermines the great cause of China's peaceful reunification." A military spokesperson talked about a retrogression in U.S.-China relations and the negative impact it would have on Sino-American cooperation in the United Nations and elsewhere, alluding to America's problems in the Middle East and the fact that because China had not used its veto in the United Nations Security Council, the United States was able to prosecute the Gulf War under United Nations auspices.

For several weeks the Chinese media castigated the United States for the F-16 sale.[9] This seemed to prevent the issue from dying and put pressure on government officials to take retaliatory measures. Foreign Minister Qian Qichen then threatened to punish the United States by canceling purchases of American-made products worth US$4 billion. He even hinted that Beijing might alter its policy of opposing North Korea's invasion of South Korea. He pointed out that North Korea had just accepted China's decision to open relations with South Korea.[10] Beijing subsequently boycotted arms talks being held by the permanent members of the United Nations Security Council. According to one observer, when announcing his country would not attend the talks, the Chinese representative indicated that China was furious over Bush's decision to sell the F-16 fighters to Taiwan.[11]

But it seems that much of this ballyhoo was simply for show. Beijing took much more significant retaliatory measures against France for its sale of Mirages to Taiwan. It closed a French consulate in China and took other harsh punitive actions. One Chinese leader explained this by saying that the United States and China had a communiqué about weapons sales to Taiwan (never mind that the communiqué in question contained a promise by the United States to decrease and ultimately end arms sales to Taiwan and the sale of F-16s blatantly violated it); it did not have such an agreement with France.

Subsequently, Deng Xiaoping personally endorsed George Bush for another term as president. Perhaps Deng was returning a favor, for the United States' assistance in 1982. Other interpretations of China's mild reaction include the notion that the United States was too important to China for economic reasons, and China's rightist reformers were again in command and could convince enough top members of the Chinese Communist Party that a restrained reaction was in China's national interest.

Others said the military had been bought off by Deng allowing the PLA to get into commercial ventures and make obscene profits from it. The military had indeed gone capitalist. The military was also fighting itself at the time. A significant number of top military leaders did not support the PLA's top general, hard-liner Yang Shangkun (who had ordered the military into Beijing, resulting in the Tiananmen massacre).[12]

Finally, it should be remembered that Deng was a part of the military's brotherhood; he had a military background and was a hero during the war against Japan and in fighting Chiang Kai-shek. Deng thus had the loyalty of many in the top ranks of the military. The support he got from the military hierarchy was apparently decisive, so Deng personally overruled a PLA proposal to retaliate in some way against the United States for the F-16 sales.[13] Making it easier for Deng to make such a decision, the blow of President Bush's announcement was softened by Bush's sending a high-level official to Beijing at this time, ending some arms sales sanctions imposed on China after the Tiananmen massacre, and vetoing a congressional bill that put conditions on the renewal of most-favored trading status for China.

Another explanation was that Beijing could bully France; it could not bully the United States.[14] Taking hostile actions toward France was sufficient to placate hard-liners, for the moment at least. Still another view of the situation, and probably the most correct one, was that the Chinese military did not choose to respond immediately in view of all of these reasons. So its reaction was a delayed one, which would cause problems later.

After the decision to sell F-16s to Taipei, senior military officers wrote to Deng and Jiang Zemin, expressing their view that only a balance of power in the

Taiwan Strait that favored Beijing would deter Taiwan from declaring independence. They pledged their determination to confront the United States if need be.[15] The F-16 decision seemed to visibly accelerate the growth of Chinese nationalism, patriotism, and anti-Americanism in China. The effect of the sale, in other words, was slow in developing, but with time it became very dynamic.

On the other side of the Taiwan Strait, Taipei was suddenly blessed with aircraft that it long had been unable to purchase. Its ability to defend the island was markedly improved, and patently that enhanced its ability to parry or reject Beijing's overtures to talk about reunification.

According to some observers, Taiwan now had more fighter aircraft than it needed. It had America's F-16. It had the French Mirage. And it had its own Indigenous Defense Fighter that it had built courtesy of President Reagan's allowing Taiwan to purchase military technology in the United States. There was even talk that Taiwan's military planes might run into each other. Obviously Taiwan now had control of the airspace over and around the island—air superiority. It also gained in deterrence capabilities, since China would now have to sacrifice much more, perhaps virtually all, of its air force to assault Taiwan. Taiwan's new air defense capabilities likewise meant that China could not use a cordon of submarines to strangle the island easily—with control of the air, Taiwan's military could effectively employ its antisubmarine capabilities.

Some in Taiwan boasted that Taiwan could now protect itself and that it would never unify with China. Weapons meant independence.

4

President Lee Visits His Alma Mater; Beijing Feels Betrayed, Benefiting Hard-Liners

In June 1995, Taiwan's President Lee Teng-hui visited the United States to attend a reunion at his alma mater, Cornell University. The visit enraged China. Chinese leaders and their media viciously attacked Lee, Taiwan, and the United States. Many of the insults were personal. Beijing was incensed that Taiwan was not being diplomatically isolated according to plan. Instead, Taiwan appeared to be successfully "breaking out" of Beijing's containment and going its own separate way toward independence.

Indeed, Lee sought to advance Taiwan's pragmatic diplomacy and shatter Beijing's plan to degrade Taiwan's international status. The visit was a coup for Lee. Making matters worse for Beijing, China's political leadership, with the military very much involved, was embroiled in a succession crisis.

People's Liberation Army leaders, enraged over Lee's sojourn and acting with the support of Communist Party elders, ordered missile tests not far from Taiwan's shores, blocking sea and air lanes into Taiwan while terrorizing the population. The U.S. response was mild. In retrospect it looked weak and timid. This gave Congress further cause to chide the Clinton administration's China/Taiwan policy.

The public reaction in Taiwan was supportive of Lee. Most applauded his boldness. The majority felt Taiwan had to take a tougher stance toward Beijing and the Clinton administration. Many, however, feared the consequences.

In any case, this event had a profound impact on both U.S.-China and Taiwan-China relations.

—◆◆◆—

June 7—President Lee Teng-hui arrived in Los Angeles for a stop on the way to visit Cornell University where he was invited to be a "special guest." Except for a transit stop in Honolulu in 1994, this was the first time a president of Taiwan had ever visited the United States.

It was supposed to be a private visit, but it was very obvious from the start that it would be much more. A private visit by the president of a "nation" that the United States officially regarded as a province of another country (an assumption, however, with which the Congress and the American public disagreed), could hardly be private. Signaling that the trip would have political overtones, Lee met Los Angeles Mayor Richard Riordan and California Governor Pete Wilson. He also made an appearance with the Los Angeles Chinese community, which was divided in its support between Beijing and Taipei, as were virtually all Chinese communities in the United States.[1]

However, regardless of where their loyalties lay, most Chinese in the United States were impressed with Taiwan's democratization and admired Lee for his contributions to this process. This included American-born Chinese, who had been acculturated in America and strongly supported democracy. It included Chinese from Taiwan, both Taiwanese, who identified with Lee because he was Taiwanese, and mainland Chinese, who saw Lee as bravely parrying Beijing's pressure and deftly handling the often-difficult process of democratization in Taiwan. Even Chinese from the People's Republic admired Lee; some of them felt that Lee personified China's hope to democratize, and many said it would be better that Taiwan remain separate so it could continue to serve as a model for China.

Hundreds of supporters met Lee outside of his hotel carrying Republic of China flags. Lee told them: "I am excited about this development and hope that it will lead to an official recognition of Taiwan as a sovereign country." This did not seem to most Americans to be a provocative statement; but it certainly was. To Chinese leaders in Beijing, it was akin to waving red in front of a raging bull. In the general context of Taiwan-China relations and Taiwan-U.S. relations, it was provocative and very portentous.

When Lee arrived in Syracuse, New York, home to Cornell University, where he had received his PhD in agricultural economics in 1968, he was met by the mayor, the president of Cornell, and three members of Congress, including Jesse Helms, Chairman of the Senate Foreign Relations Committee, Senator Frank Murkowski from Alaska, who was an expert on Asian issues, and Senator Al D'Amato from New York. Helms told Lee, "Mr. President: today, Syracuse; very soon, I hope, the capital of the United States in Washington, D.C." Helms's statement was intended to annoy the White House and the Department of State; neither was represented in Cornell that day. They were busy trying hopelessly to play down the importance of the visit, portraying it as private and therefore unimportant.

The Department of State had nixed a number of requests by Taipei for Lee to visit the United States. Spokespersons at Foggy Bottom (the slang term in Washington, D.C., for the State Department because of the fog that often settles in the area but also reflecting the view of the State Department as having a closed mind and lacking innovation) had said a Lee visit would have "serious consequences" for U.S. foreign policy. They asserted that even a private visit would be seen by Beijing as "removing the unofficiality" of Washington-Taipei relations.[2] Officials at Cornell University and the local media in contrast referred to Lee as "President Lee" and "President Lee from Taiwan." So did most of the U.S. national media.

Lee's motorcade of stretch limousines, the mob of media representatives there to see him and hear his speech, and the throng of Chinese attending the speech and interested onlookers gave the appearance of an official state visit. So did the fact that when Lee gave his address at the university, flags were waving in the audience: flags of the People's Republic of China held by opponents, flags of the Republic of China clutched in the hands of supporters, and flags of the Taiwan Independence Movement. Lee had been invited to deliver the annual Olin Lecture. He was treated as a distinguished alumnus, as a scholar and VIP, and as the head of state of an important and respected nation.

In his speech on June 9 to an audience of four thousand, Lee harkened back to his days as a student there, mentioning the long hours he spent in the library, going to class, taking walks with his wife in the evenings, and attending church. Lee cited many other memories and spoke of his recollections as "filling his heart with joy and gratitude." Lee gave a vivid and happy picture of his American experience. He underscored his positive views of the United States. Less than subtly, he suggested Taiwan had emulated and then copied American democracy.

At one point in his speech he said: "I returned to my homeland determined to make my contribution toward achieving full democracy for our society." Lee talked at length about Taiwan's successful political modernization. He proclaimed that the "Taiwan experience" was unique and had much to offer the rest of the world, that it had "profound implications" for the future of the Asia-Pacific region (obviously including China). He stated that the invitation to speak at Cornell constituted recognition of this "remarkable achievement." He referred several times to Taiwan's "political miracle." More provocative still, Lee said that the "people of the Republic of China on Taiwan are determined to play a peaceful and constructive role among the family of nations. . . . We are here to stay."

Lee used the term "Republic of China on Taiwan" throughout his talk, trying to send the message that Taiwan has a long-established legal government and is a sovereign nation. He declared, "Our people are not happy with the position accorded our nation by the international community"—indicating that he wanted to upgrade Taiwan's status. At minimum he wanted to underscore Taiwan's sovereignty, which Beijing and the U.S. Department of State denied or ignored. He declared that only "mutual respect" would lead to the "peaceful unification" of China, when China adopts democracy and freedom and creates an equitable distribution of wealth.

On a harsh note, Lee declared, "Communism is dead or dying." This was an unveiled attack on China's political system and its leaders, and it was clearly deliberate. By way of contrast, he asserted, "Democracy is thriving in my country. No speech or act allowed by law will be subject to any restriction or interference." Lee also mentioned the coming "unprecedented direct election of the president and the vice president," scheduled for March 1996, and the fact Taiwan had a multiparty system and had realized the goal of popular sovereignty. Lee obliquely noted that he was a Christian (as every other president of Taiwan had been, though he did not say this), suggesting that Taiwan was very unlike China in terms of religious freedom, a point that had long impressed many Americans who make a contrast between the two.

Lee clearly made a hit. His visit to the United States was well handled and received vast press coverage. Media reporting was very positive. Lee had put Taiwan on the map and had improved its already good image in America and throughout the world, except, of course, in Beijing.

—⚬⚬⚬—

Most of the reporting about Lee's trip to the United States focused on the presence of a leader from Taiwan, Lee's moving speech at Cornell University, and democracy in Taiwan. It was also reported that the visit caused problems in U.S.-China relations and that the White House and Congress had different views about Taiwan. But for the most part the details of this and how the visit came about were left out.

The background to the visit is illuminating. The Lee visit was made possible by efforts of the U.S. Congress. The Department of State adamantly opposed the visit and said so many times in no uncertain terms. The State Department was unabashedly pro-Beijing, and it appeared much more so at this juncture. The White House likewise did not countenance his visit but tried to veil its feelings.

The events leading up to President Clinton's bending to Congressional pressure and ordering the Department of State to issue President Lee a visa against the State Department's advice tell a story. When Clinton campaigned for the office of president in 1992, his speeches mirrored an almost ubiquitous hostile sentiment in the United States toward China because of the Tiananmen massacre as well as images of China in America as an arms merchant, a nuclear proliferator, and a nation that aided terrorist states and impeded America's efforts to make the world a better, safer, and more democratic place. China also exported more to America than it bought from the United States, causing many U.S. workers to lose their jobs. On the stump Clinton exploited what his advisors considered one of President Bush's weaknesses: his China policy. Clinton constantly made an issue of China's human rights record and repeatedly proclaimed he would not "coddle dictators."

Clinton said he liked Taiwan; he had been to Taiwan four times when he was governor of Arkansas, essentially as a salesman for Arkansas's products. Lamar Alexander, governor of nearby Tennessee, had been eminently successful in promoting his state in Asia. He had brought the largest piece of foreign investment to the United States ever in the form of a Nissan auto plant near Nashville. He had attracted buying missions from Taiwan, which ignored

Arkansas and bought soybeans and other commodities from Tennessee instead of Arkansas. Clinton had changed this through his visits to Taiwan as Arkansas's governor.

Bill Clinton had never been to China, and judging from his statements during the campaign he did not want to go. But things are often not what they seem to be. Certainly Bill Clinton's proclivities were not. Though he ran as the "economic president," Clinton soon found that he had to make foreign policy decisions, and the two intersected. He also encountered a State Department that considered China a very important country and Taiwan "an annoyance." His secretary of state, Warren Christopher, was said to hold a grudge against Taiwan for being taunted by an angry mob in Taipei after President Carter cut diplomatic relations with the Republic of China. Christopher had been sent to Taiwan to "explain" Carter's decision. Some believed that Christopher had feared for his life at the time and blamed Taiwan's Foreign Minister Frederick Chien for staging the "mob attack" on his car.[3] The State Department, at both the top and throughout the ranks, favored Beijing over Taipei, disregarding Tiananmen, arms sales, and so on. Those matters could be negotiated, and doing so would advance the power and prestige of the Department of State.

Clinton also listened to the Department of Commerce, which he viewed as having important input in formulating U.S. foreign policy. In fact, Clinton probably gave it more say than any other president in American history because of its role in increasing American exports and thus creating jobs (for which Clinton could take credit). Commerce viewed China as an important market, one without bounds, and Taiwan as a small market with little growth potential.

In late 1993, President Clinton had met China's president, Jiang Zemin, in Seattle at a meeting of the Asian-Pacific Economic Cooperation forum. It was the first important venture into the world of U.S.-China relations for Clinton, and it was an experience he wouldn't forget. The talks settled no outstanding issues of importance. Clinton, probably with the public backlash caused by President Bush's sending National Security Advisor Brent Scowcroft to China on a secret mission to China after the Tiananmen massacre in mind, did not want to appear friendly toward Jiang Zemin; as a result he appeared neither friendly nor statesman-like.

Meanwhile, President Jiang (who was also secretary general of the Chinese Communist Party) toured a Boeing Aircraft factory, dined with Boeing executives, addressed Boeing employees, and even visited the home of a Boeing worker. At Boeing Jiang made at once an appeal for better Sino-American relations and an unveiled threat that jobs for American workers hung in the balance. China would place more orders and keep the company in business and workers getting checks if Washington treated China well.

Almost simultaneously with Jiang's very effective publicity campaign (as some in the U.S. media called it), Germany's Chancellor Helmut Kohl visited Beijing with an entourage of forty business leaders from companies such as Daimler-Benz, Siemens, and others. The German government accorded a high priority to business relations with China and had not allowed issues such as most-favored nation status and human rights to get in the way. Premier Li Peng, known in the West as the "beast" who ordered the soldiers to perpetrate the Tiananmen massacre, proclaimed even before Kohl's arrival that he would be handsomely rewarded. Kohl signed eighteen contracts, worth more than US$2 billion, during his visit. Included were deals for the purchase of Airbus planes. The news of Kohl's visit and the contracts were front-page news in Seattle while Clinton was there.

Clinton had to compete or be left behind. He reckoned being able to boast of creating new jobs was more important than slamming Beijing on human rights in terms of measuring his success as president and probably his reelection chances as well. Seattle thus constituted a major conversion for Clinton, according to some analysts of his presidency. Another consideration was that a host of big American companies were doing business with China, and they would willingly make an investment in doing future business deals by donating to the Democratic Party. So in 1994, the Clinton administration pushed a strategy of putting business first. Clinton unlinked China's most-favored nation status from human rights and spoke more about the importance of U.S.-China commercial relations. This pleased China very much. It also elated American businesses, especially the big corporations that were profiting from commercial ties with China.

But there was another side on the coin. The issue of China's abominable human rights record had been the focus of an annual debate in the United States when most-favored nation status (MFN) had to be renewed, according to the arrangements made when Beijing was granted MFN in 1980. Congress enjoyed raking China over the coals; many senators and representatives were able to look humane and win support from human rights groups and other anti-China organizations in their constituencies. To unhook the human rights issue from the debate about access to America's big and very important market was not something that Congress or various human rights groups liked, even though Clinton argued cogently that trade with China should not be held hostage. The link, according to some well-known members of Congress and a number of human rights organizations, had saved numerous political prisoners from misery in forced labor camps or worse and had caused China's human rights behavior to improve.

To make matters worse for the Clinton administration, Chinese leaders in Beijing were ungrateful. They rebuffed Secretary of State Warren Christopher when he complained of human rights abuses in China on the eve of Clinton's unlinking of trade status and human rights. This was widely publicized.

In November 1994, Clinton's party experienced a rout in the election. Republicans captured both houses of Congress for the first time in decades. Clinton was blamed for the setback. After the election Clinton's poll ratings dropped to an all-time low and Democrats, in increasing numbers and in a variety of ways, abandoned him. Meanwhile, Republicans were preparing to take the White House in 1996.

Other factors also played on Clinton's decision to grant President Lee Teng-hui a visa, against the strong pleadings of the Department of State. In February, with Republicans firmly in control of Congress, the Senate Foreign Relations Committee, reflecting public sentiment that was hostile toward China, stated that Tibet was "an occupied, sovereign country" and suggested President Clinton name an envoy to Tibet. In March, Vice President Gore and Premier Li Peng (who had ordered the Tiananmen massacre) clashed viciously on the issue of human rights during a United Nations conference in Copenhagen. The U.S. media found this very newsworthy and reported in detail on the event. Subsequently the White House turned down a proposed meeting between Clinton and Jiang Zemin in Moscow to mark the fiftieth anniversary of the end of World War II. Clinton was afraid of being seen as cozy with China.

At this juncture, the White House announced that Gerry Adams, head of the Provisional Wing of the Irish Republican Army, would be permitted to come to the United States and furthermore that he could try to raise funds in the United States. He would even be granted a visit to the White House and a one-on-one meeting with President Clinton. A few days later, the Department of State announced that it would not give a visa to Lee Teng-hui.

Various editorial writers had a field day with this. Even liberal writers attacked the White House for hypocrisy. Their assessment went like this: Clinton hobnobbed with Gerry Adams. He negotiated personally with Hafez el Assad, the President of Syria, a nation the United States officially brands a "terrorist state." He sent former President Jimmy Carter to negotiate with North Korea, another terrorist state, and the United States "caved in to North Korean extortion" and promised aid if North Korea would cease its program to build nuclear weapons. Clinton also overlooked atrocities in Chechnya in order to keep a summit date with Russian President Boris Yeltsin. Yet he refused to talk to Lee Teng-hui, the president of the nation that had faithfully followed America's lead in democratizing and was admired around the world first for its "economic miracle" and now its "political miracle." Taiwan had, in the words of a multitude of reporters, become a democracy more successfully than any country in the world in recent times, as demonstrated by its getting rid of martial law, holding elections, and respecting political freedoms and human rights.

The upshot of all of this was that in early May the House of Representatives voted 396 to 0 on a resolution stating that Taiwan's President Lee Teng-hui should be given a visa to visit the United States. A week later the Senate voted on a similar resolution, with 91 senators voting for it and one opposing. Clearly Democrats were not with Clinton on this issue, partly because the moral argument so strongly favored allowing Lee to come and partly because of Clinton's unimpressive reputation in handling foreign affairs, not to mention the fact that his political stock at this time was in the basement and falling.

The Congressional resolutions were not binding, but it appeared that if they were not respected and Clinton opposed a Lee visit there would be more to come. Clinton was very afraid, petrified said one insider, of Congress. To head off a crisis Governor Charles Robb of Virginia went to the White House to talk to President Clinton about the matter. He advised Clinton to give Lee the visa. Clinton did the expedient thing and ordered the State Department to grant the visa. This happened in spite of the fact that the Department of State, including both Secretary of State Christopher and Assistant Secretary for Asia and the Pacific Winston Lord, had made personal and definitive promises to Chinese officials in the Ministry of Foreign Affairs and other top leaders in Beijing that Lee would not get a visa and would not visit the United States.

There was another inconsistency in Clinton's volte-face: it came just after the Taiwan Policy Review had been concluded. This changed Taiwan's status in the United States in some positive ways. It is noteworthy, however, that the new policy did not change one thing: "top officials" from the United States still could not visit Taiwan, and "top officials" from Taiwan were not permitted to visit the United States. The new policy, while helping Taiwan a bit, seemed to reassure the People's Republic of China that it did not have to worry about Lee Teng-hui improving Taiwan's diplomatic status with a U.S. trip.

After Clinton made the visa decision, the Department of State tried to play it down, saying it was a private visit only. Indeed, Lee did not visit Washington and did not talk to any high officials from the executive branch of government while in the United States. Still, Lee's visit caused a lot of damage. The Department of State was embarrassed. It didn't know what to say to Chinese leaders. A State Department official said off the record that the department had told Chinese officials that President Nixon had visited China in 1972 and President Ford in 1975, at which times the United States had official diplomatic relations with Taipei and "no one had said that this violated anybody's one-China principle." The explanations only made Beijing angrier. It was a gross understatement to say that China was displeased with the affair. Given the sensitivity of the issue in China and the fact that it divided the Chinese leaders along factional lines it was probably described accurately as a "bomb about to go off."

—⁂—

"China went ballistic" was the often-heard description of Beijing's reaction to President Lee's trip by the Western media. The response of Chinese leaders in Beijing was to condemn the trip in unusually harsh terms. Chinese government officials made a formal condemnation; the government-controlled media took care in propagating it. Lee's visiting United States was an "outrage," a "betrayal." Statements like these from China were sometimes overstatement for effect, but in this instance they were genuine. Chinese leaders saw their policies toward Taiwan failing. Chinese leaders were incensed at both Washington and Taipei, and at each other. The issue, in fact, became so heated that Jiang Zemin rushed back to Beijing from a trip to Shanghai. A policy response had to be made by China's several-member political elite group, the Politburo of the Chinese Communist Party.[4] Few other debates about U.S.-China policy ever, publicly at least, got to this level.

The military and hard-liners joined the chorus. Both demanded stern action against Taiwan and got it. Spokespersons for Chinese core leadership forthwith charged that the United States' allowing the visit was "grave in nature" and violated three Sino-U.S. joint communiqués and infringed on China's sovereignty.[5] Chinese leaders leveled unprecedented criticism at the United States for having lied, promising that Lee would not get a visa. They mentioned people by name. President Jiang Zemin said that Secretary of State Christopher had, seven or eight days earlier, stated unequivocally that a Lee visit would violate the joint communiqués that were the legal basis of Sino-American relations.[6] Assistant Secretary of State for Asia and the Pacific, Winston Lord, Chinese leaders charged, had also asserted on the record that Lee would not be given a visa. Foreign Minister Qian Qichen pointed out that the Clinton administration had agreed on many occasions with Beijing's contention that a Lee visit could not be unofficial. "Does the administration have any regard for international credibility when it goes back on its own words on such a major issue of principle?" he asked.[7] Foreign Minister Qian declared that the visit constituted a "carefully planned political act aimed at splitting China and advocating 'two Chinas.'"[8]

A subsequent article in China's "official" news magazine, *Beijing Review,* stated that the idea, put forth by the U.S. State Department, that the visa was given because of pressure from Congress, was "not tenable." This reflected both a shortfall in Beijing's understanding of the American political system and extreme hostility in Beijing toward Taiwan. The lack of understanding of the U.S. political system had resulted in incidents in the past, such as a very thorny one in the 1980s stemming from a successful lawsuit against China in a U.S. state court over nineteenth century railroad bonds that became worthless. Beijing perceived that state courts had little or no authority and could be easily overridden by Washington. Chinese leaders, in fact, asked the Department of State to reverse the decision.

The notion espoused by the Chinese leadership that the United States, like China, is a country where all important decisions are made at the top, together with China's bunker mentality and the low-key stance of its diplomats in the United States after the Tiananmen massacre, explains China's lack of understanding of U.S. politics. Obviously this was a recipe for problems. Factionalism in the Chinese leadership (with hard-liner leftists itching to use the Taiwan issue against rightist reformists) and rapidly growing ultra-nationalistic sentiments in China also affected China's reaction.

China's official news agency, Xinhua, declared that the United States had "dishonored" commitments made in the three communiqués. It said that the United States "prevaricated" about calling the visit unofficial. It described the Taiwan issue as "explosive as a barrel of gunpowder." An article in *Beijing Review* went on to talk about "certain people" in the United States who see China as a "potential enemy" and believe that "only by maintaining a state of division across the Taiwan Strait can Taiwan be used to contain China."[9] The strongest statement by China was that Washington's decision to invite Lee was a "belligerent act on par with the Korean and Vietnam wars" and constituted a "wanton wound inflicted on China."[10]

China was at least equally furious with Lee Teng-hui and attacked him even more harshly. Signed editorials in the *People's Daily* were more vicious than those that had been published against Hong Kong's Governor Cris Patten, whom the Chinese leadership thoroughly hated. According to one observer, what Beijing said about Lee compared to statements about Khrushchev during the peak of the Sino-Soviet dispute—they might have been worse. Lee was labeled a "traitor," "schemer," "lackey of America," a person "with ties to the mafia," and "a sinner of the millennia." Lee's father was called a "Japanese running dog"—one of the worst things someone can say about a Chinese person. Lee was a "scab"—another term Chinese leaders used to show extreme contempt. Beijing issued diatribe after diatribe against Lee, going on for days and weeks. *People's Daily* called Lee's father a "100 percent traitor" for having served in the Japanese colonial government. Xinhua said, "To sweep Lee Teng-hui into the trash bin of history is the common, historical responsibility of Chinese on both sides of the Taiwan Strait."[11] According to a later article in *Beijing Review*, Lee's speech revealed that he is "turning his ideas of 'Taiwan independence' into action." Lee was also charged with trying to internationalize the Taiwan question and using the idea of two Chinese governments to "phase-in" a "two Chinas policy."[12]

Officials in Beijing, it was said, changed their view of Lee at this time, irreversibly. He had been seen earlier as caught between the advocates of independence and unification, not favoring either, a neutral and a moderate. Some even said Lee tried to maintain a balance. Now he was viewed as a proponent of independence, and the personification of evil. Evidence of this tectonic shift in view was easy to find.

An influential magazine in China, *Outlook Weekly*, delineated Taiwan's abandoning the one-China policy, orchestrated by Lee.[13] After 1988 when Lee became president, according to *Outlook Weekly*, he tried to promote Taiwan's sovereignty under the rubric of "one country, two governments," "one country, two regions," "one country, two entities" and other formulas that translated into two Chinas, or one China and one Taiwan. Lee, the magazine contended, was determined to establish diplomatic equality between Taipei and Beijing as a way of promoting Taiwan independence. Second, Lee tried to advance a new style of diplomacy, described by various terms such as "elastic diplomacy," "pragmatic diplomacy," and "flexible diplomacy." With these new policies, Lee sought to expand Taiwan's "international space" by promoting informal contacts with nations that diplomatically recognized Beijing by giving economic assistance, or bribes. Third, Lee made a number of foreign trips to promote Taiwan's national status, meeting frequently (though often informally) with other national leaders. This was Lee's so-called "vacation diplomacy."

Finally, in 1994, Lee gave an interview to Ryotaro Shiba, a Japanese reporter with *Sankei Shimbun*, one of the few papers in Japan that stationed correspondents in Taiwan. Lee spoke of the "sorrow" of being Taiwanese. He described the

KMT as an "alien regime" in the past. Lee declared that the Chinese Communist Party had never set foot in Taiwan and the government of the People's Republic of China had never collected any taxes in Taiwan—therefore how could it insist on Taiwan's being part of the mainland?[14] Lee, in this interview, compared himself to Moses leading the Jews from captivity in Egypt when they fled to build a country in another place. This gist of this statement was certainly not lost on leaders in China. Beijing was especially sensitive to Lee talking to a Japanese reporter. Japan had ruled Taiwan for fifty years, and many Japanese leaders were thought to have designs on Taiwan. Chinese leaders were also concerned about the fact that Taiwan had suddenly become a topic of interest in Japan rather than one that Japanese seldom mentioned.

Two months after the Lee interview with Shiba, *Asahi Shimbun*, one of Japan's largest newspapers, carried a front-page story about Taiwanese writing traditional Japanese poetry. Then *Asahi Weekly* published a series of pieces on Taiwan's history and republished the Lee interview. All of this suggested that Taiwan was no longer a taboo topic in Japan and that Japan, with its "revived nationalism and militarism" (a common view of Japan in China), was changing its policy on Taiwan.

This was confirmed in the minds of many Chinese leaders when President Lee, shortly after this, sought to attend the Asian Games in Hiroshima. Beijing threatened to boycott the event and Lee was politely asked not to come. But Lee won the battle insofar as Taiwan stayed in the news in Japan, and many Japanese sympathized with Lee and Taiwan. Many more thought Beijing had been petty and that Japan could not go on pretending that Taiwan, a major economic power, did not exist. Subsequently, Taiwanese reporters stationed in Japan were for the first time allowed into the Ministry of Foreign Affairs building, and frequent references began to appear in the media about Taiwan's successful democratization.

To leaders in Beijing the situation was ominous. Taiwan and Lee Teng-hui had turned the tide in its favor in the two nations that would determine Taiwan's fate, the United States and Japan. Both were now abetting Lee's efforts to propagate the view that Taiwan was a sovereign nation-state and should rejoin China only if and when it wanted to, which Chinese leaders thought was probably never.

—ⱳ—

Chinese officials decided to conduct missile tests in the Taiwan Strait to vent their anger and intimidate Taiwan. As a prelude, the Ministry of Foreign Affairs officially upbraided the United States for permitting the Lee visit. Summoning Ambassador Stapleton Roy for a scolding, China's Foreign Minister Qian Qichen said the visit was "evidence of U.S. support for the Taiwan authorities in creating 'two Chinas' or 'one China, one Taiwan.'" Beijing in the meantime cancelled a visit to the United States by Defense Minister Chi Haotian and a trip to China by John Holum, director of the U.S. Arms Control and Disarmament Agency. Greiner International, a U.S. company, was on the verge of finalizing a US$35 million contract to supply equipment and do engineering work on the new airport in Nanking. It was canceled.[15]

China then took an extreme step. It recalled its ambassador to the United States and put on hold the acceptance of former Senator James Sasser's appointment to the position of U.S. ambassador to China. Hence, for several months neither country had ambassadors in the other's capital. It was almost as if diplomatic relations had been severed.

On June 16, Beijing announced that it would not reopen talks scheduled between the Association for Relations across the Taiwan Strait (ARATS) and Taiwan's Straits Exchange Foundation (SEF), the two organizations that had met in Singapore in 1993 to negotiate differences between Beijing and Taipei and which had created considerable optimism about the two sides resolving their differences. On July 1, ARATS notified Taipei that technical talks between the two would also have to be postponed. Beijing blamed Lee for causing the termination of the talks, saying he had "poisoned the atmosphere" between the two sides.

China's response was in some senses understandable. China had recently experienced the rapid growth of extreme nationalism; Deng and his reformists substituted it for communism. The Taiwan issue was an ultrasensitive matter, and Lee's visit was as polarizing as it was unnerving in Beijing. Furthermore, with strongman Deng Xiaoping failing in health and heir apparent Jiang Zemin lacking the support of hard-line leftists and the military, the making of policy toward Taiwan was severely impacted by Lee's U.S. visit.

Tough actions were called for. A group of high-ranking retired officers wrote a letter to Jiang demanding a tougher line on Taiwan. One commented that "the Chinese military does not take orders from civilians." It was later reported that Jiang and Foreign Minister Qian Qichen, in order to survive politically, humiliated themselves with self-criticism before the Leading Group on Taiwan Affairs.[16] To some this harked back to the days when Mao, backed by the military, forced this kind of loss of face upon errant Chinese leaders as an expression of his dominance in China's totalitarian political system.

This was the backdrop to China's PLA firing missile at targets near Taiwan's shores, in a mock up of an attack on the island. Between July 21 and 28, the PLA conducted missile tests in a circular area ten nautical miles in radius approximately eighty miles northeast of Taiwan and adjacent to sea and air lanes between Taiwan and Japan. Beijing warned foreign ships and aircraft to avoid the area. The tests included firing four M-9 missiles with a range of six hundred kilometers and two DF-21 missiles with a range of more than one thousand miles into the test area. The missiles had sufficient range to hit any and all of Taiwan's major cities. The tests were part of a larger military exercise called Blue Whale 5. A whale in the shape of Taiwan was the symbol of Taiwan's proindependence groups.[17]

Before the tests started and in what seemed to be an explanation for them, Beijing accused Lee Teng-hui of "seriously damaging" relations across the Taiwan

Strait in making the trip to the U.S. Xinhua News Agency chimed in loudly, declaring that China should "use fresh blood and lives" to prevent Taiwan from rejecting unification. Beijing's intention was to create consternation and fear in Taiwan, and it definitely succeeded. At the end of the first round of tests, Defense Minister Chi Haotian gave a speech on the occasion of the sixty-eighth anniversary of the founding of the PLA; the speech turned into a harangue. Chi said in an angry tone that China would not give up the use of force and would not sit idly by if "foreign forces interfered in China's unification and get involved in Taiwan independence" or if Taiwan authorities insist on splitting China.[18]

In August, Beijing let loose with another barrage, to again vent its spleen and intimidate Taiwan. Between August 15 and 25, the PLA fired more missiles. As before, ships and planes were warned to stay clear of the area. Artillery firing and joint air-sea combat maneuvers were added to the PLA's repertoire. Beijing not only sent a message that it opposed Taiwan "sliding toward independence," but also that Taiwan was very vulnerable to military actions that would cut its foreign trade.

At the time 99 percent of Taiwan's foreign commerce went by sea—75 percent of it via the ports of Keelung and Kaohsiung. Almost 100 percent of its oil was imported. A whopping 82 percent of its gross national product derived from trade.[19]

In addition, Beijing hinted at launching an invasion. In other words, its military exercises could instead be the real thing—part of a bigger force it would join with to assault the islands. Beijing hoped to influence Taiwan's coming elections. A legislative election was scheduled for December and a presidential election for March 1996. Finally, the feud had a personal element to it, like the long and bitter struggle between Mao and Chiang Kai-shek. Lee Teng-hui was a "new Chiang Kai-shek," said a Chinese student in the United States. The anger likewise reflected the fact that Chinese leaders in Beijing were whipping up nationalistic sentiments against both Taiwan and the United States. This gave it momentum that one observer said may make it unstoppable.

At a critical juncture, just before the end of the campaign period for the election of a new national legislature in Taiwan, according to a Hong Kong newspaper, the People's Republic of China would hold military exercises with the intent of influencing the voting. State television in China subsequently showed air force, navy, and army units in combined military exercises, not by coincidence in Fujian Province adjacent to Taiwan and where citizens of Taiwan had been visiting relatives in large numbers over the last decade. A few days later Beijing said that the planned exercises were to "safeguard the nation's sovereignty and territorial integrity"—obviously aimed at what it regarded as separatist elements in Taiwan, notably Lee Teng-hui.[20] Chinese officials declared the drills would include bombing runs. A PLA spokesperson stated obliquely that the PLA had found "blind spots" in Taiwan's radar system during earlier tests.

Chinese forces did more. Some said it was military bluster; some said it was more than that. Reflecting what the Chinese military was thinking at the time, army officers told some American counterparts and even visiting scholars that America was too preoccupied with domestic problems and Bill Clinton was too weak to do anything. One senior official said to an American visitor: "It is bullshit that the U.S. will intervene. You did nothing in 1954 and 1958 about Quemoy and Matsu, and you are doing nothing in Bosnia."[21] In November, PLA marines, accompanied by tanks and other heavy weapons, made a practice beachhead landing from amphibious landing craft, as they would do if invading Taiwan. Jet fighter planes and other naval vessels accompanied them.

Taiwan's stock market, where half of the adult population had some of their money, took a dive. So did the housing market. There was a rush to buy American dollars. Individuals and business transferred large amounts of capital abroad, to the tune of more than US$8 billion.[22]

Meanwhile, in October, a Chinese official had told former state and defense department official and China specialist Charles Freeman that China was prepared to sacrifice millions of people, even entire cities, in a nuclear exchange with the United States to prevent Taiwan's independence. "You will not sacrifice Los Angeles to protect Taiwan," he said.[23] Some observers did not take this warning too seriously, since it did not come from Deng Xiaoping any other top Chinese official. But a couple of months later an American scholar with personal ties to Qiao Shi, a member of the Politburo and a top leader with an intelligence background close to Deng and Jiang Zemin, warned that if the United States used nuclear weapons against China, Beijing would respond by bombing New York City.[24] Both of these statements were repeated in big letters by the media and made scarier by China's present intimidation of Taiwan and the anticipation of what Washington's reaction might be.

In December, apparently in response to China's military threats against Taiwan but perhaps also in a show of force in response to Beijing's threatening statements against the United States, the *Nimitz*, one of America's aircraft carriers, approached the Taiwan Strait, the first time a U.S. aircraft carrier did this since Washington and Beijing established diplomatic relations in 1979. However, this show of strength occurred after the crisis was over, nearly three weeks after the election. Washington did not officially announce it, and when news reporters demanded an explanation they were told was that it was forced to sail there because of bad weather. Some officials in Beijing referred to this as a "very timid response."

—⟋⟍—

Meanwhile, in Taiwan, citizen response to President Lee's trip to the United States in June was positive. In the eyes of the island's population, Taiwan gained in stature throughout the world, especially in the United States. Lee got loads of positive Western media publicity, and so did Taiwan. The trip demonstrated that Taiwan has influence and friends in the United States. Lee's pragmatic diplomacy was viewed as a success. When Lee arrived back in Taipei, he was given a hero's welcome. A student just back from studying in the United States described it as like a victorious general returning to Rome during the time of the

Roman Empire. Lee had made it possible for Taiwan to burst out of its isolated diplomatic predicament engineered by Beijing. Some referred to Lee's visit as a diplomatic coup. Lee himself said he returned to Taiwan with a sense of great accomplishment.

But then the shock came. Beijing launched missiles. Taiwan's reaction to Beijing's threats and the missile tests and other military exercises can best be described as astonishment in the extreme. The government had tried not to overreact to China's hostility up to that point. When Beijing opened the salvo of hate speech against Lee Teng-hui in early July, the presidential office in Taipei asked government officials not to comment and pleaded with the press to play down the story. However, typical of a flourishing democracy, the media did not listen. Due to intense public concern over this new crisis in Taipei-Beijing relations, the request would not have honored in any case.

The image of the PLA firing at targets near Taiwan conjured up frightening thoughts in many people in Taiwan, of a military invasion of the island, of a flood of refugees trying desperately to get to some other country, of chaos, and most of all a massive loss of life. Many in Taiwan had recently read author Chang Lang-ping's best-selling book *August 1995: China's Violent Invasion of Taiwan*. Chang predicted an escalation of the conflict between Taipei and Beijing and an invasion of Taiwan by the PLA. In fact, A PLA attack on Taiwan had become the subject of talk shows and debates on radio and television and was widely discussed in private conversations among citizens. It was almost as if the book were prophetic. In any case, the government realized the possibility of an attack could not be dismissed.

At this juncture President Lee became less restrained. Lee charged that Chinese leaders had slandered him and repeated an earlier pledge to build a "Great Taiwan." He stated that the Republic of China is a democratic country and that China's missile tests "increased opposition from the people of Taiwan." Lee sought to create a backlash. Lee even told the National Assembly that Taiwan should "restudy" the question of nuclear weapons.[25] Parris Chang, a legislator from the Democratic Progressive Party and a former professor in the United States for many years, chimed in to support Lee. He said, "We are institutionalizing our independence and the People's Republic of China is going to have to accept this reality."[26]

But Lee's timing was not good. At this juncture political hopefuls were announcing their candidacies. They issued statements in support of and in opposition to those of President Lee, and the press aired them. Beijing's actions thus became the subject of an even bigger public debate. The opposition Democratic Progressive Party took the position that China did not have the ships necessary to launch an invasion of Taiwan. DPP leaders contended that in any event the United States would protect Taiwan. Party spokespersons also charged that the government and the Nationalist Party were playing up the threat in order to undermine the position of independence advocates. The DPP, ironically, in one respect pitched the feud much as Beijing did: The United States did not want to see Taiwan made a part of China. It was not in Washington's strategic national interest. On the matter of whether Taiwan was historically, legally, or otherwise part of China, the two diametrically disagreed. DPP leaders chided Beijing for its ignorance of history, and reality. The New Party, which had been formed by a breakaway faction of the Nationalist Party in 1993 and was comprised mainly of Mainland Chinese, refused to sign a petition in support of Lee. New Party leaders charged that the crisis had been "provoked unnecessarily" by Lee.

The *United Daily News*, which was one of Taiwan's largest newspapers and known for its regular anti-Lee reporting, joined the fray. It charged that Lee had caused "serious public anxiety" and that he had engendered "economic anxiety" that might lead to political chaos. Other newspapers did not toe the official line.

The Ministry of Foreign Affairs, unhappy with Lee for having excluded them from policy making related to the U.S. trip and its final planning (officials in the presidential office close to Lee had orchestrated the trip), did not cooperate as it normally did to support Lee. Leaks made this public knowledge. The press reported, apparently from a leak, that, to make the trip happen Lee had exerted some very "special efforts." The Nationalist Party had spent US$4.5 million dollars on a three-year contract with the public relations firm Cassidy and Associates in Washington, D.C. Cassidy was Washington's largest such company and a firm considered to employ the best. It was charged to set up the trip in the United States. This included a full-court press to solicit the support of Congress. Democrats in the United States, many from the liberal wing of the party, interestingly, staffed Cassidy. A former aide to George McGovern headed it. President Carter's former press secretary, Jody Powell, was an employee. So was Bob Bechel, a Carter political advisor. Gerald Warburg, once an aide to Senator Cranston, managed the account.[27] This public relations firm was eminently successful in its efforts to influence Congress and get Lee a visa. In addition, it drummed up loads of previsit publicity for the trip. Cassidy and Associates even made many of the nitty-gritty arrangements for Lee after he got to the United States.

Lee's supporters felt the effort was justified. They approved of Lee's use of Taiwan's vast financial resources to enhance its diplomatic efforts. Critics, however, pointed out that this was a lot of money and Taiwan was unwisely spent engaging in "dollar diplomacy." After a fairly long and heated public debate about the wisdom of Lee's sojourn, attention shifted to other aspects of cross-strait problems. For example, could Taiwan defend itself from an invasion? A quarantine? The Ministry of National Defense expressed confidence that it could cope with the threat. Some commentators, however, said the Ministry of National Defense was using the situation to get approval for a larger budget and had tried to put on a good face in a bad situation. The military took a pro-Lee line, yet how the top brass in the military felt personally about Lee was uncertain.

In November, when Beijing announced tests just before the election, the stock market dropped by 54 points (1.18 percent of its value). There was also large selling of the National Taiwan Dollar to buy U.S. currency. There was a repeat of this when China announced that it would do bigger tests during the March 1996 election. The stock market fell by just under 66 points (1.38 percent of its value). Some commentators said that the election would resolve arguments about Taiwan's relations with the mainland and the United States, letting the people decide.

Polls were taken daily during the campaign period. Most reflected that the population favored the status quo regarding relations with China, essentially the Nationalist Party's position, Lee's position. The results of the election, on the other hand, clearly favored the view that Beijing had had an impact on the election in the way it wanted. The Democratic Progressive Party, which advocated Taiwan's independence and its permanent separation from China, performed well below expectations. Party leaders had said after the 1989 election that it would be the ruling party if the electorate were allowed to choose candidates for all seats. In 1992, party spokespersons predicted that the party would be in power in four years. In this election it made barely any headway in this direction. Many DPP activist leaders, especially those most vocal about independence, were defeated. The New Tide faction of the party, which was adamant in support of independence, saw its members do very poorly; in contrast, the Formosa faction, which is more moderate, did better. Lee Teng-hui's Nationalist Party also performed badly. It won 46 percent of the popular vote compared to 53 percent in 1992. It lost seven seats in the legislative branch of government, and there was talk about coalition building at the time the votes were being counted.[28] The New Party, labeled a "conservative party" and which advocated unification, performed very well. It tripled its number of members in the legislature.

It looked as if Beijing had won the inning, though the game was hardly over. Beijing's "victory in intimidation" had created a delayed backlash yet to be seen.

5

America Debates China Threat; China Talks About America Threat

The June 1989 Tiananmen massacre caused China to become viewed in much of the world, especially in the United States, as an evil nation, a pariah. The pending collapse of the Soviet Union, which became apparent that year and finally happened in 1991, profoundly altered the perception of China by America's foreign policy decision makers another way: Washington no longer needed China. This engendered a debate among policy makers, as well as in the media and the academic community, concerning whether China had become America's new enemy. The debate was not too serious at first, but it soon became so.

Meanwhile, China's economic miracle boom, in progress for more than a decade, engendered what many called the "China economic challenge." Then came Chinese nationalism and anti-Americanism, which grew almost like an explosive force in China in the 1990s. China's expanding military spending and its acts of aggression in East Asia further provoked America.

All of this had a huge effect. In the United States, China changed faces from friend, to challenge, to foe. Some in Washington began to see China as the opposing pole in a new bipolar system. Those that recalled the bipolar system as one that made international politics comprehensible liked this. Some said America needed an enemy. The U.S. military was attracted to it. Apprehension of China also fit the view of political realists.

China likewise changed its view of the United States. America became China's enemy and Beijing's leaders frequently said so. This added fuel to the debate in the United States. The Taiwan issue, which many said was at the heart of the U.S.-China conflict, became more important. Taiwan was the only nonnegotiable issue between the two countries.

How did this all happen? What were its implications?

—ᴍ—

The underlying factor in the United States' coming to perceive China as a threat, if not an enemy, was China's marvelous economic success beginning in 1979. China's "miracle economic growth" enabled Beijing to challenge, in one very important respect, America's global prominence and thus its world leadership. The United States claimed to be the world's foremost power based in large measure on its economic might. China's economic growth brought this into question.

China's economic miracle also had a number of important and ominous secondary effects. American businesses became enthralled by the potential of the Chinese market, and through them China had a lobby in the United States. This, and American businesses' well-placed campaign contributions, meant China could buy influence from within and corrupt American politics.[1] China's trade surplus allowed it to invest huge sums of money in the United States. Treasurey bills were a favorite, but also land and businesses. Americans began to fear China was buying up the United States as the Japanese had done in the 1980s. The trade deficit meanwhile energized organized labor in the United States against China. Unions saw jobs disappearing. Labor was a molder of public opinion and controlled a large bloc of votes for the Democratic Party, and it increasingly disliked China. Finally, China's economic success made increasing military spending possible. The United States' status as the only world superpower after the demise of the Soviet Union was thus again challenged. Multiplying the effect of this, the United States cut its military budgets—a dividend of the end of the Cold War. On the other side, China's economic successes made Chinese leaders apprehensive that the United States wanted to block China from becoming a world power. They felt that Washington was jealous of China and feared China.

How did this situation come about?

In 1976, Mao died. After a brief interregnum government led by Hua Guofeng, the head of Mao's security forces, Deng Xiaoping, whom Mao had purged from the Chinese Communist Pary shortly before he died, returned from exile to seize the reins of political power in Beijing. By the end of 1978 Deng was in full control.

Deng deeply disliked Mao's radical (in private he said "insane") left-wing communism and all that it stood for: extreme egalitarianism, national central planning of almost everything, building the "socialist man," political campaigns and movements, power struggles, persecutions. But most of all Deng opposed continuing Mao's economic program of bureaucratic planning, self-reliance, isolationism, and stagnation, which had failed China. Deng was not alone in this view. He had broad support in the Chinese Communist Party and the government, especially from those Mao had savaged during the Cultural Revolution. They, like Deng, wanted to change the country's economic policies and give economic growth a top priority, disregarding communist egalitarianism. Under Mao, Deng proclaimed, China had grown slower economically than the average country and had fallen further and further behind the rest of the world. China was poor and, relatively speaking, got poorer. China was therefore weak and was not respected.

Mao had engineered a rather impressive program of nation building after he defeated the Nationalists in 1949. But within a few years, Mao's economic schemes and his command economy led to ruin more often than economic progress. His overall record in building China's economy and making China prosper was dismal. China, in terms of its gross national product, the total production of goods and services, grew slower under Mao after China's post–World War II rehabilitation than did India—slower than most Third World countries. China's global influence through trade, foreign investment, and commercial relations in general were minuscule. The largest nation in the world in population did not rank among the top twenty in global commerce.[2]

Deng was going to fix this. Beginning in 1979, he put economic reforms in place that were to truly transform the nation. Deng's growth policies were well considered: Begin with agriculture. Establish a free market. Open China up to foreign investment. Trade.

Deng perceived that economic development would probably be accompanied by political change; but the former would propel the latter, not the reverse. Democracy would come to China some time later, or perhaps not at all. This was the Singapore model, which Deng favored. It also characterized the success of South Korea and Taiwan. It was not the model the Soviet Union followed, upon the ill-conceived advice of some Western scholars.

Deng's was also a step-by-step approach. He started in rural China. The peasants, in spite of the fact that they had brought Mao to power, were the social group least enthralled with his style of communism. They took to the free market quickly. They asked Deng for private ownership, which according to Marx is the essence of capitalism, and got it.[3] Deng next set about to reform industry. He restrained the military brass (having, as noted earlier, humiliated them with their Vietnam War) to keep defense budgets low. He needed the capital to grow the economy. Once Deng's program gained credibility and nearby Asian countries and the overseas Chinese perceived that he was on the right track, China became seen as the world's greatest investment opportunity. Money came pouring in from the rich countries nearby as though China was one great magnet.

According to the British publication *The Economist*, Hong Kong was swimming in private liquid capital—between twenty and forty times that of Germany (which by any count was considered a rich country). Hong Kong money went to China as if there were no tomorrow. Overseas Chinese from Southeast Asia sent investment money to China in huge amounts, most of it funneled through Hong Kong.[4] Japan was the richest country in the world in foreign exchange. It invested willingly and generously in China. Taiwan was second in foreign exchange holdings; it put money into a host of industries and projects just across the Taiwan Strait in Fujian Province, where the majority of Taiwan's population hails from. Taiwan investors also liked Shanghai. South Korean investors went to North China. Deng's plan was eminently successful.

China's economic growth rates, as measured by increases in the gross national product, were proof positive.

In the 1980s, China was number one in economic growth among the world's large or important countries as measured by annual increases in the gross national product. China continued to top the list in the 1990s. Comparisons with the United States began to be made. For example, during the two decades that followed Deng's rise to political prominence and the start of his efforts to make China boom (from 1979 on), China's worst year was 1989, the year of the Tiananmen massacre, when China experienced nationwide chaos and political and economic paralysis. That year was better than America's best year during China's initial boom period. During the 1990s, the major portion of which was reported by the Clinton administration and a host of American economists to be a period of "great" economic expansion in the United States, China grew nearly five times faster. Before the end of the 90s, China was the second richest country in the world measured by its foreign exchange position. Only Japan was wealthier. China was buying more T-bills in the United States than any other country, causing some real concern that a massive sale might destabilize the American economy.

Projections of China's continued economic growth were even more daunting. In 1994, the *Economist* predicted that based on growth figures from the beginning of the Deng era to that point, China would pass the United States to become the world's largest economy in 2010. China would equal 140 percent of the U.S. economy in 2020.[5] Subsequent projections put that date even earlier. John Rohwer, the author of *Asia Rising*, forecasted in 1995 that China's economy would be 150 percent of the U.S. economy in 2025. Many other writers agreed. Rohwer said China would pass the United States, Japan, and Europe combined in the not-too-distant future.[6] One had only to believe that Beijing was on the right track in terms of its economic development (which seemed obvious), that China could do what Taiwan and South Korea had done (they were similar cultures), or that global capitalism would equalize incomes and national wealth throughout the world (as many Western economists long predicted would happen and would favor entrepreneurial peoples such as the Chinese), to think that China would dominate the world economically in the twenty-first century. China had between fourfold and fivefold the population of the United States, the Chinese people were smart and had a strong work ethic (and now someplace to use it), and Beijing was now propelled by an intense desire for China to prosper and become powerful. China would certainly fulfill these predictions.

Before he died, Richard Nixon had predicted that the world's largest communist country would become the richest capitalist economy in the next century. This indeed seemed to be happening. Nicholas Kristof, the *New York Times* correspondent in Beijing, wrote in 1994, "If China can hold course, it will be the greatest economic miracle in recorded history."[7] Futurologist John Naisbett, author of *Megatrends Asia*, wrote, "The Cold War is over and the Chinese won."[8] Even American China scholars who tried to play down the China

danger and who liked Beijing and wanted to improve U.S.-China relations perceived the coming of a powerful China.[9]

Many cheered China. But many more were apprehensive. Americans were
not used to being in second place and many did not take to these predictions
kindly. One observer noted, while trying to explain the situation, that the foot-
ball team that loses the Super Bowl, the second-best team in the world, is still
considered a loser. That was going to be the United States.

—⚭—

Not only did China's economic miracle become a big concern to America, a
virulent strain of Chinese nationalism that took off in the 1980s and 1990s
became another cause for seeing China as a threat and therefore as an enemy.
Chinese nationalism grew in part out of China's economic success. China's
miraculous economic growth was something Chinese could be proud of. But
more important in terms of explaining its antiforeign, anti-American character,
Chinese nationalism found its origins in Chinese history. This made it much
more than just pride in China's economic accomplishments and its modernization. Beijing's "new nationalism," as many called it, was to a large degree generated by dismay over China's decline and national humiliation in the eighteenth
century. China was a victim of Western imperialism. To most Chinese, China
had been wantonly and cruelly abused, controlled, and disgraced by the West.
Reaction to this was the force that brought Mao and the Communists to power.
It was now being revived. New debates were being heard about how China had
been exploited, its fragile condition in the past, and how Beijing under Deng's
leadership could finally rectify this. So Deng recreated China's nationalist spirit.
It was, Deng thought, a powerful force he could use to facilitate nation building
and at the same time solidify his popularity and political base.

But it became more than just support; it took on a life of its own. Chinese
are deeply, some say irrationally, proud of their nation's history and its accomplishments. All Chinese learn this from their families and from school. Some
Chinese even say it is innate. Chinese had long felt superior to other peoples; for
thousands of years they thought this. As one American writer noted, no other
country or people has nurtured a sense of superiority for so long.[10] Before the
Opium War in 1840, which is seen as a turning point in Chinese history and
the beginning of China's decline and humiliation, China had no inkling of any
place in the world that could even remotely compare to China in science, culture,
or anything else of importance. Thus, ingrained in China's psyche in the last
hundred-plus years was a desire to restore China's place in the world to what it
once was. One only had to look at some other nations that have sought to
restore their historical greatness to understand what a force this can be, then
multiply it many-fold for China.

Central to the debate about restoring China's greatness was concern about
lost territory and how it should be recovered. As a consequence the Chinese
leadership demanded the return of Hong Kong when Beijing discussed it with
the United Kingdom in 1984. Deng and other Chinese leaders, rather than

negotiate something less than a full, immediate transfer of sovereignty, which would certainly have been better for China in terms of its economic growth plans, asked for Hong Kong back. The same went for the Portuguese colony of Macao. Both were returned to the motherland.

Taiwan was the only land not slated for recovery that was once part of China and where Chinese were a majority of the population. And Taiwan was also important for strategic reasons. It thus became the central focus of Chinese nationalism and irredentism. In contrast, Chinese leaders said (off the record, of course) that "Chinese land" in Russia could be bought or would eventually "become China" because of massive Chinese migration there. Time was on China's side. This was not, however, the case with Taiwan. Time was not on China's side.

Two other factors also help explain the importance of and the potency of growing Chinese nationalism in the 1980s and afterward. First, to repeat a point already made (but which needs to be restated), Chinese officials who were conscious of the nation's history, and nearly all were, knew that past leaders that historians recorded as great leaders had unified the country. They were China's heroes. Those who allowed China to split or its territory to be lost were not; they were China's villains. Their position on the issue of recovering Taiwan hence would brand current Chinese leaders as either heroes or villains, as valiant or cowardly.

Second, Chinese nationalism was studiously nurtured by the post-Mao leadership for a very good reason: when Deng consolidated political power in China in 1979 he immediately launched reforms which made China de facto a capitalist country economically and in many other ways. The reforms quickly undermined China's communist ideological underpinnings. Deng thus sought to weld his brand of Chinese nationalism to economic development. In contrast to Mao, who preached Communist ideals including common poverty, Deng's most widely known quotation was "To get rich is glorious." Deng declared repeatedly that China had fallen behind the rest of the world economically under Mao. Because it was poor, China had no respect, asserted Deng and his reformist supporters. Beijing's international influence as a result of its economic weaknesses was little, he preached.

Deng was determined to change China, to modernize it. And, as noted earlier, he had the support of the Chinese Communist Party, government and the military. But he needed to fill the spiritual or ideological void that making China capitalist had caused. His opponents charged that he had forsaken Communism, that he had turned his back on the party's accomplishments, that he had created a spiritual vacuum and promoted mammonism, and worse. Deng thus emphasized making China strong and respected again. He played on latent feelings of national pride and China's historic superiority complex. This was Deng's answer to his critics. Deng also needed the nationalist "glue" to hold the country together in view of the fact that he had put into motion political and economic centrifugalism by decentralizing the economy and the political system in order to facilitate economic growth.

Nationalist sentiments gained momentum. In 1989, after the government suppressed the student democracy movement, patriotism (a form of nationalism) became even more vital to the Chinese leadership. In fact, the government increasingly nurtured it and depended upon it for its legitimacy. One of Deng's first nationalistic gestures was to restore Confucianism and other religions of China's past. He said that leftism in the Chinese Communist Party had been excessive in condemning Chinese tradition, which "Chinese are duly proud of." Deng brought back the traditional Confucian virtues of propriety, filial piety, charity, and the five human relations that constituted the backbone of Confucian teachings.[11] Ancestor worship was resurrected. In fact, the government built a huge, US$750,000 mausoleum as a place for Chinese to worship their ancestors. The Great Wall, once viewed as a symbol of feudal oppression that caused many of China's lower classes to perish during its construction, was made a place of national pride. There was talk of constructing the tallest building in the world in Chongqing, the capital of Sichuan, Deng's home province. Hainan Island, now a province, was said to sport the biggest zoo in the world with five thousand animals. The Three Gorges Dam, when finished, would be the largest in the world. The museum in Nanking that displayed evidence of the Rape of Nanking perpetrated by the Japanese Tenth Army in late 1937 became a popular place for Chinese to visit, even for children.

In 1995, the year Lee Teng-hui visited the United States and set off a crisis in the Taiwan Strait, the Chinese government published a work entitled *The Selected Works for Instruction in Patriotic Education*. It contained writing and speeches of Mao, Deng, and Jiang Zemin. *People's Daily* stated that the book was intended to fill an ideological vacuum and get eight hundred million peasants to "love their country" and "not forget the humiliation of foreign aggression." It was being read and talked about when China fired missiles at Taiwan.

In 1996, the Chinese government launched a US$4 million project designed to support the argument for pushing the origins of Chinese civilization back to the Xia Dynasty, long regarded by most serious Western historians as mythical. Foreign archaeologists were excluded from the work. The goal of the project was to provide the basis for believing in China's "sacred past." Some equated this to the Japanese government's manipulation of its history before World War II to feed nationalistic sentiments and support militarism.[12]

Foreign observers, especially from Western countries, could relegate China's behavior to efforts in nation building and acting as Third World countries do when maturing. Some could anyway. Many could not. In some critical ways China was changing, becoming a very different place. Chinese nationalism, built on China's historical greatness, assumed reestablishing China's "rightful" place in the world. China therefore needed to get lost land back. China needed to expand. This meant irredentism and an aggressive, even militant, foreign policy were the natural consequence.

Modern Chinese nationalism also contained an element of xenophobia. China's period of humiliation was caused by foreigners. China had to get even and could not trust outsiders, now more than ever, as they would try to keep a rising (and challenging) China down, divided and weak. Authorities in Beijing thus became more sensitive to foreigners living or working in China and their contacts with Chinese citizens. Changes in both China's attitudes and its treatment of people from other countries were noticed. So was the obtuse nature of Chinese nationalism, antiforeignism.

In another sense Chinese nationalism was different from that cultivated in other Third World countries: it was state-nationalism. It rationalized a strong state and a strong central government. China was a huge country of numerous nationalities, dialects, and diversity. Thus, this kind of nationalism was needed, and cultivating it was justified. But it had its dark side. Dissent was not welcome. Any challenge to a growing and powerful state was not tolerated. In some other places in the world nationalism was simply pride. In many developing countries the government made few if any efforts to control it. Not so in China. Justifications for the government directing and manipulating Chinese nationalism were manifold and in many cases hardly rational.

According to official or officially approved publications that appeared at this time, China's first emperor (known as the Yellow Emperor), who united the country, created a code of human relations that became the moral foundation of Chinese civilization that all peoples, whether Han Chinese or not, partook of over the centuries. Ancient history thus justified present policies.

Another odd explanation of China's history that appeared at this time was based on a study of blood groups. It demonstrated that all of the various peoples in China (even Caucasians in Western China) came from the same bloodlines, traceable as genetic descendants of the mystical Yellow Emperor. To some this recalled Hitler's theories of race and the state. In fact, Chinese nationalism, according to many of its critics (notably in the United States), was very similar to that nourished by Nazism in Hitler's Germany. Fascism thus became a term that many in the Western media used to define China's new nationalistic ideology and indeed many, if not all, of the aggressive actions taken by Beijing.

Worse things were to come: Chinese nationalism would develop an enemy complex and the United States would be the target.

—⁂—

China's pent-up emotions, its hostility and its frustrations, bolstered Deng's efforts to nurture nationalism. As it grew it more and more needed an outlet or target. Chinese nationalism as a consequence became increasingly directed at the United States. By the early 1990s, in fact, evidence accumulated suggesting the heart or essence of Chinese nationalism had become anti-Americanism.

In 1989, as noted earlier, the Tiananmen massacre dramatically changed Beijing's relations with the United States. Anti-Americanism became a yardstick for measuring the loyalty, and even the qualifications, of Chinese leaders. Reflecting this, a shift in focus in Beijing's world outlook, one that defined America as China's enemy, emerged during the years after the Tiananmen massacre. Official anti-American vitriol and propaganda were the result. Chinese leaders repeated the warning that America was trying to spread "spiritual pollution" in China to undermine the society and the government.

Beijing's rather simplistic anti-American views soon devolved based on these kinds of criticism into more potent ideas. The criticism also became much more bitter. Chinese officials began to attack the United States for seeking "global hegemony" and for trying to contain China or to keep it territorially split and thus weak. The words used became at once more visceral and more closely connected to the issue of China's sovereignty. "American hegemonism" and alleged U.S. efforts to divide China were increasingly linked. American criticism of China's political system, its human rights abuses, its exporting missiles, and its giving nuclear weapons and nuclear technology to other nations including terrorist states and enemies of the United States, played into the hands of proponents of Chinese nationalism, in fact, never mind that America's charges were true.

Meanwhile the collapse of the Soviet Union wiped out the "strategic imperative" in Sino-American relations. At the same time, it made the United States the dominant world power, which in the eyes of Chinese military leaders gave Washington a free hand to focus solely on China in pursuing America's strategy of "peaceful evolution" (meaning democratizing, and in this way controlling, China).[13]

The Gulf War subsequently had a shocking impact on the thinking of Chinese decision makers. It demonstrated the United States was far and away the dominant power in the world and, to Beijing, made Washington "more arrogant and more dangerous." China had to beware. In late 1991, a secret ten-point document written by the Communist Party's Propaganda Department and the Foreign Ministry warned of Washington's plan to weaken China. It discouraged contacts with the United States.[14] Deng parried this "battle cry" in early 1992 with the announcement of a policy of further economic reform and opening to the outside world. But he could not hold back the floodgates for long.

The promised sale of F-16 fighters to Taiwan by the Bush administration and the election of Bill Clinton in 1992, who approved of the sale and castigated Chinese leaders during the campaign as "butchers" he promised not to "coddle," accelerated Chinese anti-Americanism. Clinton's announcement in early 1993 that he would use trade sanctions against Beijing to improve China's human rights situation and force it to democratize turned the tables against Deng. Soon after this, 116 high ranking officers of the PLA wrote to Deng and Party General Secretary Jiang Zemin, demanding an end to "tolerance, forbearance and compromise" toward the United States.[15]

In 1993, the *Yinhe* incident (provoked when the U.S. Navy stopped and "illegally" searched a Chinese ship thought to be transporting ingredients for chemical weapons to Iran) was made to look like Washington had defined China as an enemy. The incident infuriated Chinese leaders, created deep suspicions of the United States, and further fanned the flames of anti-Americanism. In early 1994, a high-level meeting was called that brought party officials from all of

China's provinces to Beijing. At the meeting party secretaries and those officials in charge of propaganda were told that the United States was China's main rival and that Beijing must establish a "global antihegemonist united front." Chief of the General Staff General Zhang Wannian spoke at the meeting. He cited "blatant interference by American hegemonists" and U.S. support of "hostile forces" inside the country and elsewhere. He concluded that China's armed forces must accordingly be strengthened.[16]

A few months later, a military incident occurred involving U.S. and Chinese military forces. The *U.S.S. Kitty Hawk*, one of America's front-line aircraft carriers, and its accompanying battle group moved into the Yellow Sea to make a show of force that would be noticed by North Korea. The purpose was to dissuade North Korean leaders from pushing ahead with their nuclear weapons program. In an unprecedented move, China scrambled F-6 fighter planes and sent submarines to stalk the *Kitty Hawk*. The chain of events reminded many observers of the dangerous and provocative war games played by the Soviet Union during the Cold War. After the incident, one Chinese official suggested that the United States military did not belong in the Yellow Sea (even though it is international space and Washington was, as China knew, a strong advocate of freedom of the seas). Another warned that "next time" China would "shoot to kill."[17] Both the rhetoric and the incident itself seemed to reflect the fact that Beijing had made the United States its foe, or at least a significant portion of the Chinese leadership had. China's military and many of its top political leaders were clearly behind the vilification of the United States and labeling America China's enemy.

At almost this same time, Chinese leaders, taking note of Washington's normalizing relations with Vietnam, attaining naval stationing rights in Singapore, and upgrading of ties with Taiwan asserted that all were part of Washington's "encirclement strategy" (of China).[18] A document published by the Chinese Communist Party Central Military Commission (where top-level strategic decisions are made) on July 10, 1994, spoke in very aggressive terms of the need to use armed force against Taiwan. This view had been germinating for a year. Discussions mentioned taking action no later than 1996.[19]

The fact the United States was almost always mentioned when military threats or aggressive actions against Taiwan were discussed and when a final date for resolving the Taiwan question was set seemed instructive. According to a number of observers, Beijing planned the 1995 missile tests months before Lee's visit to Cornell, suggesting China's apparent outrage over the visit was orchestrated, a pretext for taking military action against Taiwan. There was evidence to support this view. In September 1994, the People's Liberation Army Navy, as China's navy is called, conducted its first large-scale exercises in the South China Sea in several years. U.S. Office of Naval Intelligence analysts said the maneuvers could be connected to a planned invasion of Taiwan.[20]

In early 1995, after earlier passing legislation (the Territorial Waters Act) stating that the South China Sea was the "sovereign territory" of the People's

Republic of China, Chinese warships surrounded Mischief Reef, not far from the Philippines and claimed by that government. Chinese forces then occupied the island. Some observers said this was a deliberate affront and challenge to the United States, since Washington had in force a defense treaty with the Philippine government. The very hostile statements about the United States after Lee Teng-hui's visit to Cornell University in 1995 and missile tests done afterward to intimidate Taiwan could thus be viewed as a natural continuation or outgrowth of China's "policy" of viewing the United States as its enemy and Washington's relations with Taipei as a just cause for preparing for war. Almost simultaneous with the first missile tests, an article appeared in a military magazine in China saying that Taiwan is the "gateway" for China to move into the Pacific, which is necessary for China to prosper and wherein lies its future.[21]

Growing anti-American nationalist sentiment may also be seen to have been behind the face-off between U.S. and Chinese forces as a result of the PLA's 1996 missile tests to disrupt Taiwan's election, that created the crisis that permanently changed the landscape of Washington-Beijing relations. Coinciding with the tests, a Chinese journal published a piece (likely provided to top military and civilian leaders before it was published) describing Taiwan as a "valuable military base" useful for "breaching the chain of island democracies on China's eastern periphery."[22] Just a month later, a book that was soon to become a best seller made its debut in Beijing. Entitled *China Can Say No*, this book, obviously cleared for sale by top Chinese Communist Party officials, was written by several very nationalistic, anti-American authors. The theme that the United States was China's enemy was unmistakable.

In the book the authors accused the U.S. Central Intelligence Agency of trying to destroy China's social order. The CIA and Hollywood were said to be instruments of America's "cultural invasion" of China. The accusations went on and on. Reflecting the linkage of extreme (though also ludicrous) nationalism and anti-Americanism, the writers, in the context of discussing intellectual property rights claims the United States had made against China, proposed that the United States compensate or pay royalties to China for its inventions of paper and gunpowder centuries ago. The authors went on to criticize China for being "weak" and recommended using force to reclaim Taiwan. They also called for an alliance with Russia to resist "American imperialism." One of the authors, when talking to foreign reporters not long after the book was published, called the United States "disgusting."

Unlike an earlier book, *Can the Chinese Army Win the Next War?*, which also called for preparing for war with the United States but was given less publicity so it did not become a best seller, the Chinese government gave its official support to *China Can Say No* and even financed making a television series based on it.[23] A Chinese scholar told a Western friend he did not dare criticize the book. He said he was advised that it was safer to be a leftist and better to be a nationalist than an internationalist.[24] James Woolsey, former director of the Central Intelligence Agency, said at this time that the Chinese government "seems to have fallen under the influence of people who want conflict with the United States."[25]

Following up on *China Can Say No*, in 1997 the PLA's Defense University put out a strategic publication entitled "On Commanding Warfighting Under High-Tech Conditions." The author or authors mentioned hitting the enemy's weak points (command, control, communications, information) "as if hitting acupuncture points when in kungfu combat."[26] The enemy was obviously the United States. Admiral Prueher, later commander in chief of U.S. forces in the Pacific, said that the PLA was "heavily into acupuncture warfare" because China wanted to "put at risk the things other people care about and then leverage that." According to U.S. reports on this subject that followed, China had established a base on the Pacific island of Tarawa and could deploy ground-based lasers to shoot down U.S. military satellites.

At about this same time, the PLA began simulating computer virus attacks in its military exercises. One Chinese general even claimed to have invented the term "information warfare." An expert in both Western and Chinese military technology observed that China watchers had been "periodically surprised" by China's military's technological breakthroughs, such as its joining the nuclear club in 1964, putting a satellite in orbit in 1970, and testing an intercontinental ballistic missile in 1980. He concluded that the history of technology has demonstrated that latecomers often catch up during a paradigm shift.[27]

In 1999, another anti-U.S. book hit the bookstores in China, this time detailing China's war plans. Two military officers, Colonel Qiao Liang and Colonel Wang Xiangsui wrote and published the treatise *Unrestricted War*. Both officers had been in Fujian Province in 1996 when missiles were fired at Taiwan, and both were concerned with the question of how China could prepare more quickly for war with the United States. They suggested using "other kinds of weapons" such as terrorism, drug trafficking, environmental degradation, spreading germs and viruses, and causing the collapse of the global financial system. They declared that unrestricted war "surpasses all boundaries and restrictions." The book cited twenty-four different types of war and recommended using them in combination, such as terrorism plus a media and financial war, depending upon who was the enemy and upon the circumstances. The authors declared that different tools of war must be employed against the United States since in conventional or Western terms America is stronger than China.

Connecting their views to China's history and nationalist feelings, they said that "unrestricted war" was a modern version of China's traditional way of fighting as detailed in Sun Tzu's classic book *The Art of War*. The authors perceived that their ideas could, and should, be put into practice. One of them, Qiao Liang, told a newspaper in China that Yugoslav President Slobodan Milosevic during the NATO air attacks on his country should have sent terrorist groups into Italy to attack NATO air bases, and he might have also considered terrorist actions against population centers in Germany, France, and Belgium.[28]

Following the U.S. bombing of the Chinese embassy in Belgrade in May 1999, another book appeared in bookstores in Beijing and other cities in China. Its title was *China's Road: Under the Conspiracy of Globalism*. One of the writers of this book declared that the embassy bombing constituted "probing" (by the United States) of China's reaction preparatory to using force in Tibet and Taiwan. The author went on to say that the United States would not admit a non-Western country like China, which has the potential to become a great power, into the global order. China, therefore, must prepare for conflict with America.

China's Road contained a map showing three new countries carved out of Chinese territory (East Turkistan, Tibet, and Manchukuo), alleging it was the Western media's effort to show how to split up China. The authors also asserted that Harvard scholar Samuel Huntington's "class of civilization" thesis is a "crypto-call for race-based Western unity against the only non-white power that can threaten the West's dominance—China." One contributor even accused the United States of developing race-specific biological weapons to use to commit genocide against China.[29]

—⁓—

Just as anti-American sentiment grew in China, anti-China feelings proliferated in the United States. After the 1989 Tiananmen massacre, public opinion in the United States toward China, especially in the media, in academe, and in Congress, shifted dramatically. Prior to the massacre and the subsequent manhunts, China, as measured by various public opinion polls, was well regarded by Americans. In fact, before Tiananmen, China was held in higher esteem than Japan, Taiwan, South Korea, and the Soviet Union.[30] Afterward, however, Americans came to view China much less highly than any of those nations. A sudden shift of opinion in the United States about China had occurred. Nearly 90 percent of Americans at this time felt the PLA's actions were wrong and unjustified. Only 22 percent believed that China would make the transition to a multiparty system, while 68 percent doubted China would become more democratic.[31]

As noted in chapter 2, the U.S. media was deeply disappointed with China, an important country thought to be heading toward democracy that had instead regressed to "Communist dictatorship." To many in the American press, China became an international ogre, a pariah. To explain what occurred or rationalize it in terms of their own ideological view of the world, the liberal Western media called the orthodox Communist hard-liners who did the dirty work "conservatives." The rationale: They were trying to block progress. But this was confusing to the reader of newspapers and the audience of television news because China's reformers were turning China to the right with free-market capitalism, openness to trade and foreign investment, and so on. They abandoned communism, exalted those with education and who worked hard, and allowed a bigger gap between rich and poor. In China, they were also called conservatives. One observer pointedly asked: Why did the Western media not call Teddy Kennedy a conservative for trying to preserve policies of the 1960s? Furthermore, he said, Kennedy resembled the hard-liners in China. These verbal gymnastics mirrored a changed situation: that China was now bereft of any political constituency in the United States.

The Left had long supported China. It promoted Beijing's joining the United Nations. It called for U.S. diplomatic recognition of the People's Republic of China and America dumping Taiwan. Now the Left abandoned China because of what it alleged was a brutal, "fascist" government. The right, or conservatives, in the United States, did not turn to support China, notwithstanding its gargantuan political move from the left to the right to adopt capitalism and some basic political liberties because, they thought, China was still a communist country.

Reflecting this odd but very unenviable situation, one very well-known political commentator declared that liberals and conservatives in the United States and the West should unite against China.[32] The academic community almost in unison attacked China for its rejection of democracy and its human rights abuses. Academics who defended China openly became the targets of a barrage of criticism from colleagues. The majority in academe thus switched from an earlier friendly view of China and from promoting good U.S.-China relations to condemning China. A well-known very pro-Beijing, pro-Marxist scholar, who turned against Beijing as a result of its massacre of students, began to regularly call the regime "fascist." Many others followed in using this term.[33] The academic world, which was at one time very pro-Beijing, was no so more. China, it seemed, was now deemed an evil fascist, perhaps even a Nazi, country.

As noted earlier, Congress, reflecting public opinion in America, became increasingly hostile toward Beijing after 1989. Congress was the place where special interests could vent their feelings and exercise influence. Special interest groups that did not like "Communist China," were outraged by the massacre, or had their own special reasons and got into the business of berating and condemning China. China, prior to the Tiananmen massacre, had the edge when it came to human rights criticism. No longer. When the media mentioned China, its human rights abuses were almost always cited directly or indirectly.

China went on the offensive and presented its own view: that human rights must be seen in the context of that nation's history and culture (an argument that should have appealed to U.S. liberal scholars who championed multiculturalism). But China's point of view was seldom read or given credence by anyone in the West. Meanwhile Beijing was assailed in the media and by Congress for having friends among terrorist states, for selling arms, and for causing nuclear proliferation. China was increasingly labeled an "arms merchant" even though Beijing sold only a fraction of the arms peddled on the world market by the United States, Russia, France, and some other countries. The mood of the country was simply anti-China, and nothing short of a miracle would change this.

The year 1991 was the turning point. The "Tiananmen massacre syndrome" might have faded and China might have experienced an improved image in the eyes of Americans, but this was not to be. In fact, the opposite was true. The Gulf War and the final collapse of the Soviet Union amplified America's hostility toward Beijing and its negative view of China. China was not on board with the democratic trend of the future. That was an odd view since during the run-up to the Gulf War, Beijing might have used its veto in the United Nations Security Council, thereby blocking U.S. efforts to use the aegis of the world body and make the effort look like a world community one instead of an American one. China's abstention was even seen to some as a hostile act. Its subsequent criticism of Desert Shield and Desert Storm, though apparently not genuine, certainly not harsh, and done mostly to win friends in Arab countries according to China's longstanding policy, did not sit well with Americans because of the media's interpretation of it.

Even more important was the fact the American victory, as interpreted by the well-known futurologist Alvin Toffler, changed the nature of warfare forever. Toffler wrote about three stages of the history of war: Stage one, when brave soldiers fought wars; stage two, when wars were decided by materiel and the winners were the most-industrialized nations; and stage three, the era of "knowledge wars."[34] In the last period, the present, the United States reigned supreme. The Gulf War also to a large degree erased America's guilt complex, its malaise, and lack of national confidence caused by the Vietnam War. The American government and the general population of the United States, in the words of one commentator, "were ready to take on the world." "The United States," he said, "was instilled with confidence."

Coinciding with all of this, Japan entered a period of severe recession. In the 1980s, Japan had been seen by many as America's nemesis. To Americans who looked at the world in economic terms instead of military terms, Japan was the enemy, not the Soviet Union. This indeed became a popular viewpoint as the end of the Soviet bloc became evident in 1989 and after. One writer had observed, "The Cold War is over; Japan won." But this point of view was erased with Japan's economic bad times and China's good times. Japan's recession, in fact, amplified China's economic and military challenges to the United States.

Another monumental event occurred at this time: the formal demise of the Soviet Union in 1991. This event meant that the United States was unquestionably now king of the mountain. After all, the world had been bipolar and lost one of its poles. Now it was unipolar. Thus, America need not brook criticism from anyone. It could mold the world in its own image. It could define moral conduct, popular culture, and good and bad countries.

The only opposing voice was China's. Beijing, in contrast, thought the world should be a multipolar one. It did not discount Russia as an international power. It put Europe, Japan, and itself on par with America. As noted above, China's economy was booming, its leaders were energized with nationalist sentiment, and the country was rife with growing anti-Americanism. China would not be subsumed into the category of lesser power. In this context, China's economic boom was a big factor in America's perception of the country. It was dangerous. Its economic growth was translated into increased defense spending at a time when all of the other major powers, including the United States, were cutting their military budgets as a consequence of the end of the Cold War. The U.S. media reported frequently on China's annual double-digit increases in military spending, its purchasing expensive Russian weapons, and so on. Americans wondered why China was doing this. Certainly it could not harbor good intentions.

Beginning in about 1993, perhaps even earlier, China began to be seen as a growing military challenge to the United States. Clearly China was not the military equal of the United States, but it was catching up. It would compete with the United States someday, perhaps very soon.[35] That year the Pentagon's Office of Net Assessment sent a new alarm: China was making significant advances in military technology and was more confident, and arrogant, because of it.

In early 1995, an East Asia Strategy Report done by the Department of Defense noted that other Asian nations "may feel a need to respond to China's growing military power."[36] This seemed to lay the groundwork, or provide the justification, for the United States to seek allies in East Asia against the People's Republic of China. The two Taiwan missile crises, in 1995 and 1996, gave energy and direction to this cause.

In 1997, a "big debate" ensued in the United States as to whether China should be seen, and treated, as a U.S. enemy. The publication of the book *The Coming Conflict with China* by Richard Bernstein and Ross Munro that year stimulated profound discussions about China's strengths and China's view of the United States as its future implacable enemy. Bernstein and Munro found many supporters. Popular columnist George Will declared that the "strategic aim of U.S. policy is, and must be, the subversion of the Chinese regime."[37] Will was reflecting what many Americans thought about China: the "evil" nature of its government, its growing economic and military power, and its hostile statements about the United States. U.S. military planners, and almost the entire military to some extent, began to see the China threat as invoking a return to the bipolar system. That would make military strategy easier to formulate and bring large defense budgets. Many others supported the argument simply to be cautious. "Keep the powder dry" was the thinking of many; China had been behind but was now quickly catching up, so the best policy was to get ready ourselves.

Critics of Bernstein and Munro said that the so-called China threat argument was woefully premature. China was far behind the United States economically, militarily, and in other ways. It would be decades before China could catch up. Some even said China was not catching up but rather was falling further behind the United States in military strength.[38] But few believed this. One observer called such an argument unbelievable and "pure peacenik desperation." Opponents of the China enemy view also warned that making China out to be a threat and an enemy was perilous. It would be a self-fulfilling prophecy. If China were treated as an adversary it would become one, whereas it would not otherwise. But the China threat school retorted that this was appeasement and recalled the actions of various European nations toward Hitler in the 1930s. Some even charged that those who contended China could not catch up in the fore-seeable future were "racists" for thinking China incapable of becoming a formi-dable power. The two sides became further polarized in ensuing months and the controversy became more and more vicious.

The debate meanwhile entered the ranks of the State Department. The word there was that China was not America's enemy and should not be so treated. And those who disagreed should keep their mouths shut or leave. But Congress took quite another view, almost diametrically opposed. This added to the already serious alienation between the two branches of government.

The American public, and to a lesser degree the media, sided with the China threat advocates. Both China's actions and the U.S.-China relations supported their view.

—ᗡᗡ—

As the 1990s came to a close, thorny issues and periodic crises continued to amplify the views in the United States that China was America's foe and in China that the United States was the enemy.

On March 6, 1999, the *New York Times* published an riveting story on the detention of Wen Ho Lee, a Chinese researcher at the Los Alamos National Laboratory in New Mexico, America's most sophisticated and most secret nu-clear weapons production facility. Labeled a "Chinese spy," Lee was said to have provided Beijing with "tons of information" on virtually all of America's nuclear weapons and missile technology. Chinese intelligence work with Lee as an op-erative was said to have resulted in China's being able to upgrade its strategic weapons quickly, a process that otherwise would have taken many years and might have been too costly. In particular, Lee's act of stealing America's most highly classified weapons technology gave China miniaturization capabilities and thus helped it develop multiple-targeted warheads and submarine-launched ballistic missiles, both of which were essential for China to strike U.S. cities with nuclear bombs. This put the American people in imminent danger.

Lee's case defined China as a hostile enemy country. It conjured up scenes of nuclear Armageddon that characterized U.S.-Soviet relations during the Cold War. Some said it was worse because the United States had understood Russia, to some degree at least; America did not understand "oriental China."

Reports followed that China's intelligence network had targeted the United States. Chinese agents had been stealing secrets en masse for years. China, the media noted, was the largest in the business. This proved that China viewed the United States as its enemy and that China should thus be seen as America's adversary. It was the start of the Cold War again, some said.

China denied it was spying on the United States, saying it did not need American military secrets and wasn't in that kind of business anyway. U.S. offi-cials rejected this reply since all countries spy on each other, while noting that the evidence showed China was doing it more than any other country in the world. Some said Beijing's denials constituted Chinese arrogance combined with efforts to cover up China's own weak scientific capabilities, not to mention the country's penchant for bold-faced lying about stealing technology from the United States (about which there was surfeit documented evidence). Beijing replied that singling out Lee and making accusations of stealing aimed at China constituted "official racism" on the part of the U.S. government and reflected jealousy about China doing so well scientifically, especially in weapons research. Chinese leaders also connected it to America's seeing China as a threat and American efforts to "keep China down."

In April, China's Premier Zhu Rongji visited Washington on a trip aimed at negotiating World Trade Organization membership for China. In the context of the Wen Ho Lee case and a report being prepared in Congress on Chinese spying (the Cox Report), parts of which had been leaked, President Clinton let Zhu "hang out to dry." According to both Western analysts and the Chinese government, Zhu had made large concessions on trade issues to get U.S. support and was snubbed and humiliated by the U.S. government. In fact, some say that Zhu's political position was so damaged by the U.S. rebuff that in the days and weeks after he returned to Beijing he was close to falling from power. Zhu was indeed thoroughly embarrassed by the failed trip. He and other pro-U.S. reformist leaders in China lost credibility and saw the incident as a sell-out and worse. Critics said that Clinton didn't care or didn't understand China's domestic political situation, or that he worried too much about public opinion in the United States.

Meanwhile, in the spring of 1999, NATO intervention in Kosovo, led by the United States in its military dimension, caused many Chinese officials to see America as "wildly aggressive" and much more as a "hegemonist power hostile to China." Chinese leaders expressed alarm. They generalized from America's bombings and other military actions. They saw a connection with both North Korea and Taiwan: U.S. forces might take military action against North Korea for similar reasons (seeing the North Korean government as a rogue state, causing grief for its people and threatening international peace) and, based on similar principles and logic, protect Taiwan.[39]

It was in this context as well as a milieu of seriously strained relations between Washington and Beijing for a host of other reasons, that U.S. planes, on May 7, 1999, dropped smart bombs on the Chinese embassy in Belgrade. At least this was the interpretation of officials in China, backed by the government's information bureaucracy and the state-controlled media. They charged that the attack was a deliberate act of war by the United States against China.

China first made issue of the fact that journalists were killed. Some officials even charged that the attack might have been aimed at them specifically. At least, the lack of sympathy displayed for their colleagues by American journalists indicated systematic ill felling or hatred toward China not to mention, of course, racism. The government harped on the issue daily. According to one observer, the government-run media etched the pictures of the burned-out embassy compound on everyone's minds in China and to some extent in some Third World countries, just as the West had done with the picture of a dissident standing in front of a tank, daring the driver to run him down before the Tiananmen massacre.[40]

The Chinese media said that the bombing could not have been an accident; American technology could not make such an error. Most people in Asia and in Third World countries were prone to believe China. Beijing thus refused to accept President Clinton's apology or his explanation of the incident. Instead China set difficult conditions before it would let the issue rest. Chinese leaders sought to keep the bombing of innocent civilians by U.S. planes before the public view in China and throughout the world. They chose not to let the matter die.

The U.S. view was that the bombing constituted a mistake, the kind that often happens during combat. It occurred because of a faulty or dated map. Clinton's apologies and the United States's paying reparations should close the matter. That Beijing refused to accept Washington's assessment and its efforts to deal with the "accident" was proof that Beijing's leaders found it highly beneficial, because of growing nationalist and anti-American feelings in China, to fan the flames of hostility toward the United States. To many in the U.S. media China sought to use the event to divert attention away its own dirty deeds. The tenth anniversary of the Tiananmen massacre was just around the corner. Chinese leaders indeed anticipated demonstrations in June and used the Belgrade bombing incident as justification for police vigilance and suppression, and for staging anti-American demonstrations in front of the U.S. embassy in Beijing and elsewhere. Americans, both the population and government officials, did not take kindly to this. After all, the bombing had been an accident.

U.S. officials also noted that China almost exclusively blamed the United States for the incident, when it was in fact a NATO operation.[41] Others explained that China's reaction must be seen in the context of the "spy scandal" in the United States and accusations against China in Washington. Tit for tat, in other words. One American policy maker said that China was "acting like a child" in retaliating in such a way about U.S. legitimate accusations of Chinese intelligence work in America. Later that same month a seven-hundred-page report issued by the Cox Committee described Chinese spying in the United States. China had stolen America's "legacy codes"—which contained all of the data the United States had gathered in fifty years of nuclear testing. Chinese agents also got all of the designs for current nuclear weapons, plus satellite and guidance systems.

This theft of America's most precious secrets was said to have facilitated China's moving at warp speed from a 1950s nuclear power to one with the most modern thermonuclear technology in its possession. The People's Republic of China, the report said, built a neutron bomb using stolen technology from the United States, improved the accuracy of its missiles (which endangered Taiwan as well as other countries in Asia), and would now be able to build missiles with miniaturized nuclear warheads that could be fired from mobile intercontinental ballistic missiles, which would make American cities vulnerable targets to missiles fired from deep within China.

Further, the report said, China had more spies in the United States than any other country. Chinese intelligence agencies operated through some three thousand "front companies" and had friends (whom it bribed) in U.S. high-tech companies doing space research. China sought to make agents of Chinese traveling to the United States (of whom there were eighty thousand every year). Beijing had for many years used a "vacuum cleaner" approach to getting all the technology and secrets it could without restraint.[42] According to the Cox Report U.S. security was "in shambles."

Among government officials as well as ordinary citizens throughout the rest of the country, the reaction was huge. Most Americans were flabbergasted and irate. China's response made the situation even worse. The Information Office of China's State Council issued a rebuttal entitled "Facts Speak Louder than Words, and Lies Will Collapse by Themselves." This report stated that China had long ago mastered the technology for building a neutron bomb and that China had developed this on its own, not through the theft of U.S. nuclear secrets. A subsequent report saying that the Cox Committee had gotten information about the loss of America's most sophisticated U.S. thermonuclear warheads by a "walk-in" Chinese spy who ostensibly was acting under orders of a Chinese intelligence agency and was told to give this information to the U.S. Central Intelligence Agency, confused the issue. Beijing, some said, wanted the U.S. Government and the public to know that it was a nuclear power on par with the United States and to send the message that Taiwan was vulnerable, and if Washington tried to block reunification, it would risk a devastating war.[43]

Another incident that revealed the depth of anti-U.S. feeling in China and anti-China feeling in the United States occurred in April 2001, when a U.S. reconnaissance plane collided in mid-air with a Chinese fighter aircraft, causing the fighter to crash and the American plane to make an emergency landing on China's Hainan Island. Beijing immediately blamed the United States for causing the accident, comparing it to an incident in 1998 when a U.S. Marine plane hit a ski gondola in Italy, killing everyone aboard, and to an American submarine hitting a Japanese fishing boat just weeks before. In both cases the United States was at fault. Foreign Minister Tang Jaixuan called U.S. Ambassador Joseph Prueher to his office and said that the United States "had made repeated errors." Jiang Zemin declared that the United States should apologize and bear all responsibility. He later commented arrogantly (according to the American media) that he was not worried about the incident since "if he [President George W. Bush] gets out of line his father will talk sense to him."

The Chinese media went on the attack, calling the United States "high-handed." A Chinese paper published a carton showing the pilot of the American plane looking at a map when the crash occurred. The caption read "another map error" (making reference to the U.S. explanation for bombing the Chinese embassy in Belgrade in 1999). China's top military newspaper was much harsher. Internet polls were conducted in China that showed that less than 4 percent of respondents wanted the release of the crew and an immediate peaceful solution. Chat rooms buzzed with hate language: "Kill the crew. Kill George W. Bush."

An enlarged Politburo meeting that included the Military Affairs Commission was called. According to diplomatic reports, the generals blocked three attempts by the Foreign Ministry to reach a settlement. China demanded an apology. Beijing refused to release the crew. After eleven days the crew left, but the plane didn't. The PLA demanded that the United States stop spying on China, calling it a violation of China's privacy and an encroachment on Chinese territory. Finally, civilian authorities interpreted what the United States said as an apology (mistranslating some words) and agreed to return the plane in pieces, but not before saying that the United States was "on a dangerous course."

The United States took a very different view of the incident but, like China, was angry and cast blame. The Bush administration took the position that the plane was flying legally in international air space. The Chinese pilot of the F-8 fighter was at fault because according to international law, the smaller plane should move to avoid a collision. U.S. officials added that the Chinese pilot had a reputation for "hot-dogging" and had caused near misses with U.S. aircraft in the past. The incident also occurred in a milieu of China recently challenging U.S. reconnaissance missions both in international air space and in international waters. Washington also connected it to political turmoil and irrationality in China, as indicated by the government's stepping up religious persecution (against the Falun Gong, a religious cum exercise movement) and detaining Chinese-born American citizens for spying; there was also anger in the Chinese military over the recent defection of an intelligence officer that confirmed Chinese technical assistance to Saddam Hussein.

President Bush took a hard stance, demanding that the crew and the plane be returned. He said he would not apologize. A large majority of Americans agreed with him. Congress, reflecting widespread hostility toward China, took an even tougher line. Senator Nichols canceled a visit to China. Senator McCain called Chinese behavior "reprehensible." Senator Daschle said that trust between the two nations was severely damaged. Representative Richard Gephardt condemned China for not abiding by international law. Several members of Congress proposed using the trade weapon against China. Many called for increased arms sales to Taiwan.

Shortly after this President Bush agreed to sell arms to Taiwan, with US$14 billion including offensive weapons (submarines). This was the largest deal for Taiwan since 1992, when the first President Bush agreed to the sale of F-16s. It broke precedent because the Taiwan Relations Act requires that the United States only sell "defense weapons" to Taiwan.

PART III

AFTER THE CRISIS

Taiwan's Voters Elect Their President Directly; Beijing Says Foreign Forces Are Trying to Split China

Beijing conducted threatening missile tests and military exercises before Taiwan's 1996 election. Chinese leaders succeeded in causing alarm, even panic, in Taiwan. But Lee Teng-hui won the election. China, in fact, generated a backlash and helped Lee win. Many in Taiwan said this. They also asserted Beijing looked foolish.

The United States, not to mention the international community, dramatically changed its view of Taiwan. Taiwan was now viewed as a full-fledged democracy, said one expert, "with all of the benefits therefore appertaining." The Western media labeled the election a historic event: democratization.

And, as a consequence, Taiwan moved further toward separation from China. According to various public opinion polls, the missile tests made a much larger number of people in Taiwan favor independence. The bottom line: Taiwan had democratized and it was now less willing to accept any deal with "undemocratic China."

Beijing and Washington grew further apart. Political factions in the two made the formulation of foreign policy—and compromise—more difficult. There was certainly less mutual understanding than before the election, perhaps less than ever before.

—⚉—

On March 23, President Lee Teng-hui and his vice presidential running mate, Lien Chan, won a "big victory" in Taiwan's first-ever direct presidential election. They garnered 5,813,699 votes out of around ten million cast, or more than 54 percent of the ballots in a four-way direct presidential race.[1] The Lee ticket won twenty-four of Taiwan's twenty-five counties. Lee won a majority in every county save Nantou, Taipei County, and the two counties in the Offshore Islands. Lee won a larger percentage of the popular vote than the very popular James Soong had won running for governor of Taiwan two years earlier. The Lee team won twice as many votes as the number two team, and more than the other three pairs of candidates combined. It was a momentous victory, a landslide, in an election that captured the attention of Taiwan's electorate not only because of its being the first such election but also because China had conducted missile tests in an attempt to disrupt it.

More than 76 percent of the eligible voters cast ballots. The turnout was almost ten percentage points above the most recent legislative election and six percent higher than the pollsters and the Election Commission had predicted. After the votes were tallied, one of Taiwan's largest newspapers called Lee's win a "resounding victory." All of Taiwan's newspapers, radio stations, and television broadcasters pretty much echoed this view. Peng Ming-min, representing the Democratic Progressive Party (DPP), Taiwan's main opposition party, conceded that Lee had won an unquestionable victory before the vote counting ended. Lin Yang-kang, often called Taiwan's best Taiwanese politician and a consummate campaigner, and also considered very charismatic, was the third largest vote-getter. After the election, Lin said that he accepted the "people's choice." Chen Li-an, the fourth biggest vote-getter among the presidential candidates, said he recognized Lee's "overwhelming" win.

In his victory speech, Lee said that the twenty-one million people of Taiwan "have written China's new history." He went on to say that the "big door of democracy is entirely open in Taiwan." Lee defined the occasion as the "most precious moment in Taiwan's history." It was a euphoric time for Taiwan.

It was not for China. One observer noted that Lee, who had been portrayed during the campaign in a mural on the side of a large building as a "caped crusader" stopping PLA missiles with his bare hands, signifying he was Beijing's nemesis, won the election handily. "For the next four years," said another observer, "Lee would have a mandate to resist Beijing's overtures and reject unification." "He will be Beijing's antagonist," said another. Proving that the day after the voting, Lee declared proudly, "The people had spoken. My win proves that the population of Taiwan does not favor unification with China at this time, but rather supports the status quo."

Lee won the election for a variety of reasons. But the most important ones had to do with relations with Beijing and the Washington-Taipei-Beijing triangle. Critical to explaining Lee's victory was the fact the United States helped Lee. It wasn't direct help or what might be labeled interference, but it was important. The White House feared a win by the DPP, which advocated independence, was certain to strain U.S.-China relations even further. No longer did U.S. officials say that the cause of democracy was furthered by the opposition doing better at the polls. America had promoted democracy in Taiwan. The United States had favored the opposition because of that. Now things were different. The DPP could no longer play the "democracy card." Washington, in a word, dumped the DPP. This was clearly a new factor in a Taiwan election. Most voters in Taiwan respected the United States and generally agreed with U.S. views.

Probably a much more important factor, however, was this: Chinese leaders had assisted Lee. The missile crisis and Beijing's outpouring of hostility, their ugly words and threats aimed at Lee, unquestionably made him more popular with voters. One Nationalist Party official noted that Beijing had been Lee's "best campaign aide." A member of Lee's campaign staff stated publicly that the "Beijing factor" (meaning the missile tests) had helped Lee win the election by a much bigger margin.[2] "The PLA gave Lee an added five percent," one said. A Lee opponent and cynical commentator said, "The stupid asses in Beijing really assisted Lee; they gave him a big election victory and a mandate he would not have had otherwise."

People in Taiwan were scared. But more, they were angry. The former emotion prevailed in 1995. Not this time. Beijing's actions were perceived differently. On this occasion it seemed singularly a case of Beijing trying to disrupt and impede Taiwan's democracy. Taiwan's citizens didn't like that.

Another important factor was that the missile tests were not a surprise. A second round of intimidation did not have the shock effect it had the first time. Taiwan's populace was ready and responded very differently. More precisely the feeling in Taiwan was expressed this way: The electorate strongly supported the status quo. And it wanted the government to do so also. And the government, led by Lee, did. Also, rather than the military threats by Beijing creating confusion and distrust of the government, it created a sense of a need for unity in the face of danger.

Lee Teng-hui understood the public mood well. Less than a month before the election he told an audience that they should not be afraid. They listened. Thus Lee became a fountainhead of stability at a time of extreme crisis. Some said Lee assumed the role of a "wartime leader." Lee also exploited the widespread feeling in Taiwan that Beijing was trying to stop Taiwan's democratization and was interfering with Taiwan's "historical" election. Lee spoke often and critically of Beijing's unwanted intrusions in Taiwan's domestic affairs.

Adding to this argument, Lee and his supporters pointed out a contradiction in Beijing's reasoning. How often have people in Taiwan and elsewhere heard Beijing's protestations about the United States and other countries that complain about human rights conditions in China? Chinese leaders accuse the United States of wanton and illegal interference in China's domestic affairs and violations of China's sovereignty? "What hypocrisy," said one observer—what about China's interference in Taiwan's internal affairs? Beijing's stance was not really inconsistent, though, since it regarded Taiwan as part of China. Yet most listeners believed Taiwan's point.

The people of Taiwan were also turned off by Beijing's name calling. Having preserved traditional Chinese culture in Taiwan, people were not used to the very ugly terms Beijing hurled at President Lee (notwithstanding rough political campaigns since 1980 and name-calling and slander in legislative sessions). Visibly voters did not approve of Beijing using the vile epithets toward Taiwan's popular president. In particular, they did not appreciate things said about his family. Some replied in kind, directing names like "Commie dogs," "uneducated rogues," "scumbags," and so on at Chinese leaders in Beijing. Some Taiwanese used the term "Chinese pig," showing contempt but at the same time suggesting Taiwanese were not Chinese.

One Taiwanese commented that Taiwanese are not, in fact, Chinese. "DNA research indicates that," he said. "Because centuries ago the Chinese government prohibited women from migrating to Taiwan, Taiwanese became a mixed race people.... We are not Chinese," he protested. Beijing thus had no business claiming Taiwanese as its people. "Taiwanese are special and need their own nation," he said.

To call Lee's father a traitor for having served in the Japanese colonial government was not well received by Taiwanese either. Taiwanese, who are 85 percent of Taiwan's population, do not recall the Japanese period as a bad time. They contrasted modern Japan and backward China. Japan modernized Taiwan; they perceived. Beijing's propagandists did not seem to understand this.

Beijing's charges that Lee supported Taiwan's independence also lacked credibility in Taiwan. Most people in Taiwan had long viewed Lee as a moderate or as sitting on the fence on this issue. Most saw Lee's position on the subject of Taiwan's being part of China, or not, as the majority one. Lee favored of the status quo, a wait and see position. Meanwhile, the population was very aware of the U.S. position on the missile tests and on Taiwan's democratization. They were assured (or so they thought) that the United States would defend Taiwan and the democratic processes. This was another reason to vote for Lee.

It is noteworthy that the opposition DPP interpreted Lee's victory as a victory for independence. A DPP spokesperson declared after the votes were counted that Peng (the well-known father of Taiwan's independence) and Lee (who, Beijing said repeatedly, supported independence) together got 75 percent of the vote. "The two candidates opposing separation got only 25 percent," he noted. Many DPP supporters, as postelection analysis showed, voted for Lee because they liked his stance on relations with China. Though they also felt the DPP's candidate, Peng Ming-min, could not win.

Some noted experts seconded the "three fourths" (for independence) interpretation. There was supporting evidence: Because the DPP made gains in the concurrent National Assembly election (and in its platform was a plank calling for Taiwan's independence), the electorate supported "legal and final separation" from China. The bottom line was that whether or not Lee supported independence, according to this interpretation he had a huge mandate to keep Taiwan separate. Most people in Taiwan took Lee's victory to be a watershed event and considered it a rebuff to Beijing. They deemed it now more likely that Taiwan would remain independent and sovereign in the foreseeable future.

Finally. before Lee's victory, especially during the campaign, a considerable measure of the political debate in Taiwan centered on whether Lee would gain a "credible" win. Many, in fact, were predicting that Lee, although he would not be beaten by another candidate, would not do all that well. Many said that Lee would not have a real mandate if he won less than 50 percent of the vote. Constitutional experts and political pundits talked about the need for a run-off election if no candidate got half of the vote. The Lee–Lien ticket's big victory thus gave Lee a mandate. He would be a stronger leader for the next four years. This was reason for alarm in Beijing, all the more so because Beijing intensely disliked Lee personally and had made this plain during the weeks and months leading up to the voting and because Chinese leaders now viewed Lee as for sure supporting Taiwan's independence.

—⚏—

This evokes two important questions: Why did China dislike Lee so much? What would this mean in the long term?

Lee Teng-hui had become president from the position of vice president when Chiang Kai-shek's elder son, Chiang Ching-kuo, president for a decade from 1978 to 1988, died. Lee was Chiang Ching-kuo's protégé. He was loyal to the KMT and supported Chiang Ching-kuo's policies. But, many in Beijing did not take Lee seriously at the time. They doubted Lee's ability to lead and questioned his mandate. The old guard in the KMT, who were adamantly anticommunist (but that hardly mattered anymore), espoused a one-China view. They would control Lee. At first Beijing had no strong objections to Lee, but some officials were concerned, even alarmed, because he was Taiwanese. "Ethnic" Taiwanese were thought to favor independence because Taiwan was a part of Japan for two generations before 1945. They had been "Japanized."

Beijing misjudged Lee. A few months later Lee became unchallenged head of the ruling Nationalist Party. This marked the beginning of his rise. In 1990, Lee was "reelected," or given another term in office by the National Assembly, which was a partly elected body of government but hardly a U.S.-style electoral college. At that time, the National Assembly was still "stuffed" with KMT holdovers from the days when the Nationalists ruled all of China. It did not represent democracy at work; on the contrary . . .

In 1991, Lee, as noted earlier, ended the state of war between the two Chinas, the Republic of China and the People's Republic of China, or Nationalist China and Communist China, or Taiwan and China. According to some observers, this was the first step in their legal separation. In 1992 the Constitution was amended, on Lee's urging, to provide for a direct presidential election for the first time in Taiwan's, China's, history. To Beijing, this was part of Taiwan's democratization *cum* independence process. It made Taiwan look like a sovereign nation (which Beijing denied it was) and widened the gulf politically between Taiwan and China. Why would Taiwan have a direct election of its president unless it was a sovereign nation-state? Chinese leaders understood the implications of this and knew others, including the United States, did also. "This was not good," one Chinese official said.

In Beijing's view Lee departed from the KMT's long espoused one-China policy in another way when he embarked upon what was called "flexible diplomacy," seeking "international space" for Taiwan. In January 1995 Lee ignored then rejected Jiang's eight points for reunifying Twiain. Jiang lost face. Lee's visit to the United States shortly thereafter was the "last straw." It, in the eyes of Chinese leaders in Beijing, showed that Lee unabashedly sought to pursue Taiwan's permanent separation or independence. Why else would he have made the spectacle he did in the United States? Why else would he have said the things he said? Beijing had come to see Lee as cunning, deceitful, and ruthless in the pursuit of an independent Taiwan, so Lee was China's enemy.

In 1996, when Lee was elected directly by the people of Taiwan while winning international acclaim and special accolades from the United States, Beijing suffered a big blow. The election gave Lee, whom Beijing had come to despise and to some extent fear, according to one observer, a "great mandate." He no longer had to pay obeisance to the National Assembly. His mandate was separate, like the American president's. Psychologically Lee's new status was even more impressive. After the election Lee was lauded by nearly everyone in Taiwan. He had overwhelming public support. Some referred to him as a savior. Others said he was the "greatest person in Taiwan's history." This being the case, if Beijing were right about Lee being a supporter of Taiwan's independence, Taiwan in the future would certainly be going in the direction of permanent separation from China. Lee, China's nemesis, was in charge of that.

Another way of looking at the situation was that Beijing had made an enemy of Lee. They had vilified him. They had deeply insulted him. They had tried to engineer his defeat. What could they expect from him now? Either way there were grave implications.

In the process of electing the nation's chief executive directly, though this was in considerable part a matter of extralegal power given to the president by virtue simply of a separate election, Taiwan's political system became more a presidential one. This meant, not to mention the tremendous acclaim and prestige Lee personally gained by the election victory, that Lee Teng-hui's political powers were greatly enhanced.

Putting the election in a still different perspective, the ruling Nationalist Party or KMT had not performed well in the two most recent national elections: in the 1992 and the 1995 legislative elections. It seemed that in 1996 Lee Teng-hui had reversed the declining fortunes of the ruling Nationalist Party. As a result Lee was fully in control of the ruling party. There had been doubts about this in the past, but those were now resolved.

From Beijing's perspective, the KMT was a "reconstituted" party—one that represented local interests, was Taiwanese in make-up, and reflected a "Taiwan identity" and most of all did not favor unification. Lee's election victory indeed gave new life to the KMT. Lee's opponents had left the party to form the New

Party in 1993. The New Party performed quite well in 1995 legislative election. In 1996, it did not do well. Lee was now truly in control, as Chinese leaders in Beijing saw the situation. From their perspective Taiwan had a dominant party or a one-party system. The KMT had many advantages in keeping power: talent, money, and more. In short, Lee could stay in power as long as he wanted.

Policy makers in Beijing looked for alternatives. Political debate in China's leadership hierarchy was intense. What if, given the increased powers of the president that the election had given Lee, the opposition Democratic Progressive Party should win the next election? DPP leaders had long supported a direct election and a stronger presidency with the expectation that they would win this office in the near future. Some DPP officials said at this time that they wanted to have a DPP member in the presidency in order to fulfill their desire to make Taiwan an independent country by creating the "Republic of Taiwan."

Even if the DPP did not win the presidency, there was cause for apprehension in Beijing. There had been speculation in Taiwan, no doubt heard in Beijing, that Lee was friendly with DPP leaders. There was even talk after the election, though mostly coming from Lee's critics, about the KMT and the DPP merging to become one party. The DPP had helped elect Lee. DPP leaders did not try to dissuade their supporters from voting for Lee, or at least not very much. Several top DPP leaders, who got along with Lee very well and considered him a close friend, spoke highly of him. Lee's victory, moreover, did not hurt the DPP's future, according to a number of its leaders' pronouncements at the time. After all, the DPP was made a legitimate and popular party by Lee. Some remarked that "Lee's KMT" was Taiwanese, as was the DPP. Lee had chased many Mainland Chinese out of the KMT; they formed the New Party. "Why not cooperate for an independent Taiwan?" one DPP official asked.

Finally, the election was something that the large majority of the population was very proud of. Voters who were interviewed after the election spoke of it being a "momentous event." They echoed statements made by Nationalist Party leaders and the media, including the foreign media, that it was the first and only election "of a top executive leader in 5,000 years of Chinese history." Judging from their tone of voice, many who said this were deliberately insulting Beijing. Many said the election had made it even more clear that Taiwan and China were not the same politically, socially, and in many other ways, and should not be forced into unification. Others said that the election made it more obvious than ever before that Taiwan was China's democratic model and that until rulers in Beijing realized this and implemented the model themselves there could be no reconciliation or unification. Still others commented that the whole world had seen what Taiwan had done and that the unprecedented direct election of the nation's executive leader had increased global support for Taiwan's right to choose its own future.

The election was indeed a defining event in terms of Taiwan's national identity. a point that deserves further discussion.

—ᴍ—

The election not only gave Lee Teng-hui, Beijing's nemesis, a historic election victory, it was also a taking-off point in the growth of nationalism in Taiwan and the maturation of its self-identity, both of which could, to anyone (including Chinese leaders in Beijing) looking at this phenomenon, be translated into Taiwan's more permanent separation from China.[3] President Lee and this election personified both.

Why was it the beginning point? Taiwan's history reveals that, for a variety of reasons, a national identity did not develop early among the island's population, as it had evolved elsewhere in the world. Migrants from Southeast Asia, or possibly from some other place or places first populated the island many millennia ago. The Aborigines, or the original inhabitants of Taiwan, did not have a common language or culture and were not in the process of building a nation when Chinese migrants arrived. Their situation was something like the American Indians when Europeans arrived in what is now the United States.

Chinese who migrated to the island beginning around a thousand years ago, were of two different ethnic or subethnic groups: Fukien Province Chinese and Hakka, who didn't have a province. These groups spoke different dialects of Chinese that were mutually unintelligible. They took up residence in different areas on the island. They did not interact very much or try to develop a common culture, language, or identity. Mountains fragmented the island. There were no roads linking various parts of the island. Powerful families wielded power and the political system was feudal in nature.[4]

In the mid-17th century, Taiwan was colonized by Holland for forty years. But no Aborigine or Chinese identity or any form of nationalism developed in response to foreign rule as it did in many other places. Perhaps it would have if Western colonialism had lasted longer. In 1683, Taiwan became self-governing, though the ruling Chinese regime was loyal to the recently overthrown Ming Dynasty. In fact, it was preoccupied with overthrowing the new Manchu Dynasty that conquered China in 1644. It did not promote a local identity. In any case local Chinese governance was also very short-lived. China subsequently ruled (though *misruled* might be a more accurate term) Taiwan for more than two centuries. Local Chinese, or Taiwanese, developed a disdain for the "interlopers and cruel officials" from China and frequently revolted. Still no local or island perspective developed, other than a dislike of China's rule.

From 1895 to 1945, Taiwan was a Japanese colony. During this period a sort of national identity seemed to gradually grow. But it was hampered by ethnic divisions among the Chinese population, efficient Japanese rule (which many local Chinese liked and certainly accommodated to), and Chinese culture that focused loyalty on the family.

Perhaps also explaining Taiwan's not developing a real national identity, the Chinese population in Taiwan did not have much access to information about decolonization movements elsewhere or about nation building. Finally, democracy did not become a rallying call for change in Taiwan at this time.

After World War II ended, Taiwan was made part of China again. But the local Chinese, now calling themselves "Taiwanese," did not speak the Chinese national language, Mandarin Chinese. And after nearly two generations of Japanese rule they were no longer familiar with Chinese law and did not know many Chinese customs. In 1945, most of Taiwan's population did not understand the main concern of Chiang Kai-shek's regime, fighting communism, or many other things about Chinese rule imposed on them. Local Chinese, Taiwanese, generally supported the Chiang regime but could not easily identify with it, having previously had little contact with it.

Then their support quickly waned. In February 1947, local Chinese or Taiwanese revolted against the government, an effort that was suppressed with massive killing, including a generation of Taiwan's would-be local political leaders. The incident left scars of hatred and exacerbated ethnic division and tension among the Chinese population. It also delayed the development of a national identity. The ruling Nationalist Party mollified ethnic ill feelings to some extent by promoting economic development. The "Taiwan economic miracle" became a unifying factor and an emblem of pride and national unity. Within a decade or so economic development begat political change in the form of democratization. More than economic development, democracy became the basis for a new Taiwan identity.

Taiwanese oppositionists wanted "full democracy." It favored the Taiwanese or locally born Chinese, who were in the majority by a ratio of more than 6 to 1. (Taiwanese constituted nearly 85 percent of the population, Aborigines less than 2 percent and Mainland Chinese 14 percent.) They also wanted Taiwan to be formally and legally separate from China. They advocated a Taiwan identity. But they learned a lesson in 1991, when they so blatantly made independence the central issue in a political campaign, and lost.

The Hakka Taiwanese, early immigrants themselves, also dampened the Fukienese Taiwanese extreme and anti–Mainland Chinese views. They opposed Taiwanese becoming the national language, as many of them did not speak it. Businessmen also cautioned against getting rid of Mandarin Chinese and espousing extreme views, especially antiforeign ones (which many said characterized Taiwanese politicians' attitudes toward China), which might hurt foreign commerce. Others pointed out that all ethnic groups were in the same boat in facing China's threats.

Meanwhile KMT memberships had become mostly Taiwanese and, in 1988, the party's chairman and the country's president became Taiwanese—Lee Teng-hui. The ruling party changed quietly, without a revolution. President Lee represented a coming together of views about Taiwan's identity. He was Hakka Taiwanese; yet he was the leader of the Mainland Chinese Nationalist Party. Lee was a unifier. He also sought to build a Taiwan identity which included, some said, Taiwan nationalism. Taiwan's national identity was thus late in forming, and Lee Teng-hui built it. How he did this is instructive.

In 1992, under Lee's direction, the government issued a detailed public report of the February 28, 1947 incident when the Taiwanese revolted against the Nationalist Chinese governor Chen Yi. Between eighteen thousand and twenty-eight thousand had been killed, said the report. Lee later apologized on behalf of the government. At his urging, the Legislative Yuan passed a bill compensating victims' families. A monument was also established. Under Lee, school textbooks were rewritten and Taiwan's history books began to emphasize events that occurred on the island rather than mainly records of what happened in China. Lee, who had a special interest in education, personally oversaw many of these changes. Lee meanwhile supported constitutional reform that made the president an official to be elected directly by the people and one who would represent Taiwan exclusively and democratically. During the early 1990s, as noted in previous chapters, Lee set about publicizing Taiwan's democratization and its right to have space and status in the international community.

In 1994, Lee supported James Soong in the first election for Taiwan's "provincial" governor. Soong was a Mainland Chinese, born in China. During the campaign, to bridge the ethnic gap, Lee spoke of Taiwanese as being anyone loved in Taiwan. In fact, Lee went into great detail on this issue. During that election Lee frequently used the term *New Taiwanese*. He meant by it anyone born in Taiwan or who had lived there for very long and identified with Taiwan (rather than with China, he implied). Lee was successfully building a Taiwan national identity that was not based ethnicity and which was inclusive.

In 1995 and 1996, Taiwan's nationalist sentiment increased markedly and the development of its national identity began evolving in a different direction. It emphasized Taiwan's democratization. But it also assumed China's hostility to it and the fact a democratic Taiwan would likely be an independent Taiwan.

While Lee Teng-hui became more and more the molder of the national identity he was increasingly hostile toward China and more proindependence. After the 1996 election, Lee boasted proudly and loudly about Taiwan's accomplishments. It was the first ever election of a top executive official, and Taiwan did it. "China was not able to do this," one of Lee's aides said. "This set Taiwan apart from China," another said. Lee sent the message that Taiwan was a nation (otherwise how could there have been such an election) and that its relationship with China would from now on be different.

Lee chided leaders in Beijing, saying in an interview with *Newsweek* that "inside they feel defeat, but don't speak out." He also declared that Taiwan was not a model of Asian democracy, disagreeing with Singapore's Lee Kuan Yew. He proclaimed that Taiwan was a "beacon for Chinese democracy."[5] In another interview, this one with CNN, Lee asserted that China is "ruled by two distinct political entities." He said of the Normalization Agreement concluded with Beijing by the Carter administration, which reiterated America's one-China policy, that it was "outdated." He compared it to clothes outgrown by a child. He went still further when he compared nationalism in China to Nazism and declared that Taiwan would still seek admission in the United Nations.[6] Lee's assistants announced on other occasions that people should not think of Taiwan so much as a part of China (if at all), but rather as a model for China to emulate, and when it did perhaps the two could find more areas of cooperation and maybe form a "commonwealth" or "Chinese community." But these terms assumed Taiwan had sovereignty and would keep it.

In his inaugural speech, Lee talked about a "new era of 'popular sovereignty.'" He spoke of Taiwan's contribution to the international democratic camp and the causes of freedom and democracy. He spoke of Taiwan's pride. Lee's message was that Taiwan was unique, and a unique people with a homeland should be a sovereign nation-state and Taiwan was in no way going to be inferior to China or accept being treated as a runaway child or a rebel province, as Beijing contended. "Taiwan has stood up," said one of Lee's people, paraphrasing Mao's statement of October 1, 1949, when he established the People's Republic of China after defeating the Nationalists.

Shortly after Lee's victory he replaced his foreign minister, Frederick Chien, who was a strong advocate of one-China. The new foreign minister was more of Lee's mind about Taiwan's new national identity. After the election, Lee repeated his "Go South" policy (promoting trade with Southeast Asian countries rather than the People's Republic of China). He pressed large enterprises and even some smaller companies not to invest in China.

In December, Lee called a National Development Conference, a kind of town hall meeting, attended by scholars, officials, and opposition politicians. The Democratic Progressive Party was well represented. At this meeting, it was decided to eliminate the provincial government on Taiwan. This "local government" (which had duplicated to a large extent the national government) had existed, many said, only because of the pretense that Taiwan was a province of China. This move was controversial inasmuch as the provincial government had just been democratized. But "streamlining" the government, Lee said, was needed. Observers suggested he intended to get rid of the "myth" of Taiwan being part of China, and that was more important. The DPP cooperated closely with Lee in the effort.

In early 1997, February 28 was made an official holiday. In so doing Lee sent the message that early autocratic "Chinese rule" of Taiwan had not been a good thing, and that it would be repeated if Taiwan were reunified with China. In his subsequent public speeches and pronouncements, Lee spoke more and more of Taiwan's national identity, its sovereignty, its nationhood, and it being a model of democratization. All were connected.

—⁓—

Beijing's ex post facto reactions to Taiwan's first direct presidential election and to Lee's victory were astounding and revealing. China's official news agency, Xinhua, reported the outcome of the election without comment, obviously seeking to play down its importance. It stated simply that the results were to be expected given Lee's "advantage in controlling various resources."[7] The government's Taiwan Affairs Office proclaimed with indignation that the election did not alter Taiwan's status. "Neither the changes in the way in which Taiwan leaders are produced nor the result can change the fact that Taiwan is a part of China's territory," a spokesperson said. *Beijing Review*, China's state-controlled international news magazine, did not report on the election during or right after the vote counting. In fact, it did not say anything about Taiwan at all in the issue immediately following the election. In an early April issue, the magazine carried a hardly noticed half-page article that merely reiterated what Premier Li Peng had said a week before the voting, the gist of which was that no matter what the outcome Taiwan's leaders must refrain from activities that would create two Chinas and that the Taiwan issue is an internal affair.[8] "Old hat," said one commentator in Taiwan.

Quoting Li Peng, who was widely blamed for the Tiananmen massacre, an observer in Taipei said that "Beijing wanted to send the message to Taiwan that its democratization would have the same end result as the democracy movement in Tiananmen Square in the spring of 1989." In subsequent press briefings by China's Ministry of Foreign Affairs officials, the military exercises as well as tensions with the United States were said to be a consequence of President Clinton's dispatching aircraft carriers to the Taiwan Strait. Nothing was said about the election or democracy in Taiwan.

The Politburo of the Chinese Communist Party discussed the election and concluded that the missile tests reduced the number of votes won by the opposition Democratic Progressive Party and "dampened the arrogance of those in power" (obviously referring to Lee Teng-hui). Beijing officials also argued that the results of the election proved that the population of Taiwan did not favor independence. Their logic: The Democratic Progressive Party won only 21 percent of the vote. The teams supporting one-China or "reunification" together got 79 percent. This argument seemed foolish. In fact, it was self-contradictory inasmuch as the Chinese media had for some time, and especially during the campaign, accused Lee Teng-hui of favoring Taiwan's independence. This, further, did not make sense in view of the fact that in the concurrent National Assembly election the DPP won a higher percentage of the vote than it had in the previous national election, suggesting that many DPP voters voted for Lee because they thought their candidate could not win and Lee, who supported an independent Taiwan, was a good second choice.

Chinese leaders in Beijing said nothing about the fact that they had opposed a direct presidential election because it represented a break from China or a separate, sovereign Taiwan. Similarly they failed to reply to the Western media's favorite comment that the election was a "final step in Taiwan's democratization." Even more poignant was that nobody in official Beijing said anything to the effect that Taiwan, because of its Chinese people and culture, was not suited to be a Western democracy. This had been stated many times by official spokespersons in Beijing. Beijing was completely silent on this point, even though the Western press made much of this. Western commentators, as a matter of fact, said that the election was proof that Western democracy worked in East Asia and that "Asian democracy," as advocated by many in the region, was not as good a model as Taiwan.

Nor did Chinese leaders admit that the election gave Lee Teng-hui a mandate, or that it strengthened his leadership, or that he would be an even tougher foe in the future. Beijing likewise did not mention that the election was evidence that a unique and a separate national identity was evolving in Taiwan, which the press in Taiwan and the Western media commented on frequently both during and after the election. Beijing did not even comment about money politics in Taiwan. Before the election, government spokespersons had said critically that the election process was "run by money and the mafia." No official in China, nor any media source, commented about the fact that Beijing's actions helped President Lee Teng-hui to win. This was said very often in Taiwan and was regarded as true by the Western media and foreign scholars. This was odd, in view of the fact that pundits in Taiwan had discussed the "Beijing factor" at length. In fact, there was general agreement in Taiwan that China had created a backlash, which helped Lee Teng-hui win appreciably more votes than he would have otherwise gotten, many said five percent more, and some said as much as ten percent. If it was five percent, assuming Lee needed fifty percent or more of the popular vote to have a mandate, as was widely proclaimed by pundits before the election, then Beijing had provided his mandate. One KMT official quoted in the media after the votes were counted said in this context, "We should give Jiang Zemin a medal. He was a super campaign aide."

Scholars in China did not talk about this, or if they did it was not heard outside of China or published anywhere. Similarly Beijing's impact on Taiwan's domestic politics was not discussed, at least in the open. The Taiwan media had earlier observed that Beijing's actions caused an alliance between the Democratic Progressive Party and the New Party that had existed before the missile tests to abort.[9] Had this not happened, many said, the KMT would have done poorly in the election and Lee would surely not have had more than 50 percent of the vote. No comment from China.

Beijing did not talk about the election being part of the evolution of Taiwan's political system. Chinese officials failed likewise to respond to criticism of their interference in the democratic process or in the Taiwan's internal affairs. Not only did Beijing deliberately ignore the election's implications, Chinese officials tried, in spite of the overwhelming tide of positive world opinion, to put another spin on it.

A researcher from the prestigious Academy of Social Sciences in Beijing wrote that "many countries held a mild, understanding, and even positive attitude toward the military exercise." The author noted that United Nations Secretary-General Boutros-Ghali called on Western countries not to interfere in China's internal affairs and asserted that this was the view of most countries and virtually all Asia-Pacific countries.[10] The Politburo concluded that the military exercises in the Taiwan Strait and its intimidation of Taiwan at a time of an election was popular in China and that it had aroused patriotism. Communist Party officials further perceived that it had "duly punished Taiwan's traitors."[11]

Some days after the election, a foreign ministry official compared China's view of Taiwan to the American civil war when officials sought to protect the territorial integrity of the country and opposed the sale of weapons to the south by European countries. Beijing even issued a delayed warning to the United States about the "danger" of dispatching the wrong signal to "Taiwan authorities" and said that by sending aircraft carriers to the area the United States had supported Taiwan's independence.[12]

Three months after the election, a spokesman for the Taiwan Affairs Office of the Central Committee of the Chinese Communist Party stated that the missile tests "had been a success."[13] The gap between the views of Chinese officials in Beijing, at least as reflected by what they said and what was reported in the media, and opinion in Taiwan and the United States, seemed to indicate serious problems in the triangular relationship and even a dangerous postelection "understanding gap."

—m—

In the United States and around the world the reaction to Taiwan's watershed direct presidential election was quite different, in fact, diametrically, different from Beijing's. That is, except for the Department of State and to some extent the White House. The State Department's reaction was that because the United States does not have diplomatic relations with Taiwan, no formal congratulations would be offered.[14] State Department officials were instructed not to make laudatory public remarks about Taiwan's unprecedented democratic election. Secretary of State Warren Christopher did, however, comment. He said, "It is my hope that with the Taiwan elections behind us, there will be a lessening of tensions in the area, and we will be able to return to contacts and discussions between China and Taiwan."[15] Christopher completely ignored the "democratic breakthrough" made in Taiwan as reflected by the election. He shunned its historical importance. "He saw the election as a troublesome event in U.S.-China relations," said one observer. A White House spokesperson was a little more responsive. Mary Glynn congratulated the people of Taiwan on their "great strides toward democracy," but she also expressed hope that tensions in the Taiwan Strait could be reduced in "days to come."[16]

Congressional reaction was markedly different. Members of Congress praised Taiwan's election, calling it "historic" and indisputable proof of democracy in Taiwan, more evidence of the difference between good Taiwan and bad China. Several members of Congress even discussed offering a formal invitation to President Lee to visit the United States. Others spoke of the need for the United States to establish diplomatic relations with Taipei. On March 28, just days after the election, the Senate approved the Foreign Relations Authorization Act, and included provisions in it for inviting President Lee to the United States, improving relations with Taiwan, and toughening human rights pressures on

Beijing. It even called for sending a special U.S. envoy to Tibet and provided for
Radio Free Asia broadcasts to China. The bill passed in both the Senate and the
House.[17]

The U.S. media also praised Taiwan's election. All of the major newspapers
carried lengthy stories and virtually all were very positive. They described the
election as "contributing to Taiwan's democratization." Many used words such as
"historic," "watershed," and "a milestone." Most described it as the final step in
Taiwan's democratization process. Almost unanimously the media described the
event as a victory for Lee Teng-hui and a setback for Beijing and the PLA. It was
called variously a "defeat" for Beijing, a "rebuff" of China's intimidation, and "a
stinging rejection of China."

The *New York Times* in a page-one news story declared that the election
served as a "forceful rebuke to China," gave Lee a mandate, and was cheered in
other countries in East Asia.[18] Editorially the paper said the election reflected
Taiwan's voters' opposition to the PLA's intimidation and threats and asserted
that "China's belligerence backfired not only on Taiwan, but across Asia and
in Washington." It also opined that the United States was correct in sending
aircraft carriers to the Taiwan Strait.[19] The *Wall Street Journal* editorially described the election won by President Lee as "the culmination of an extraordinary story of human perseverance and political maturation." It declared Taiwan
is on the "right path to democracy" and criticized the ambiguity in U.S. policy
toward Taiwan and China. Another editorial stated that Taiwan "needs the U.S.
to show support." One of the editors of the paper called Lee an "unreconstructed
democrat" and said his vision was "Taiwan leading the mainland back into the
fold, not the other way around."[20] *USA Today* carried two stories. One was titled
"Chinese threat helped Lee with victory cut across age, ethnic lines." Another
was headed by the words "Taiwanese voters verify the appeal of independence."
The former said Beijing had succored Lee's victory; the other declared that the
election indicated Taiwan was going further in the direction of separation from
China.[21] The *Washington Post* described the event as a "landslide victory for
incumbent President Lee Teng-hui, in an election that completed Taiwan's
transition from dictatorship to democracy and underlined its differences with
Beijing." The paper noted that Lee won more than 50 percent of the popular
vote, which Beijing had tried to deny him, and that it marked a "setback for
China's Communist leaders."[22]

The press elsewhere was equally effusive in its praise for Taiwan and gave
similar interpretations to the election's meaning and significance. The *Times* of
London called the election a "landslide victory" for Lee, a "blow" to Beijing, and
a "call for independence."[23] The *Financial Times* described the election as a
"sweeping victory" for Lee and wrote of the "courageous defiance" by voters. It
said the election reflected moderation in Taiwan and indicated that Beijing must
talk to Taiwan.[24] The *Guardian* wrote that Beijing had deluded itself into
thinking that it could use intimidation to influence Taiwan's voters and contradicted itself in chiding Lee before the election as a supporter of independence

and then claiming the election was a victory for prounification forces.[25] The *Daily Yomiuri* in Tokyo spoke of Lee's mandate. It also described as "very meaningful" the fact that Lee had been chosen directly by popular vote. The *Straits Times* in Singapore described the turnout as impressive in view of China's intimidation and described the election as "historic" and a big victory for Lee.[26] The *South China Morning Post* in Hong Kong (now under Beijing's jurisdiction) spoke of Taiwan as a "model" and it "realizing the dream of republican government." It even called Beijing's intimidation wrong.[27]

In summation, the reception to Taiwan's historic election in the United States was extremely positive. So was the reaction in most other countries. It demonstrated Taiwan's successful democratization. Beijing did not look good by comparison. Regarding America's future Taiwan policy the election provided clear evidence: Congress, the media, and citizens praised Taiwan's "accomplishment" profusely. The Department of State did not.

President Clinton Visits China, Polarizes Taiwan Issue

In June 1998, President William Jefferson Clinton visited the People's Republic of China. The trip was a landmark event but it also vividly illustrated how one event could be seen so differently by contending players and subplayers in the Washington-Taipei-Beijing triangular relationship.

In the United States, the president, according to the White House spin-doctors, made a statement on human rights that was the first ever heard widely in China; he reached agreements on weapons proliferation, the environment, and other important matters; he brought back with him commercial contracts that would create jobs for American workers. At the same time he impressed Chinese, both leaders and the common people, with his charm.

To China, President Clinton erased the stigma of the 1989 massacre by appearing in a public ceremony in Tiananmen Square. He was made to look foolish at times. He slavishly praised China's communist bosses just as they had asked him to do. He appeased China on Taiwan. He got promises from Chinese leaders that he should have known they did not plan to keep.

In Taiwan, there was some fear that the American president had sold out Taiwan. Most government officials, however, saw the visit as primarily a goodwill trip and an effort to dampen advocacy of Taiwan's independence across the Taiwan Strait. They knew it would have little impact.

In Congress and among critics of the Clinton administration, the trip was seen as an effort to divert attention from the president's personal and other problems. It also mirrored a confused China policy and created a backlash in Congress that made U.S.-China relations more contentious.

In most East Asian countries, the trip was seen to reflect a U.S. "tilt" toward China and away from Japan and Southeast Asia that was puzzling, to some frightening.

To the seasoned observer, the visit represented unreality, when reality was needed. It caused polarization and misunderstanding, and subsequent actions by the United States contradicted policies announced during the trip.

—⁓—

On June 24, 1998, President Clinton; his wife, Hillary; and his daughter, Chelsea, embarked on a sojourn to China. They arrived on June 25. It was the president's longest trip abroad—nine days (eleven counting travel time). It was, according to some reports, the longest trip abroad in recent memory for any U.S. president. It was also the most-accompanied trip by a U.S. president ever. Several cabinet members, 225 staff members, hundreds of military and security people, and more than four hundred journalists went.

The visit was given massive publicity by the White House, much of it picked up by the media. For weeks, even months, before the trip, White House public relations people, together with the Department of State, published tidbits about the trip: the agenda, purposes of the trip, personal interest items, and so on. The read: President Clinton was breaking out of his image as a domestic-only president. He was now a foreign policy president as well.

Clinton was returning a visit from the head of state of the world's largest country, a country second only to the United States in importance. Jiang Zemin had visited the United States in 1997; Clinton was properly reciprocating the call. The White House and President Clinton's press relations staff made the point again and again that the U.S.-China relationship was the most critical one in the world; it had to be managed well. The world would be a more peaceful place because of this trip. A Department of State spokesperson said at the beginning of the trip that the President's visit would result in the "de-demonization of China." There was a basis for this statement: China's image in the United States was bad. U.S.-China relations were at a low point, and that could be translated into likely hostilities.

In the sense of putting on a good show, the trip was an overwhelming success. It won accolades at home and in the Western media generally for the President's talents at showmanship and shrewd diplomacy. Some media reports even read that future historians may record Clinton's China trip as the high point in his presidency. The polls also showed the trip a success. Even looking beyond the superficial, the president attained essentially all of his stated objectives. He got through to the Chinese people, to the man on the street, as no other Western official ever had. The Chinese government did not block or censor most of what President Clinton said. He presented his, and America's, views on human rights, democracy, good government, the environment, and more. He talked about Hong Kong.

All of these discussions were allowed to go onto the airwaves via radio and national television. No other U.S. leader had ever gotten permission from the Chinese government to address the Chinese nation. Through personal magnetism Bill Clinton got China's leader Jiang Zemin to shed a lot of the baggage of history and speak as a friend. An American scholar on the trip described it as an "electrifying feeling" and a signal "that possibly something had changed."[1]

More important than this person-to-person breakthrough but perhaps because of it, the president got Chinese leaders to agree to join the Missile Technology Control Regime, a kind of treaty signed by many of the world's important nations, which sought to stop the proliferation of missiles that had been threatening international peace in recent years. President Clinton obtained a specific pledge by China not to provide missiles to Pakistan. Chinese leaders even promised, in return for a like U.S. pledge, not to target any of China's missiles on U.S. cities. Americans could now sleep easy with no nuclear-tipped missiles pointed at them anymore. To cap off the strategic agreements, China concurred with Clinton's position regarding chemical and biological weapons and promised that sales of U.S. high-tech items to China would not get into the hands of their military.

More important than any of these items, at the moment at least, President Clinton managed to enlist China's cooperation to deal with new nuclear powers in South Asia: India and Pakistan had both tested nuclear weapons just days before the Clinton trip. Getting China's assistance could, declared White House politicos, end the horrific danger caused by nuclear proliferation in South Asia. Beijing tacitly promised to help and more, not resume its own nuclear testing. Chinese leaders averred they did not intend to build more intermediate range missiles in response to India's new nuclear status.

As if to celebrate their successes, President Clinton and President Jiang Zemin together called for a "strategic partnership" between the United States and China. This new policy symbolized Clinton's success, White House spokespersons said, in making the U.S.-China relationship a happy one and turning the "most important nation in the world to the United States" into a friend that would help America promote peace and stability. "Clinton had taken historic steps toward the goal of world peace," said one of his people. Some even suggested he should get the Nobel Peace Prize.

President Clinton also left with some big contracts to help American business and workers. He had gone to China to promote U.S. commercial interests, among other things. He even got an agreement from Beijing whereby the United States could monitor trade to be sure that China was not cheating or violating any trade agreements with the United States. Perhaps most important in the commercial area were China's renewed assurances to Clinton that China would not devalue its currency. A Chinese decision to adjust the value of their currency downward, Americans had been told by the economic experts and the media, might trigger more devaluations and, with Asia already in a state of meltdown after several countries in the region experienced a serious economic downturn in mid-1997, might be the catalyst for destabilizing the entire global economy. At the time of the trip this seemed to be an especially acute problem because the Japanese yen had been falling, making Japan's exports compete better with China's. China was expected to retaliate.

   Clinton, in addition, engaged in preparatory but important talks about China's joining the World Trade Organization. This would serve two critical purposes: it would make China a cooperative member of the international community and would resolve the big trade deficit the United States was registering with China each year. The details were left to be worked out in the future.

   Clinton accomplished a lot.

   For those interested in more details, the context of the trip, or its place in history, there was something for them too. Jiang Zemin had visited Washington in October 1997 and had made a good impression. He was seen as important. Returning the visit thus helped President Clinton look stately, a man of the world, in the context of other news that had had just the opposite effect. Before the trip to Washington, China signed on to the United Nations Covenant on Economic, Social, and Cultural Rights and invited some religious leaders from the United States to visit China and discuss religious freedom. This had helped Clinton. Jiang had agreed when he was in Washington to resume a dialog with the United States on human rights. He even invited Newt Gingrich to visit Tibet. Jiang also brought some other goodies: he announced the purchase of fifty Boeing planes for US$3 billion, promised to cut tariffs on U.S. computers to zero by the year 2000, and talked of buying large amounts of American-made power generation equipment.

   Many Americans remembered Jiang's trip. This, plus the fact that most Americans perceived that China was a big and important nation, it appeared Clinton was right when he invited Jiang and should, in the American view of returning a favor, go to Beijing. Those with a little more knowledge of China were told that following Deng's death in February 1997, Jiang was unquestionably in control. There had been some doubt about that before. Thus with the leadership question having been resolved in China, Clinton's visit was timely and appropriate.

   Clinton aides also talked to the press about the visit representing a "turning point" in U.S. relations with China. They said that relations had been strained and the president's visit would change that. They also mentioned Clinton's policy of engagement, in contrast to ambiguity, which had been scrapped as U.S. policy on China, and isolationism, which was undesirable, hinting that opponents of U.S. China policy and critics of the trip were advocating America's retreat from international affairs.

   Clearly President Clinton's trip was well presented. "It was extremely well choreographed." said one observer.

—◆◆◆—

President Clinton's visit from Beijing's outlook was decidedly, profoundly, different. This was, of course, partly because Chinese leaders had their own perspective of the world and had a quite dissimilar set of objectives to be reached during his visit. Beijing also put its own "spin" on the trip. The state-controlled media in China reported that this was President Clinton's longest foreign trip just as the U.S. press did. But the conclusions to be drawn were very different. It was not because Clinton had so much to do—rather it was because China was such an important nation. Chinese newspapers and news magazines reported repeatedly that Clinton took over a week, almost two weeks, out of a very busy schedule to visit China. They noted the very large size of his entourage. They emphasized the importance the White House assigned to the visit. They boasted that at the behest of Chinese leaders, Clinton had agreed not to stop in any other country en route to China or back to the United States.[2] President Clinton, at Beijing's request, canceled a trip to Japan. Japan was Beijing's major strategic competitor in East Asia (after the United States) and a nation many Chinese leaders strongly disliked. So Clinton's not making a stop in Tokyo was a coup for Beijing. Moreover, observed the Chinese, the time of the trip had been moved forward. The state-controlled media said it was because of the importance of relations with China. The Chinese press did not say this had to do with the scheduling of the Paula Jones court date.

Beijing, like the White House, gave its interpretation to explaining the reasons for the trip. It was noticeably different from Washington's spin. President Jiang Zemin had visited Washington the previous year and the two presidents talked about a "constructive historical partnership." Clinton had to return the visit to China to "consolidate" this partnership. Explaining the need (by the United States) for this partnership, China's official spokespersons stated that China was playing an increasingly important role in the world, one the United States could not deny or control. Some cited the economic boom that would soon make China the number one economy in the world. Others mentioned China's new military strength.

There were other angles. Said one Chinese official, the "well-being of the Asia-Pacific region and the world" would be enhanced by a better relationship between the two countries, and the United States knew this; the only wars America fought in during the past fifty years were in Asia, and the region accounts for more trade than any other (nearly double Europe), and the percentage is increasing. Further elaborating on commercial relations, Chinese government officials and the media almost in unison talked profusely about China's role in maintaining economic stability in Asia in the midst of the "Asian economic crisis." This amplified the theme of China's importance.

Both officials and the media suggested repeatedly that the United States (confirmed to some extent by the Western media) was desperate to get China not to devalue its currency, as this would create an economic crisis. However, instead of citing global instability in trade, they said it might paralyze America's stock market and inaugurate a recession or even a depression in the United States.

Chinese spin-doctors noted that Clinton brought with him a huge "retinue" of commercial experts, business leaders, and so on, proving China's new economic importance. Often those in the retinue were portrayed as supplicants who needed, even begged for, Chinese trade and other economic favors. One writer even declared that if the United States canceled most-favored nation status for China, the United States would suffer even worse than China from this (a diametrically opposed view from Washington's as well as the rest of the world).[3] The Chinese media matter-of-factly suggested on several occasions that their government set preconditions for Clinton to be invited to China, which, it declared, were met. For example, Chinese media sources stated that the United States had increasingly recognized that Taiwan independence activities would endanger Sino-American relations and, therefore, in the months preceding the trip, the White House sent "relevant messages" to "Taiwan authorities" via former high-level officials visiting Taiwan. One magazine declared that the United States "seems ready to make its 'indistinct strategy' on Taiwan clear."[4]

The Chinese media also noted that President Clinton had agreed to meet Chinese leaders and attend a ceremony in Tiananmen Square. There was no discussion about the massacre there in 1989, but the message was clear: the United States, which had so loudly condemned the Tiananmen massacre and had refused to send high-level officials to China after that (even lower-level Americans refused to be seen in Tiananmen Square), had finally given in to China's supreme importance. Some officials even portrayed Clinton's presence in Tiananmen Square to constitute an apology and an admission of having made a mistake for condemning China in 1989 for the massacre of prodemocracy demonstrators. One said that Clinton had accepted the Chinese statement that the democracy movement was a counterrevolutionary rebellion.

As a prelude to the visit, official Beijing delineated various sources of Sino-American disagreements, seemingly to have a rationalization in case the visit did not turn out as well as expected. "The United States is a 'hegemonistic' nation that seeks to dominate Asian and global affairs and impose its views on others while constructing a new world order in its own image, and based on American culture and values," said one top diplomat. Chinese officials, as if they had consulted America's political correctness handbook, and to subtly make fun of Washington, said: "China instead wants diversity." China also, they said sarcastically, advocates the ideal of equality among nations. Instead of a U.S.-dominated world system, Chinese scholars and officials, the Chinese media said, seek to promote a "balanced, mutually-constraining multi-polarized world framework."[5]

Chinese news organizations blamed much of the discord in Sino-American relations on the U.S. Congress, pointing to congressional moves to obstruct White House efforts to improve relations with China. They specifically pointed to various bills passed by Congress promoting better relations with Taiwan as well as motions, senses of the Congress resolutions, and statements about China's spying and illegal campaign contributions.

During the time President Clinton was in China, especially the first part of the visit, the Chinese media said much less than many expected. More analysis followed the visit when it was clear there were no major snafus. This underscored the fact the media in China was controlled, if anyone did not know this already. While Clinton was in China, China's news people provided major reports on the first anniversary of Hong Kong's reversion to China, applauding the "one country, two systems" formula for the incorporation, while suggesting it would work to deal with Taiwan's reunification. Major issues that were discussed between Clinton and Jiang were cited in the press, with, of course, a Beijing spin.

On June 27, when President Clinton restated Washington's commitment to a one-China policy, this was given broad and detailed coverage. President Jiang was quoted as saying that by "scrupulously abiding by the three communiqués," the Taiwan issue could be handled. No mention was made of the Taiwan Relations Act. President Clinton was quoted as saying that he agreed that "Tibet is an autonomous region of China." He was further put on record saying that he "understood" why the acknowledgement of that was a Chinese precondition for dialogue with the Dalai Lama.

President Jiang said that the United States and China, both members of the Security Council of the United Nations, needed to cooperate on strategic issues and that two countries with "complementary economies" needed to promote commercial relations. Jiang's views on human rights, namely that they depend upon the country's history, social system, and culture, were reported. Clinton's contrary views did not get much media attention.[6] President Clinton was permitted to talk about human rights, but government-controlled media organizations did not relay this to local television stations or newspapers or even let them have a transcript.

Chinese analysts said later that what Clinton said had very little impact because no commentary or analysis was provided. Chinese scholars also explained that what Clinton said about human rights didn't matter because democracy and civil liberties were no longer at issue in China. Recent polls, in fact, showed that hardly anyone felt the right to protest was something people were born with. Furthermore, criticizing China on human rights grounds strengthened Chinese nationalism, which Chinese leaders wanted.[7]

In presenting an ex post facto analysis of the trip, the Chinese media cited the large number of agreements signed, while repeating comments about the time Clinton spent in China and the number of people that accompanied him. President Jiang's handling of the issues was given special play. One observer remarked that Jiang was a superb "barbarian handler." The amount of the trade deals was widely cited also. In fact, some Chinese newspapers portrayed Clinton as a "salesman." Some observers made a comparison with the use of this term in a derogatory way by the United States and various European countries to describe Japanese prime ministers visiting abroad in the 1970s and 1980s.

President Clinton's statement of concurrence (made to look like obedience to the "Chinese emperor" by the Chinese media) with China's "Three Noes" on Taiwan was given top billing. One newspaper in a political cartoon likened Clinton to a puppet on the end of strings moved back and forth by Jiang Zemin. The cartoon was copied by other newspapers throughout the country and shown on television.

In the realm of subtleties, the Chinese media made a lot of the places Clinton went: Xian, to pay obeisance to past Chinese Emperors; Beijing's

Tiananmen Square, for obvious reasons; Shanghai, to show the importance of Sino-American commercial relations; Guilin, to see the beauty of China; Hong Kong, to show American support for China's unification.[8] A professor of history at Beijing University wrote at the time, in a story that was carried widely by the Chinese media, that Clinton went first (even before he got to Beijing) to Xian, as barbarian guests did in the past, to see the graves of China's past emperors and pay respect to China's greatness. Xian, others noted, is also a city where few Chinese go due to the inauspicious nature of the place; it is a "cemetery of graves of China's past." Clinton was taken there to humiliate him as the United States had humiliated China in the past. Clinton was made to appear a barbarian supplicant and was duly insulted. Along the way the Chinese media reported that Clinton was fed a diet that Asians know often makes foreigners ill. So much for Chinese respect for Mr. Clinton.

Not long after the Clinton trip, in fact just a month later, China published a White Paper on military and national security issues that was very revealing in terms of Beijing's view of the United States. It spoke of "hegemonism and power politics" (code words for the United States) as the main forces causing threats to world peace and stability. It rebuffed military alliances (aimed at NATO and the U.S.-Japan alliance).

According to one commentator, the report made Clinton's idea of a "strategic partnership" between Washington and Beijing "appear naive, at best, if not downright foolish" and advanced the view that China should displace the United States as the dominant power in Asia.[9] Another quipped, "Apparently Clinton's charm didn't work in China or didn't last very long."

In sum, China's view of the trip was starkly at variance with the White House's presentation of it. Both, of course, gave it lots of spin. But to anyone seriously observing, they had disagreed strenuously on issues of substance and continued to do so after the trip. This did not suggest the trip led to a better understanding "between East and West."

—w—

To other Asians Clinton's trip also looked very different from the White House version. Rather than appearing the consummate politician and diplomat, Mr. Clinton was an oaf taken in almost totally by his Chinese handlers. He said and did things that undermined U.S. Asia policy and sullied America's reputation in the region.

First, Mr. Clinton met Chinese leaders in Tiananmen Square. The president told South Korean President Kim Dae Jung, who visited the White House earlier, that he was a guest of the Chinese government and should allow China to plan the ceremonies. "That was their right," Clinton said. His apologists subsequently explained that going to Tiananmen was the normal course for conducting diplomatic business. In the Asian mind, Clinton represented the most powerful nation in the world and could have easily declined. By going to Tiananmen, particularly on the anniversary of the massacre, and subsequently making a spectacle of himself by directing the PLA Band for a few minutes, he, deliberately or otherwise, acknowledged that China was once again a great power—the dominant power in Asia—and had to be accorded that status. The Tiananmen visit was thus seen as a repudiation of American supremacy in the area and worse: a signal that the United States was retreating from East Asia and China will fill the void. In other words, Clinton's actions symbolized the end of the "American century" and the rise of the "China century."

One Asian newspaper matter-of-factly repeated what a Chinese diplomat had said a couple of years earlier about Henry Luce's oft-repeated statement to the effect that the post–World War II era was the American century—that he was only "half right."

The Asian press also noted the hypocrisy in Clinton's going to Tiananmen Square. Recalling Clinton's condemnation of China's human rights abuses when he ran for president and in the first year or so of his presidency, they noted that he had changed. They assumed that America really didn't care about human rights abuses in Asia, as Asians had thought all along.

Second, President Clinton agreed in advance, again at the behest of his Chinese hosts, to make the trip to China without stopping in Japan. This, of course, played well in the United States, and Asians understood this. In the 1980s, Japan embarrassed the United States with its superior business acumen, high-quality products, technological skills, and education; now having fallen from grace, the Western press and especially Clinton's audience at home were quite willing to have the president snub Tokyo. Few Americans saw anything wrong with this. But to Asians Mr. Clinton had played a much different tune. The message constituted a denial of former U.S. ambassador to Japan Mike Mansfield's statement of more than a decade earlier that Japan was America's most important ally anywhere. Tokyo apparently doesn't play an important role to the United States in strategic terms anymore because China had passed Japan militarily, said an Asian observer. Never mind the fact that the United States and Japan have a defense treaty and Japan's military budget is four to five times larger than China's according to official figures (though probably about the same in real terms). Forget the reality that a threatened or jilted Japan could decide to go nuclear and that would severely destabilize East Asia. Or ignore an ally and send the message that the United States is abandoning Japan at a time when its influence is more welcome and more needed than ever.

According to the Asian perception, Japan had slipped from its economic pedestal in the president's mind. China, Mr. Clinton apparently perceived, was more vital to stabilizing East Asia economically than Japan, as long as Chinese leaders do not devalue their currency. In the eyes of most Asians, this was absurd. Japan was still the biggest economic force in Asia, proven by the fact that it is the world's largest aid giver and the number one foreign investor. By other measures Japan was still the economic giant of Asia. There was widespread concern, if not downright apprehension, felt throughout Asia about the fall of the Japanese yen (and little concern about the value of China's currency). China's boasts about its economic growth, Asians surmised, had bedazzled Mr. Clinton.

Third, President Clinton, in his own view, made a smart move on the Taiwan problem when he said that he did not support Taiwan entering any international organization "for which statehood is a requirement." This, in the president's mind would cool troublesome independence advocates and would likely evoke constructive talks between Beijing and Taipei. That, in turn, would reduce the probability of a future crisis in the Taiwan Strait, like the one engendered by the 1996 missile tests when the United States sent aircraft carriers and the United States and China faced off.

To Asians, however, Clinton had given in to another of President Jiang Zemin's requests with no apparent quid pro quo. Worse, he had acknowledged China's right to expand its borders and increase its territory to what it was at its historical high-water mark (twice what it had been in normal times). In other words, Clinton did not stand in the way of Chinese irredentism. Asians thus surmised he had given Beijing carte blanche to claim the entire South China Sea and to continue to bully legitimate Southeast Asian claimants as Beijing had been doing. So much for an America that opposes big power chauvinism and demands resolving territorial disputes peacefully.

Clinton's statement was also read by Asians to mean that Taiwan did not possess sovereignty. As a matter of fact, however, most nations in the world, including the majority of the countries of Asia, assumed it did, having only taken note of or acknowledging Beijing's claim to Taiwan rather than "recognizing" it (the required legal term). Thus, said one Southeast Asian leader, America under Clinton had blatantly turned its back on Wilsonian diplomacy in favor of big power realpolitik, and didn't practice that well either. The fact that Taiwan had democratized faster than any nation in the region in recent years and was recently applauded as having the freest press in East Asia (in stark contrast to Beijing, which barred some unfriendly journalists during President Clinton's visit) similarly didn't seem to matter to Mr. Clinton. "Pleasing big China is more important than democracy (even one America helped build)," wrote a Taiwanese commentator. This, Asians felt, was another example of American hypocrisy and a departure from traditional values in making United States foreign policy. One Asian reporter asked: What happened to the America that protects the weak against tyrants?

Fourth, Clinton engaged in talks and made public statements about China's cooperation in dealing with nuclear proliferation, arms sales, and global instability evoked by some rogue countries. In enlisting agreement on these matters from his Chinese hosts, he helped make the world safer, more secure, and more peaceful. At least this is what he apparently thought. Western pundits generally agreed or did not voice any loud criticism. To Asians, this was another sign of Clinton's once again turned his back on democracy—siding with autocratic China and its ally autocratic Pakistan against democratic India. India was sacrificed because of China's perceived importance just the way Taiwan was.

More relevant still, Clinton seemed to abandon a strategy of balancing power in Asia and in that way trammel China's appetite for domination in the region.

Asian military experts recalled that in February 1995, the U.S. Department of Defense issued a report entitled "U.S. Strategy for the East Asia-Pacific Region" stating that the United States would put America's alliances, particularly with Japan, on a firm basis and that Washington would help develop multilateral institutions in Southeast Asia. From that "position of strength" the United States would deal with China. By suggesting now the United States needed China strategically, Mr. Clinton gave the impression that China could not be constrained and that these earlier announced policies, which almost every nation in East Asia had taken seriously, were defunct.

The pomp and ceremony of Clinton's visit were also seen very differently from the eyes of Americans and Asians. To Asians, his hosts made Clinton's activities look trivial. They made events look important, yet it was obvious to Chinese most of it was show and not sincere. "They snookered him," said one Chinese. One cartoonist pictured Clinton as the face on Jiang's dog. A local commentator wrote, "President Clinton was a fool and didn't even know it." Another observed that he was defeated, using Sun Tzu's tactics, without a fight. A host of Asian writers also implied that he was "bought and paid for," indicating they believed the reports of China's military giving money to Clinton's campaign fund.

Some observers concluded there were lessons to be learned from this: that even presidents and their wise advisors do not know how Asians will view such events as this trip. Alternatively, they didn't think ahead or didn't care. One observer said: "Asians don't matter as Mr. Clinton seemed to demonstrate when he turned his back on his Asian fundraisers" (referring to Clinton's betraying Johnny Huang and others who raised money for his campaign).

Another explanation: Mr. Clinton was in so much trouble at home that only the U.S. view of the trip mattered.

—∞—

Congress and Clinton's critics at home took an even different view of the president's trip to China.

Even before the trip began, members of Congress critical of the Clinton administration or President Clinton himself noted that the president had timed the trip so as to be gone during the Paula Jones sexual harassment trial. That trial was scheduled for June 1998 and was certain to embarrass the president. In fact, many charged, as did the press, that Clinton moved the trip ahead to June, from its original November schedule, solely for that reason.

In other words, Clinton was escaping to China. Some even compared Clinton's going to China to some known fugitives running from the law. They mentioned in the same breath Johnny Huang and Charlie Trie, who had allegedly arranged illegal contributions from the PLA to the Clinton presidential campaign and the Democratic Party, who were missing in China at the time.

Others found different reasons for criticizing President Clinton's China visit. Human rights advocates in Congress and elsewhere excoriated President Clinton for what he didn't say and do while in China, citing his earlier strong statements about terrible human rights abuses in China. Various influential human rights groups, many on the left of the political spectrum, had said he should not go to China. Many accused the president of hypocrisy. Some said they were sickened by Clinton's willingness to meet Chinese leaders and attend a ceremony in the "bloodstained infamous Tiananmen Square." They declared that Bill Clinton had "colluded with Chinese leaders to erase the legacy of the Tiananmen massacre." Nancy Pelosi, the point person for human rights groups in Congress and one of the most vocal critics of Clinton's China policy, said bitterly, "Bill Clinton gave China a public relations coup."[10]

Meanwhile, human rights groups, together with a host of members of Congress, made much of the fact that three journalists from Radio Free Asia, who were scheduled to accompany the president, were denied visas at the last moment by the Chinese foreign ministry. Radio Free Asia, a congressionally funded operation established in response to China's poor human rights record that had been, in the eyes of many, set up specifically in reaction to the Tiananmen massacre, was in this instance a victim of China's human rights policies and its authoritarian system. Many members of Congress, in fact, expressed displeasure about Beijing's denial of visas to Radio Free Asia reporters and viewed it as typical of China's callous views about human rights and its rejection of concerns expressed by people elsewhere in the world.

In the midst of this controversy, a human rights group in Hong Kong reported that a large number of dissidents in China had been detained in advance of President Clinton's arrival in order to guarantee a smooth presidential visit and to avoid any embarrassment to President Jiang Zemin. In fact, dissidents were arrested in every city Clinton visited.[11] President Clinton's National Security Advisor, Sandy Berger, was even quoted at the time as saying that China "was acting as if people were debris to be swept up for a visitor."[12] Clinton's critics in Congress and in human rights organizations took this to be an open admission of guilt by the White House.

Other critics pointed out the fact that the trip had cost American taxpayers US$40 million and Clinton's working part of the trip was only a few hours, the rest being play and sightseeing. The conclusion was that Clinton was making a "show trip" and that it was for public relations, not serious business, at government expense. Some compared this sum to the money Kenneth Starr had spent, which had evoked endless White House derision.

Clinton opponents also challenged the White House argument that the trip was a resounding success. They said, for example, that though President Clinton had "addressed the nation" while in China and had mentioned human rights concerns in his speech, his comments did not appear in local newspapers or on local television or radio, and some of his points were mistranslated.[13] The impact of talking to the Chinese people was, therefore, superficial.

Most members of Congress stated, in contradiction to the White House's contention that the U.S. public's response to the trip was very positive, that their mail did not reflect this conclusion at all. Nor did public opinion polls, said congressional critics. According to one opinion survey, only 30 percent of those asked said the Clinton visit had been a success in terms of making relations better (unusually low for a presidential trip, especially one of this magnitude). Almost 60 percent said later that U.S.-China relations were the same or worse.[14]

Critics and members of Congress, referring to the time when the United States took China as an ally against the Soviet Union asked whether "strategic partnership" wasn't a Cold War mentality. Others suggested that since Sino-Soviet relations were now very good, the strategic partnership must be aimed at Japan—ostensibly China's most serious enemy. If that were the case, then Washington had turned against a nation with whom it had a formal security treaty, one many believed to be our most important ally. Still others pointed out that the Clinton administration had, "almost like magicians," turned relations with a large number of nations into strategic partnerships. This included Russia and even a number of small, inconsequential nations. Hence the term was meaningless, they said. In fact, one critic called it just another example of the Clinton administration's "foreign policy fluff." One observer pointed to the fact that Secretary of State Warren Christopher had earlier scratched the term *strategic partnership* from the title of a meeting he had in China. It was now back in vogue, indicating vacillation and disarray in making foreign policy decisions.

Congress, Taiwan's supporters, and advocates of a U.S. foreign policy in support of spreading democracy throughout the world (the so-called Wilsonians) were especially troubled by President Clinton's statement on June 30 in Shanghai: "We do not support Taiwan independence, two Chinas or one China and one Taiwan, or Taiwan's membership in international organizations where statehood is required for membership." Many called this selling out Taiwan, a long and loyal friend of the United States. Some said the United States had abandoned a nation that had produced an both economic and political miracles—both of which benefited its people immensely, making them the envy of much of the world while promoting the idea that Taiwan was a model for Third World countries. They also noted that the United States was instrumental in making Taiwan a democracy. Washington had cajoled, pressured, and helped Taiwan to democratize. Taiwan was an "exemplary student," said one observer, "and deserves to be treated accordingly." Taiwan supporters in the aforementioned groups charged that Clinton's statement, which had turned China's Three Noes Policy into a tenet of American foreign policy, was entirely uncalled for. "President Jiang had asked for it and Clinton gave it," one said. Still others said it was bought with campaign donations. Those taking a rule of law approach to foreign policy making said Clinton had violated U.S. law: the Taiwan Relations Act (TRA). Indeed, The TRA promised U.S. support for Taiwan's participation in international organizations.

There was also considerable cynicism expressed regarding Clinton's specific accomplishments. For example, President Clinton got a promise from the Chinese leadership to sign the Missile Technology Control Regime agreement (to prevent the spread of missiles). Yet the Chinese leadership called this agreement "formulated by Western nations" and "discriminatory" in its terms and stated that China should not abide by it while the United States sells weapons to Taiwan. On the issue of China's agreeing to help President Clinton stop nuclear proliferation, skeptics said that China had already recently done an extensive series of nuclear tests and did not need more. They also said that China had been the cause of the most unprecedented and dangerous case of nuclear proliferation in three decades by helping Pakistan go nuclear. Congressional critics said pointedly that the Clinton administration had ignored China's nuclear help to Pakistan and that this had led to India's series of nuclear weapons tests in May. Indian officials, in fact, had provided evidence for this when they said at the time of their tests that the decision to do this was inspired by China and China's help to Pakistan.

Members of Congress and others also questioned the supposed "breakthrough" Clinton made in getting Beijing not to point any of its strategic missiles at U.S. cities. They noted that Clinton had earlier stated in a public speech that no nuclear missiles anywhere were aimed at American cities. If China had agreed to not target American cities it must have had them aimed at U.S. cities before and, therefore, Clinton had lied earlier. In any event, this agreement was meaningless inasmuch as strategic missiles not targeted at cities in the United States (if it is true they weren't) could be pointed at American population centers in a matter of minutes.

On July 3, Christopher Cox, a heavyweight in foreign policy matters, especially China policy, and who later published the "Cox Report" dealing with Beijing's spying in the United States and illegal campaign contributions by China, wrote an open letter to President Clinton. Cox quoted Clinton's June 30 statement that "we think reunification has to be done peacefully." Cox then pointed out that the Taiwan Relation Act reads, "the future of Taiwan will be determined by peaceful means." Referring to Taiwan's future on the one hand and unification on the other, Cox said sarcastically: "There is a big difference." According to Cox's view and that of most members of Congress, Taiwan's future, whether reunification, independence, or something else, was yet to be decided. He further stated that Clinton gave the impression that the United States and the People's Republic of China had "plotted Taiwan's future and it would be unification." Cox followed up by saying that American policy must "uphold unequivocally the right of the people of Taiwan to determine their own future."[15]

Even before Clinton returned from the trip to China, Congress started the ball rolling to counter the impact of the trip. Congress passed legislation bolstering the Taiwan Relations Act and pressed ahead on antimissile defense (aimed at China). There was talk of other actions. It is hardly an exaggeration to say that Congress reexamined the Taiwan and missile defense issues as a direct response to what President Clinton said on his trip to China. Likewise it would not be hyperbole to say that Congress and most of Clinton's critics and many others observers saw the alleged successes of the trip as White House hype and the trip as bad and dangerous for Taiwan. In view of the already very strained relations between the two branches of government, the trip further damaged White House-congressional relations.

—⚂—

The reaction in Taiwan offers an interesting and still different perspective on President Clinton's trip to China. Officials in Taipei had long been apprehensive of presidential initiatives in making China policy and presidents' trips to Beijing. This was especially true of this trip, given what they saw as Bill Clinton's proclivity to make foreign policy decisions based on personal political considerations rather than principles or the U.S. national interest. Notably, leaders in Taipei felt Clinton was in debt to Beijing for campaign contributions. The public also believed this. They had read in the newspapers that at the time of the 1996 election campaign that a Clinton aide had been to Taipei for money and had not gotten any. Liu Tai-ying, manager of the Nationalist Party's funds, had stated publicly that a Clinton advisor, Mike Middleton, had asked for a large campaign contribution and was turned down. Some newspapers even predicted that Clinton would sell out Taiwan because of this.

Still, cool heads prevailed in Taipei, that is until Clinton's shocking statement on June 30. When in Shanghai speaking to a roundtable discussion attended by academic and religious leaders and set up to debate a broad range of issues, President Clinton stated, "We don't support independence for Taiwan, or two Chinas, or one China, one Taiwan; and we don't believe Taiwan should be a member in any organization for which statehood is a requirement." He further declared that he had told President Jiang Zemin in Beijing at an official meeting on Saturday that this was "the heart" of U.S. policy on Taiwan. The Ministry of Foreign Affairs in Taipei immediately issued a statement saying that it was not proper for the United States to negotiate with Beijing over issues concerning Taiwan. More precisely, the harshly worded official announcement said, "The United States and Communist China have no right and are in no position to negotiate bilaterally on any affair concerning our side (the Republic of China)." The proclamation went on to say that the United States should consult with Taipei; otherwise it would have a negative effect on cross-strait relations.[16] The ministry also asserted that Clinton's comments were unnecessary, implying that he had ulterior motives and he was not acting in Taiwan's interest nor facilitating better relations between Taipei and Beijing.

Editorialists writing in Taiwan's major newspapers chided Clinton's remarks, interpreting them as denying that the Republic of China, or Taiwan, has sovereignty. One asked sarcastically, "Should not U.S.-Taiwan contacts be considered 'interference' in China's domestic affairs?[17] Another writer asked humorously whether the American Institute in Taiwan, Washington's pseudo-embassy in Taipei, should not be renamed a consulate of the People's Republic of China. Still another suggested that U.S. arms sales to Taiwan were brought into question, since it would not be proper to sell weapons to a province of a country without the approval of its central government.

Clinton's statement caused many to recall the TRA. President Clinton, they said, had violated it. The TRA pledged U.S. arms sales and support of Taiwan joining international organizations. Similarly challenged was the often-stated (by the White House and the Department of State) policy that the United States does not want to get directly involved in the Taiwan issue—that it should be "resolved by the Chinese themselves." Wasn't Clinton, in his Three Noes statement, getting involved?

There was also apprehension as a result of Clinton making the statement that the United States did not support an independent Taiwan. Washington had consistently since 1979 only "acknowledged" Beijing's position and had stuck to the stance of not responding to questions about support or nonsupport of Taiwan's independence.[18] Officials complained, mirroring broad public sentiment, that Clinton, after having portrayed himself as a president that supports democratic countries over authoritarian ones and backing the spreading of democracy around the world, gave no consideration to Taiwan's tremendous progress in political reform and democratizing, or China's lack of progress.

The upshot was widespread doubt whether Clinton really supported a democratic world as he said he did and as has been American policy for years. The answer in Taiwan was a resounding no. Reflecting its democratic political system and the above arguments, Taiwan's political parties separately issued statements in response to Clinton's declaration.

Hsu Hsin-liang, chairman of the opposition DPP, said that the party's platform states that Taiwan is a de facto independent political entity and that it should be established as a de jure independent, autonomous Republic of Taiwan by plebiscite to seek permanent political separation of Taiwan from the Chinese mainland. He further asserted that this was a basic tenet of the party and it would not be changed. The candidates running for mayor of Taipei and others already campaigning for the December election also issued very critical statements about Clinton's remarks. Taipei Mayor Chen Shui-bian was restrained. He said simply that he did not support the president's comments. Parris Chang, a DPP legislator active in foreign policy issues, remarked that Taiwan had "taken greater strides toward democracy than anyone else in Asia." He went on to say that "Clinton should be ashamed of himself. The United States talks about democracy, yet Clinton is colluding with the communist dictatorship to harm Taiwan."[19]

At this juncture, the opposition DPP published an opinion poll on the issue of independence. According to the poll, almost 40 percent favored independence, while only 25 percent favored unification with China. It was the highest pro-independence voice ever recorded in the party's opinion surveys.[20] One DPP stalwart said, "Clinton did this. He helped the cause of independence in Taiwan immensely." Another opposition leader, citing Secretary of State Madeleine Albright's statement that Taiwanese anxiety was an overreaction, said, "Albright is stupid, naive and loves communist dictatorships." Clearly the controversy, which President Clinton precipitated by his Three Noes comment, was disquieting, coming as it did when an election campaign was just starting in Taiwan.

President Lee Teng-hui did not comment immediately about Clinton's trip or his remarks on June 30 in Shanghai. But those close to him said he was obviously not pleased. When Lee finally spoke, he expressed gratitude to Clinton for keeping his promise not to "impair the ROC's interests." He noted especially that Clinton had pledged to continue arms sales to Taipei and maintain Washington's current Taiwan policy. President Lee also pointed out that Clinton called for a peaceful resolution of cross-strait problems and encouraged Beijing to become democratic and respect human rights.[21] Lee was obviously trying to put a good face on a bad situation. He clearly wanted to avoid a controversy with the United States, for the moment at least. In retrospect it seemed he was saving his reaction for July 1999.

President Lee, however, did not stop other high officials from responding. Minister of Foreign Affairs Jason Hu said that the United States should restate its Taiwan policy, including the "Six Assurances" made by the Reagan administration. These assurances, he noted, included Washington's pledge not to play any mediating role between Taipei and Beijing, not to alter its position regarding sovereignty over Taiwan, and not to exert pressure on Taipei to enter into any negotiations with Beijing (all of which the Clinton administration seemed to be doing). Taipei considered the Six Assurances set forth by President Reagan in 1982 as a cornerstone of U.S. China/Taiwan policy, along with the Taiwan Relations Act. Clinton's repudiation of the assurances was serious. One observer said that President Nixon had chosen to be equivocal about whether there was one China or not and President Clinton did not, and this constituted a change in U.S. policy.

The bottom line was that Taipei perceived that Clinton's China policy was slavishly pro-Beijing. Some officials voiced the opinion that Clinton disliked Taiwan and was not a proponent of democracy, human rights, or anything else he had said during his campaign for the presidency. They said he should not be trusted. Others even referred to him as "Taiwan's enemy."

But officials in Taiwan were also very aware of the backlash Clinton had caused in Congress and that legislative-executive relations had deteriorated badly in recent months. Some said Taiwan should be calm but exploit the rift.

8

The Taiwan Relations Act Is Refurbished; America Will Protect Taiwan

On July 10, 1998, just days after President Clinton returned from China, the U.S. Senate voted 92 to 0 to reaffirm provisions in the Taiwan Relations Act (TRA). The House passed a similar resolution on July 20. The votes constituted a rebuff of Clinton's China policy initiative and mirrored the serious and worsening rift between the executive and legislative branches of government.

The TRA, the most formal document relating to U.S. China and Taiwan policy, had redefined U.S. ties with Taiwan in the wake of President Carter's breaking diplomatic relations with Taipei in early 1979. It afforded Taiwan various U.S. guarantees (economic and political) and treated Taiwan as a sovereign nation-state in contraposition to the Normalization Agreement negotiated by the White House. It was leverage in Congress' hands and a pain in the neck for the Department of State.

After 1989, the Taiwan Relations Act gained added importance in the China policy debate. The press cited it more often. Congress referred to it frequently. It took on even more salience after the missile crisis of 1996. The TRA's security pledge, some said, amounted to an "if" declaration of war on China (if it attacked Taiwan). Chinese leaders despised it. Leaders in Taiwan felt it guaranteed U.S. protection. President Chen felt it gave him immunity to goad China to the brink of war if it suited him.

—∞—

On December 15, 1978, President Jimmy Carter, in a hastily arranged, nationally televised announcement, declared to the American people that the United States would forthwith establish formal diplomatic relations with the People's Republic of China and simultaneously would break official ties with Taiwan. Two weeks later, on January 1, 1979, Washington and Beijing issued a joint communiqué formalizing their "normalization of relations." The Normalization Agreement, among other things, declared that the United States "acknowledges the Chinese position that there is but one China and Taiwan is part of China." This is what Beijing demanded.

The Normalization Agreement immediately sparked concern. It seemed to sell out Taiwan. It certainly left important questions unanswered. Most vital among them was the political or legal status of Taiwan (especially whether or not it was a sovereign nation-state) in the eyes of the United States. The agreement said only that the United States would "maintain cultural, commercial, and other unofficial relations with the people of Taiwan."

Congress, as the Carter administration anticipated, took the initiative to fill the vacuum in U.S. China policy. The American public as well as many in Congress felt that the White House had treated an old friend and ally wrongly. The United States had extensive commercial and other relations with Taiwan that needed attention. There was much more . . .

President Carter's stock in Congress was very low at the time. He had used nearly all of the favors he was owed to get the Panama Canal Treaty passed in the Senate, succeeding by just one vote. He was at odds with Congress over an important arms control treaty, which he eventually withdrew from Senate consideration, knowing he could not muster the votes to get it passed. Both Iran and Afghanistan presented Carter with serious foreign policy messes that engendered further doubts about the administration's competence in making foreign policy.

Meanwhile, details on the background leading up to Carter's decision to establish diplomatic relations with Beijing were leaked and published in the media in considerable detail. The story was embarrassing. Carter's political advisors told him how Nixon improved his image (and in retrospect looked like a good president and might, be so rated by future historians notwithstanding Watergate) by engineering a breakthrough in U.S.-China relations. They advised President Carter that he could do this too.

Michel Oksenberg, Carter's China advisor on the National Security Council, was quoted as saying that the United States would ultimately establish formal diplomatic relations with Beijing and he wanted to be the one to accomplish that. This was interpreted as meaning the administration would disregard principles, the national interest, and anything else. Richard Holbrooke, then assistant secretary of state for Asia and the Pacific, wanted to establish diplomatic relations with Beijing and Hanoi at the same time. Holbrooke had an interest in Vietnam. Years earlier he had resigned from the Foreign Service to protest U.S. Vietnam policy. He was labeled a war protester, which didn't help his image at the State Department.[1] Zbigniew Brzezinski, the president's national security advisor and Carter's most trusted person on foreign policy, wanted to use China as leverage against the Soviet Union just as Nixon had done, even more so if possible. This, in fact, was of paramount importance to Brzezinski and the grounds for his push to establish formal ties with Beijing.

Brzezinski took control of U.S. China policy. He didn't accept others' opinions easily or any challenge to his authority. He openly belittled and embarrassed both Oksenberg and Holbrooke whenever he had the chance and kept important information from them. He engaged in a turf war with Secretary of State Cyrus Vance, which he won. In any event, Beijing strenuously opposed Washington establishing relations with Hanoi, as the two were bitter enemies at the time. Beijing, it was said, would nix a "double deal." Officials in China liked the national security advisor's views. In any case, Beijing wanted to deal with the top foreign policy person in the Carter administration, and that was Brzezinski. Thus they assisted him in marginalizing Vance, Oksenberg, and Holbrooke.[2] The infighting, which resulted in confusing signals on China policy, was picked up by the press.

Meanwhile Carter's poor image in making foreign policy, especially in the eyes of many members of Congress, declined even further as the result of a constitutional challenge by Barry Goldwater. During the summer Goldwater had acquired information about Carter's negotiating with China in secret. Goldwater went public, contending that President Carter could not on his own authority terminate the U.S. defense treaty with Taiwan because of the Senate's "advise and consent" role laid out in the U.S. Constitution. This evoked a miniature constitutional crisis. Carter ignored Goldwater and the constitutional issue and continued to negotiate with China in private. Congress was miffed.

President Carter alienated Congress further by announcing the decision to establish formal relations with Beijing just before Christmas when Congress was on recess in order to delay congressional debate on the subject. Carter then presented the decision as a fait accompli. He said this was the way an important foreign policy matter such as this was often handled. Congress saw it differently— as the White House inappropriately maintaining secrecy in making foreign policy and eschewing democratic debate on an important issue.

Making relations with Congress even worse, Carter made a serious gaffe. Just after the announcement of establishing diplomatic relations with Beijing on national television, he turned to someone nearby and said that the American people would be happy with what he had done (suggesting Congress wouldn't be), not knowing that he was still on the air.

Congress was in a bad mood: it was displeased with Carter personally, the White House in general, and the Department of State. Moreover, members of Congress felt they had an important job to do in fixing things. The result was an unprecedented law: Public Law 96–8 or the TRA. The work was bipartisan but led by Democrats, since the Democratic Party had a majority in both houses of Congress. Senators Ted Kennedy and Jacob Javits spearheaded the effort. Senators John Glenn and Frank Church were major players. Republican Senators Howard Baker, Charles Percy, and Richard Luger offered valuable input.

Passed by Congress in March and signed by President Carter in April, the TRA became the first-ever legislation to set guidelines and parameters for U.S. foreign policy toward a specific foreign country. It was a landmark piece of legislation. The TRA gave Congress an unprecedented responsibility in making China policy or at least the Taiwan portion of it. In addition, it gave Congress the authority to do so.

President Carter, during the congressional debates on the TRA, threatened to veto the law if it contradicted the Normalization Agreement, which it did. But the vote for the TRA in both houses of Congress was so large it looked like an override would be a certainty if President Carter used the veto. Carter did not want to be humiliated by Congress.

The TRA contained what came to be called military, economic, and political provisions. First, the military provision restored America's responsibility for Taiwan's security. The Carter administration, coinciding with the agreement establishing diplomatic relations with Beijing, had given Taipei notice that the United States–Republic of China Defense Pact, signed in 1954 after the Chinese PLA assaulted Quemoy and Matsu, would expire one year from January 1, 1979. The "security clause" in the TRA, which in essence replaced the defense pact, was very controversial. It promised arms sales to Taiwan and suggested Taiwan's status related to the U.S. national interest. Some said it was better than the U.S.-Republic of China treaty because boycotts and embargoes (which many said were more likely than an invasion) would trigger an American response and because it pledged the United States would maintain a military presence in the region to back it.

Second, the TRA provided for maintaining U.S.-Taiwan economic relations: trade, investment, and other commercial ties. Its immediate effect was to shield Taiwan's economy from a protracted shock that might have derailed its economic viability and growth. President Carter's breaking formal relations with Taipei had sent Taiwan's economy into a tailspin. The TRA thus restored stability to Taiwan's thriving economy. In fact, Taiwan continued to boom economically as a result, giving Taiwan more reasons to reject talks with Beijing about reunification.

Third, the TRA contained a provision asking for Taipei to improve its human rights record. By implication this meant Taiwan should democratize. Members of Congress had stated during the debate that Taiwan should move away from authoritarianism and became a democracy, and by including a human rights provision in the TRA made this a formal request. The TRA also spoke of supporting Taiwan against "threats to its social system." This meant that Taiwan had American guarantees it would help Taiwan deal with any effort to make it communist. Finally, it stated that the United States would support Taipei's participation in international organizations.

Looking at all of this, it became clear that the TRA had created a potent dichotomy in America's China policy. Some said that it created two China policies—one advanced by the executive branch of government, and one by the legislative branch, or Congress. The former viewed Taiwan as part of China; the latter didn't. This dichotomy in U.S. China policy, though confusing, was in some respects convenient. It made it possible for American diplomats to blame the Congress for the United States' maintaining close relations (and in many respects official ties) with Taiwan, and the State Department frequently did this.

The TRA, however, created a rift in official Washington. Some said it poisoned executive-legislative relations. It certainly made relations between Congress, the White House, and especially the State Department contentious, even nasty at times. After 1979, U.S.-China policy, to the Department of State, became viewed as founded on three documents: the Shanghai Communiqué, signed when President Nixon visited Beijing in 1972; the Normalization Agreement; and the Taiwan Relations Act. Later the State Department also included the "August 17 Communiqué"—the controversial deal negotiated in 1982. The State Department talked and acted as if the communiqués and the Taiwan Relations Act had equal status. Congress viewed the TRA as having special status because it was a law; the communiqués weren't. Members of Congress frequently said the TRA was legally superior to the communiqués. Congress was right, but it was not in a position to enforce its view or even keep up with China policy on a daily basis. The State Department and the White House always had an edge because of this, and both knew it. But Congress had its means of getting even or making its views known.

The establishment of a foundation for Taiwan policy certainly sent a message to Beijing and Taipei that two branches of the U.S. government disagreed about China/Taiwan policy. Could Beijing exploit these differences? Could Taipei? As one diplomat put it, in retrospect the TRA "transformed an intent by many policy makers to fashion a short-term policy that would provide Taiwan a 'decent interval' before capitulating to Beijing, to one which assumes a direct American commitment in the Taiwan Strait for a long time."[3] The former was China's hope and expectation. To Taiwan, it was the latter.

—❦—

In 1979, most pundits opined that Beijing would have plenty of time and many opportunities in coming months or years to weaken, marginalize, or perhaps even nullify the TRA.[4] It didn't start out that way, though. Beijing's response to Congress debating the TRA was almost no response at all. Officials in the Chinese embassy in Washington attended the hearings and debates in Congress, but they said little about what was happening and offered almost no meaningful input. There were two reasons for a near absence of criticism or comment by Chinese leaders: First, the People's Republic of China was at war with Vietnam. Second, Beijing, more specifically Deng Xiaoping, had adopted a policy of pursuing friendly relations with Taipei.

Almost at the moment Congress took up the issue of U.S. Taiwan policy, Deng ordered the Chinese PLA to invade Vietnam (incidentally embarrassing President Carter, who had presented the Normalization Agreement to the press and the American people as "representing a major step toward peace in Asia.")

The PLA did not fare well against seasoned Vietnamese forces. The conflict thus preoccupied Chinese decision makers for some time and dampened interest in the Chinese Communist Party and the government about the Taiwan issue.

Meanwhile, just after President Carter announced the United States would establish formal diplomatic relations with Beijing and break its ties with Taipei, Deng Xiaoping launched a friendly diplomatic offensive toward Taiwan. He offered trade, aid, and other ties. He even extended a gift of landing rights in Beijing and Shanghai to aircraft from Taiwan. Last but not least, he promised that China would "not pursue an aggressive policy toward Taiwan." Deng ostensibly calculated that the U.S. decision to establish formal diplomatic relations with Beijing had put Taipei in a very difficult predicament and that Taiwan's government could not refuse to negotiate. Alternatively, he wanted to give the impression that Taipei would "submit" to talks leading to reunification. This would justify the new relationship with the United States and head off critics who periodically charged that Deng had "abandoned the sacred mission" of getting Taiwan back.

In January after Washington and Beijing established formal ties, Beijing issued a "Message to Taiwan Compatriots" stating that China hoped Taiwan would "return to the motherland" and "work together for the great cause of national development."[5] The message pledged that Beijing would consider "present realities" in Taiwan and respect the status quo there. China's National People's Congress (its so-called representative or democratic organ of government) in the interim made provisions for the establishment of appropriate administrative organs to manage mutual visits, postal and transportation links, and trade—the "three exchanges." At this juncture, Beijing, in a friendly gesture of a different sort, announced that it would end its alternate-day artillery shelling of the Nationalist-held island of Quemoy, which had been going on since 1958. This was another olive branch.

When President Carter signed the TRA into law in April, the Chinese government delivered a formal note of protest to U.S. Ambassador Leonard Woodcock in Beijing. The language was not very strong, though: the TRA, the note said, was "unacceptable." It said little else.[6] The response from the press in China, however, was noticeably different, harsher. This reflected major differences over Taiwan policy between the Left, which controlled the media, and the Right, or Deng's reformist supporters, in the Chinese Communist Party and the government. Deng was also under pressure from the Chinese military, which took a hard line on the Taiwan issue. The PLA didn't like the TRA and said so.

To placate his opponents, Deng publicly, though somewhat belatedly, charged that the TRA violated the Normalization Agreement and proclaimed that it would undermine U.S.-China relations. He made some other critical remarks about what Congress had done.

In the coming months, Deng, on various occasions, was chided by the Left for his "betrayal" regarding Taiwan. His friendly overtures to Taipei were ridiculed as producing no results and his "conciliatory policy toward the United

States" was described as "surrendering on the Taiwan issue." It thus became evident that Deng was walking a tightrope and that the Taiwan issue was a very divisive political matter in China, one that would affect and trouble U.S.-China relations in the future.

Before the year was out this situation evoked an interesting, even ironic, change in one aspect of Beijing's Taiwan policy. In December 1979, when an antigovernment demonstration supported by Taiwan independence forces broke out in the southern city of Kaohsiung, Deng sided with the Nationalist Party and the government against the demonstrators. For years Beijing had condemned the KMT's domestic policies and had encouraged so-called native-born Taiwanese to overthrow the government. Deng now supported the KMT, which, even though very critical of communism, espoused at least nominally a one-China policy.

Was this shift in policy wise? It made it appear that China opposed Taiwan's democratization. In the United States, Beijing was pictured as opposing political change and progress away from authoritarianism in Taiwan. It was also doubtful what effect supporting the KMT would have, if any. Deng and his advisors apparently didn't realize that it was going to be difficult, perhaps impossible, to deal with KMT leaders, that the Nationalist Party was the major force behind democratization, and that the KMT and the advocates of Taiwan separatism talked to each other and agreed on one important thing: a communist China should not govern Taiwan. Furthermore, views were fast converging on the matter of Taiwan's future and its relationship with China. The opposition in Taiwan had earlier defined independence as getting rid of the KMT, but it now meant avoiding any ties with China that might affect Taiwan's sovereignty. In the past, the opposition had contended that knocking out the KMT would mean that China would not bother Taiwan any longer. This was clearly not the case, as everyone could now see.

Deng meanwhile tried to put the Taiwan issue into a broader context where he could handle it better. In January 1980, Deng referred to the reunification of Taiwan as a "great issue." Later, he linked it to peace in Asia.[7] In so doing, Deng tried to broaden the Taiwan issue and make his Taiwan policy part of China's overall foreign policy and thus less contentious.

But this didn't work. In the summer and in late 1980, the political left in China was provided with more ammunition to use against Deng on the Taiwan question. In mid-year, President Carter announced a resumption of arms sales to Taiwan (frozen at the time that diplomatic recognition was granted to Beijing). Deng's opponents were energized and highly critical of his Taiwan policy. Deng made more tough statements about Taiwan, hoping he could defuse the issue. The White House and the Department of State understood Deng's position and did not respond or criticize Deng. Congress was attending to other business. In October when the United States granted diplomatic privileges to Taiwan's "representatives" in Washington, the Left in Beijing went on the attack again. *People's Daily* said this move represented a two-China policy and opined that it would "reverse the good trends in U.S.-China relations."

When Ronald Reagan became president the situation got even worse. Reagan had taken a pro-Taiwan stance during the campaign and had criticized the Carter administration for "betraying" Taiwan. He even suggested he would reestablish diplomatic ties with Taipei. The Chinese media, speaking for the political left, which had become politically more aggressive in recent months partly due to Ronald Reagan's pro-Taiwan statements, immediately became harsh and vocal. China's press warned that Reagan would "wreck" Sino-American relations. It strongly chided the U.S. for arms sales to Taiwan. It blasted Congress for its views on Taiwan. It complained about almost any Washington-Taipei contact.

Congress was not happy about this, when it noticed. However, it said and did very little in response to Beijing's tough talk. In the spring, when Secretary of State Alexander Haig visited Beijing, various Chinese newspapers charged that U.S. arms sales constituted a "de facto policy of reestablishing the defense treaty." The Chinese media carefully ignored the fact arms sales were promised in the Taiwan Relations Act and there had been no change in U.S. policy as a result.

In June 1982, former Senate leader Howard Baker visited China. Deng told him of the difficulties he and his supporters faced because of his "capitalist" reforms. He also talked about U.S.-China relations and the Taiwan issue. He suggested to Baker that Congress amend the TRA. In July, on the occasion of the sixtieth anniversary of the founding of the Chinese Communist Party, General Secretary Hu Yaobang scored the United States "for not seeing a contradiction between the TRA and the Normalization Agreement."[8] What he said was obvious, but saying it suggested Deng was in deep trouble with the hardliners.

Deng was playing a tough game—trying to sidestep his opponents at home on the Taiwan issue by giving them the impression that he sought to (and could) persuade Washington to alter its China policy and this would help Beijing "bring Taiwan back into the fold." Deng was in a serious bind because there was no chance he could get Congress to rescind the TRA or even amend it to his pleasure. It was here to stay. And it was ammunition for the hardliners to use against him, which they did. Leftists said that the TRA "overturned" the Normalization Agreement. They grumbled that it gave Taiwan back its sovereignty. They charged that the security provision in essence reestablished the U.S.–Republic of China defense pact or better, since it cited threats to Taiwan apart from a direct military attack. Secretary of State Alexander Haig sought to succor Deng by proposing a communiqué agreeing to limit arms sales to Taiwan.

The result was the August 17 Communiqué of 1982. As noted earlier, in it the United States declared that it did "not seek to carry out a long-term policy of arms sales to Taiwan" and that such arms sales will decline and eventually end. The document also restated Washington's policy of not "infringing on China's sovereignty" or "pursuing a two-China policy." Though it wasn't signed and for other reasons lacked legal status, the August Communiqué helped Deng get through a crisis.[9]

In the ensuing years, Chinese leaders periodically complained that the United States was not abiding by the August 17 Communiqué. They certainly had a point. At times Foreign Ministry spokespersons said that the August 17 Communiqué canceled the provision in the TRA promising arms sales to Taiwan. However, they did not state this very loudly, as Congress might hear it and seek to prove them wrong.

Deng and other Chinese leaders meanwhile had given up trying to influence Congress to change or weaken the TRA. Beijing stacked its hopes on its friends in the United States, such as Henry Kissinger and a host of others from the Nixon and Ford administrations, together with pro-Beijing scholars they thought would help gradually erode the TRA in favor of the communiqués. In fact, China seemed to count on this. Chinese officials also reckoned the Department of State to be on its side (even if the Reagan White House was not) and that Congress was asleep at the wheel most of the time when it came to foreign policy issues and would not notice the TRA was being ignored and marginalized. Beijing took the position that the Taiwan Relations Act was domestic legislation and for that reason, in terms of defining U.S.-China relations, was inferior to the communiqués. This, of course, proved Chinese diplomats as well as its foreign policy were "out of touch" with Congress. The Chinese Foreign Ministry also at various times promoted the idea of a "fourth communiqué" to dilute or, some said, to nullify the Taiwan Relations Act. Ministry officials waited for an opportunity.

—ᴍ—

Taipei's response to Congress's debating and finally rendering the TRA into law was markedly different from Beijing's. It was quietly supportive. To understand Taiwan's view it is necessary to first examine its reaction to the United States' establishing diplomatic relations with Beijing and breaking formal ties with Taipei.

When President Carter announced that the United States would establish formal diplomatic relations with the People's Republic of China, Taiwan was stunned. Most citizens felt that their country had been jilted, betrayed.[10] Taipei thus reacted with both anger and surprise—even though there had been talk of the United States establishing ties with Beijing for a number of years. Many people in Taiwan had been optimistic that President Carter would not kowtow to Beijing. Many thought Carter's moral perspective in foreign policy making ("Human rights is the soul of American foreign policy," he had said) would favor Taiwan. How wrong they were. When the shocking announcement was made, President Chiang Ching-kuo was given only a few hours warning. He had to act quickly and head off panic. Chiang promptly put the military on alert, closed the stock market, and canceled an important national election. This was necessary given the potential for political and economic instability in Taiwan at the time.

After a few days, Taipei issued a formal policy statement. It called the decision "regrettable" and said that Washington should "change its mind." It said further that the Republic of China would "under no circumstances" enter into talks with Beijing. Officials in Taipei repeated the country's tough Three Noes policy: no contacts, no negotiations, no compromise (with Beijing). Taipei then announced the establishment of a "defense fund" to compensate for the pending cancellation of the U.S.-Republic of China defense treaty (even though this was not to happen for a year). The government asked for public contributions.

Some days later when Deputy Secretary of State Warren Christopher visited Taipei to work out the details of unofficial relations between Washington and Taipei, an angry crowd pelted his limousine with eggs and stones in an unusual demonstration of public outrage. Some observers said the government had staged the event, or at minimum had encouraged it. Clearly President Carter's decision had undermined the credibility of the government in Taiwan and many officials were irate.[11] The public was apprehensive and angry. Some said government actions were intended to vent public outrage and ire. Others said it was a spontaneous public reaction. It was both.

As ill feelings began to subside a bit, on December 28, President Chiang Ching-kuo announced five principles (continuity, reality, security, equality, and governmentality) upon which future relations with the United States should be based. These principles were vague but represented a calmer and more rational response on Taipei's part. They were rejected by the State Department. They were examined by Congress and, in fact, became the central components of the TRA, which was written over the course of the next few months.

During January, February, and March, while Congress was working on the TRA, Taipei made only a few comments. Regarding relations with the United States, its formal position was that the United States had "made a mistake" and that formal diplomatic relations should be restored. This quite unrealistic response can be explained: Officials still needed to encourage feelings of anger and disappointment in the population to prevent a shocked citizenry from blaming their government for the loss of ties with Washington. Government leaders also at the time feared the opposition might try to exploit the situation.

When President Carter signed the TRA, it was evident that Congress had in essence restored Taiwan's sovereignty and had guaranteed Taiwan's security and its economic health. Still, Taipei did not react in an openly positive way. Officials noted the fact that the TRA throughout referred to "Taiwan" and did not use the country's formal name, "Republic of China." It spoke of the "people on Taiwan"; it should have, one critic said, talked of "the people of Taiwan" or "people in Taiwan," which would have suggested a more permanent and legitimate relationship. Some called this insulting. In the heated environment derecognition had caused, this was understandable.

Taipei's representatives in Washington kept abreast of the debate in Congress on the TRA and carefully analyzed the legislation from various perspectives, including most of all its impact on U.S. Taiwan policy. They provided input behind the scenes. When Congress passed the legislation, they supported it—though without fanfare. In Taipei, most top government officials, including President Chiang and Premier Sun Yun-suan, were pleased with what the U.S. Congress had done, though they continued to talk tough. Taiwan's lower-level officials as well as the general populace soon became resigned to the "facts of life." Many felt things might have been worse. They were happy about the TRA, perceiving its provisions provided sufficient guarantees that Taiwan needed.

Taipei then began to send different signals. Clearly, top officials calculated, expressions of anger, if carried on too long, might create a backlash. Taiwan also wanted to appear reasonable, especially in light of Beijing's "peaceful" overtures. The government toned down its anti-Communist propaganda. Officials in Taiwan and the press stopped referring to the government in Beijing as a "bandit regime." In a few months, government officials began to take note of the fact that the foreign press had been uncharacteristically "understanding" of Taiwan. The Western media, in fact, had not taken the position that Taiwan had lost its sovereignty or that the U.S. decision to break diplomatic relations with Taipei could be interpreted as supporting the opposition in Taiwan. One official noted that while the White House and the Department of State had characterized U.S. policy toward Taiwan as "unofficial," this word did not appear in the TRA. As a result, Taipei began to make policy statements based on U.S. policy as set forth in the TRA. It also began to make logical arguments. Taiwan's leaders began to say that the TRA protected Taiwan. One said it was Taiwan's "shield." Others said it was the country's "weapon for dealing with Beijing."

In reply to Beijing's subsequent overtures, Taipei made some of the following points: If, as Beijing suggested, Taiwan could have its own military after a reunification agreement, then why should Beijing oppose the weapons sales provision in the TRA? If China wanted Taiwan to prosper (another provision in the TRA), why should it try to isolate Taiwan and endeavor to have Taipei expelled from international organizations, many of them financial? And why did Beijing continue to threaten Taiwan with military force and thereby challenge the TRA?

A policy of quiet support for the TRA evolved. The rationale for less than enthusiastic acclaim being, said officials in Taipei, Taiwan should not give the impression that it is dependent for its survival on the U.S. Congress.[12] Officials in Taipei also realized that Congress was a legislative body and did not normally make, and certainly did not conduct, U.S. foreign policy. U.S. China policy would continue, they reckoned, to be made primarily by the executive branch of government, with the TRA serving as guidelines or a constraint.

The ruling Nationalist Party soon found that U.S. China policy, however objectionable, could be used advantageously for domestic political purposes. In 1980, after the period of crisis had passed, some government officials began to argue that the TRA (in tandem with the Normalization Agreement, of course) did not support, but rather opposed, a two-China policy. They thus used it to cool independence supporters. They similarly pointed out that Beijing would not allow Taiwan to declare independence and that the United States would not help independence advocates because of Washington's view of the importance of its ties with China.

Others contended that reform was under way in China, beginning with Deng Xiaoping's ascendancy in 1978, and that Taipei had to take cognizance of that. Deng had launched an "economic miracle" in China. Perhaps reconciliation with Beijing was both possible and desirable. However, more than anything, there was a widespread feeling in Taipei that Taiwan had to democratize. The TRA demanded this. Congress called for it. Political change needed to keep pace with economic modernization anyway. Scholars had often spoken of a "dangerous gap" between economic and political change (or the large magnitude of the former and the dearth of the latter).

Others said democratization would increase support for Taiwan in the United States, especially with Congress, the media, and the American people, and Taipei had to offset the support for Beijing in the White House and the Department of State. The KMT acknowledged the need to democratize and Congress's encouragement. Thus there were common grounds between it and the opposition. Commentators and even some officials proclaimed that Taiwan's survival depended on it democratizing.

In late 1980, little more than a year and a half after the TRA became law, Taiwan held its first competitive national election. It held its second competitive national election in 1983. In 1986, President Chiang Ching-kuo promised that the ban on forming new political parties would be lifted. Immediately, the DPP formed and challenged the Kuomintang in the December election. The result was the first ever two-party national election in Taiwan; in fact, it was the first two-party election ever in a Chinese nation.

Soon Nationalist Party officials in Taiwan, to whom Beijing directed overtures to negotiate party-to-party, replied cleverly that Taiwan was no longer a one-party system and only the government could negotiate such matters. They learned some new vocabulary from the Western media and talked of Taiwan as having a "pluralist" political system. They cited public opinion polls at will. In 1987, Taiwan ended martial law and canceled the ban on travel to China. In mid-1988, the Kuomintang held its thirteenth Party Congress and instituted reforms that democratized the ruling party, in some ways beyond that of Western parties. Restrictions on newspapers were lifted that year.

Meanwhile, in September 1981, when president Ye Jianying of the People's Republic of China issued a nine-point statement regarding the reunification of Taiwan, Premier Sun responded that this could be possible "on the basis of Sun Yat-sen's Three People's Principles" (meaning on the basis of democracy). This statement constituted a major departure from the Three Noes policy. Moreover, it represented a degree of confidence not seen before on the part of the leadership of Taipei.

In 1989, the DPP, as noted earlier, won an election victory, increasing its representation in the legislature while capturing a number of local executive offices. In 1991 and 1992, Taiwan held important plenary elections for the National Assembly and the Legislative Yuan, having persuaded older members of both bodies that represented districts in China to step down (thus, to many, ending the fiction Taiwan was tied to China).

In the case of all of this progress toward democracy, officials in Taiwan said the TRA was the catalyst. The act had called for democracy. Taiwan was doing it. Taiwan also made serious efforts to comply with the TRA's call for improvements in its human rights conditions. Not long after the passage of the TRA, Taipei established a human rights organization and made genuine efforts to improve its human rights condition.[13] In ensuing years, when Beijing, or others mentioned the issue of reunification, Taipei's standard response was to cite human rights abuses in China. Tibet was specifically mentioned. They pointed out that Tibet was an "autonomous region" in the People's Republic of China, just as Taiwan would be after reunification, according to Deng Xiaoping. "What would be the human rights impact on Taiwan?" they asked rhetorically.

In the late 1980s, Taipei began officially to praise the TRA for "helping Taiwan overcome a diplomatic crisis in 1979" and establishing what it called a "statutory basis for continuing the U.S. commitment." Government publications said that the "Republic of China had become one of the top ten exporting nations in the world, that foreign exchange controls were being lifted, that there were meaningful elections, and that visits to the People's Republic of China would be approved." The TRA was cited, in this context, as "welcoming a new era."[14] In 1991, when Taipei officially ended the state of war with China, observers noted that the TRA had "provided the stability Taiwan needed to do this." Others remarked that the TRA was a contributing factor to democratic reform in Taiwan and in particular that it enabled Chiang Ching-kuo to end the "Temporary Provisions" that had circumvented constitutional guarantees of civil and political rights.[15] It thus had become clear Taiwan was a strong supporter of the TRA and credited it and Congress for Taiwan democratizing. "More than this," said one official in Taipei, "it saved Taiwan's life!"

—ɯ—

Before Congress became interested in and influential in making China policy following the Tiananmen massacre and the collapse of the Soviet Union, it seemed that the TRA was gradually being forgotten and marginalized. Beijing asked its consultants and friends in the United States, including such luminaries as Henry Kissinger, to "destroy" the TRA. It seemed that might happen.

The Department of State in private, and sometimes in public, revealed its view: it abhorred the TRA. In any case, its dislike of the TRA was transparent, and it was clear that the department wanted it weakened. State Department people spoke of it in the same sentence as the communiqués, suggesting they had equal weight. Often they cited, or listed, the TRA last. They seldom mentioned its specific provisions. They didn't regard its guarantees as constituting a genuine U.S. commitment.

Congress didn't pay much attention to foreign policy most of the time. Before 1989, it didn't say much about the State Department's efforts to marginalize the TRA. Furthermore, for ten years after the TRA became law, Beijing's influence in the United States increased; Taipei's declined. To many the TRA's future was in doubt.

This situation suddenly and dramatically changed in 1989. Beijing's stock in the United States fell, said one observer, like a ton of bricks, like the stock market in 1929. The United States reviled China, and Congress acted on this. Individual members of Congress enhanced their popularity by castigating China. The end of the Cold War and human rights considerations justified Congress' new role in formulating China policy. The TRA served as the legal grounds for Congress' new role. The TRA also gained in stature as a result of Taiwan democratizing. Taiwan's critically timed 1989 election was a key event. Many in Congress understood that the TRA had aided Taiwan's democratization. Put another way. the TRA was directly responsible for the demise of authoritarianism in Taiwan, boasted members of Congress who had been involved in writing the TRA and many others that favored Taiwan over China.

Taiwan's democratization clearly helped close the gap in views on China and Taiwan between Republicans and Democrats in Congress. Both felt that Congress had played an important role and felt good about it. Others argued that it justifiably provided security guarantees to Taiwan. The TRA was frequently mentioned, directly or obliquely, when addressing Beijing's defense buildup. In fact, the defense provision in the Act seemed to take on new meaning. Later, some said the security promises in the TRA became the "heart and soul" of U.S. Taiwan policy and the main source of friction between Washington and Beijing. Beijing understood it could not get very far in calling for negotiations with Taipei if the latter could defend itself, and the TRA seemed to guarantee that.

The TRA was mentioned in 1992 when President Bush decided to sell F-16 fighter planes to Taiwan, although not by the president himself. Observers noted that the administration was now abiding by the TRA and not the August Communiqué.

As relations between the White House and the Congress became more combative regarding China policy, the TRA was cited with increasing frequency by the latter. Enforcing it became Congress' rallying call. This situation persisted after Bush left office and Bill Clinton became president. In fact, it accelerated.

In mid-1993, to ensure that President Clinton pursued a China policy not detrimental to Taipei (as there had already appeared doubts about this), the Senate Foreign Relations Committee adopted an amendment to the TRA proposed by Senator Murkowski of Alaska stating that the promise of arms sales to Taiwan in the TRA "shall supersede any provision of the August 17, 1982 Joint United States-China Communiqué." The full Senate subsequently approved the amendment, though in conference with the House of Representatives there was some wrangling and a sense of the Congress declaration resulted instead of a formal bill.[16]

The following year, in April 1994, a conference bill, which included provisions from Congress' earlier declaration, was passed and reluctantly signed into law by President Clinton. Before the president signed it, however, the Department of State registered its opposition. State was concerned that the word "supersede" would nullify all of the communiqués. The wording was altered to assert the "primacy" of the TRA. To get this change, Secretary of State Warren Christopher wrote a letter to Murkowski "reaffirming" the TRA's "legal standing over the August Communiqué."[17] Thus, by the secretary's admission, the relationship between the TRA and the communiqués was resolved in favor of the TRA. Christopher's letter was shown to the press and subsequently quoted by members of Congress on appropriate occasions.

Soon after, the Clinton administration finished the Taiwan Policy Review. Congress expressed grave disappointment. As noted earlier, most members of Congress concerned with Taiwan policy considered the policy review cosmetic rather than substantive.[18] Some members of Congress expressed anger, saying that the administration was still not abiding by the spirit of the TRA. There was speculation at that time that Congress might seek to amend the TRA in ways very advantageous to Taipei and to the extreme displeasure of Beijing.

The White House and the State Department struck back. Seeking to avoid a deterioration in relations with Beijing, the Clinton administration adopted some patently pro-Beijing policy initiatives. Several appeared to violate the intent if not the letter of the TRA. For example, in negotiating with Beijing on the Missile Technology Control Regime in 1994, it was reported that Clinton agreed to discuss the U.S. sale of F-16 fighter planes to Taiwan with Beijing. The TRA had specifically given this power only to the White House *and* Congress in order to keep others out of the process, especially Beijing. Subsequently President Clinton, in a letter to Chinese President Jiang Zemin, said that the United States was committed to a "unified China." U.S. policy up to that point supported a peaceful resolution of the "Taiwan issue" but did not back any specific outcome. A number of members of Congress were upset to the say the least. Several blew their cool and said unkind things about President Clinton. Most became suspicious.

Fanning the flames of congressional ire, State Department spokesperson Michael McCurry used words that evoked still further concern. He said that the United States "accepted" China's claim that Taiwan is part of China, rather than using the term "acknowledge" which had been in common usage.[19] These friendly gestures from the executive branch toward China (some said they were more than this) caused many members of Congress to see disturbing signs in the Clinton administration's Taiwan policy and came to deeply distrust the president regarding Taiwan. The administration apparently thought Congress was not paying attention and it could retrieve its dominant authority over making China policy by doing business on the sly, while pretending not to oppose congressional oversight. This was clearly wrongheaded and led to deeper antagonisms between the executive and legislative branches.

After the Republican victory in the 1994 election and even more so following the PLA's missile tests near Taiwan's shores in 1995, U.S. Taiwan policy frequently became the focus of attention in Congress. With its new powers at hand Republican leaders in Congress sought to do something for Taiwan. Although the TRA was not amended and, in fact, no serious attempts were made to do that (though there were some efforts in that direction in the form of proposed amendments) the TRA took on a significance it had not had before. It was more often invoked in statements about Taiwan and U.S. Taiwan policy. In fact, it was cited many fold more times by Congress and the media than it had been in previous years. It seemed now to have unquestioned status as the basis of China/Taiwan policy.

At this juncture it appeared there was no possibility of it being marginalized. Moves made by the Clinton White House and the Department of State to alter it through understandings with Beijing or via changes in the language or provisions in U.S. China policy were regularly stopped in their tracks. As a matter of fact, it appeared to one observer that "after being whipped," the Department of State was "falling into line" in accepting the TRA and ending its portraying either the TRA and the communiqués as having equal status or the TRA to be something less than a genuine American commitment to a "sovereign" Taiwan.

In December 1995, State Department spokesman Nicholas Burns said that "according to the TRA the U.S. had committed itself to Taiwan's security and would consider any effort to determine the future of Taiwan by other than peaceful means, a threat to the peace and security of the Western Pacific and of grave concern to the United States."[20] It thus appeared that the White House and the Department of State had completely changed their stance on the TRA. A few months earlier both had tried in various ways to undercut it, and now they supported it. How long would their new stance last? Many in Congress wondered.

—⚹—

When the U.S. Navy sent aircraft carriers to the Taiwan Strait in March 1996, Clinton administration officials conveyed the impression that the United States was "obligated under the law"—meaning the TRA—to respond to Beijing's threat. National security advisor Anthony Lake used the phrase "grave consequences" when warning Beijing—employing a word found in the TRA: "to consider any attempt to resolve the Taiwan issue other than by peaceful means as a threat to the peace and security of the Western Pacific area and of grave concern to the United States."[21]

Assistant Secretary of State for Asia and the Pacific Winston Lord, in testimony before a House committee in early 1996 declared that the TRA "forms the legal basis of U.S. policy regarding the security of Taiwan." It was considered noteworthy that he did not even mention the communiqués. Moreover, Lord stated: "Its [the TRA's] premise that an adequate defense of Taiwan is conducive to maintaining peace and security."[22]

The assistant secretary of state went on to say that he opposed ambiguity in U.S. China policy, thereby hinting that the TRA obligated the United States to protect Taiwan and that Taipei possessed sovereignty. This view contradicted the opinion held at the time by many in the executive branch of government and most in the Department of State regarding the breadth of the TRA's commitments. Deputy Assistant Secretary of State for Asia and the Pacific Jeffrey Bader, also in testimony before Congress, said that the TRA "sets forth our abiding interest in the peace and security of Taiwan and the Western Pacific." He went on to say that U.S. arms sales to Taiwan had helped maintain a cross-strait military balance.[23] His statements, like Lord's, seemed to suggest that the United States has a solemn obligation set forth in the TRA to defend Taiwan. This had always been in doubt in the executive branch of government. The State Department and the White House had on many occasions spoken as if the TRA did not necessarily oblige the United States to act to protect Taiwan.

Congress shortly after this passed a joint sense of the Congress resolution that criticized the People's Republic of China for the missile tests and declared that the United States was "committed to the military stability" of the Taiwan Strait and declared that the President should, "consistent with the TRA, consult with the Congress on an appropriate U.S. response" (to the missile tests and the threat caused to the peace and stability of Taiwan).[24] Congress also recalled that the TRA stated that U.S. policy is based on the expectation that the future relationship between Beijing and Taipei would be resolved peacefully. Members of Congress even said that the People's Republic of China should, therefore, in order to arrive at a peaceful solution (though obviously not the kind of agreement Beijing sought) engage in negotiations with Taipei.[25]

In 1997, House Speaker Newt Gingrich visited East Asia. He said during his stop in Hong Kong that the TRA "being a law passed by the Congress and signed by the president would take precedence over a communiqué that was not in treaty form."[26] Gingrich also said in very clear words that the United States would intervene militarily if Taiwan were attacked. The White House responded, saying that Gingrich was "speaking for himself," but forthwith issued a statement saying that it is the policy of the United States to "meet its obligations under the Taiwan Relations Act."[27]

It indeed appeared that the TRA was unlikely to be downgraded, weakened, or ignored; rather it seemed destined to play a central role in U.S. China policy. Still, disagreements between the White House and Congress persisted. Some observers said that the White House and Department of State "toed the line" on the TRA during the crisis to avoid Congress demanding an even more positive response than sending two aircraft battle groups. There was also concern Congress might pass legislation aimed at punishing Beijing. However, after the crisis passed, the executive branch shifted back into a pro-Beijing, anti-Taipei mode. This was apparent when Jiang Zemin visited the United States in 1997 and even more so when President Clinton visited China in 1998.

During the Clinton visit to China, as noted in chapter 7, the president of the United States made public statements that deeply troubled Taiwan's supporters in the United States and many in Congress, especially his "three noes" comment.

Congress took Clinton's move as "violating" the TRA. Some said it constituted a flip-flop from the administration's earlier statements of strong support for the TRA. In reaction, on July 10, 1998, just days after Clinton returned to the United States, the Senate voted 92 to 0 to reaffirm important provisions the TRA. The House passed a similar resolution on July 20. Senate Majority Leader Trent Lott on the occasion said that "sending a message" was needed in view of Clinton's visit to China and what Clinton had said there. Clearly, the votes, though not binding, constituted a rebuff of Clinton's China policy and mirrored the continuing contention between the executive and legislative branches of government regarding U.S. relations with Beijing and Taipei. In fact, this stand-off led Congress to pass a spate of legislative actions to protect Taiwan and obligate the executive branch of government to abide by the TRA. Some provisions added to appropriations bills make it hard for President Clinton to veto them or ignore them.

Yet to some in Congress, having been burned before, this was not enough.

—⟋⟋⟍—

In May 1999, Representative Tom DeLay of Texas and a bipartisan group of fourteen cosponsors introduced a bill called the Taiwan Security Enhancement Act (TSEA), or House Resolution 1838. Within a few weeks seventy-seven members signed on to cosponsor the bill. At the same time Jesse Helms and Robert Torricelli introduced an almost identical bill in the Senate.

A few months later a revised version of the TSEA was proposed by Benjamin Gilman, a Republican from New York and chairman of the House International Relations Committee, and Sam Gejdensen, a Democrat from Connecticut. The committee passed it by a vote of 32 to 6. The intent of the legislation was to reverse the erosion of Section 3 of the TRA, which pledged making available to Taiwan defense articles and services to enable it to "maintain a sufficient self-defense capability" and stated that the "President and Congress shall determine the nature and quantity of such defense articles and services."

Congress felt that various presidents, but especially Bill Clinton, had been lax both in working with Congress to ascertain Taiwan's needs and in informing Congress as required according to provisions in the TRA. Members of Congress said that President Clinton had sought to keep Congress out of the loop and had "illegally" consulted with Beijing regarding arms sales to Taiwan. They concluded that Clinton did not seriously consider Taiwan's security needs in the course of making U.S. China policy. Senator Helms, chairman of the powerful Senate Foreign Relations Committee, said that the administration prefered to "curry favor with Beijing" at Taiwan's expense. The attitude of the administration was demonstrated vividly, said members of Congress, in statements President Clinton made during Jiang Zemin's visit to the United States in 1997 and during Clinton's visit to China in 1998.

The Taiwan Security Enhancement Act addressed still another problem: the absence of formal and effective lines of communication between the U.S. military and Taiwan's Ministry of Defense or its military. This gap had been revealed during the 1996 missile crisis when the United States dispatched aircraft carriers to the area. U.S. naval personnel were not able to talk directly to top defense people in Taiwan. This piece of legislation would, if passed into law, also correct this situation. Specifically, it would formalize U.S. military relations with Taiwan (mandating military contacts between the two sides, liaison, and the coordination of policies, which, incidentally, were also absent during the 1996 missile crisis, which had prevented the United States from making a full response to help Taiwan).

Referring to Clinton's moves to adjust Taiwan policy, several members of Congress commented that the TSEA would also make up for what the Taiwan Policy Review had failed to do.

Last but not least, the TSEA was seen to almost guarantee Taiwan participation in Washington's theater missile defense plan in cooperation with Japan and South Korea. During debate on the bill, Representative Gilman, in fact, called on a Pentagon advisor on Asia policy and asked him pointedly whether the administration had refused to provide Taiwan with missile defense systems.[28] In any event, the TSEA became linked to subsequent reports that Taiwan's defenses were inadequate and to the missile defense issue.

The White House and the Department of State, naturally, were both adamantly opposed to the TSEA. Clinton aides attacked the bill as "unnecessary" and described congressional actions as a move that "could have unintended negative consequences." Susan Shirk, deputy assistant secretary of state for East Asian and Pacific Affairs, said it might be seen as a revision of the Taiwan Relations Act, which had successfully governed the U.S. role in cross-strait issues.[29] Subsequently Secretary of State Albright said that TSEA should not be voted into law and that that the TRA should be strengthened instead. Some in the Clinton administration took the position that there was no good solution, political or otherwise, to the problem and that the president should punt— meaning downplaying the issue, delaying as much as possible, and dumping it into the hands of the next administration.

The Foreign Ministry in Beijing made its strong opposition to the bill known. It said that it "violates China's sovereignty and brutally interferes with China's internal affairs." A ministry spokesperson said that the bill was "an excuse for the U.S. to provide advanced weapons to Taiwan and expand direct relations between U.S. and Taiwan military forces." He concluded that it was an "American plot" that would "support the arrogance of Taiwan's independence aims" and was an effort to "create an obstacle to China's plans of reunification."[30]

When George W. Bush assumed the presidency in 2001, the TSEA ceased to be a burning issue. In fact, it soon faded from view. Observers said it had served its purpose in pressuring the Clinton administration to fulfill the spirit and the letter of the TRA. Now it was no longer needed.

President Bush had voiced very strong support for the TRA during the campaign and he was seen as a chief executive that would honor it. The question was: Would it push him toward a tougher policy toward China that might lead to conflict?

The Missile Defense Issue Involves Others in "Taiwan Issue"

The 1996 missile crisis, not to mention its other effects, drew attention to Taiwan's dire need to defend itself in the event of an actual Chinese missile attack. Taiwan's reaction was to both build and buy more weapons. Antimissile missiles were its top priority.

The Clinton White House, with its penchant for selling arms, delivered much of what Taiwan wanted. To China, Taiwan's acquiring more and better weapons, especially a missile defense system, was distressing. Beijing's leverage over Taiwan via its missile juggernaut would be lost. Chinese officials were especially enraged over the possibility of Taiwan linking up with other nations in the region. Beijing didn't want other countries to commit to Taiwan's defense.

Most worrisome for China was a Taiwan-Japan connection. Taiwan and Japan had a history that Beijing, to put it mildly, found insufferable. Furthermore, Japan was China's competitor for influence in East Asia. Taiwan's acquiring the means to defend itself also had domestic political ramifications in China. It would enhance the clout of hard-liners and the military in Beijing, and it portended of an arms race.

There was still another side to the story. Taiwan's alternative was deterrence in the form of weapons of mass destruction it might use against Chinese cities. This made the Taiwan issue in U.S.-China relations more explosive.

—⁂—

When the Chinese PLA conducted its first missile tests near Taiwan in 1995 in response to President Lee Teng-hui's visit to the United States, it fired two DF-15 missiles daily for three days. DF stands for *dong feng* ("east wind"; which Mao, when he was alive, spoke of as "blowing back the West Wind" or the influence of the West, in particular the United States). The DF, a mobile missile, has a range of around six hundred miles.[1] DFs resemble the SCUD missiles used by Iraq in the Gulf War. Both were mobile; they could be launched from a trailer or other conveyance. They were not easily detectable by aerial reconnaissance because they could be moved quickly and easily and could be camouflaged. Also, like Saddam Hussein's SCUDs, DFs were not very accurate.

One missile fired in 1995 had to be destroyed in flight due to a guidance malfunction. Two hit at the very outside edge of the target zone. Three hit inside the target perimeter, though not in the center. But the PLA learned very quickly from these tests or by other means.

When it did firings in March 1996 to disrupt Taiwan's presidential election campaign, missiles were shot at two separate targets and they hit with uncanny (given the earlier tests) pinpoint accuracy. According to one observer, China had accomplished in eight months what it had taken the United States and the Soviet Union twenty-five years to do.[2]

In the 1950s, U.S. and Soviet missiles had a "miss distance" of approximately one mile, something similar to China's missiles in 1995. In the 1980s, both American and Russian missiles could hit targets with a margin of error of a few hundred feet. By March 1996, less than a year after its first "Taiwan test," Beijing's missile accuracy rivaled that of Moscow and Washington of the 1980s. How China improved its guidance systems and other technology so quickly remains a mystery. Beijing apparently got help, perhaps from the United States via spying on U.S. weapons facilities or from Russia. It may have worked out the kinks itself, but this seems highly unlikely. In any case, Beijing made its rapid advances known to Taiwan (and everyone else) with public announcements about its progress, just in case the military in Taipei did not report this to civilian leaders or it was not picked up by Taiwan's media.

Chinese leaders in Beijing wanted to capitalize on the implications of its new military prowess to cow Taipei. Beijing could now force Taiwan to negotiate reunification, or so Chinese leaders hoped.

Indeed, the DF was Beijing's ideal weapon for some very special reasons. First, during the March 1996 tests, the PLA declared that ships should not enter the waters where the tests were being conducted for a period of ten days, from March 10 to 20. They didn't, and Taiwan was virtually quarantined for a fortnight. Beijing in this way sent a signal to Taiwan: China could close Taiwan's ports and shipping lanes for an extended period anytime it wished. Missile intimidation could economically strangle the island. Taiwan would have to negotiate on Beijing's terms. Second, Taiwan's military preparedness had not given missile defense a high priority, partly for historical reasons, partly for other reasons. Now it was too late!

This situation had an interesting history. In the spring of 1950, Mao had forces poised to invade Taiwan using small boats carrying thousands of soldiers trained to swim the last mile to shore carrying a gun and some bullets. Mao was compelled to adopt such a strategy because the Nationalists had taken the

Chinese navy, including nearly all its large ships and its landing craft, to Taiwan with them in 1949. The Korean War, which precipitated a volte-face in U.S. foreign policy, stymied Mao's plan to seize Taiwan. But Mao did not give up. Later he planned to assault Taiwan the same way he had intended to in early 1950: with a fleet of small boats and hordes of soldiers.

Taiwan prepared for this by purchasing artillery that could be shot over the Taiwan Strait to spray the water below with tiny metal fragments. This would be deadly to incoming swimmers. Taiwan's military also had napalm that would burn on water, and it mined the beaches. Finally, a backup line of defense was built near the island's shores. Beijing thus had to look for other military strategies.

Nuking Taiwan was one, but Chinese officials said they would "never use nuclear weapons on their own people." Probably they meant it at the time. Bombing Taiwan with nuclear weapons had some big downsides. It would kill hundreds of thousands, maybe millions, of people and would leave Taiwan in a shambles, thus negating its economic value to China. It would probably make Beijing the ogre of the world for a century. Leaders in China, especially the reformist faction, were concerned about China's global reputation. A neutron bomb, which China acquired at some point (whether by stealing U.S. secrets or not), resolved the problem of obliterating much of the island and its infra-structure. But it was still an "image buster" and was undesirable in other respects (including the fact that Taiwan was important economically in large part because of its human talent).

Beijing's best strategy was, therefore, to blockade or quarantine the island and cut Taiwan's economic lifeline. It could do this with submarines or with submarines in combination with surface ships. But it needed air superiority over the Taiwan Strait and the island itself to make this work effectively. Noting this, Taiwan's defense strategy focused on obtaining good fighter planes and credi-ble antisubmarine warfare capabilities. To a large extent the latter depended on the former. During the 1970s and 1980s, Taipei had some difficulties guaran-teeing control of its air space. But it greatly enhanced its capabilities in this realm with the acquisition of top-of-the-line U.S. and French fighter planes in 1992.

Beijing's strategy shifted as a result of Taiwan's purchases but also as a prod-uct of its improved missile technology. Hence, the Chinese PLA chose to use mis-siles as the weapon of choice in 1995 and 1996. In fact, after 1996 it seemed that any future action by China to intimidate Taiwan or vent its anger at the United States or someone else would involve using missiles.

Certainly with its growing arsenal the PLA could, with a single test or simply by announcing one, immediately scare away foreign ships and planes. This would deny Taiwan the use of its ports, causing its economy to freefall while creating an energy shortfall and a general panic or crisis. The PLA could then escalate the conflict, if the United States did not intervene, and strike at military targets, destroying Taiwan's air force and navy through attrition with its big advantage in number of planes and ships.

Assuming the United States might at some future time be too preoccupied somewhere else in the world or get too fatigued to continue to come to Taiwan's rescue every time Beijing made a threat or military feint, became fearful of American casualties, or became isolationist or divided, Taipei would have little choice but to surrender.

At least this was a likely scenario. It was one Taipei worried very seriously about.

—⁂—

Taiwan's response, rather than accept defeat, was to build or buy antimissile weapons, perhaps both. Even before China's PLA fired missiles at targets near Taiwan's shores in 1995, Taiwan had some experience with both building and deploying missiles. In the 1980s, Taiwan built the Sky Sword air-to-air missile. It was fitted to locally built (under contract with Northrop Corporation) F-5E fighter planes.

Taiwan also manufactured the Sky Bow surface-to-air missile. Like the Sky Sword, it was produced by Taiwan's premier research facility, the Chungshan Institute of Science and Technology located in Lungtan near Taipei. The Sky Bow was subsequently upgraded and called Sky Bow II. It was said to be able to track and intercept flying objects up to one hundred kilometers away while flying at a velocity of four times the speed of sound. Tested in the field in 1998, it demonstrated its capability to shoot down another missile in flight. A Sky Bow II fired from Pingtung in southern Taiwan destroyed a missile fired from a base in southeastern Taiwan. The test impressed Taiwan's military planners.

Officials in Taipei sought to build the country's own weapons in some measure for political reasons. The Ching-kuo or Indigenous Defense Fighter was a product of Taiwan's local defense industries. It had made it possible for the United States to argue, when talking with Chinese leaders in Beijing, that Taiwan was building its own weapons. Hence, the United States could not prevent Taiwan's growing military strength and its ability to defend itself. Or in case a future administration in the United States became hostile toward Taiwan or unconcerned, Taipei had an option.

In fact some decision makers in Taiwan perceived that the United States was often "inscrutable" about arms sales, even fickle. Many also felt that producing weapons locally would serve as a tripwire to ensure a U.S. commitment, just as France's nuclear weapons had during the Cold War.

Meanwhile Taipei purchased a number of U.S. missiles and missile defense related technology. Many defense specialists and political leaders preferred, in fact, to "buy American." It was cheaper, the weapons' quality was better, and presumably arms sales increased Washington's commitment to Taiwan (based on the argument that the prestige of U.S. weapons would be at stake).

Also, not long after China's 1996 missile intimidation it looked like missile defense, including theater missile defense, was "on go" in the United States. This was good news for Taiwan. For some years there had been, in the United States, both among foreign policy experts and the public, growing sentiment favoring national missile defense as well as theater missile defense (for protecting American troops abroad). Advances in technology and new threats from rogue states were the catalysts.

In 1992, after the fall of the Soviet bloc and in response to "new threats," President George H. W. Bush redefined the Strategic Defense Initiative (SDI) program to focus on "complete defense" against an attack of less than two hundred warheads instead of partial defense against a Soviet massive attack with thousands of missiles and aircraft. It was designed to protect not only the United States but also U.S. forces overseas and U.S. allies. Taiwan benefited from this policy. Raytheon Corporation, a large U.S. weapons producer, received U.S. government permission to help Taiwan upgrade its Sky Bow missiles. The next year, the German government approved the sale to Taiwan of Patriot missiles built under a joint agreement with the United States.[3] Subsequently, Raytheon, taking the cue that Taiwan was to get more arms, negotiated a large deal, worth over US$1 billion, with Taipei to replace its Nike air defense system.

So Taiwan bought more missiles from the United States. It also deployed its own Sky Bow missiles. Both were intended to defend the country against Beijing's aircraft and missiles.[4]

Immediately after China conducted missile tests off Taiwan's coast in July 1995, Taiwan defense officials said they wanted much more. In particular they sought to purchase a big, "comprehensive" missile defense system from the United States, including a high-altitude system to defend the island against missiles fired from long distances.

In August, Taipei announced that it would deploy the U.S.-made Modified Air Defense System, a Patriot system, adapted for Taiwan. This was intended to counter missiles fired from shorter distances than those China fired at Taiwan in 1995. The Clinton administration did not mind selling lower-tier defensive missiles. Arms sales employed Americans, and Congress favored strengthening Taiwan's military capabilities. Finally, Beijing did not say much.

Though in October officials in Taipei set off a firestorm when they stated publicly that Taiwan was interested in participating in the development of the U.S. Theater Missile Defense system. Beijing was spitting mad. For the next several months, officials in Beijing designed policies to counter what one official called "an awful trend." Some even threatened the United States if it went ahead with theater missile defense and included Taiwan. Late in the year it was reported in the press that Taiwan had decided to appropriate more than US$10 billion for new weapons and that defensive missiles were a first priority: both locally produced missiles and missiles purchased from the United States.[5]

After the PLA missile tests in March 1996, Taipei gave an even higher priority to the acquisition of antimissile missiles. Taiwan's military procurement people began to look to various sellers, even Russia. They probably hoped this "looking around" would prompt U.S. companies and Congress to press the Clinton administration to offer more to Taiwan. Anyway, in May, the Ministry of National Defense announced that Patriot missiles had arrived and bases were being placed around Taipei to protect the city, even though some politicians, including Taipei Mayor Chen Shui-bian from the opposition DPP, argued that this would create more danger than it would offer protection.[6]

In early 1997, Taiwan received more Patriot missiles in addition to Avenger air-defense missile systems (which employs Stinger missiles) from the United States. In January 1998, Taiwan received still another shipment of Patriot missiles. Two months later, in March, Taipei announced that it had tested the Brave Wind II missile that uses the Satellite Global Positioning System to find its targets. Late in the year, Taipei began talks with the United States for the purchase of four Aegis-equipped destroyers that carried an elaborate system of antimissile defense at a staggering price of over US$1 billion each. This would be a major breakthrough for Taiwan in its efforts to join theater missile defense if approved by Washington.

In March 1999, Taiwan's Defense Minister Tang Fei estimated that it would cost US$9.23 billion over eight to ten years to build a low-altitude missile defense system capable of destroying 70 percent of missiles aimed at Taiwan.[7] He recommended starting immediately, or "it will be too late for us to consider whether to join TMD." According to an opinion poll conducted at that time, 86 percent of the population said China's missiles threatened Taiwan, and a majority favored Taiwan's participation in a regional antimissile defense arrangement.[8] In September, Defense Minister Tang said that TMD was Taiwan's "highest priority." Later in the year, the Ministry of National Defense announced that Taiwan might build its own "Taiwan Missile Defense" system. But this looked like a ploy to get the United States to include Taiwan in whatever it did. Subsequently President Lee Teng-hui proclaimed that Taiwan was committed to missile defense. Meanwhile, Chen Shui-bian, now the opposition DPP's presidential candidate, announced his support for the plan.

In April 2000, the Clinton administration denied Taiwan's request for Aegis ships at least temporarily. A month later, Taiwan's new Defense Minister Wu Shih-wen said Taiwan would develop a missile system by itself. He noted that it was an "essential deterrent to a Chinese attack."[9] Clearly Taiwan was determined to defend itself against Chinese missiles one way or another, arms race or no.

—⚍—

During the Cold War, China constructed missiles to deliver nuclear weapons. Since this (as well as its nuclear weapons) came mainly after Sino-Soviet relations had soured in the late 1950s and early 1960s, Beijing built almost exclusively intermediate-range ballistic missiles that were targeted on the Soviet Union. China did not give a high priority to either intercontinental or submarine-launched missiles that could hit targets in the United States because the Soviet Union was its "paramount enemy."

With the end of the Cold War, Beijing revamped its strategy and began to build more intercontinental missiles to hit the United States. But it constructed more short-range missiles to intimidate countries (especially U.S. allies) in East Asia and/or strike U.S. military installations and personnel in the region. Taiwan was on the top of the list of targets.

As noted earlier, with almost carte blanche offers to purchase arms from the Soviet Union and with the availability of American missile and related technology, which China got through the Internet, bought, or stole, Beijing was able to acquire better long-range and short-range missiles very quickly.

Meanwhile, in fact as early as 1990, the PLA began to amass forces and weapons in China's southeastern provinces. Following a deal with Moscow to reduce tensions on their border, Beijing transferred much of its military capabilities, both manpower and weapons, from North China to Fujian Province (across the strait from Taiwan) and to inland areas in China still striking distance to Taiwan. In 1994, Chinese troops repositioned to areas close to Taiwan conducted military exercises using code names "Conquest 96" and "Doomsday of the Aircraft Carrier." *Ninety-six* was said to refer to the time it would take, ninety-six hours, to conquer Taiwan. Others said it was the year 1996, when the offensive would be launched. *Aircraft Carrier* referred to Taiwan (called an unsinkable aircraft carrier by the Japanese during World War II and by General Douglas MacArthur later). Military maneuvers employing troops earmarked as "invasion forces," were conducted on an island little more than seventy miles from the Nationalist-held island of Quemoy. No efforts were made to prevent Taiwan from knowing about this.[10]

Not only were army and air force units shifted from one part of China to another (closer to Taiwan), navy installations were also moved and either rebuilt or expanded. Part of the reason for this connected to Beijing's strategy of giving its naval development the highest priority in its defense planning and its desire to attain military dominance in the South China Sea to scare off Southeast Asian nations asserting territorial claims there. Some said Beijing claimed the South China Sea so that it could also say the Taiwan Strait was its territory before it "liberated" Taiwan. In any event, the South China Sea and Taiwan were related in the minds of Chinese leaders.

Subsequently Beijing created new military units that combined land, sea, and air forces. They were placed in Fujian Province in the Nanjing Military Area. Control over the units, which also included missile units recently moved in, was placed directly under the Central Military Commission of the Chinese Communist Party. The area was labeled a war zone.[11]

What happened in 1995 and 1996, to some observers, was simply the culmination or the natural consequences of China's military build-up aimed at Taiwan. After 1996, the build-up continued unabated. In late 1998, according to a January 1999 U.S. Defense Intelligence Agency report, China, among other military exercises, practiced launching DF-3 and DF-4 missiles (much improved missiles compared to those used in 1996) at Taiwan.[12]

A month later Congress released a Pentagon report that stated that China was rapidly improving its military capabilities in the Taiwan Strait area and that it was preparing to fight with "precision weapons," especially missiles. The report went on to say that the balance of power had shifted in favor of Beijing and against Taiwan. The authors of the report predicted that by 2005, the PLA would possess the capability to attack Taiwan with air and missile strikes "which would degrade key military facilities and damage the island's infrastructure."[13]

In November 1999, a U.S. newspaper reported that the PLA was in the process of placing some one hundred new advanced short-range missiles across the strait from Taiwan. It quoted Dennis Blair, commander of U.S. forces in the Pacific, who said that China was going to eventually put five to six hundred missiles in the area. The newspaper, in addition, cited a Pentagon study that confirmed this: China would deploy six hundred and fifty missiles there within six years.[14] The conclusion seemed inescapable: China was going to overwhelm any effort Taiwan made at erecting a credible missile defense system.

Meanwhile, in fact even before the PLA's military buildup in areas of China close to Taiwan, Beijing began making a concerted effort to block U.S. efforts to develop antimissile defense, especially anything that would help Taiwan defend against China's newest best weapon. Prior to its missile tests in July 1995, Foreign Ministry officials in Beijing declared that getting rid of the restrictions on building missile defense in the Anti-Ballistic Missile Treaty in force between the Washington and Moscow "would be destabilizing to East Asia, will trigger a new arms race, and will do no good to the nuclear armament process."

After the subsequent U.S. tests, Chinese spokespersons said that theater missile defense (high altitude) would threaten China and consequently Beijing would be forced to increase its nuclear arsenal. Shortly after the 1996 missile tests and in the context of Washington sending antimissile weapons to Taiwan, Beijing declared that "theater missile defense will lead to an arms race" because it would increase the nuclear superiority of big powers (meaning the United States). Chinese leaders also asserted that the U.S. and Japanese contention that they want to defend against North Korea was untrue and what they were doing was aimed at China. In 1998, Beijing tried to negotiate a pledge from the United States not to share theater missile defense technology with Taiwan in return for China halting ballistic missile cooperation with Iran, but Washington didn't take the offer.

In early 1999, the PLA's newspaper called Taiwan's participation in missile defense with the United States a "serious encroachment on China's sovereignty and territorial integrity."[15] Shortly after that, China Daily warned the United States about bringing Taiwan into the Theater Missile Defense plan, saying, "If there is an action, there must be a reaction." Beijing later asserted that "by bringing Taiwan in, the U.S. would forge a de facto military alliance with Taiwan" and that the "path of nonproliferation of weapons of mass destruction which the United States has been following is in danger of being reversed."[16] What Beijing was saying was that it would lift restraints on selling or transferring nuclear weapons technology to nations the United States considered terrorists states if the United States included Taiwan in its theater missile defense plans.

Two months later, the head of China's Department of Arms Control and Disarmament in the Ministry of Foreign Affairs, when asked about theater missile defense, said, "In the case of Taiwan, my God, that's really the limit." U.S. moves "would provoke the entire Chinese people" and that it would "bring severe consequences."[17]

—⚏—

For technical reasons as well as costs, not to mention the fact that Beijing was absolutely committed to aiming more missiles at Taiwan than Taiwan's military could defend against, Taipei did not find it feasible to go it alone on missile defense. For political reasons as well officials in Taipei saw a big advantage for Taiwan to join or become part of a regional theater missile defense system. How to do this was the question.

Since Washington was pursuing a program of theater missile defense in co-operation with Japan and possibly South Korea, hopefully Taiwan could jump on board. That possibility had been discussed in Taiwan and in the United States. Japan had long been reluctant to undertake missile defense for a variety of reasons, including its pacifist foreign policy and the fact that leaders in Beijing would see its participation in theater missile defense as a provocation. However, this policy began to change as Tokyo's military strategy started to evolve in a new direction that defined China as Japan's adversary.

This became apparent to some degree after 1989, but much more so after 1996. Following the 1996 Taiwan missile crisis and as a direct result of it, the U.S.-Japan defense treaty was upgraded. For its part, Tokyo revised its guidelines for military cooperation with the United States and widened its responsibilities to the Taiwan Strait. In July, apparently in response to Japan's policy shift, Beijing reignited the dispute over the Senkaku (in Chinese, Diaoyutai) Islands—very small islets north of Taiwan thought to be near or on top of large undersea oil deposits and claimed by both Japan and China. To Japanese leaders, China, it seemed, was blatantly trying to intimidate Japan. Tokyo, in fact, interpreted the "Senkaku crisis" as Beijing sending a signal that it could and would raise a serious issue that might lead to a crisis in relations between the two countries if Tokyo misbehaved. Tokyo took this to mean also that China's threat to Taiwan extended to Japan. A few months later a Japanese government spokesperson made a very public correction to a Diet member's statement that Taiwan and the Taiwan Strait were "off limits to Japan." Some saw this as a riposte to Beijing for making issue of the Senkakus.[18]

In August 1998, as noted earlier, North Korea conducted a missile test that sent shockwaves throughout Japan. The missile passed over the densely populated part of Japan and on to the Pacific Ocean east of Japan. It might have been carrying a nuclear warhead. This had apocalyptic implications for Japan. As a result of the test the defense landscape, in Japanese defense planners' eyes, changed dramatically, as did the public's perception of missile defense. Forthwith the Diet passed a resolution calling on the government to "take all measures to ensure the security of the Japanese people."[19]

The thinking in Japan was that North Korean missiles carrying atomic bombs (assuming North Korea had them, which was the conventional wisdom in many quarters) could, and might, hit Japanese cities and kill a huge number of Japanese. To most Japanese, given the ill feeling Koreans harbored toward Japan due to its colonization of Korea early in the century, its harsh rule of Korea after that, events during World War II (such as forcing Koreans into the Japanese military and to work in factories in Japan and recruiting "comfort women" as forced prostitutes for the Japanese military, and so on), it seemed plausible that North Korean leaders might actually do what Japan most dreaded.

Some Japanese military leaders in private, however, said they did not take North Korea's test too seriously. They went on to say that it constituted a good excuse to arm against their real enemy: China. In a very uncharacteristic statement, Professor Masashi Nishihara of Japan's National Defense Academy proclaimed: "Even if the North Korean threat subsides, we need to be wary of China."[20] Japan subsequently "signed on" or accepted Washington's proposal to build a theater missile defense system. Tokyo forthwith appropriated US$280 million to start the joint effort. Mitsubishi Heavy Industries and Raytheon in the United States signed an agreement.[21]

For Taiwan this was fortuitous. Japan's changed policy was a distinct advantage. The "Japan connection"—if there could be one—would be very useful to both political and military leaders in Taipei that wanted to participate in theater missile defense. But it was a road filled with potholes and dangers due to the fact that Beijing so vehemently opposed the prospects of Japan and Taiwan being linked in any way, shape, or form. Chinese leaders, in fact, fulminated with rage at the very idea. It evoked thoughts of Taiwan under Japanese rule and the possibility of that recurring.

On Tokyo's part, because Japan's oil lifeline to the Middle East passed through the Taiwan Strait, it could not afford to see Taiwan in "enemy hands." Much of its other trade went through the strait. Also pundits had argued for years that if Japan were ever to exert increased military influence (and some said political or economic influence as well) in East Asia again, Taiwan had to remain separate from China. That meant supporting an independent Taiwan in whatever way possible was in Japan's national interest.

Inasmuch as the United States controlled Taiwan's fate, Japanese seldom expressed any concern over or overt interest in Taiwan. The reality was that Taiwan's future was in Washington's hands, so Tokyo followed America's lead on Taiwan. Nor did Japanese leaders want to unnecessarily rile Beijing. They clearly understood that Taiwan was a very sensitive issue in Sino-Japanese relations. Still, many leading Japanese politicians (supported to some degree by public opinion) maintained close ties with leaders in Taiwan and often subtly (sometimes not so subtly) expressed support for the status quo (meaning separation from China).

It had also been reported in the media that at least a hundred members of the Diet were secretly supporters of a separate Taiwan. Not many opposed the idea. This gave rise to frequent speculation that Tokyo had a hidden agenda regarding Taiwan.

Support for Taiwan in Japan grew as public opinion soured on China. After the Taiwan missile crisis of 1996, 51 percent of Japanese polled said they did not feel friendly toward China (compared to 18 percent in 1985).[22] More Japanese than Americans thought Taiwan was an "independent country."[23] Meanwhile politicians in Taiwan encouraged political and military ties with Japan. This included President Lee Teng-hui. Lee talked about Taiwan and Japan having a common destiny. He said Taiwan and Japan should be closer in both political and military ways. Others in Taipei said Japan would help guarantee Taiwan's security because of the formal and very important U.S.-Japan defense relationship, which perhaps extended to Taiwan. During the 1970s, an agreement between President Nixon and Prime Minister Sato had put Taiwan within Japan's "defense perimeter" in terms of U.S.-Japan military cooperation. This "pact" was never repudiated by any subsequent Japanese prime minister.

Not long after Beijing's second round of missile tests, former Cabinet Secretary Seiroku Kajiyama said that Japan's defense responsibilities in the U.S.-Japan treaty "certainly include Taiwan." The Foreign Ministry at the time said that it followed guidelines established by Prime Minister Kishi in 1960, which put the line of demarcation just north of the Philippines.

—⟡—

Beijing's response to Taiwan's possibly acquiring significant antimissile defense capabilities by joining a Northeast Asia theater missile defense system was telling. It mirrored how much Chinese leaders hated Japanese or feared Japan's military revival, or both. Some observers reported they had never seen leaders in Beijing so "bent out of shape and full of rage" when talking about defense linkages between Taiwan and Japan. To Chinese leaders, especially military hardliners, the idea of Japan being joined by Taiwan in a Northeast Asia theater missile defense system, in terms of their efforts to "reunify" Taiwan, was a "worst case situation."

To understand Chinese leaders' perceptions and the problem generated by missile defense becoming a Washington-Taipei-Japan matter, one must comprehend that Chinese in China espouse very different attitudes toward Japan from Chinese in Taiwan or Taiwanese. Japan humiliated China in war in 1894–95 (and acquired Taiwan in the peace treaty), colonized Korea (once a Chinese vassal state) in 1910, tried to de facto colonize part of China after World War I, and imposed various "imperialist" controls on China at this time. In 1931, Japan stripped Manchuria from China and incorporated it into the Japanese empire. In 1937 Japan invaded China proper. Japanese military forces subsequently caused horrendous loss of life and damage in China in an effort to force China into Tokyo's Greater East Asia Co-Prosperity Sphere, a codeword for Japanese imperial dominance of East Asia.

The Chinese military under Chiang Kai-shek's leadership resisted the subservience Japan sought to impose on China. But Nationalist Chinese forces fared poorly against Japan's superior military machine. Chiang resorted to a policy of strategic retreat, in some cases a "scorched earth" policy, to overstretch Japanese supply lines. Communist forces under Mao fought guerrilla warfare against Japanese forces. Japan regarded both as reflecting Chinese cowardice. In the midst of a "sea of Chinese," the Japanese military had to resort to terror tactics to try to bring China to its knees.

Japanese atrocities, though scarcely reported in the West, were vividly known to virtually all Chinese living in China. The Rape of Nanking, one of the now most notorious cases of human rights abuse in modern times, cast the Japanese as brutal, bloodthirsty, and the bitter enemies of China and the Chinese people. Most Chinese (in China) came to thoroughly revile Japan and Japanese. But because Japan was defeated at sea by the U.S. Navy and the war was brought to an end by the American bombing of Japan, including the use of atomic bombs, neither Chiang nor Mao tasted the fruits of victory. Japanese forces simply left. Though in ruins after the war, Japan was, in the minds of Chinese, still a potential aggressor. Many feared Japan would rise again.

When Mao took control of China, he forthwith signed a military agreement with Moscow known as the Sino-Soviet Alliance. It cited Japan as the enemy even though Japan was a destroyed and occupied nation. This mirrored a latent fear of Japan in China. Memories of Japan's military prowess and Japanese draconian rule of much of China could not be erased from Chinese minds.

In subsequent years, Chinese leaders, like the population at large, worried about the revival of the Japanese military machine. This did not seem reasonable to many in the West, since Japan was disarmed, neutered, and permeated with pacifism, and its leadership and population were devoted to economic development and a peaceful (if any) role in the world. But Chinese had their reasons for thinking this way.

For example, to most Chinese Japan never accepted guilt or apologized for World War II, as Germany did. Textbooks used in grade school and high school, which are approved by the Ministry of Education in Tokyo and are standard throughout Japan, had been revised to speak of Japan's invasion of China as an "incursion" (suggesting it was not Japan's fault) and its atrocities as "vexing" China. Many Japanese, including government leaders, even denied the Rape of Nanking and other atrocities committed by Japanese forces in China really happened. Top political leaders in Japan periodically visited shrines for Japan's war dead, including the infamous Yasakuni Shrine in Tokyo, where class-A war criminals were buried. Prime Minister Hashimoto went in 1996. In China, the prime minister's visit was seen to be paying respects to the despised General Tojo while tacitly supporting nascent militarism in Japan. Recent books, such as one portraying Tojo as a hero, and the frequent public displays of Japanese nationalist sentiment have also been disconcerting to China.

In 1998, shortly after President Clinton visited China, President Jiang Zemin went to Japan on a state visit. It was the first visit ever by a Chinese head of state to Japan. Foreign Minister Tang Jiaxuan said before the visit that Sino-Japanese relations hinged on two things: Japan's attitude toward history and its stance on Taiwan. Jiang expected to use good press coverage of the trip to bolster his image at home as the China visit had done for President Clinton. Prime Minister Hashimoto had visited China the previous year to celebrate the twenty-fifth anniversary of the signing of the Peace and Friendship treaty in 1972. Everything seemed well prepared. Jiang sought an apology for the harm done to China by Japan during World War II. He also expected to get the Japanese government to concur with China's "Three Noes" regarding Taiwan, as President Clinton had.

Prime Minister Obuchi, however, refused to issue a formal apology for the war, even though he had made one a year earlier in Korea. He also declined to repeat the "Three Noes." It was a serious rebuff. Jiang's trip was seen at home and by the international media as a flop. His newly appointed foreign minister, Tang Jiaxuan, who was a Japan specialist, was injured politically by the failed trip, not to mention Jiang himself. The two left Tokyo with an unsigned communiqué.

Why the diplomatic disaster? In Japan, Jiang's demands created a backlash. It evoked renewed hard feelings toward China in Japan. Japan's apology, which China had already accepted, was contained in the 1972 joint communiqué between the two countries. Japanese leaders said it "hurt the people" for Beijing to keep asking for Japan to apologize. Many Japanese also saw China's "incessantly talking about past Japanese misbehavior" as extortion. China really wanted money.[24]

Jiang had delayed his trip to Japan for two months, using as a pretext floods in China keeping him at home. He wanted to put pressure on Japan. As it turned out, this was a monumental blunder. In the interim President Clinton had visited Japan. He and Japanese leaders talked about theater missile defense. At the end of the visit, a joint communiqué was signed. It said that Clinton and Prime Minister Obuchi had consulted on international issues, including Russia and China. Two days later, the Pentagon issued its fourth report on "U.S. Security Strategy for the East Asia-Pacific Region." It attached a new significance to Japan. So much for President Clinton's pro-China leanings when he visited Beijing in the summer. Some observers said Japan was willing to make concessions to China before the Clinton visit but not after.[25]

Meanwhile, the Chinese Communist Party, in the midst of a worsening legitimacy crisis, had come to recognize that it needed a unifying issue and perhaps an enemy. Japan was it. Jiang's failed trip thus became the pretext for more anti-Japanese declarations. Party leaders subsequently encouraged consternation and ill feelings toward Japan. A spate of anti-Japanese diatribes followed in the press. Much said this was planned.

Japan and China were natural enemies. Certainly they were competitors for leadership (and political and military control) of East Asia. Since China's economic boom that began in 1978, the two quickly became economic rivals. When China's military spending took off after 1989 they became, or were poised to become, military contenders.

In reply to those who said Japan was a military weakling and its population largely pacifist, Chinese leaders pointed out that Japan's defense spending made it the second ranking military power in the world after the United States. And, unlike the United States and various European powers, Japan did not cut its defense spending in response to the end of the Cold War, they said. Answering those who argued that Japan is pacifist and is not a nuclear power, Chinese analysts replied that Japanese pacifism is a sham, only "skin deep." They charge that Japan can, when it wants to, since it has (purposely, say Chinese leaders) built mostly breeder reactors among its numerous nuclear power plants, build an arsenal of nuclear bombs overnight. Moreover, said many military leaders in Beijing, with antimissile defense Japan does not need to go nuclear to be a world-class military power.

China's fear of Japan's military power had grown rapidly in recent years for some other reasons, most having to do with it assuming a bigger defense burden from the United States and perhaps even replacing U.S. military power as Washington "draws down" in East Asia.

It is noteworthy that Chinese leaders "changed their minds about Japan" at a critical juncture: at the time of the first Taiwan missile tests. This "change of heart" had to do largely with Japan's perceived intentions toward Taiwan. But there was a broader context. After early 1995, when the U.S. government issued the so-called Nye Report (or the East Asia Strategy Report) that gave a new emphasis to the U.S.-Japan alliance and included a major provision for theater missile defense, China's attitude shifted dramatically. A U.S.-Japan decision to build theater missile defense truly riled Chinese leaders.

Cognizant of the importance of this development, Chinese leaders stated, with a voice that reflected alarm, that they did not believe that missile defense was stabilizing, as U.S. and other military strategists claimed. Rather, it consti-tuted "breaking the norm of self-restraint on Japan's part" and would lead to a comprehensive Japanese military buildup, which would be destabilizing and dangerous. And the United States would be the "coconspirator" in this devel-opment. Thus China's missile tests in 1995, or even the more shocking ones in 1996, may not have been the cause behind U.S.-Japan TMD cooperation. Or perhaps Washington and Tokyo saw these events coming.

In any event, in 1997 the United States and Japan agreed on "guidelines" for defense cooperation and made theater missile defense "situational," (read to include Japan as a participant in any help the United States might want to give to Taiwan). Jiang Zemin declared that China was on a "high alert" regarding changes in the U.S.-Japan alliance.

In 1998, when Japan signed on to theater missile defense and allocated money to pursue it, Beijing promptly said it did not believe that it was designed to counter North Korea's missile capabilities. Chinese leaders asserted that it was aimed at China and was intended to counter Beijing's most effective weapon against Taiwan. Beijing's suspicions were doubly aroused by Taipei's interest in theater missile defense. Part of this came from Chinese leaders' personal dislike and distrust of Lee Teng-hui. They noted Lee had graduated from Kyoto Uni-versity and speaks Japanese fluently. (In fact, many in Taiwan have observed that he speaks it better than Mandarin Chinese and that the first newspaper he reads every morning is a Japanese paper.) Furthermore, Lee had served in the Japanese military. Beijing put two and two together: Lee's pro-Japanese views and his advocacy of Taiwan's independence, and Taiwan's interest in theater missile defense.

For Beijing, the tables had seemingly turned, from having a special weapon to force Taiwan to negotiate, to losing its leverage to force Taiwan to talk reunification. China would have to build more missiles.

—⁓—

The issue of building a theater missile defense program that Taiwan might join put the Clinton administration in a bind, to put it mildly. It was certain to strain U.S.-China relations, perhaps irreparably. But the White House faced a torrent of pro–missile defense sentiment, more than it had prepared for. Initially the administration thought it might delay missile defense by signing on and then dragging its feet. This did not work. Taiwan was part of the reason.

After the missile crisis of 1996, it was reported frequently in the U.S. press that China was increasing its forces in the area of China across the strait from Taiwan. Much was made of China's transferring its military personnel and weapons (including missiles) to areas of the country adjacent to Taiwan. This had not been reported on much before. The U.S. media also carried stories about the number of missiles China housed on bases close to the Taiwan Strait and the fact new ones were coming in.

According to some of the reports, the increases were not just incremental; they were geometric, in the range of fourfold in a short time. Taiwan needed to defend itself, and it had the right. And America should help. The Clinton administration had to respond. Taiwan was under increased threat and Congress was paying heed. The public favored democratic Taiwan over authoritarian China and supported arms sales to Taiwan.

In July 1996, just four months after the second Taiwan missile crisis, President Clinton signed the National Missile Defense Act to go ahead with a plan for missile defense "as soon as it is technically feasible." The adverbial phrase seemed a cop-out. But was it going to be that? Clinton had signed on.

When Clinton became president, national missile defense had been almost a dead issue. It was revived by technological breakthroughs and by an increase in the acquisition of weapons of mass destruction by rogue states, plus debate about the China threat (recall that Chinese leaders had talked about nuking Los Angeles) and by China's intimidating missile tests aimed to pen in Taiwan. These all became linked, creating a powerful parallax of forces favoring missile defense beginning at the time of Beijing's threatening missile tests near Taiwan's shores.

After the 1996 missile tests, Clinton announced a "three plus three" program. The United States would develop and then deploy a national missile defense system in three-year phases such that deployment would never be less than three years away from a serious intercontinental ballistic missile threat by another country. It was clear that China was the one that this was aimed at. Momentum subsequently grew for reconsidering a full-fledged "star wars" program based on both political and military considerations.

In the summer of 1998, a bipartisan Commission to Assess the Ballistic Missile Threat to the United States, chaired by then former Secretary of Defense Donald Rumsfeld, released a report saying that within five years certain rogue states might develop missiles that could carry weapons of mass destruction and hit U.S. cities with little warning. With this backdrop, in August North Korea tested its three-stage Taepo-Dong I missile over Japan. In January 1999, the administration announced that it would make a decision regarding missile defense deployment in the summer of 2000. At this time, because missile defense could presumably counter missile threats from smaller states with fewer missiles than the Soviet Union, which no longer existed anyway (and with its demise so went the mentality of a bipolar confrontation), the voices saying "missile defense is dangerous" were not considered relevant.

Small rogue countries and the proliferation of delivery systems around the world were a serious problem. So was China. To some they were connected because China had helped a number of "rogue states" acquire weapons of mass destruction. Or so the evidence seemed to indicate. President Clinton could not very well oppose missile defense on the grounds that an opponent or opponents could build offensive weapons faster and cheaper than the United States could build defensive ones. Small states could not. It wasn't certain whether China could or not. Beijing was on record as saying it would not engage in an arms race on America's terms. It would fight unconventional war instead.

In any case, how could a president that so clearly understood spin not favor putting resources into a weapon that could save American lives, including U.S. military personnel abroad (numbering above thirty thousand in Korea and more than that in Japan and Okinawa just north of Taiwan)? Clinton's advisors at the time reminded him of the fact that the most serious losses incurred by U.S. forces in the Gulf War came from Iraqi SCUD attacks. Congress began talking in these terms. American forces in East Asia had become vulnerable. The same could be said about American cities.

Finally, missile defense was popular with the American public. The opinion polls said so. China was considered a growing threat to the United States. And the two were related in the public's mind.[26]

At this juncture an event occurred that further dashed doubts that missile defense would work. In October 1999, after a flight of four thousand miles from California over the Pacific Ocean on a path that would lead it to China, a Minuteman missile was destroyed in flight by a high-tech American "exoatmospheric kill vehicle" (EKV) fired from Kwajalein. At a velocity of sixteen thousand miles per hour, the EKV hit the Minuteman missile flying at supersonic-plus speed 140 miles above the ground. The EKV was going so fast that it did not need to carry a bomb to cause a giant explosion; the impact alone did that. This successful test was a tremendous boost for missile defense. Meanwhile it was becoming increasingly apparent that America's strategic problems were in Asia, not Europe, as evidenced by Pentagon studies on major threats. Certainly the world's flash points (the Taiwan Strait and the Korean Peninsula) were in East Asia.

There was an additional reason for giving a high priority to theater missile defense in Northeast Asia: an arms control agreement, the Anti-Ballistic Missile Treaty signed in 1972 between Washington and Moscow, that impeded the development of national missile defense. It did not prevent the United States from building defensive weapons or placing them in another country or at sea, and this is what theater missile defense in Northeast Asia was about.

There was still another twist. Including Taiwan in TMD helped fulfill the U.S. "obligation" under the TRA to provide for Taiwan's defense. The downside was that including Taiwan would make it more obvious, perhaps unmistakably so, that the system was aimed at stopping Chinese missiles, not just North Korean ones. And that was politically explosive.

Finally, there was also the matter of money. Taiwan had lots of cash and could pay its share, making the whole system more feasible in terms of both its workability and the problem of its cost. In fact, some Pentagon officials argued that "getting Taiwan on board" was essential to financing the system.

Which way would the Clinton administration go? What would "swing the deal" one way or the other?

For the Clinton White House it appeared it may be a choice of theater missile defense being designed to cover a larger area and thus being more effective or not. There was also the choice between markedly increasing U.S. defense spending to build a Northeast Asian system or getting money from Taipei.

Clinton was at this time under pressure from a number of U.S. companies that saw the opportunity for huge contracts to manufacture the system and profits from doing business with Japan and Taiwan, both flush with cash. Lobbyists went to work and campaign donations were mentioned. But Beijing viewed Taiwan's getting missile defense as politically portentous and something that would discourage talks leading to unification and directly supporting those advocating Taiwan's independence. Chinese leaders were bitterly hostile to the idea. Beijing was also committed to beating it by building more missiles. This, of course, could be translated into an arms race between the United States and China in the region. But since Beijing was also advocating fighting unconventional war against the United States, some defense planners in Washington said that the United States could compete with China and indeed should, to get China to focus on Western concepts of war. In other words, it would stabilize the military relationship between Beijing and Washington. It was also argued that focusing China's attention on theater missile defense and Taiwan would draw attention away from America's national defense project and thus make it easier to build the latter.

The bottom line: In the United States there were a host of good reasons for building a theater missile defense system in Northeast Asia and including Taiwan in it.

Shortly before Bill Clinton left office another antimissile test was done. Problems arose in advance of the actual firing. Clinton found this a convenient reason for delaying a final decision on missile defense, essentially making it one for the next administration to deal with.

—⚏—

Since the early 1950s, Taiwan was known to possess some measure of deterrence against an attack by China's PLA on the island. Taiwan had a strong military and could slow a Chinese attack long enough, it was thought, to allow the United States time enough to act. Taiwan also had a strong air force. In dogfights during the Offshore Islands crises in 1954–55 and 1958 and some other skirmishes, it chalked up a decidedly favorable "kill ratio" against the Chinese air force.

For Beijing's leaders, Taiwan's military could certainly make an assault on the island costly in terms of the planes, ships, and soldiers it would lose. The PLA was, thus, reluctant to attack Taiwan in view of the fact such losses would weaken its defenses on China's northern and southern borders.

China's "breakthrough" advances in missile capabilities as demonstrated during the missile tests in 1996 created a new ball game. Taipei could no longer cope with China's threats. Meanwhile, improved Sino-Soviet relations caused Chinese decision makers to have less worry about its northern border, the biggest of Beijing's worries prior to the late 1980s. This further weakened Taiwan's deterrence because China now presumably did not have to worry so much about its military losses.

Taiwan had to plan. What if missile defense did not materialize? Taiwan had to think about other options. The main one was building "offensive deterrence" in the form of weapons it could use to attack China and cause significant loss of life and destruction there.

Taiwan had several choices. The first that came to mind to many observers was the possibility that Taiwan may possess nuclear weapons or at least had a potential to build them, and would do so if denied missile defense. In 1964, after China went nuclear, Taiwan became very concerned about China's nuclear threat and embarked upon a project to build its own nuclear weapons. According to one source, Taiwan did this in secret, even from its own president, Chiang Kai-shek. Chiang's son, Chiang Ching-kuo, who became president later, allegedly approved a nuclear weapons project without telling his father.[27]

The U.S. Central Intelligence Agency said that in 1974, Taiwan had an "advanced" nuclear program, thought capable of building a bomb in five years or so.[28] Subsequently, Taiwan, under extreme pressure from the United States to cease its work, supposedly stopped its efforts toward building a nuclear bomb. At the time there were rumors that the promise got a quid pro quo: a guarantee by the United States to protect Taiwan in the event of an attack by China. Some said this included either a Chinese assault using nuclear or conventional weapons.

There is good reason, however, to believe that Taiwan continued work on weapons of mass destruction even though it closed the facility in question and Washington apparently accepted its word that it would not produce nuclear weapons.

The fact the United States did not ultimately accept Taiwan's repudiation of its desire to become a nuclear power was revealed in a sensational action by the United States in 1988, when it "kidnapped" a nuclear physicist from Taiwan, said to be working on a nuclear project.[29] It was later reported that the project to build nuclear weapons or at least develop that capability continued after Lee Teng-hui became president. Given Beijing's hostility toward Lee, he may have kept it going or even upgraded it. In any event, Lee, after China's first threatening missile tests in 1995, told the National Assembly that Taiwan "should consider nuclear weapons as a long-term option."[30]

Former chief of staff of the military, defense minister, and premier Hau Pei-tsun later wrote in his memoirs that Taiwan had developed a nuclear capability similar to Israel's, but it was put on hold, he said. Some experts interpreted that to mean that Taiwan had developed a nuclear weapon though it had not done an actual test (except by computer) or that it had developed the ability to build one very quickly. Taiwan had nuclear power plants and could divert fissionable materials from them into bombs. According to China, Taiwan could build ten bombs. This added further to Taiwan's "nuclear option" credibility.[31]

In fact, Taiwan seemed to have several options.

First, Taipei could claim that the United States made a commitment to protect Taiwan since it did not develop nuclear weapons. It might even produce some sort of documentation (assuming there was a deal made). Officials from Taiwan could certainly make a case that it did not have a bomb and thereby win support from Congress and the American people saying it was being intimidated by a nuclear power. Thus the White House would be under pressure to come to Taiwan's rescue.

Second, Taipei might announce that it had built nuclear weapons secretly and would use them against China if attacked. This would ensure that Beijing's threats against Taiwan would not be ignored by the international community or the United States. Washington would probably intervene, and in the course of doing so Taiwan would be shielded and its continued sovereignty ensured.

Third, Taiwan might do a test or even drop a bomb on China either as a warning (in a desolate area or in the ocean) or on a city.

Taiwan also had still other cards. It had conventional bombs that it could drop on cities on the mainland. Hong Kong and Guangzhou are less than five hundred miles away. Shanghai, China's largest city, is within range of Taiwan's fighter planes, which can be equipped to carry bombs. Taiwan's leaders, in fact, talked about the possibility of striking Chinese cities during the 1996 missile crises. It was discussed during the 2000 presidential campaign both before and after China threatened Taiwan. The Nationalist Party's candidate, Lien Chan, advocated developing long-rang missiles that could be used to bomb targets even in Western China.[32]

Military leaders in Taiwan long ago argued that Taiwan must maintain a measure of deterrence, meaning the ability to attack Chinese cities and military bases. Many have said repeatedly that Taiwan cannot rely on a defensive strategy alone.

One can also assume Taiwan has done some work on chemical and biological weapons (although it denies this, others, including Beijing, suspect it), or it has some access to them from other countries or arms merchants, which is not difficult to imagine. This makes sense from the perspective of China's being vulnerable to such attacks because of its dense population in the eastern part of the country. Chemicals or bacterial weapons could also be transported to China through intelligence agents or even tourists, or they could be dropped from balloons. A truly worrisome scenario is that Taiwan might send agents to China and keep them in place and when faced with an extreme danger to its existence such as an invasion, detonate explosives near or at China's Three Gorges Dam. Taiwan might also hit the dam with missiles. Some Chinese leaders have said that such an action, brought up when Sino-Soviet relations were not good, might kill one hundred million people because it would cause floods through the heartland of China for thousands of miles. China is extremely vulnerable to flooding because the beds of its large rivers are higher than surrounding populated areas due to silting and the building of levees over the centuries.

Taiwan also has the capacity to engage in various other forms of unconventional war against China. Its military leaders have discussed this in public. It would no doubt use such tactics to defend the country. In fact, Taiwan already has tested unconventional weapons—doing damage to China's computers, wrecking websites, and so on in retaliation for Beijing doing the same to Taiwan. Taiwan, being one of the world's biggest producers of computer products and having thousands of software geniuses, possesses a recognized capability in this area.

All of this presents a dilemma to those who oppose providing sophisticated missile defense to Taiwan. The alternative is worse. This, of course, increases support for Taiwan's having missile defense or joining a U.S.-Japan-South Korea system and creates commensurately a nettlesome problem for Washington in view of Beijing's commitment to block it.

PART IV
THE PRESENT STANDOFF

President Lee Comments That Taipei-Beijing Talks Should Be Nation-to-Nation; Beijing Is Furious

On July 9, 1999, President Lee Teng-hui sparked a bitter and lasting feud when he proclaimed that talks between Taipei and Beijing henceforth must be on a "special state-to-state" basis. Lee's declaration meant that "the Republic of China on Taiwan" was a nation and possessed sovereignty and, furthermore, that Beijing must acknowledge this.

High officials in both Beijing and Washington became instantly unglued—Chinese leaders "foamed at the mouth," said one commentator. Chinese leaders proclaimed angrily that China's military was preparing for action against the island. The Chinese media issued a cavalcade of threats and criticisms. The Clinton administration assailed Lee for provoking a conflict. The Department of State, as expected, did likewise. Congress behaved very differently, supporting Lee, as did almost all of the U.S. presidential candidates running in the 2000 election. So, generally, did the U.S. media.

The essence of what Lee said was that Taiwan was a nation despite Beijing's claim that it wasn't and America's one-China policy. There are, insisted Lee, two Chinese governments; one was Taiwan, and it was sovereign.

This badly upset relations between Washington and Taipei and Beijing and Taipei. It widened the gulf between the executive and legislative branches of government in the United States over China policy. It worsened relations between hard-liners and reformists in China. Lee's statement showed how fragile Washington-Taipei-Beijing relations were. What if Lee had made a declaration of independence?

—⚏—

On July 9, 1999, President Lee Teng-hui was reported by the media throughout the world to have told a news reporter from Deutsche Welle, a popular, government-owned and -operated radio network in Germany, that the relationship between Taipei and Beijing must be seen as a "special state-to-state relationship" and that talks between the two, which were ongoing, would henceforth have to proceed based on this assumption.

Lee was immediately portrayed in both Beijing and Washington, by the Western media, and by some newspapers in Taiwan as having thrown a wrench in the delicate machinery of cross-strait negotiations. President Lee, in short, created a monumental fuss, possibly one leading to an armed conflict in the Taiwan Strait. But what Lee said was much more complex than the reporting of it suggested.

In the interview with Deutsche Welle, Lee replied to the following question: "Taiwan is considered by Beijing's government as a 'renegade province.' This is a cause for present tensions and threats against your island. . . . How do you cope with these dangers?" Lee said he would answer the question from two perspectives: historical and legal. The "historical fact," said Lee, is that the "Chinese communist regime" has never ruled the territory under the jurisdiction of Republic of China: Taiwan, the Pescadores, Kinmen (Quemoy), and Matsu. Not only was this statement true, it had been stated and put in writing a multitude of times by officials in Taipei, not to mention scholars in Taiwan and in the West.

In 1949, after the civil war between Communist and Nationalist forces, Mao assumed political jurisdiction over the territory that today comprises the People's Republic of China (except for Tibet, which the Chinese PLA invaded in 1950 and brought under Beijing's control). His army never conquered any of the territory the Republic of China currently ruled. Nor did his government establish jurisdiction, even temporarily, over any of the land the Republic of China now claims to be its sovereign domain. All of Republic of China's territory has been under Taipei's jurisdiction since 1945. Then why all of the controversy?

In 1949, Mao claimed to be the successor government to the Republic of China, which was defeated and rendered defunct. In fact, this was the basis of Beijing's legal claim to Taiwan. The problem with this argument was that the latter government still existed. Moreover, Mao himself, by establishing a new government that he named the "People's Republic of China," contradicted, and thus undermined, the successor government claim. An observer in Taipei noted that Taiwan and the Pescadore Islands (Penghu)—more than 98 percent of the Republic of China's territory—had not been under Chinese sovereignty for fifty years before the end of World War II. He said, "Taiwan was not ruled by China as long as Mongolia was. . . . Beijing didn't claim Mongolia is Chinese territory."

Further, both Taiwan and the Pescadores had been transferred to Japan "in perpetuity" in 1895 following the Sino-Japanese War. This was written in the Treaty of Shimonoseki. Japan assumed permanent sovereignty, and Western nations and the international legal system recognized this transfer as legitimate. At the end of World War II, both territories were taken from Japan and turned over to Chiang Kai-shek's Republic of China as promised in the Cairo Declaration and the Potsdam Agreement. They could not have been given to the People's Republic of China because it didn't yet exist.

Matters were further complicated. Because the transfers were "wartime statements," some scholars questioned their legality. Also the transfer described was "incomplete" in the sense that it was not put into the surrender agreement between the Allies and Japan at the end of the war or in a final peace treaty concluded later. And, as some have noted, the Cairo Declaration was not signed and two of the participants did not take it seriously (Churchill and Stalin both laughed at FDR's unilaterally making China a big power). Also, nothing was done about Taiwan's legal status after World War II. All of this contributed to the argument that Taiwan's future was not legally decided and thus a claim based on occupation and governance was even stronger, and it favored Taipei.

Mao, furthermore, was on record as implying that Taiwan was not part of China. He told Edgar Snow in the late 1930s, when discussing the task of regaining lost territories, "We do not, however, include Korea. . . . The same thing applies for Formosa."[1] Mao even said later that he "regretted" having changed China's national title in 1949 to the People's Republic of China because Beijing would have had a better claim to Taiwan had he not done this. He thereby seemed to admit that he created two Chinese states. Thus the historical argument clearly favored Lee's position that there are two Chinese governments. In fact, no serious Western historian or legal expert has ever said otherwise. Thus, the Republic of China's (Taiwan's) claim to the territory it governs is, according to most historians and legal experts, quite valid.

But Lee went further. He noted that in 1991 an amendment to Taiwan's Constitution limited the nation's territory to only the areas the government actually controlled. It terminated any claim to territory controlled by the People's Republic of China and recognized the legality of its government and its jurisdiction over the territory it ruled. It further declared that members of the National Assembly and the Legislative Yuan (the lawmaking branch of government) would henceforth be elected from the "Taiwan area" only.

At the time Beijing hardly reacted to these constitutional changes, probably seeing them at the time as inconsequential, although it's possible that Chinese leaders did not know how to respond or did not want to dignify them in any way. The Western media reported very favorably on the constitutional amendments, creating the popular (and technically accurate) interpretation that Taipei was "ending the state of war" with China. This was a peaceful act, the Western media said, and should be applauded. It also represented an enlightened policy by Taipei in contrast to Chiang Kai-shek's claim that all of China belonged to the Nationalist Chinese government and he would liberate the mainland portion. Some Western media sources at the time even encouraged Beijing to respond with a pledge (which Washington had long asked for) not to use force to resolve the Taiwan issue.

Lee further stated in the interview with Deutsche Welle that subsequent constitutional amendments passed in 1992 (which made the president and vice president positions directly elected by the people) gave the executive branch of government a mandate from the people of Taiwan. This had nothing to do with the people or government on the mainland (in the People's Republic of China). This further disconnected Taiwan from China; however, it was necessitated by Taiwan's democratization.

Beijing responded negatively at the time to this amendment, saying that Taiwan was still a local government. The Western media either ignored or laughed at Beijing's position and lauded "Taiwan's progress toward democracy."

President Lee might have also declared that Taiwan, or the Republic of China, has sovereignty based on the traditional qualifications: territory, population, government, and diplomatic relations. Taiwan, though seemingly small, is close to the size of the average nation in the world. Its population is considerably larger than that of the average nation. Its government is stable and there have been only legal and peaceful transfers of power. It does not have formal diplomatic relations with many countries, but quite a number of members of the United Nations have only as many embassies or fewer in their capitals. Clearly, Taiwan, by these criteria, possesses sovereignty. And since the legal requirements for sovereignty have been weakened, or the qualifications for nationhood made easier to achieve in order to accommodate decolonization and now the end of communism, so that many new and not very viable nations could qualify, Taiwan is unlikely to see its status affected by recent interpretations of international law or shifts in diplomatic practices.

Lee may have implied these points. But he seemed to think more in terms of Taiwan having become a democracy; therefore, its government has a mandate and, hence, it cannot be considered anything other than a legitimate nation-state and should be treated that way. He stated that the constitutional amendments cited above have made cross-strait relations a state-to-state relationship, or at least a special state-to-state relationship, "rather than an internal relationship between a legitimate government and a rebel group, or between a central government and a local government." He concluded, therefore, that "Beijing authorities' characterization of Taiwan as a 'renegade province' is both historically and legally untrue."

Lee made some other statements to the German radio station, including some that Beijing should have wanted to hear. For example, he said that there was no need for Taiwan to declare independence. He talked about cross-strait exchanges and promised dialogue and consultations (as leaders in Beijing had asked). However, no one seemed to hear these words.

Lee also made some unfriendly proclamations such as accusing Beijing of a smear campaign and refusing to renounce the use of force against Taiwan. He rejected Beijing's "one country, two systems" formula for resolving the Taiwan issue—which he said contains "intrinsic contradictions, violates the basic principles of democracy, and denies the existence of the Republic of China."

Lee even talked about Taiwan's defense, the Chinese market, Beijing-Taipei economic ties, and purchasing submarines. None of these things, however, stirred any controversy. His statement that relations should be on a state-to-state basis caused a humongous flap, even though it seemed to be nothing new and at face value nothing controversial. It was Lee's image in Beijing, his intent (or alleged intent), and the political milieu at the time (meaning sensitive Washington-Taipei-Beijing relations) that made his statement so provocative.

—⚹—

After President Lee's interview with the Deutsche Welle there was some speculation that he had spoken without thinking and that what he said could simply be relegated to the category of a mistake. But that was hardly the case. Lee's statement was, as most analysts subsequently concluded, deliberate. It was well thought out. It was planned (some say for a long time) and well timed.[2] The question then arose: Why did President Lee say what he did? He must have known that it would create a stir, if not a serious crisis in Beijing-Taipei, Washington-Taipei, and Washington-Beijing relations.

Lee as a matter of fact had a multitude of reasons for demanding that Taipei-Beijing relations be viewed as state-to-state relations. One relates to an informal agreement Taipei had, or thought it had, with Beijing to the effect that Taiwan be given "international space" or that the People's Republic of China would not endeavor to completely destroy Taipei's diplomatic status.[3] There had existed such an agreement or a "working understanding" since at least the 1980s, as far as Taipei was concerned. Beijing adhered to the understanding, it was said, in exchange for generally improving cross-strait relations and for Taiwan's investing huge amounts of money in China and aggressively pursuing economic exchanges.

Early on it had been Deng Xiaoping's stated assumption that economic contacts and friendly diplomacy would dampen independence sentiments in Taiwan and would lead eventually to reunification. In fact, for a number of years this seemed a reasonable proposition and it appeared to be working. In any case, Deng used this argument to parry his critics' charges that he had abandoned the cause of Taiwan's reunification for better Sino-American relations. However, as nationalist sentiment grew in China in the early 1990s, dissatisfaction with this assumption grew. Some said it was not working. Others were simply impatient. Some said China's status as a "rising power" justified a more aggressive policy. Some were upset about Taiwan "showing off" its democracy. The military in particular grew unhappy with the idea of waiting. More important though, military leaders began to perceive that time was on Taipei's side and that reunification might never happen. Taiwan might even become a base for a foreign power.

Beijing thus adopted a policy of putting pressure on Taipei by "closing its international space" or by "killing" its diplomatic relations with other countries. In 1991, Beijing tore Saudi Arabia away from Taipei; in 1992, South Korea; in 1996, South Africa. Losing diplomatic relations with these three countries, Taipei had remaining formal ties with no important country in the world.

Panama was considered the only country of strategic significance with whom Taiwan still had diplomatic relations. Malawi, with a population of eleven million, was the largest. The number of nations that maintained ambassadorial ties with Taipei fell to below thirty, a figure some called a water line. Of the nations that had diplomatic relations with Taipei, most were very small and of little importance in international politics. In fact, the total population of twelve of the countries with which Taipei had diplomatic ties was less than two million.

Beijing also refused any type of dual recognition. In some cases, China bought diplomatic connections while it hypocritically accused Taipei of practicing "dollar diplomacy." In the case of South Africa, the last nation of importance to make the switch from Taipei to Beijing, Beijing offered a commercial deal, or bribe, to get Pretoria to push the timetable ahead and leave Taipei without even meaningful informal relations.[4] Meanwhile, Beijing made every effort possible to exclude Taipei from various international organizations, even going so far as to force the United Nations, the World Bank, and other institutions to desist from publishing economic and social statistics on Taiwan.

Many in Taiwan regarded this as petty, as "dirty pool," and as part of an effort to utterly destroy Taipei's status as a nation and isolate it from the international community. Doing this to a nation that was an economic model (recall that Taiwan had long been known as an "economic miracle") and a political model (having democratized very fast and without bloodshed) was, many said, outrageous. The media in Taiwan, reflecting public sentiment and opposition parties' criticisms, widely publicized Taipei's predicament. Officials in Taipei, including President Lee, responded by reassessing Taiwan's economic ties with China. The government put limits on investment in the mainland and halted further steps to increase trade. Barriers were erected, or not lifted, on financial transactions and in other areas that affected trade and investments. In 1993, Taipei, at Lee's personal urging, announced the "Go South" policy: investing in Southeast Asian countries instead of China.

Taiwan also sought to embarrass both Beijing and the international community by making application to the United Nations. That same year Taipei applied to "participate" in the U.N. Through friendly sponsors, it made a bid annually after that. After all, the "new world order" was supposed to be inclusive and the U.N. thus should be open to all "nations." But Beijing had the veto (which applied to membership) by virtue of being a permanent member of the Security Council, and it could keep Taipei out. Yet it could not quash the view that Taiwan's twenty-two million people should be represented in the world body and that it was perpetrating a myth that Taiwan did not exist (like the myth of an earlier time that the People's Republic of China did not exist).

The breakdown of the "understanding" between Taipei and Beijing thus started a new "diplomatic war" between the two. This war escalated after President Lee's visit to the United States in 1995 and the subsequent missile tests. President Lee and other officials in Taipei had already begun to perceive that the National Unification Guidelines passed into law in early 1991, which set forth a

policy of one China (but two "political entities") and included a plan for unification in three steps, were a mistake. Beijing, in Taiwan's eyes, had cunningly
exploited Taiwan's one-China proclamation. It proclaimed (although Chinese
officials had already been saying this for some time, but less often and with less
force) that "China" (in the phrase "one China") meant the People's Republic of
China and that Taiwan was a local government and, therefore, did not possess
sovereignty or nation-state status. In Taiwan's eyes, "China" meant historical or
cultural China. "China" did not mean the People's Republic of China. Lee thus
sought to promote this interpretation of Taiwan's one-China policy while rejecting Beijing's definition of China. Most importantly, he endeavored to foil
Beijing's efforts to deny Taiwan international status.

Obviously Lee had other motives and he certainly considered the circumstances, the timing, and the opportunities involved before making his statement.
For example, President Lee had a mandate after he was elected by a substantial
popular vote in 1996. Lee may have been reflecting his personal confidence and
his belief that he personally knew what was best for Taiwan. Or he may have
perceived that the statement was what the public wanted. Lee's term of office
was drawing to a close. He may have felt that he needed to make an imprint on
Taiwan's foreign relations before he left office, to leave with a splash. Lee's
detractors said he sought glory and a place in Taiwan's history, and this was a
way of accomplishing that. Alternatively, Lee may have sought to establish a
cross-strait policy that would be lasting. In August, Lee had the two-states policy
framework put in to the Nationalist Party's charter. There was speculation that
Lee planned to put it into the constitution.

News analysts in Taiwan suggested that Lee wanted to help Vice President
Lien Chan win the ruling party's presidential nomination and be elected his
successor in Taiwan's second direct presidential election eight months hence.
Lien's ratings in public opinion polls were not good. Lien's main challenger,
former governor James Soong, had very high ratings (the highest of any potential
candidate for president), but Lee strongly disliked him. Since Soong had a
reputation for wanting closer relations with China, Lee's move could adversely
affect his chances of becoming the next president. (Lee's statement came at a
time when Soong had just announced his candidacy.)

Lee may have been seeking to promote better relations between his party, the
Nationalist Party or KMT, and the opposition DPP. Or he may have intended to
undermine the DPP's public appeal (and possibly win the 2000 presidential
election if the two KMT candidates split the vote) by stealing one of its issues or
by creating tension with Beijing. In retrospect it appears that Lee may have sought
to help independence candidate Chen Shui-bian. At the time a member of the
pro-unification New Party said it would destroy the KMT's candidate, Lien Chan.
His reasoning was that Lee had won the 1996 election in some part because the
KMT was viewed as the party that could best manage cross-strait relations and
keep the peace, and Lee changed this. It is certainly worthy of note that Chen
Shui-bian, at this time the DPP's candidate for president (when visiting the

United States in April), had described China-Taiwan relations as "special international country-to-country relations." And when Lee made the announcement, the DPP claimed it was a "gift" to Chen.[5]

Another possibility is that Lee may have perceived that talks with Beijing were going nowhere and that China's negotiator, Wang Daohan, who was due to arrive in Taipei in October to continue talks restarted in the fall of 1998, would not come. So he was risking nothing. Lee may even have thought that Wang's visit would be delayed so as to help Beijing save its influence until the coming presidential election or that October was already too close to the March 2000 election. Anyway if the visit were to occur, Lee wanted to set the groundwork or define the talks such that they would add to Taiwan's national status rather than detract from it. Lee had long argued that the term "negotiations" as that word is defined in international law and in diplomatic practice assumed the equality of participants. If Taipei were to engage in talks, they should be real negotiations, and Taipei should be treated as an equal and should accept nothing less. Another factor was that Lee may have wanted to set the agenda in broader cross-strait talks. Other issues were being discussed at the time.

Finally, hardly anyone doubts that Lee deliberately made his controversial statement to a German press organization. His choice of venues drew attention to the "German formula" for unifying China. The two Germanys before they became one had both been viewed by the international community as having sovereignty and equality, and they recognized each other and treated each other as separate sovereign states (unlike the Koreas, which do not and have had many bloody encounters). In this way they were able to engage in meaningful negotiations that led to a resolution to the "German problem."

Lee no doubt considered the timing of his statement. Certainly Washington-Beijing relations were a major consideration. Relations between the United States and China were very obviously at a low point. There were serious differences over U.S. military actions against Kosovo. Washington said its mission was to eradicate "ethnic cleansing." Beijing viewed it as a case of putting human rights above sovereignty and used its veto to prevent Washington from acting in the name of the United Nations. China subsequently blasted U.S. "unilateralism" and suggested that America might seek to do the same thing in Tibet or fight a similar "no casualty campaign" to protect Taiwan.

Another issue was the "accidental" U.S. bombing of the Chinese embassy in Belgrade in May and subsequent "staged" anti-American demonstrations in China, which, especially when the U.S. embassy in Beijing became a target, "even made the Department of State angry for a change," said one observer.

In addition, the Cox Report had just been released (documenting Beijing's theft of U.S. nuclear weapons secrets) and because of it, President Clinton delayed Beijing's entrance into the World Trade Organization (seriously embarrassing Premier Zhu Rongji during a visit to Washington in April), and human rights violations in China had recently energized critics in the United States, including Congress. Topping this off, the Falun Gong religious sect was being viciously suppressed, according to the Western press. Its leader, Li Hongzhi, lived in the United States. A former director of the Central Intelligence Agency voiced his opinion at the time: that Beijing's treatment of the religious organization "undermined the notion that engagement helped human rights." Relations between the White House and Congress over China policy were thus more strained than they had been for some time. They were impacted by the Cox Report, Congressional hearings on China's illegal campaign contributions to the Democratic Party, Clinton's visit to China, and more.

Dick Morris, President Clinton's erstwhile favorite political advisor, said at this time that Chinese spying on the United States was an act of "foreign aggression." He called it the "espionage equivalent to Pearl Harbor." He connected it to "politicians too dependent on campaign donations to act in our own national interest" and to "national spinelessness."[6] Members of Congress at this juncture were getting into campaign mode, and presidential candidates from all parties were on the stump and talking about issues, including foreign policy matters. The two parties were choosing their presidential candidates. China policy was front and center and, reflecting public sentiment, Taiwan had a big advantage.

Lee probably noted also that the U.S. policy of "strategic ambiguity" had been so thoroughly discredited, having been condemned as causing the missile crisis of 1996, that it was scrapped. Therefore, he should help add clarity to Taipei-Beijing relations (or at least he would have some sympathy among the Congress and the American populace for doing this). Lee may have, in addition, wanted to send a signal to the White House and the Department of State that he did not like the idea of an "interim agreement" between Taipei and Beijing, which had been recently floated. Su Chi, chairman of the Mainland Affairs Council, was in Washington, D.C., two days before Lee's announcement, listening to the assistant secretary of state for Asia and the Pacific detail an "interim accord" (between Beijing and Taipei).[7]

In a much more serious vein, Lee may have calculated that China would respond with military displays and threats as it did in 1996. Perhaps Beijing would go further. If a clash should occur with U.S. military forces, U.S.-China relations might be severely, even irreconcilably, damaged. In that context, Taiwan, like Kosovo and South Korea, could get a firm U.S. strategic commitment, which would translate into Taiwan's status changing to that of a sovereign state, like South Korea, in U.S. eyes.[8] Finally, Lee must have been cognizant of the fact that U.S. aircraft carriers were in the area, just in case Beijing blew a fuse and ordered an attack on Taiwan. They had not been a couple of months earlier.

—⚬⚬⚬—

Beijing reacted to Lee's proclamations with a fury seldom seen before and certainly not expected by most. Wang Daohan, head of the Association for Relations across the Taiwan Strait and a close associate of Jiang Zemin, said Lee's comments "wiped out the foundation for contacts." Tang Shubei, vice chairman of the association, who had been negotiating with its Taipei counterpart, the

Straits Exchange Foundation, accused Lee of "playing with fire." He further declared that Lee's comments constituted a "crude destruction" of the one-China principle and that Lee was an "incorrigible splittist" and had moved Taipei and Beijing "to the edge of war."[9]

The state-controlled media in China went into an attack mode, placing scare stories in Hong Kong papers and elsewhere. During the next sixty days there were more than two hundred stories in major newspapers condemning Lee and his "two states" pronouncement. A number of papers published pictures of simulated military landings on Taiwan's shores and soldiers singing, "We will liberate Taiwan."[10] *Beijing Review*, a publication aimed at readers outside of China, said Lee's statement "exposed his political malice, intention to split the Chinese territorial integrity and sovereignty, and his attempt to separate Taiwan from China [sic]."[11] *People's Daily* said Lee was "blinded by lust for gain." An article in the paper also called Lee "the scum of the nation, who is intent on splitting the motherland, and who will be infamous for 10,000 years."

China's main military newspaper carried an article saying that Lee had "completely removed the camouflage" and "bared the ugly features of being a Taiwanese independence element" in a "vainglorious and foolhardy manner." The paper declared that the Chinese PLA "will not permit even a square inch of territory from being split from China."[12] The author of the article also charged that Lee had "brazenly defied world opinion," Taipei being the largest purchaser of weapons in the world over the past two years (citing the Stockholm Institute for International Peace). This would not work, he charged, because of China's military prowess and the will of the Chinese people. Hong Kong papers subsequently reported that at an emergency meeting of high-level Taiwan affairs officials in Beijing, top Chinese leaders discussed military exercises "on a scale greater than 1996." Coinciding with this meeting the official media in China spoke of a "monumental disaster for the people of Taiwan."[13]

One Western source reported that hard-line military leaders in China accused Jiang and Premier Zhu Rongji of "betraying China." In fact, senior military officers were said to have labeled the Foreign Ministry the "ministry of selling out the country." This seemed a manifestation of a power struggle like several in the past that immobilized foreign policy making and led to irrational and aggressive actions abroad.[14] The Chinese Foreign Ministry, apparently in an effort to save itself, or at least avoid being branded spineless, said one observer, joined the chorus. The Foreign Ministry certainly could not go against the current of rage that had enveloped China. The ministry thus announced that what Lee had said constituted "extremely dangerous steps to take on the road to independence."[15] Western reporters, quoting Chinese leaders' "ultra-hostile" statements, said that Beijing seemed to be more incensed by Lee's comments than by his visit to the United States in 1995—which was followed by missile tests off Taiwan's shores.

On July 12, the Politburo of the Chinese Communist Party met to discuss "the deterioration of the political situation in Taiwan." Two days later the State Council (China's cabinet), the party's Central Committee, and the party's

Central Military Commission all reviewed the results of the meeting and passed them on to lower echelons.[16] The upshot of the meeting was that the Politburo had concluded that Lee's special state-to-state proclamation "meant Taiwan independence" and "constituted an effort to split China." Further, "it is a declaration of war on the whole nation and the whole Army." Politburo members were quoted as saying they had exposed the "hideous features of the instigators" who want to split the motherland and pledged to "resolutely shatter" Taiwan independence.

A week after Lee's proclamation, China announced officially for the first time that it possessed neutron bomb technology. Since this kind of weapon is designed to kill people and not destroy buildings or infrastructure, it would presumably be ideal for Beijing, said several observers, to use to resolve the Taiwan issue.[17] At this time Taiwan reported violations of its airspace by Chinese fighter planes. The PLA added to the tension this had caused when it referred to Taiwan as the "rebel island."

A fortnight later, the Chinese Navy seized a Taiwan ship near the island of Matsu, where fighting broke out in 1954 and 1958 between Communist and Nationalist forces, which ultimately dragged the United States in. The ship was carrying supplies to Taiwan's military forces, ten thousand strong, on the island.[18]

On August 2, the pro-Beijing Hong Kong newspaper, *Ta Kung Pao*, reported that China was seriously contemplating an economic blockade of Taiwan.[19] That same day, the PLA conducted a test of a long-range ballistic missile capable of hitting any part of the United States with a nuclear weapon. The Western media reported this and it caused a stir in Congress. "Was China preparing for nuclear war with the United States?" one observer asked.

Meanwhile, an incident was reported in the air over the Taiwan Strait: A PLA Air Force Russian-built Sukhoi Su-27 fighter aircraft locked its targeting radar on one of Taiwan's French-built Mirage-2000 fighters. Taiwan's Air Force was in a state of panic for a while. U.S. officials expressed grave concern about this incident in the context of the increased number of fighters from both sides flying over the Taiwan Strait and crossing the midline between Taiwan and the mainland, which both sides had heretofore respected and had seldom crossed.[20] On August 4, Beijing announced that it was henceforth refusing to let U.S. military aircraft land in Hong Kong. It gave no reason for its action, though a U.S. embassy official was summoned at this time to hear a protest about U.S. arms sales to Taiwan. A few days after this, it was reported that China's "preparations for war" with Taiwan were complete.[21]

In mid-August Chinese government officials warned the Clinton administration that Beijing might well take military action against Taiwan to punish it for moving toward independence.[22] At this time, according to Hong Kong newspapers, the PLA had put submarines in the Taiwan Strait in "attack positions," mobilized reserves, and moved military personnel and weapons from other parts of China closer to the Taiwan Strait.[23] Later in the month, *Beijing Review* carried a long article refuting Taipei's Mainland Affairs Council's explanation for Lee's special state-to-state relations. The article explained the history of China's territorial problems and agreements between Taipei and Beijing to maintain China's territorial integrity. It concluded that Lee's statement "deliberately sabotages cross-strait relations" as well as "peace and stability in the Asia-Pacific region."[24]

On September 1, Beijing warned Taiwan that if it put the special state-to-state idea in its constitution, it would be tantamount to a declaration of independence, and military action would follow. The "prerequisite for peaceful reunification would no longer exist," the message said.[25] Shortly after this warning, the Chinese Communist Party said that if Lee did not back down, "a fatal attack is a certainty."[26] Some said that China's sensitivities to Taiwan "slipping away" were made worse by the fact that the fiftieth anniversary of the founding of the People's Republic of China was approaching in October.

Chinese officials also noted that Lee's statement also followed only weeks after NATO's victory, with U.S. help, over Serbia. To Chinese leaders in Beijing, there were implications for Taiwan.

China was also preparing for the return of the Portuguese colony of Macao in December. It was to be the last piece of territory to be recovered, except for Taiwan. There was lots of talk at this time about the "one country, two systems" formula for China's territorial recovery, which Lee Teng-hui had repudiated.

In early September, the PLA, using coordinated air, sea, and land forces, conducted a large military exercise in South China. In fact, a mock invasion was done in the military region where preparations to invade Taiwan would be made. The military commander of the area said that a hundred thousand ships (including civilian craft) could be mobilized to "meet the needs of a large-scale sea crossing and landing operations." Other top military leaders cited Lee's comments and his efforts to split China.[27] In following months, Beijing continued to show its anger over Lee's statement. Threats persisted.

Thus Lee's declaration was not a matter that was going to pass easily or quickly. In fact, it seemed like something that would be remembered for a long time and would continue to fester and poison relations with both Taipei and Washington.

—⁂—

After "shocking the world" with his special state-to-state relations proposal, President Lee tried to placate those who were upset by what he said with some "explanatory comments" about unification and seeking closer Taipei-Beijing relations. But this did not last long, and for the most part Taipei continued on the attack. Only a few days later, Mainland Affairs Council Chairman Su Chi said, "We feel there is no need to go on using the one-China term."[28] Other officials in Taipei followed suit. On July 14, Su Chi said that the "one-China framework" had long been "obstructing and destroying cross-strait relations." Foreign Minister Jason Hu added, during a Nationalist Party Central Committee meeting, that Lee's comments had "given inspiration to Republic of China diplomats all over the world."[29] The next day, Premier Vincent Siew declared that Taipei needed to "clearly define the status of Taiwan and the mainland, in accordance with reality." He called on "Chinese mainland authorities" to "rationally face the political and legal realities of cross strait relations."

It appeared that Taipei had planned to retreat briefly in order to avoid being seen as too provocative and then go on the offensive again. In a speech to the Rotary Club in Taiwan on July 20, President Lee reiterated his special state-to-state comments. He further declared that Beijing's one-China policy, by which it means the People's Republic of China is "China" and, according to that view, Taiwan is a "renegade Province," is "the fundamental impediment to any improvement in cross-strait relations." On July 30, Koo Chen-fu, chairman of the Straits Exchange Foundation, the organization that had held successful talks with its counterpart in Beijing, the Association for Relations Across the Taiwan Strait, in 1993 and again in 1998, said that President Lee had "clarified the reality that the Republic of China is a sovereign state." He further asserted that Beijing had "expanded its definition of one-China to deny our existence," meaning that China was already unified and that the Republic of China was a local government. He charged that it was agreed upon in 1992 that each side could adopt its own definition of "one China"; therefore, Lee was simply stating Taipei's view according to this understanding.[30]

On July 25, a senior adviser to President Lee, Liu Tai-ying, in response to reports in the Hong Kong press that Beijing planned more war games in the Taiwan Strait near Taiwan, told the international media that Taiwan should "lob some missiles into waters near Hong Kong," that this would cause jitters there which would result in an outflow of foreign capital and might topple China's government.[31] President Lee then quipped to news reporters that because of his special state-to-state remarks, the whole world took notice, and that was a good thing. That the comments aroused so much international attention would "raise the island's international profile," he said. Lee went on to explain that what he had done was to define Taiwan's status so that whoever succeeded him would "not be bothered by ambiguity." Lee then took another jab at Chinese leaders in Beijing, saying that his ultimate aim was to transform China and "let the Taiwanese experience blossom there."[32]

In August, Foreign Ministry spokesperson Henry Chen refuted statements by China's ambassador to the United States, Li Zhaoxing, to the effect that Taiwan was "stroking tensions," saying that it was Beijing that was acting aggressively by not repudiating the use of military force to resolve the Taiwan issue.[33] In September, the Mainland Affairs Council issued a statement refusing to rescind the statehood claim. Chairman Su Chi asserted that there was no need to have it withdrawn because it was aimed at safeguarding the national interest and the country's dignity. He further stated that 70 percent of respondents, according to a number of opinion surveys, supported Lee's statement. He added that Taiwan was not seeking independence, but rather parity.[34]

Subsequent opinion polls showed even stronger public support for Lee's pronouncement. In a survey conducted by the Mainland Affairs Council and given to the media, 85 percent of respondents said Taiwan should stick to Lee's demand for parity while 84 percent said that Taipei's negotiating position would be better if the two sides were considered equals. The Mainland Affairs Council concluded that people feel "more and more disgusted" with Beijing saying that cross-strait problems can be resolved only using the "one country, two systems" formula.[35] Soon after this, Foreign Minister Jason Hu blamed the United States at least in part for the brouhaha. Hu asserted publicly that Beijing's reaction to President Lee's statement had been so strong because it had been "emboldened" by Washington's "pandering"—an unveiled reference to the "Three Noes" statement President Clinton made when he visited China in 1998.[36]

In November, an article entitled "Understanding Taiwan," written by Lee Teng-hui, appeared in the prestigious U.S. journal *Foreign Affairs*, which has the reputation of being extremely influential and read by most of the foreign policy elite in the United States. Lee, or whoever wrote the piece (it was probably a collective effort by Lee and his advisors), made a number of key points: that Taiwan has democratized and has a sense of identity separate from China; that in formulating foreign policy he and other leaders have to consider public opinion (which favors his special state-to-state idea); that if negotiations between Taipei and Beijing (which the United States had been pushing) are to succeed the People's Republic of China must accept Taiwan's equality in such talks (since this is the norm of global diplomacy and the people of Taiwan demand it); that Beijing's intimidation affects public opinion in Taiwan toward independence (and the government must also move in this direction, Taiwan being a democracy); and, finally, that Beijing's efforts to isolate Taiwan were not in accord with efforts to maintain peace and stability in East Asia and the new world order.[37] Lee also reiterated the points he made in his special state-to-state interview and asserted that "New Taiwanese" are "willing to fight for . . . survival of their country." He declared that Taipei's relationship with Beijing had already been one of a state-to-state nature and that Beijing should abandon its policy of treating Taiwan as a "renegade province" and "embrace (Taiwan's) democracy rather than trying to contain it." The article both presented Lee's logical arguments and made an appeal to the United States and the international community to recognize Taipei's right to "international space" based on law and Taiwan's attainments in democratizing.

The *Foreign Affairs* article seemed to confirm that Lee's statement was carefully planned, perhaps months in advance. Following a Nationalist Party high-level meeting shortly after Lee's pronouncement, one member stated that the "two states" concept was the product of a year-long study by the "Select Group on Strengthening the Sovereignty of the Republic of China" headed by the secretary general of the Presidential Palace, Huang Kun-huei.[38]

And there seemed to be a follow-up plan. In ensuing months, Lee repeated his state-to-state relationship idea. Other leaders, including opposition politicians, almost unanimously supported the idea. The topic was discussed during the 2000 presidential election campaign and the main contenders unanimously lent their support, Chen Shui-bian in particular.

—⧓—

The reaction to Lee's statements from the White House and the State Department was one of unmistakable and unabashed hostility. According to one source, neither was informed in advanced that Lee would make such a statement (or any statement) and felt blindsided.[39] Others, however, said the State Department was simply looking for an excuse to denigrate Taiwan.

In any event, a number of high-level officials at the State Department spoke of Lee's "hubris." One Department of State official, when talking to the press, called Lee's declaration "dangerous language." President Clinton and a number of his advisors reportedly cursed Lee. Clinton, to show his displeasure, immediately canceled a visit by Undersecretary of the Treasury Timothy Geithner to Taiwan. Clinton then telephoned Jiang Zemin to reassure him of America's commitment to the policy of one China. After the call he told the press that he had had very positive conversations with Jiang and declared that U.S. policy had not changed. Clinton further asserted that "we would take very seriously any abridgement of peaceful dialogue" called for by the TRA.[40] The Department of State's spokesperson, James Rubin, followed up. He stated and restated Washington's Three Noes policy (no Taiwan independence, no two Chinas, no membership for Taiwan in international bodies that assume statehood), in what some observers said was an effort intended to "slap Taipei down." A few days later Secretary of State Albright sent Assistant Secretary for Asia and the Pacific Stanley Roth to Beijing and the head of the American Institute in Taiwan office in Washington, Richard Bush, to Taipei. Roth, in particular, had a reputation for being unabashedly pro-Beijing.

During the next few weeks the Clinton administration continued to show its anger and on every available occasion took Beijing's side in the feud. Secretary of State Albright publicly stated that Taipei's explanations "don't quite do it."[41] One observer at the time noted that the policies and actions coming from the U.S. executive branch of government mirrored the attitude of Admiral Dennis Blair, commander-in-chief of U.S. Pacific Forces, who had said cynically a few months earlier: "Taiwan is the turd in the punchbowl of U.S.-China relations."[42]

In September, to further display its ire toward President Lee, the United States spoke out and voted against Taiwan's annual bid to participate in the United Nations. This was unprecedented. Washington had heretofore said little about this and had always abstained when a vote was called. Meanwhile, both the White House and the State Department generally ignored or played down Beijing's hostile and provocative acts toward Taiwan after Lee's statement. Sometimes they agreed. Their attitude was clearly that Lee had provoked it. Even the White House reaction to China's testing a missile that could hit targets in the United States at this time, which should have created major concern, was very mild. It was almost ignored. Instead, there was talk of cutting arms sales to Taiwan. In fact, the Department of State recommended this.[43]

The response in Congress, and from other leading political figures, and from the media was starkly different. Support for Taiwan was not as strong as had been in 1996 because there was a perception that Lee Teng-hui had provoked or at least had initiated the crisis, rather than Taiwan being the innocent victim. Also the incident could not be linked to a visit to the United States. There was, nevertheless, sympathy and support expressed for Taiwan very different from the hostility and blame emanating from the White House or State Department.

In fact, Lee found many solid supporters. Amid reports that the Clinton administration planned to hold up the shipment of arms to Taiwan, on July 21, Benjamin Gilman, chairman of the House International Relations Committee, announced that he would block approval of all U.S. arms transfers until the matter got resolved to his satisfaction. Jesse Helms, chairman of the powerful Senate Foreign Relations Committee, saluted President Lee "for having the courage to state the obvious." He further asserted that everyone should know that Taiwan is a "de facto sovereign state." Helms added that the Clinton administration is "paralyzed by its own anachronistic policy, better known as appeasement."[44] Another member of Congress stated that the president had "kissed every rear-end in Beijing" and had "tried to push Taiwan down the drain." He continued: "But he (Clinton) didn't refute President Lee's statement because he didn't dare. Congress would have taught him a lesson."

Meanwhile Congressional committees continued to debate the Taiwan Security Enhancement Act—legislation that would have substantially strengthened the U.S. military commitment to Taiwan and guaranteed Taipei arms sales. It did this in spite of a spate of bitter criticism of the bill by the White House, the Department of State, and Beijing. Congress was not going to be pushed around. In August, Representative Benjamin Gilman, as head of the House International Relations Committee, led a congressional delegation to Taipei. There he stated publicly that his group backed Lee's statement. He also opined that the two sides should "engage in dialog as equals." In September, Gilman wrote a letter to President Clinton calling on the White House to urge China to renounce the use of force against Taiwan. The letter also included Gilman's personal view that the United States should not commit to a "mediating role" between the two sides. One observer said that Gilman's comment reflected the view in Congress that President Lee Teng-hui was right in assuming that the White House wanted to force Taiwan into negotiations that were not in its interest. Gilman also expressed in the letter to Clinton concern about the United States participating in a joint statement with China when President Clinton met with President Jiang Zemin later in the month in New Zealand, in that it might perpetrate the "misperception" that the United States acknowledges Beijing is the capital of one China.[45]

On October 26, the House International Relations Committee approved, by a vote of 32 to 6, a measure that would establish direct military communications between the United States and Taiwan and would expand provisions for training

Taiwan's military officers in the United States. Patently the view in Congress of Lee's statement was at odds with Foggy Bottom and the White House.

Elsewhere, all of the candidates in the running for president in 2000 were queried about Lee's statement in the following weeks and all except Al Gore made positive statements indicating they supported Taiwan. Presidential front-runner George W. Bush, campaigning in Iowa, declared that if elected, he would "defend Taiwan against aggression from China." He said he would be "resolute" and "honor our commitments in the Far East." Bush called President Clinton's earlier decision to make China a "strategic partner" a "mistake."[46] Bush con-cluded unequivocally: "I would help defend Taiwan." John McCain declared that the United States would "defend stability and freedom in Asia." Steve Forbes, when asked if he would defend Taiwan if attacked, replied: "Of course." He further stated that he would sign the Taiwan Security Enhancement Act into law if he were president. Elizabeth Dole, Gary Bauers, and Pat Buchanan spoke as strongly or more strongly in favor of Taiwan. Bill Bradley declared, "We are committed to helping Taiwan."

The U.S. media was divided but generally supported Taiwan. *Time* magazine carried several pieces that were pro-Beijing, blaming Taipei for starting the crisis and arguing that Taiwan should stick to its one-China policy and only that will work to keep peace.[47] The *Washington Post*, however, editorialized saying that the source of instability is "China's unwillingness to follow Taiwan on the path to democratization." It further stated that Clinton administration is "always eager to placate Beijing" and that it is a "fiction that Taiwan is not a separate country."[48] The *Post* also spoke of the "pretense" in China's policy as well as America's. One *Washington Post* writer said that in dealing with Beijing, President Clinton "should help those leaders understand the United States must support the Taiwanese people's right to determine their own future." The author further suggested in regard to Taiwan's election that Clinton should tell China that if they would "accord their own people that right, the chances of rapprochement between Taiwan and China would increase."[49] The *New York Times* carried an article assessing the situation as alternatively one of President Lee Teng-hui stating a "new reality," or just repeating a version of what he had said before. The writer stated that the situation was volatile because Beijing refused to rule out the use of force.[50] The *New Republic* magazine stated that "Lee had spoken honestly." "There is no dogma more dogmatic for the Clinton foreign policy apparatus than the creed that nothing should be permitted to interfere with the American courtship of China and its holy market."[51] The *Christian Science Monitor*, two months after the crisis, editorialized applauding Lee's "truth-telling" and declared that Taiwan's nonstate status should "be put onto the fiction best seller list."[52] The *Los Angeles Times* carried a number of stories on the case, almost all positive about Lee's statement. It even published a piece written by Taiwan's represen-tative in Washington who said that Lee's statement simply "reflects the historical, political and legal facts that constitute the basis for relations . . . between Taipei and Beijing." The paper hosted another piece written by a specialist at the

Taiwan's 2000 Election: Taiwan Gets Secessionist President

In March 2000, Taiwan held another presidential election, its second direct election of the nation's president. The campaign, and even more the results, created a tinderbox out of Taipei-Beijing relations. It was worse in many ways than the 1996 election, when Beijing fired missiles at Taiwan's shores in anger.

The opposition party's candidate, Chen Shui-bian, an open advocate of Taiwan's independence, won. Chinese leaders in Beijing reviled him. His victory was ominous. China had hoped that one of the other candidates would win. In fact, Beijing had unabashedly tried to prevent Chen's victory. Just before the balloting, Premier Zhu Rongji sternly warned Taiwan's voters not to vote for Chen, but they cast ballots for Chen anyway. There was a spirit of rebellion among the electorate. They were not to be pushed around by China.

In the United States it was very apparent that the White House and the State Department worried about Taiwan's election provoking a fight with China and drawing the United States into the fray. Congress, the media, and the public had another opinion: Taiwan had taken another big step on the path to democracy, and that was good.

Political forces in China were divided. The military viewed the situation as much more dire than civilian leaders did. Hard-liners on the political left took a more hostile view than reformers.

There were no missiles fired during the campaign or after the election. But China did military exercises afterward to show its displeasure. There was a feeling of pending doom.

—⚏—

March 18—the polls closed in Taiwan at four that afternoon. There was a feeling of excitement, but also apprehension, throughout the island.[1] Many felt that the opposition DPP's candidate, Chen Shui-bian, was sure to win. What would that mean? What would Beijing do?

The vote tallies from the districts poured in—almost simultaneously—to election headquarters. Analysts were making projections, but they really didn't need to. The computer counting was done so quickly that the results very soon became official. In fact, by 5:30 the winner was announced. The television and radio stations reported it with great fanfare; Chen Shui-bian and Annette Lu would be the next president and vice president. There was euphoria, jubilation in the Chen camp. Some of Chen's supporters were speechless. They could not believe what had happened. Some said they thought that the election would be stolen from them. Others said they were not prepared for the victory.

DPP leaders, spokespersons, and workers thanked everyone. They said it was a "people's victory." They said that the party had planned, toiled, and sacrificed for thirteen years, since its creation in 1986, for this day. Supporters had risked their lives. They had given their hearts and souls. Some said proudly that the era of KMT's "white terror" (meaning political oppression) was over. It was a new day, a new era. Now Taiwan was free. Democracy was finally realized. Some talked of the advent of majority rule, by which they meant Taiwanese rule, as opposed to Mainland Chinese, who had come to Taiwan after World War II. One DPP stalwart said, "The Chinese swine won't control us from now on." Chen supporters said that there would no longer be any pretense that Taiwan was part of China. "That stupid notion has been washed away," said one on-looker who was obviously happy about the poll results and Chen's victory.

Taiwan's newspapers, whether pro-Chen or not, reported the heady stuff of the election results. One headline said the election "changed heaven and earth." "Executive power had changed hands. Taiwan politically will never be the same," said a radio station announcer in a fit of excitement. Almost in unison the media reported that what had happened was "momentous," that it would have lasting impact, that it would make a difference, that it was "historic."

James Soong won the second largest number of votes. But that was a defeat. He conceded and congratulated Chen. He tried hard to put a good face on his loss. His supporters were visibly upset. They felt Soong should have won, that the election was taken from him. They blamed the KMT and Chen.

Lien Chan, the KMT's candidate and the sitting vice president, came in an embarrassing third. He and his supporters were sober. Many were in a state of shock. How could the KMT have lost, with its talent, experience, and money? They thought they could pull out a victory even though the opinion polls had shown throughout the campaign that Lien would lose. "We never lost before," said one of Lien's fans. "We didn't think it could happen."

When the final vote tally was made public, Chen had won just under five million votes, or 39.3 percent of the total. James Soong won a bit over three hundred thousand less, for 36.8 percent of the whole. Lien Chan got less than three million votes for 23.1 percent.[2]

More than eighty percent of the electorate had voted, even more than in 1996 when China sent missiles roaring over the Taiwan Strait to intimidate voters who went to the polls in very large numbers anyway.

Who did the people vote for?

Chen was born in Taiwan, unlike the other two major candidates. He was young to be running for high office in a Chinese country; born in 1951, he was not yet fifty. He hailed from south Taiwan. He was born into a poor family, but he excelled in school and upon graduation was able to attend Taiwan's most prestigious university, Taiwan National University. He majored in law and finished at the top of his class. He gained fame nationally in Taiwan before he was thirty, defending the dissidents that were arrested during the Kaohsiung Incident in 1979. He wasn't one to shy away from controversy or political struggle. Later he was accused and convicted of libel for speaking out against an opponent. He served eight months in jail.[3]

Chen knew where his heart was and his politics. He grew up under martial law, which he defied. He joined the DPP at its founding. He later represented the party in the legislature for two terms, from 1989 to 1994. In 1994, he became a politician of the first order and a recognized leader of his party when he won the race for mayor of Taipei. So doing, he became the chief executive of the capital city. President Lee and most top KMT brass resided in his jurisdiction. His mayoral victory was a controversial one. Some newspaper commentators said he hadn't really won—rather the other candidates lost.

The New Party, which had split from the KMT in 1993, irate over President Lee's leadership of the party and what they thought to be Lee's independence views and policies, had a strong candidate: Jaw Shao-kong. Jaw was well known. He was a good campaigner. He looked to be an easy winner according to the polls. So the KMT abandoned their own unpopular candidate and threw their support to Chen. Or so it looked; most observers said that was the case. President Lee was said to have orchestrated the plan.

Chen did a good job as mayor. According to the opinion polls, he fairly consistently maintained a seventy-percent positive rating—though his critics said he paid too much attention to his popularity. Still Chen lost a reelection bid in 1998. The KMT made a comeback. It wasn't a three-way race this time.

But Chen wasn't to be discouraged. He saw the defeat as an opportunity and soon started campaigning for the party's nomination for the presidential election. He had no trouble getting it.

Chen picked Lu Hsiu-lien, or Annette Lu, as his vice presidential running mate. Lu was also born in Taiwan. She was also young, and she supported an independent Taiwan strongly. Her credentials were as good as they were interesting. She got a good local education, then went to Harvard University in the United States to study. She was an activist and very proindependence. She joined the Formosa Movement and participated in the Kaohsiung Incident. She was arrested and tried in court. Chen, in fact, defended her. She was convicted and sentenced to twelve years in prison. She served five. She said it was the KMT that jailed her. Interestingly, she also asserted President Jimmy Carter was to blame. He had stripped Taiwan of U.S. diplomatic recognition without warning or justification, she charged, engendering the massive Kaohsiung protest parade. Lu was elected to the legislature in 1992. Later she concurrently served as a senior advisor to President Lee Teng-hui, with whom she became friends. In 1997, Lu was elected magistrate of Taoyuan County, the site of Taiwan's International Airport. Here she got executive experience. Lu had still more on her vita. She had founded the feminist movement in Taiwan.

Lu was the first serious female vice presidential candidate. She would deliver the female vote, observers said. She also spoke English, which Chen didn't. She had foreign experience, and this would help the ticket. Lu was energetic beyond belief, many said. She was a good speaker and debater. She was aggressive and provocative.

James Soong was born in China, but he could barely remember it.[4] He grew up in Taiwan, and got his advanced university degrees in the United States at Berkeley and Georgetown. Soong was a decade older than Chen. He had made his political career under Chiang Ching-kuo and then Lee Teng-hui. He had headed the very visible Government Information Office, where he early on attained name recognition. Women spoke of his good looks. Soong later became secretary general of the party. He was in that position when Lee Teng-hui became president and Lee was challenged by party hard-liners, mostly Mainland Chinese who didn't trust him. Soong put his career on the line when he spoke boldly in favor of Lee. Some thought he was too young to speak out this way. In appreciation Lee appointed Soong provincial governor. Then the office became an elective one. In 1994, Soong won a big election victory, with Lee's help. After that they had a falling out.

Soong had grassroots support. He had broad Taiwanese support. He was one of the few Mainland Chinese who did. He was the most charismatic of the candidates running. Until late in the campaigning he led in the polls, usually by a good margin. However, his candidacy was derailed by the exposure of a money scandal. President Lee and Lien Chan engineered this. It hurt Soong badly because his campaign thrived on his personal popularity and image. Soong had been regarded as a clean politician, faithful to his wife, and hard working.

Lien Chan was born in China, but was considered Taiwanese because his father was Taiwanese.[5] He was the oldest of the three major candidates, but certainly not too old for Taiwan politics. Like Soong he received a good beginning education in Taiwan and went to the United States for MA and PhD degrees at the University of Chicago. He had been Taiwan's youngest cabinet member ever. He had more experience in politics than any of the candidates, probably more than any politician in Taiwan had ever had at his age. He had been minister of the interior and foreign minister among a big list of other positions. He had been premier. He was the standing vice president. Lien had won the ruling party's nomination. He had the support of President Lee Teng-hui, presumably.

But Lien was also stiff. His critics said he was arrogant and filthy rich, implying that there was some question about his family fortune. It was widely rumored that he frequently beat his wife, a former Miss China. His friends said he was a good person at heart, bright and experienced and obviously the best qualified for the job. But they admitted he didn't communicate very well and had an image problem.

There were two other candidates, but they were not serious. They did make the campaign more interesting and exciting though.[6]

Analysis of the vote count days after the election was revealing in terms of how Chen got the presidency. Soong won every voting district in the northern part of Taiwan and in the eastern and central parts of the island, except for Yilan County. He won in the Offshore Islands. He won among every "ethnic" (actually subethnic) minority: Mainland Chinese, Hakka, and Aborigines. He won the female vote. But Chen won very big in the south. He won the majority Fukien Taiwanese vote. And he won the vote of younger people and those without party identification. Voters saw Chen as the "Taiwanese candidate" even though Lien was Taiwanese, technically. The electorate clearly viewed him as a supporter of independence among the three, even though Chen didn't campaign on this issue.

—〜〜—

After the election observers pondered how Chen Shui-bian had won. There was a chain of events that seems to help explain it. In July 1999, as noted earlier, President Lee announced that Taiwan's relationship with China was a state-to-state one. This evinced a very hostile reaction in Beijing and created serious cross-strait tension that lasted for a number of months. As a result, Taiwan's electorate came to dislike China more than usual.

On September 21, an earthquake of 7.3 on the Richter scale hit Taiwan. Its epicenter was close to beautiful Sun Moon Lake in the central part of the island. Everyone living in Taiwan felt it. It was the worst earthquake in a century. The tremor killed more than two thousand people and destroyed at least twenty thousand buildings. It left in excess of one hundred thousand people homeless. In dollar terms, the quake did US$31 billion in damage—an amount equal to ten percent of the nation's gross national product.[7] Initially, victims and the media criticized the government for not acting quickly. But then the government and the KMT stepped into action. Rescue and cleanup efforts stopped the election campaigning for a while.

China gave itself a black eye from the event. Beijing offered Taiwan US$100,000 for relief efforts. Taiwan's press observed, with barbed tones in its language, that a number of individuals had donated more. News reporters compared the sum to the US$50 million or so that Taiwan had contributed to China during each of several tragedies there in the recent past.[8] Citizens in Taiwan called Chinese leaders in Beijing cheapskates. Several commented that Taiwan didn't need that kind of assistance. Others said it mirrored how Beijing would treat Taiwan if it ever became part of China. People in Taiwan were even angrier when Beijing interfered in relief efforts organized by several other countries, which were told they needed clearances from the Chinese government before they could do anything. The families of many of the victims blamed China for the deaths of their loved ones trapped in the rubble. They might have been saved by a quick response, which "Beijing's pettiness had precluded." One official in Taipei described Beijing's behavior as "tantamount to kicking the wounded and stomping on the sufferer."

The year 1999 ended with the return of Macao to China. Beijing made a fanfare of the event and tried to impress Taiwan. Chinese leaders pointed out that this was the last piece of territory to be recovered, except for Taiwan. Citizens in Taiwan were not impressed. Neither was the government. Both talked about the differences between Macao and Taiwan, the former being a colony and not having sovereignty or any means to defend itself. Taiwan was starkly different, they pointed out. Lee Teng-hui and other top leaders repeated what they had said when Hong Kong returned to China in 1997: Taiwan was not a colony. It would not follow Hong Kong's lead—no dice to one country, two systems.

Meanwhile, early in 1999, James Soong, who was registering the highest numbers in the public opinion surveys measuring support for potential presidential candidates, ended his term as governor. He left office "prematurely." Under President Lee Teng-hui's leadership, with the opposition DPP's cooperation, the provincial government was abolished (actually dramatically downsized). The governor was to be appointed again. This action was widely seen as another effort to make Taiwan legally independent. Without a provincial government apparatus, which existed because the Republic of China was almost synonymous with Taiwan but stood for China, Taiwan would now be seen as a nation apart from China. Abolishing the provincial government was justified from the perspective of cost-efficient government but was emblematic of Taiwan further separating from China. More immediately, it resulted in intense feelings of hostility between President Lee and Governor Soong. Observers said it reflected Lee's hatred of Soong and his determination to see that Soong would not be his successor. No one knew exactly why Lee's feelings toward Soong changed so dramatically. Some said Lee did not want a Mainland Chinese ever again to be Taiwan's president. Many said it was personal.[9]

This happened amidst rumors that Lee wanted to stay on. Some of his supporters said that the constitution should be amended so that presidential and legislative elections would be held together. That would mean extending Lee's term for a year and a half.

Many said that if Lee did this he might think of another reason to continue in office after his extension expired. It was reported that the U.S. government expressed its opposition.

In any event, the polls showed half or more of Taiwan's electorate wanted Lee to bow out and preferred Soong for the presidency (with only a quarter favoring Chen and ten percent liking Lien). Soong thus pressed on. In May supporters formed a "Friends of James Soong Club." It was clear, however, that

Soong would not get the KMT's nomination with Lee setting the party agenda and maneuvering to have his vice president, Lien Chan, nominated. Meanwhile, Chen Shui-bian received endorsements from his party's top hierarchy that mirrored broad support for him among party members.

In November the KMT chose its presidential candidate. Naturally it was Lien Chan. Soong decided to run as an independent and in so doing provoked harsh accusations from KMT leaders. President Lee was behind the attacks on Soong. KMT stalwarts accused Soong of splitting the party, of being disloyal, and worse. Soong replied that the era of martial law and dictatorship were over, that democracy had prevailed in Taiwan, and that the people favored him. So he would not retract his "go-alone candidacy."

As the next four months passed the feud between Soong and the KMT escalated into a destructive struggle. In December, in an unveiled effort to undermine Soong's candidacy (with him still running high in the polls) a KMT legislator accused Soong of channeling over one hundred million Taiwan dollars into an account at the Chung Hsing Bills Finance Corporation. The account was in his son's name. Soong, the legislator said, did this when he was secretary general of the party. There were follow-up accusations. Soon the government got into the act to investigate. Soong explained that the money in question had not been used. He said that other funds that he was accused of taking had been allocated for use by former President Chiang Ching-kuo's family.[10] President Lee jumped into the fray, refuting Soong's explanation. Lee even called Soong a thief. The scandal damaged Soong irreparably. But it also hurt the KMT, drawing public attention to its deep pockets and its questionable use of big money for political purposes.

Lien promised to put KMT money into a trust. But few believed him; at least most doubted this could or would be done before the election. It thus looked like a political ploy. Indeed this would not have been an easy task.

All of this and the fact Taiwan's economy seemed healthy, especially in the context of the "Asian economic meltdown" that had affected other countries in the area, but not Taiwan, turned voter attention to "black gold," or the links between criminals and politicians and the vile corruption in politics that had become a blight on the country over the previous decade or so. Chen benefited.

The other major campaign issue was cross-strait relations or Taiwan's links, or lack thereof, with China. Behind this issue was, of course, Taiwan's status as a sovereign nation state or not. On this matter the KMT's Lien Chan should have been the best candidate. Chen was perceived to be too extreme in advocating Taiwan's independence. Various polls showed this. A declaration of independence, which Chen in the past had advocated in various forms, would prompt an immediate reaction by Beijing, possibly in the form of military action, even an invasion. Soong, a Mainland Chinese, was seen as seeking unification with China and in the process surrendering Taiwan's sovereignty and nationhood, though there was little or no evidence of this other than the fact that he had in the past endorsed the KMT's view on this. The bottom line was that it was his "ethnicity."

Both Chen and Soong espoused very moderate positions during the campaign and to a considerable extent allayed public worries about their respective position vis-à-vis China and Taiwan's status. Chen, however, was more effective in doing this than Soong as it turned out because of China's behavior during the campaign.

Beijing patently favored Lien or Soong. Actually, Chinese leaders favored Lien because he represented the KMT, which Beijing thought would negotiate reunification (without Lee Teng-hui, of course). Mainland Chinese advisors also surrounded Lien, while Soong was close to Taiwanese, many of whom had been with him when he was provincial governor.

Meanwhile, internal politics in China, meaning civilian-military relations, seemed to dictate a tough line on Taiwan. On February 21, two days after the campaign officially began, Beijing issued a White Paper on the Taiwan issue. It stated that China would use military force against Taiwan if officials in Taipei refused to negotiate reunification. Heretofore, Beijing had not mentioned such a condition. China had cited only a declaration of independence, allowing foreign bases on Taiwan, or Taiwan going nuclear as reasons for attacking. The paper warned that China "will not permit the 'Taiwan issue' to drag on."

This was seen in Taiwan as an ultimatum. Opinion polls at this time showed that eighty percent of the population favored the status quo in terms of cross strait relations. Thus Beijing's new policy was contrary to what the majority in Taiwan thought it should be. The stock market fell by over three percent. People braced for another series of missile tests or some kind of military action. References to "Commie bandits" and worse could be heard on the street. But there was no panic. As before during such crises when Beijing intimidated Taiwan, people looked to the United States for moral support and military help, if needed.

Under the shadow of possible congressional action and strong expressions favoring Taiwan on Capitol Hill, White House spokesperson John Lockhart declared that the United States rejected any use of force or threats of force. Assistant Secretary of State for Asia and the Pacific Stanley Roth asserted that Beijing's White Paper was contrary to the "bedrock of our relations with China and Taiwan." One official in Taipei said he doubted Roth's sincerity but accepted that what he said was U.S. policy nevertheless. A less than polite lower official in the Foreign Ministry said laughingly that Roth "must have had a conversion."

Senator John Kerry of Massachusetts, one of the Democratic Party's leaders and a person some said would possibly be a future presidential candidate, called Beijing's statements in the White Paper "unacceptable." The Pentagon issued a statement mentioning "incalculable consequences" if China followed through on its threats. Judging from the American reaction to China's bluster, it was clear that Taiwan's protector was wide awake and could be depended on.[11]

China then rebuffed Washington's "threats." The *People's Liberation Army Daily* said that two and a half million soldiers were "urged to contribute to protecting the motherland." Statements by lower officials and scholars were much harsher. The "war of words" seemed to make the matter more one of a conflict between Washington and Beijing than one between Taipei and Beijing. This relieved the electorate in Taiwan. Meanwhile, Chen softened his position on relations with China after the White Paper was made public. Soong hardened his. Lien continued his moderate line.

A week and a day before the voters were to go to the polls, Lee Yuan-tseh, the head of Academia Sinica, Taiwan's most important and prestigious think tank and academic institution, announced he would be an advisor to Chen. Lee was the only Taiwanese ever to win a Nobel Prize, and his support was received with very obvious glee in the Chen camp. In fact, it seemed at this juncture there was a groundswell of support going Chen's direction. Lee Yuan-tseh's announcement created a palpable sense of a turning of the tide of momentum for Chen. Chen also benefited from growing anti-China feelings among potential voters. His past independence views didn't seem to engender fear anymore. He was also seen as the best candidate to deal with black gold, which now was a decisive issue to voters. Several top business leaders at this time jumped onto the Chen bandwagon.

Rather than strike a deal with Soong, or at least end their feud, the KMT continued to attack him. Even though Lien had been way behind in the polls during the period when publicizing polling data was still legal (ten days before the election), party leaders said that Lien had momentum and Soong had no chance of winning. Some even insinuated that this was based on secret polls.

Just then China made another startling move. Two days before the voting, during a ninety-minute news conference to mark the end of the meeting of China's National People's Congress, Premier Zhu Rongji appeared before television cameras and made what was for Taiwan a shocking announcement. Taiwan's voters, he said, should "shun the pro-independence candidate." Zhu was seen on television and heard on radio throughout Taiwan at the time. Everyone understood he was ordering people not to vote for Chen Shui-bian. Zhu went on to declare that Taiwan "would not get a second chance." Chinese were "ready to shed blood," he insisted. Television viewers in Taiwan saw the face of an angry and fierce-looking Chinese official direly warning Taiwan. The next day Zhu's picture, with a hostile countenance, was on the front page of Taiwan's major newspapers. His ominous words were repeated over and over.

Chen Shui-bian responded that China was "playing the terror card." He added that "Taiwan won't be scared by threats of force." The other candidates also took a hard line. But their responses were not as credible as Chen's. It wasn't clear at the time whether Zhu's terrifying words would provoke a backlash and help Chen or not. Beijing apparently calculated it would hurt Chen. When the votes were counted, however, pundits almost unanimously said that Zhu had added votes to Chen's column, perhaps three percent, just enough to give him victory.

Beijing had made a huge blunder. Taiwan's foremost advocate of separation would be the president in two months. Now what would China do?

—⚹—

As expected, China's response to Chen's historic election victory was negative in the extreme. The Taiwan Affairs Office of the Central Committee of the

Chinese Communist Party, where Taiwan policy is formulated, declared that the election did not change the fact that Taiwan is a part of Chinese territory. Its statement went on to say that independence "in whatever form will not be allowed." Two days after the election Defense Minister Chi Haotian inspected units of the PLA in Fujian Province adjacent to Taiwan. These were soldiers that would assault the beaches of Taiwan if so ordered. Meanwhile, there were reports of massive troop movements and large numbers of military aircraft flying in the area. Either the army was preparing for action against Taiwan, or this was a feint that was to give the impression an assault was about to come. Alternatively the military could have been just letting off steam.

A few days later hundreds of Chinese fishing vessels suddenly intruded into waters near one of Taiwan's offshore islands. The PLA had said that it would mobilize thousands of boats for an invasion of Taiwan. It repeated that boast. The vessels surrounding the small island were, it seemed, to look like an attack. Or it was a mock drill of an invasion of Taiwan. Civilian leaders were meanwhile telling the military to remain cool. They advocated a wait-and-see policy. Chen was not president yet. Let him make some announcements of policy. "Let's see what his colors really are," a Beijing official was heard saying. Another mentioned that Chen's inauguration speech would be telling. "We will see then," he asserted.

Xinhua, China's official news agency, subsequently provided an in-depth analysis of the election. This it appeared would become China's official version of what happened and signal how Beijing should treat Taiwan. It was not a view that augured well for Beijing-Taipei relations with Chen Shui-bian as president. The news agency talked about the seriousness of black gold in Taiwan and "confusion about cross-strait relations." These two things explained Chen's victory. But it also had more ominous things to say. It focused on Chen's relationship with Lee Teng-hui and answered the question whether Chen was a "separatist" and a "splittist" or not or whether he had "changed his heart."

The conclusion was that President Lee Teng-hui had helped Chen win the election and that he did so because he thought Chen was a supporter of Taiwan's independence. Behind this lay Beijing's view that Lee had been cunning in stringing China along with talk of unification and a purported one-China policy while actually pursuing a policy of separation. Now Lee had now gone one step further. He had arranged for a successor who would carry on his policies. Lee was so ruthless and driven that he was willing to destroy his own political party, the KMT, to accomplish this. Official news sources in China offered "concrete evidence." The DPP had regarded Lee as a "fellow traveler" before the election. It had heartily endorsed Lee's "two state" view. Chen and President Lee had met often, over lunch and on other occasions.

Lee Yuan-tseh, whose support gave the Chen campaign a vital lift at the last minute, was President Lee's good friend. He would not have done what he did without Lee Teng-hui's approval. Most important, President Lee got rid of the provincial government and refused to allow the KMT to nominate Soong, even though he was far and away the most popular presidential candidate and had been Lee's close friend in the past. Then Lee ruined Soong's candidacy by digging up information about Soong's questionable, but not unusual, financial dealings. Chen, in Beijing's eyes, had won the election because the KMT split. And Lee personally engineered it for Chen. Beijing had strong evidence to support this view, much of which came from Taiwan.

In 1994, Lee had orchestrated the dumping of the KMT's candidate to give Chen the mayoralty of Taipei. The New Party propounded this view long after the election. Most people believed it. In 1997, three years before the election, Lee had told a Japanese reporter that his ideal successor was Chen Shui-bian.[12] Hsu Wen-lung, a pro-independence businessman and a close friend of Lee's, called a press conference during the late days of the campaign. He stated that Chen, not Lien, was the best person to continue President Lee's policies. He influenced many Lee supporters to help and vote for Chen.[13] The pro-DPP *Taiwan Daily* published an article during the campaign quoting what President Lee had said earlier about the "peaceful transfer of power." Lee had used the analogy of Moses and Joshua finding a homeland for the Jews and ruling them after that respectively. Lee had earlier referred to himself as Moses. He had asked Chen to study the works of Joshua, Moses' successor.[14] At an American Chamber of Commerce meeting a few days after the election, Julian Kok, policy adviser to Chen, told the audience that his party had the KMT's chairman, Lee Teng-hui, to thank for the election victory.[15]

Lien Chan believed the reports of Lee's alleged actions to help Chen. So with the help of many angry KMT loyalists, Lien forced Lee to resign as chairman of the party immediately after the election (if Lee is to be believed; Lien offers a different story).[16]

Understanding Beijing's bitterness and anger and, some say, the possibility that civilian leaders might not be able to hold the military at bay, the United States came to the rescue. According to rumors in Taipei, U.S. officials "advised" and "strongly pressured" Chen to make some accommodating statements to cool China's hostility. Chen obliged. Some said that American diplomats wrote his inauguration speech. Most scholars in Taipei said that they at minimum read it and recommended changes before Chen presented it. It indeed read like Chen wanted to make Washington happy. A number of government officials told friends and observers another interesting story, that the United States had "advised" Chen through intermediaries that Parris Chang, a possible candidate for foreign minister in the Chen administration, was "unacceptable." He was seen as too provocative and too pro-independence. Chang did not get the job.

Indeed, Chen adopted conciliatory policies. He declared a new Three Noes policy: no declaration of independence, no amendment to redefine Taiwan's status, and no plebiscite to decide the island's future. To prove his sincerity, Chen promised to disassociate himself from any organization that advocated independence. He thereupon announced he would give up his positions in the DPP. He added that he would not be a "party president." Chen dumped two of Lee Teng-hui's most notorious policies: a ban on the "three direct links" and his "be patient and no haste" policy that sought to curtail investments in China. He endorsed Beijing's one-China policy as a "topic of negotiations." He even talked of Taiwan and China forming some kind of political union, mentioning a confederation. But could Beijing believe him or trust him?

Chen Shui-bian sent a secret envoy to China right after the election. It accomplished nothing. Beijing demanded that talks be based on the one-China principle. Chen's representatives could not comply. The director of the Taiwan Affairs Office of the State Council in Beijing said that there would be no meetings with Chen or his party until after his swearing in on May 20. One official in Beijing noted that in his four-thousand-word victory statement after the election, Chen used the word *Taiwan* more than twenty times and the term *Republic of China* only once—and that was in mentioning his official title.

Beijing didn't trust the United States either. The Clinton administration warned Chen about advocating independence. Perhaps it was serious, perhaps not. Washington didn't push for reunification either. One official recalled that the Central Intelligence Agency, just before President Chiang Ching-kuo's death in 1988, had squelched secret talks between Chiang and Beijing officials that were to promote unification.[17]

—⁂—

The reaction to Chen Shui-bian's election victory in the United States was a positive one. But the White House also expressed caution. Congress was enthusiastic. The media was impressed; it was very laudatory.

President Clinton congratulated the "future president and vice president, Chen Shui-bian and Annette Lu." Clinton spoke in a positive tone about the election results being a contribution to democracy. A critic, however, said that a Clinton aide told him that this is what American academics would say, so he should say it first. He did. A White House observer reported that Clinton told a State Department official "Chen was better than that ass . . . Lee. Chen can be manipulated a lot easier." What he meant was uncertain at the time.

The State Department official later said that with divided government in Taiwan now the United States would be able to maneuver more. "Chen won't be able to do much. He certainly won't be able to promote independence with any authority." Clinton also showed the other side of his personality. He said publicly that Chen's victory would result in no change in China policy and that the United States would retain its one-China stance. He went even further, saying that Chen should negotiate Taiwan's future with Chinese leaders and should accept Beijing's one-China formula.[18]

There was another slant to the story, however. One news reporter commented that Clinton had good cause to be angry at China. He had sent his old college buddy Strobe Talbot, now deputy secretary of state, to Beijing with a part-civilian, part-military delegation. They were to discuss U.S.-China policy and Taiwan. Three days later, without telling them what was going on, Beijing issued its White Paper warning Taiwan that if it did not negotiate reunification China would take military action. Some in the media wondered aloud why

Clinton was not angry. Was it because Beijing was being too good to him in other ways?

Secretary of State Madeleine Albright congratulated Chen. But she also was quick to assert that U.S.-China policy had not changed. She, as one Taiwan observer noted, "aped Clinton's mantra that it was U.S. policy that there was one China." Albright spoke approvingly about Chen's first public comments after the election, which she said helped diffuse cross-strait tensions. One observer in Washington said that she should be happy; after all, the Department of State had scripted what Chen said.

The response from members of Congress was different. It was congratulations and praise minus the one-China policy bit. Jesse Helms sent a telegram to Chen saying, "Your election will serve as a wake-up call. The people of Taiwan made clear this weekend that, if there is still 'one China' there are without question two Chinese states." He added. "The time has come for the United States to adopt a China policy which recognizes this undeniable truth."[19] Tom DeLay, the Republican Party's whip, went further. He called the Clinton administration's one China policy "appeasement" and recommended a two-China policy. Senator John Kerry, a few days later, said that the United States "will never accept a roll-back of democracy and freedom in Taiwan." Nearly every member of Congress, Democrats and Republicans alike, expressed congratulations and support of Taiwan's democratization. The House of Representatives sent a formal letter to president-elect Chen stating that "Taiwan should not be compelled to accept Beijing's 'one country, two systems' formulation." The House also passed a resolution, by a 418 to 1 margin, congratulating Taiwan and reaffirming the TRA, while suggesting that Beijing renounce the use of force against Taiwan.[20] Putting its money where its mouth was, according to one observer, the House also voted US$75 million to build new facilities for America's representative office, the American Institute in Taiwan.

The U.S. media was almost as supportive of Taiwan as Congress was. Editorially, the *Wall Street Journal* called Chen's victory "convincing." It advised the U.S. government not to treat Taiwan as an "embarrassing troublemaker" any more. It pointed out that when the United States has given strong support to Taiwan, China has engaged in cross-strait talks. The *New York Times* spoke of "democratic evolution" (mocking China's use of the term *peaceful evolution* to describe America's efforts to split China by encouraging democracy there). It also noted that Beijing had "failed in its efforts to defeat Chen." The *Times* called the Chen election victory a "problem in U.S.-China relations." *USA Today* recommended the United States continue to use economic leverage against China in view of its intimidation of Taiwan and considering the fact that Taiwan would continue to be a "hot topic." The *Washington Post* said that the election constituted a major step in Taiwan's "consolidating its democracy." It observed that "China's efforts to keep Chen from winning had backfired."

Time magazine carried an article entitled "Taiwan Takes a Stand." It quoted Chen's postelection comment that his win constituted "the greatest victory in

Taiwan's democracy movement." *Newsweek* lauded the election as the "first democratic transfer of power in China's 5,000-year history." It also described Chen's victory as "an event that threatened the principle honored in Washington and Beijing that Taiwan is just a wayward province." *U.S. News and World Reports* said of the election that "it created a national identity for a 'renegade province.'"[21]

—⁂—

By summer the crisis phase in U.S.-China relations had passed. But relations between the legislative and executive branches of the U.S. government had worsened when it came to China policy. In China the tension between the military and civilian leaders likewise remained. It appeared in both countries internal divisions were more permanent.

Adding to the difficulty of managing the Washington-Taipei-Beijing triangle was a new unfriendly relationship between the president and the legislature in Taiwan. In fact, there was now a face-off that was to be long lasting. Taiwan had a severely divided government.

Jiang Zemin and other civilian leaders in China were able to "cool down" the military a bit as election fever and post-election anger faded. They argued that China's admission to the World Trade Organization was necessary to maintain China's continued economic development. Membership in WTO had broad support, even in the military. Congress was scheduled to vote on permanent normal trade relations with China in late May, which would pave the way for China to join the WTO, just at the time when Chen Shui-bian would be sworn in to be the Republic of China's tenth president.

Another hot-button issue stirring the seething cauldron of U.S.-China relations was the matter of China selling missiles to Pakistan. After the elder President Bush had reversed U.S. policy of cutting arms sales to Taiwan in 1992 and allowed Taiwan to purchase one hundred and fifty F-16 fighter aircraft, Deng Xiaoping, under hostile pressure from the PLA, sent M-11 missiles to Pakistan. The Central Intelligence Agency later leaked information about this "major Chinese transgression." This incited a running battle with the State Department, which, the CIA argued, was undermining U.S. law and flaunting Congress by not acknowledging China's acts.

Senator Jesse Helms, who had acquired the nickname "Mr. No" for blocking Clinton appointments, somewhere along the line struck a deal with the White House to allow the nominations of Robert Einhorn for assistant secretary of state for non-proliferation and Joseph Prueher for U.S. ambassador to China. In return, a task force would make a determination on applying sanctions against China. Helms did not like nuclear proliferation and was going to hold Clinton's feet to the fire on this one, China policy be damned.[22] Clinton needed a concessionary statement from Beijing to deal with Helms. Civilian leaders in China had to put pressure on the military or make some kind of tradeoff to be able to help President Clinton. The problem was finessed, but China's military as well as top leaders had their feathers ruffled.

Meanwhile, notwithstanding the diversions, there remained bad blood between Beijing and Taipei. Beijing blamed the United States for the "splittist" Chen presidency. Taipei continued to insist that Washington would support and protect Taiwan, with which Congress agreed but the Clinton administration did not.

The two months between Chen's election and his inauguration were telling. The policies stated in his inauguration address, its style, and the message it actually conveyed were very noticeable to analysts in Beijing. Chen declared a policy position called "Four Noes": no declaration of independence, no change in the island's name, no constitutional amendment to legalize Lee Teng-hui's "two states" theory, and no referendum to alter Taiwan's status. Chen added a fifth. He pledged to adhere to the National Unification Guidelines adopted in 1991 that propounds a one-China policy. In his inauguration address, Chen repeated most of the pledges he made earlier. That was supposed to make Beijing and the Clinton administration happy. However, there was a dark side (for Beijing) to Chen's statements and his actions.

It was revealing that Chen did not say he would uphold the one-China principle. He only said he would not change the National Unification Guidelines, which asserts there are two separate political entities. Any thinking person would recall that President Lee Teng-hui had penned the guidelines; afterward Lee made his own interpretation. Chen also talked about expanding Taiwan's "international space." To Beijing this was anathema and smelled of Taiwan independence.

Looking at Chen's subsequent appointments was also revealing. Defense Minister Tang Fei was chosen to be the new Chen administration's premier. Tang was a member of the KMT, and his appointment seemed to send the signal of moderate policies and cooperation with the KMT. But there was another way of looking at the choice: Lee Teng-hui recommended Tang. After Chen announced Tang's role in the new government, some political pundits said this meant a "Chen-Lee co-rule arrangement." It did not translate into a coalition arrangement with the KMT.

Tien Hung-mao was picked to be Foreign Minister. He had been close to Lee Teng-hui. In fact, he was known for formulating Lee's "pragmatic diplomacy"—which Beijing called "separatist diplomacy." Tien had been head of the National Policy Research Center, which some called the "center for the study of Taiwan independence."

Chen Po-chih was given the job of chairman of the Council for Economic Planning and Development. He had a long-standing close relationship with advocates of independence. He had written extensively about how to achieve it. He was the origin of Lee Teng-hui's "no haste, be patient" policy of limiting capital investment in China.

Tsai Ying-wen, a legal expert, was made chairwoman of the Mainland Affairs Council (responsible for Taiwan's China policy). She was reputed to have been the brains behind Lee Teng-hui's special state-to-state relationship bombshell. Worse still, from Beijing's perspective, Lee recommended her to Chen.

And still there was more. Of the forty members of Chen's cabinet only five were not Taiwanese (who as an "ethnic" or "subethnic" group have a strong tendency to support Taiwan's separation from China, as opposed to the Mainland Chinese who prefer unification). One critic noted that Chen had less diversity in his cabinet than "dictator Chiang Kai-shek had." Taiwanese business leaders who had supported Chen for reasons of his stance on independence were visible at high-level meetings. And while technically there was nothing in Chen's inauguration speech that would anger Beijing (since the U.S. State Department had written it or had overseen its production), Chen nevertheless sent some powerful signals at the time which people both in Taiwan and China got.

Officiating at the inauguration was Peng Ming-min, the "father of Taiwan Independence." Peng was arrested in the mid-1960s for writing a Taiwan independence "manifesto." He was convicted of treason and jailed. Later he was let out but was put under house arrest, after which he fled to the United States. Peng returned to Taiwan shortly before the 1996 election. He was the DPP's candidate and ran on an independence platform. After the election he founded his own party, which advocated separation from China more strongly than did the DPP. In his speech, Chen said one-China is an "issue," not a principle. He pledged he would continue expanding Taiwan's international space (Lee Teng-hui's policy). Chen also talked about Taiwan's "four-hundred-year history"—in other words, Taiwan's history began with the Western discovery of the island. China's contact with the island before that didn't count. Neither did the fact that Chinese resided on the island beginning a thousand years ago. A four hundred-year history was the view of the separatist movement. Independence advocates liked the non-Chinese term "Formosa," which Chen used. Chen also referred to the history of China and Taiwan as two separate ones, very much contrary to China's view. Chen used the word "Taiwan" thirty-five times in his speech. He used "Republic of China" nine times and "Formosa" twice. He did not talk about "China"—prompting an observer to say that "he felt at home without China." At the end of his speech he shouted, "Long live the people of Taiwan." Even Lee Teng-hui had not gone this far. Entertainment at the inauguration festivities was Taiwanese. Ah-Mei, a local celebrity, sang the national anthem with a Taiwanese flair.[23] Could the Department of State not grasp all of the nuances? Some said it did with consternation.

All of this put Jiang Zemin in a bind. It was reported a month after the inauguration that the gist of some discussions in the Chinese Communist Party Central Committee had been that the victory of the DPP could be attributed to the "complete failure" of Jiang Zemin's Taiwan policy. Jiang was also openly criticized by hard-liners and the military for relying too much on "great power diplomacy," referring to his reliance on the United States, which they believed did not want Taiwan to be part of China. Beijing consequently adopted a policy of showing its dislike for Chen.

Some say Jiang Zemin and other top civilian leaders appeared they had been hit by a stun gun. They didn't know what to do. They had to adopt a tough mien toward Chen in view of sentiment in the army and the fact Chinese nationalism was determining China's foreign relations to a considerable degree. So Chinese leaders referred to Chen as an advocate of independence and his presidency as a "Lee presidency without Lee." They adopted a policy of not trusting Chen or dealing with him. China invited members of the KMT, now the opposition party, to visit Beijing or Shanghai or wherever in China there was reason for them to go. They also sent invitations to members of James Soong's newly formed party, the People First Party. Members of both parties went. In so doing they took on the role of managing foreign relations, at least relations across the Taiwan Strait. And for Taiwan these were the most important "foreign" relations there were, except for the United States.

Chen was faced with another "situation." He had to keep most Ministry of Foreign Affairs personnel for two reasons: They had civil service protection, and the DPP did not have enough people that had experience in managing foreign policy, much less a sufficient number that spoke English. Thus the KMT remained to a considerable degree in charge of foreign policy implementation, though Chen's own people, inexperienced as they were, made it at the top.

Beijing wouldn't budge from the position that Chen was an advocate of independence unless he would agree to its one-China policy. Beijing took out its anger toward China by discriminating against Taiwan companies and business-people involved in commerce with China that supported Chen. They became the targets of tax and safety rules and a host of others that were not enforced against anyone else. And they did not do this with subtlety; it was in the open.[24]

Chinese leaders assailed Chen's past independence advocacy. They would not brook any notion that he had changed. They talked about his so-called moderate policies as phony. They spoke of his relationship to Vice President Annette Lu as being a "good cop, bad cop" show. Chen, they said, spoke honey words. Lu spoke otherwise.

On May 28, Lu gave a public address saying that Beijing's one-China policy was "a thing of the past." She said that "Taiwan's 23 million people had an 'unshakeable responsibility' to reject it." A reporter in China recalled that she had gone to Japan in April 1995 to "celebrate" the hundredth anniversary of the infamous Treaty of Shimonoseki and thanked Japan for defeating China in the war that ended with that treaty which transferred Taiwan to Japan. Beijing labeled her a "Japanese running dog." Chinese leaders, for this and other things she said, called her "scum." They were not going to deal with her or Chen.

The future of cross-strait relations and the prospects for keeping peace between China and Taiwan at this juncture didn't look good.

Taiwan's 2004 Election: President Chen Wins Reelection amid Controversy while America Is Distracted Elsewhere

In 2004, in March and December, Taiwan held two important elections: a presidential/vice presidential election and a legislative election. Previous elections campaigns had exacerbated relations between Taipei and Beijing and Washington and Beijing. The situation was worse this time.

In the case of the presidential election, President Chen and his party were desperate. They were thus more provocative than usual, especially in pressing Taiwan's independence by calling for referenda and rewriting the constitution. The United States was preoccupied elsewhere—in the Middle East. China had serious cause to doubt the United States would protect Taiwan.

In the wake of the election Taiwan suffered severe political instability with the opposition claiming (with good reason) that the election was stolen. Relations between the ruling party and the opposition were extremely strained. This undermined Taiwan's unity and its ability to fend off China's overtures and threats. Chaos reigned—a situation China had long said would prompt it to take military action to resolve.

The legislative election in December did not resolve Taiwan's political paralysis. Meanwhile China became even more confident it could force Taiwan back into the fold and it showed that in some new and scary ways.

The United States had to deal with a more reckless regime in Taiwan and a more belligerent one in China. This portended miscalculation and conflict.

On March 20, Taiwan held its third direct presidential and vice presidential election. Taiwan's previous presidential elections had been crisis events in U.S.-Taiwan, U.S.-China, and China-Taiwan relations. This one was no less so.[1] The run-up to the election explains this.

After a brief interlude following the 2000 election, Lien Chan reconciled with James Soong and their two parties, the Nationalist Party and the People First Party (PFP), which Soong had formed in the election's aftermath, joined to contain the new elected President Chen. They charged that President Chen and Vice President Lu Hsiu-lien had won by default. Indeed they had; the conservative vote had been split. Furthermore, they said, had there been a provision in the Constitution for a runoff election Chen would not have become president.

"Pan-blue"—Lien's and Soong's parties—also said the Constitution set forth a parliamentary system. It did, generally. Thus Chen, they contended, should exercise very little executive power, since the legislature was the supreme body of government. Chen had a reply: If the system was constitutionally parliamentary or a mixed parliamentary, presidential and cabinet, system it had worked as a presidential system before Chen was elected. Why not now?

Chen and his supporters claimed that relenting to pan-blue's claims would be tantamount to surrendering. Chen was not about to do that. But his party held only a third of the seats in the legislature. The president thus had to try to build a coalition, or, alternatively, rule as a populist president. Chen tried both. He appointed members of the other parties to his cabinet. His premier, Tang Fei, was from the KMT. President Chen left his positions in the DPP. He went to the people with every issue he could. Nothing worked.

Six months into his presidency, the issue of building Taiwan's fourth nuclear power plant came to a head. Chen and the DPP had long railed against nuclear power. They did so during the campaign. Chen promised, if elected, to halt work on the plant. But provisions for building the plant, including such things as contracts with foreign companies to provide essential parts of it, had been duly signed by the previous administration, and approved by the legislature. And Taiwan needed the electricity. When Chen announced terminating the project, pan-blue became enraged. They sought to stop him at any cost. Chen had thrown down the gauntlet and they took the challenge. Pan-blue impeached the president. But there were not enough votes to convict him and remove him. Taiwan's constitution does not make that easy.

The effort polarized Taiwan's politics even more. Gridlock in the extreme followed. This and the worry caused to the business community precipitated an economic downturn. In 2001, Taiwan was in recession. Few alive in Taiwan had seen a serious one. Now they did. The economy contracted almost two percent. Unemployment rose to a figure few had ever witnessed and even fewer thought would ever happen. The opposition blamed Chen. Chen credited pan-blue's incessant obstructionism that paralyzed political decision making, plus the worldwide economic downturn that was especially pronounced in the high tech arena.[2]

Both Chen and pan-blue said the voters should decide. And they would do so in a year-end legislative election. Leading up to the election Lee Teng-hui offered his name and help to found a new political party—the Taiwan Solidarity

Union (TSU). Lee boasted that it was the only party with "Taiwan" in its name. It was more rabid in support of independence than the DPP. There was now no doubt that Lee sanctioned a separate Taiwan and reviled the idea Taiwan should become part of China. Lee defined "localization" (which he promoted as president) unabashedly to mean separation from China and called on KMT members who agreed with him to leave the party and join his TSU. Together the Democratic Progressive Party and the Taiwan Solidarity Union became known as "pan-green," for the DPP's party color and advocated separation.

The DPP made gains at the polls. The TSU did fairly well, especially for a new party. The Nationalist Party, or KMT, did miserably. Soong's PFP did very well.[3] After the election the DPP was the largest in the legislature. But Soong's PFP made even bigger gains. And pan-green still didn't have a majority in the lawmaking body of government. Making matters worse pan-green was determined to win by hook or by crook, and according to pan-blue it was "by crook." The DPP prevailed by "fishing in troubled waters," stirring up tension with China. It also got votes by fanning the flames of ethnic tensions, which harsh words with China facilitated. And pan-green used vote allocation (asking voters to vote for certain party candidates and not others, especially popular ones that were going to win anyway, to increase the number of seats they could garner). This was a very undemocratic practice made possible by Taiwan's single vote, multimember electoral system. Pan-blue called it a "dishonest victory." Perhaps it was. Or was all fair in politics? Either way, gridlock persisted.

After the election pan-blue almost daily complained of Chen's failures and his inability to get things done. They called him the "do-nothing president." Never mind that they blocked his agenda at almost every turn. The opposition also made hay of Chen administration scandals. And President Chen provided grist for their mill.

Chen had used his political influence to get his son assigned to a legal section in the military—even though his test scores were not high enough. Newspapers that favored pan-blue wrote in detail about this when there was a slow news day. They relayed to the public information about Chen's relatives, not government employees, using government vehicles "illegally." And the media reported that Chen's wife and a number of the Chens' friends made huge amounts of money in the stock market in what appeared to be insider trading. This seemed like serious corruption.

The press, whether pro- or anti-Chen, had a field day when information was leaked from somewhere about Chen's rendezvous with a young female aide. The First Lady said it wasn't true, and if it were, she would "take stern measures against her husband." Some said Chen needed an "outlet" because his wife was paralyzed. Others said the scandal made him look much worse because his wife's paralysis had been the product of past KMT "white terror"—though this was never proven and the First Lady did not say this. Attracting more publicity to Chen's "tryst," a popular magazine that led the charge on the story said it got its information from Vice President Lu.

Lu had been marginalized from the decision-making core and was in an angry mood. From the get-go she had been ignored and treated badly. Chen's people assailed her for her "childish" behavior. They said she was put on the ticket "to use just in case": "She was not to have any power; she knew that." Some said she "ought to find a man." Others called her ugly names. So it seemed plausible that she was the source of the story.

Meanwhile, to please the business community President Chen adopted a policy of facilitating trade, investment, and other commercial relations with China. His opponents said he needed and wanted campaign donations. One said that he often repeated what he called a "bromide of American politics"—that the candidate with the most campaign money won ninety percent of the time. Chen was looking ahead to reelection in 2004.

But Lee Teng-hui, Vice President Lu, and many others in the pan-green camp felt that economic ties with China would weaken the cause of independence. They regarded it dangerous for Taiwan to "get hooked." Pan-blue harped on the theme that Taiwan's economic recovery was dependent upon commercial ties with the mainland. Otherwise Taiwan could not get out of the recession. They argued that Chen was trying to push China away politically and build links economically. "Impossible," said pan-blue.

Pan-blue put their pincers on Chen in other ways that related to the economy. They voted on bills that would break Chen's budget. They blocked funds for welfare, undermining Chen's support in several of his big constituencies. They called for tax cuts and spending controls to restore the country's economic health. Pan-blue said at every turn that they had created the Taiwanese economic miracle only to see Chen destroy it. They said Chen had played havoc with the working class and the country and so should be removed.

Chen fell back on inciting local nationalist sentiment and stirring up ill will toward Mainland Chinese and China. He used these tactics in tandem. As ethnic relations worsened, a number of Mainland Chinese in the military and intelligence services defected to China and took military and other state secrets with them in what became sensational news. Chen administration spokespersons called them traitors. Many Chen supporters said all Mainland Chinese were. Pan-blue said Chen wanted to split China and preached ethnic hatred.

During the run-up to the 2004 election, one pundit observed that Taiwan was "in chaos . . . a perfect situation for China to take over."

—m—

Leading up to the 2004 presidential election, the pan-blue and pan-green campaigns drew their battle lines. Unlike previous presidential elections, there were no other contenders. Lien Chan and James Soong got together and formed a joint presidential ticket. They reached an accommodation. Some even said they got along. Lien was older and had the bigger party, so he was on top of the ticket. There were reports that if they won the election Lien would delegate power to Soong, who was considered politically savvier and was more charismatic and energetic. Lien was also to step down after one term, leaving Soong an opportunity to run for president.

The duo calculated that if each could bring in the votes they had won in the 2000 election their "combined ticket" would win the election easily. Their split had given Chen the victory in 2000. Chen reckoned he had a big advantage in incumbency. He and his party no longer needed to grovel for money or press attention. Chen could also control the political scene to his advantage. Thus he could win reelection.

Lien and Soong devised a platform that put the economy front and center. At every campaign stop, they talked about the "economic miracle" that they had engineered and that Chen had destroyed. They promised to put growth back on track. Taiwan's economy had recovered from the 2001 trough to some degree, but most said it still wasn't in good shape. Lien and Soong calculated that even though making the economy their main issue had not worked in the legislative election of 2001, it would now. Their pitch had sunk in.

They also promoted social stability, which the polls showed was likewise their strong suit. They would control crime. They would execute the worst criminals, as opinion polls showed the voters wanted. They promoted a multi-ethnic society and harmony among ethnic groups—which, they contended, Chen and his pan-green camp had deliberately undermined. They said they would avoid war with China, insinuating that pan-green would start one. They regularly queried those who attended campaign rallies: Do you want to die? Do you want your sons to die? Pan-blue characterized Chen and pan-green as provincial, uneducated, lacking intelligence, low-class, narrow-minded hoodlums. They pointed out that Chen had not lived or studied abroad and did not speak English. Lien and Soong had attained PhDs from top American universities.

Lien and Soong tried to offset an advantage pan-green had on the issue of national identity by acquiescing to the idea that Taiwan had a separate identity and that it was a sovereign nation-state. They abandoned the idea of reunification, at least in the short run. China could find solace in neither side, one observer said.

Pan-green's strategy was to win on the local nationalism issue and democratization. President Chen and pan-green leaders portrayed themselves as "Taiwan leaders." They were very aware of polls that showed voters had increasingly come to think of themselves as Taiwanese rather than Chinese and less and less favored identifying and unifying with China. Chen and the DPP also took credit for making Taiwan a democracy. "Democracy had been consolidated by the 2000 election," they said. They spoke of ending authoritarian KMT rule and the inferior position Taiwanese were in during the past when they were ruled by "Mainland Chinese dogs." They boasted of terminating KMT "white terror." They labeled Lien and Soong "foreigners." They called Lien "half-Taiwanese" because his mother was Chinese. They said Lien thought of China as his home, so his advisors were mostly Mainland Chinese. They pointed out that Soong was Mainland Chinese, born in the same province as Mao, who by some accounts had "murdered" more people than the populations of England and

France together, making him the number one human rights villain in human history. Soong was of the same "tribe" that ruled Taiwan with oppression and dictatorship from 1945 until 2000, they noted, and they made fun of his accented Taiwanese.

Chen charged that his opponents had offered no help over the last four years in fixing the economy or enacting political reform, which Taiwan sorely needed. They functioned only as obstructionists. Chen asked for a chance to accomplish his agenda.

Taiwan was polarized politically, socially, and in almost every other respect during the campaign, as much, many people thought, as it could be. "It was about to snap," said one talk-show pundit. To further stir up ethnic and nationalistic feelings to his advantage, Chen called for putting referenda on the ballot. He reckoned if he called for voters to decide whether Taiwan should be an independent nation or unify with China, they would vote the former and vote for him at the same time. President Chen also called for writing a new constitution. The present constitution was "written for China, not Taiwan." "It is out of date and needs to be replaced," he said. These two issues were incendiary. Referenda smacked of a declaration of independence. The DPP had long called for a referendum on the issue. A new constitution would obviously not say that Taiwan was part of China. China castigated Chen and warned against "starting a conflict." China's military spoke of "Chen's acts of war."

Pan-blue opposed both referenda and a new constitution. But the referendum issue had public support. It was also an important trapping of democracy. The constitution had a provision for referenda, but it had never been defined. Were they to be simply advisory? Or did they have the status of law? Nobody knew. So pan-blue, which controlled the legislature, proposed a referendum law.

In November, four months before the election, pan-blue delegates in the legislature passed a referendum bill that defined the procedure. It made it difficult, almost impossible, to use a referendum to change the country's name or flag or define its territory. In addition, the legislature had to initiate the procedure with a three-fourths majority to change the constitution. President Chen was livid; the bill hamstrung him. But he found a way out. Article 17 of the new law allowed the president to call for a referendum if the nation's security were threatened. Chen said it was—by China's positioning several hundred missiles in South China within range of Taiwan. So he put forward two "defensive referenda" in the form of questions: whether to accept China's one country, two systems formula for Taiwan's reunification, and whether to ask China to remove its missiles aimed at Taiwan.

Pan-blue cried foul, saying that "slippery" Chen had violated the law. There was no security threat. But Chen went ahead anyway. Observers said he was desperate. Pan-blue thought the referenda would hurt him rather than help him, as opinion polls suggested. In fact, the many polls taken all showed pan-blue's

Lien and Soong would win the election. Not only did polling suggest this, the TAIEX, Taiwan's stock exchange, concurred. The market was going up, indicating a pan-blue win—reflecting the view that Lien and Soong would better manage the economy. The stocks of specific companies linked to (or partly owned by) pan-green or pan-blue were even more revealing: pan-green companies' stock prices fell; pan-blue companies' stock went up. Confirming the polls and the stock market's signals, the odds provided by those gambling on the election said the same thing. Gambling on elections is illegal in Taiwan; still, there was a lot of it, and it was easy to figure the odds, which favored pan-blue. In the United Kingdom it is legal to bet on elections; there the odds makers said Lien and Soong would win.[4]

Chen Shui-bian thus seemed to be destined to be a one-term president. Future historians would no doubt rate him a failure. But nineteen hours before the voting was to start, in what seemed like a bolt from the blue, the situation dramatically changed. President Chen and Vice President Lu, while on the campaign trail, were both shot.

As if orchestrated in advance, the pan-green campaign machine went to work in southern Taiwan. Here was its base of support; but voters lacked enthusiasm because of serious disappointment with Chen's governance. But, they could be energized. DPP campaign officials blamed the communists (Chinese) for the assassination attempt, in collaboration with pan-blue. Campaigners conveniently did not report that the president and vice president had suffered only superficial wounds, so the incident generated a sizeable sympathy vote. This was enough to change the election results. Chen and Lu won by a margin the width of a hair. They got 0.2 percent more votes than pan-blue. China had not interfered in the campaign; yet Chen used the "China bogeyman" to win.

Foreign reporters said that Chen and Lu being shot was "too good to be true." Pan-blue charged the shooting was staged.[5] The circumstances certainly engendered suspicion. Both Chen and Lu had been wearing bulletproof vests earlier that day, but not when they were shot. The gun used to shoot them was a low caliber and the bullets did not contain much explosive power. This said there was no intent to kill. Though the incident happened in broad daylight and was on film, the police did not make any arrests. President Chen did not order the airports or harbors closed. He did not refer to an assailant. He ordered his driver to a hospital, but not the nearest one. He went to a hospital owned by a friend. A nurse said later that "official looking people" had been around to check on the hospital the day before. One of Chen's closest associates announced that there was a bullet lodged in the president's body, alarming the public by suggesting that it was a life-threatening wound. The bullet was really in his coat.

After the election, pan-blue charged that the election had been stolen. Opinion surveys showed that most people questioned the truth about the shooting. Pan-blue supporters protested for days, tying up the capital city and cities elsewhere. Anger was apparent on their faces. Many cried. Taiwan was again in chaos.

—m—

Only days later when the Election Commission had declared that Chen and Lu had won did the United States send a message of congratulations. And there was a caveat—"pending resolution of legal challenges." The message did not specifically mention Chen and Lu. Vice President Lu complained publicly that the United States should send a personal message of congratulations as was customary. Going through the back door, the Chen administration in early April solicited a formal letter of congratulations "bestowed on Chen and Lu" from the director of the American Institute in Taiwan (the organization that handles U.S. relations with Taiwan, located just outside Washington, D.C.), Teresa Shaheen. Shaheen was subsequently fired.

Meanwhile, President Chen, in an interview with the *Washington Post*, proclaimed that the election had given him a mandate to press ahead with plans to "develop Taiwan as an independent, sovereign country." He rejected the idea of one China and said that China's rule of Hong Kong since 1997 was a "negative example" for Taiwan. Chen also promised to go ahead with his proposal to pen a new Constitution. The Department of State, according to an official there, felt it was "thrown a curve" with Chen's "belligerence." Officials at Foggy Bottom had thought that Chen had been tamed.[6]

The new Hu Jintao leadership in China was challenged. It did not want the military to take matters into its hands—which seemed very possible. Hu's strategy was to ask the United States to control Chen in return for China's support on terrorism, North Korea and more. The United States needed China, so Hu thought. Would this work?

In December, President Bush had, in the presence of China's Premier Wen Jiabao, who was visiting Washington, warned Chen about "trying to change the status quo in the Taiwan Strait." Bush suggested that President Chen was a troublemaker. The State Department subsequently issued warnings every time Chen talked about a referendum or a new constitution or otherwise called for an independent Taiwan. They did so immediately and in anger. The Bush administration, labeled the most pro-Taiwan ever in 2001, was so no more. Chen was now seen as causing unwanted trouble.

After the *Post* interview, the State Department immediately reacted. It said it was holding Chen to his 2000 inauguration promises not to declare independence, write a new constitution, and so on. The tone was very hostile. In what was judged by most observers to be a delayed response, Undersecretary of State for Asia and the Pacific James Kelly, in testimony before Congress, asserted that there was a "misunderstanding" in Taiwan that the United States would "defend them at all costs." It was clear that the U.S. government was suspicious about the election result and that it regarded President Chen as having taken advantage of the United States to get reelected. Some called him a "loose cannon." Others said he was a "danger to the United States." One observer compared him to Chiang Kai-shek, who, he said, wanted the United States and China to go to war so he could pick up the pieces. Another said Chen didn't care if he sparked a crisis; that would ensure Taiwan's independence. Still another asserted, "Washington should let it be known that if there were to be a conflict with China the United States should decide the time and the place, not Chen." Some compared Chen and Taiwan to the start of World War II.

China finally responded to Chen's *Post* interview, calling his proposal to write a new constitution a "timetable for independence that we will never tolerate." A top official said that Taiwan had "crossed the line." Beijing saw that the United States had shifted course on Taiwan. Some in China said the United States had to have China's support on global issues. Would the United States sacrifice Taiwan?

Beijing would test this theory. Two days later Chinese security officials arrested two high-ranking military officers for spying for Taiwan. The timing did not seem random. The government then leveled an attack on Taiwanese businessmen who "think they can make money in China to support independence in Taiwan." Chi Mei Corporation and its head, Hsu Wen-long, whose hospital took care of President Chen after the shooting, were cited. News commentators in China speculated that Chinese leaders perceived that Taiwan's investment in China was no longer important or that they were willing to sacrifice some of China's economic growth to "deal with Taiwan." This contradicted the notion that China was restrained in its actions because of its overriding concern with economic development. "So much for that theory," said an observer in Taiwan.

China's big "probe" of U.S. policy came in July. The Chinese PLA, announcing its intentions in advance, launched a gigantic war game simulation of an invasion of Taiwan. Coinciding with the exercise, former president and former head of the Chinese Communist Party Jiang Zemin (who had remained in charge of military policy) set a date for Taiwan's recovery. This had never been done before.[7] It was reported in the Chinese press that eighteen thousand troops took part in the drill and that it had been several months in preparation. Land, sea, and air "practice runs for an island invasion" started on Dongshan Island off China's southeast coast. Dongshan resembled Taiwan, according to onlookers. It was also disclosed that the participation of the Chinese Air Force was aimed at proving something new: that China could maintain air superiority over the Taiwan Strait—a new challenge to both the United States and Taiwan.[8]

The Bush administration was angry at Taiwan but could not ignore China's affront. Bush sent National Security Advisor Condoleezza Rice to China ahead of the military exercises to persuade China not to go ahead. Chinese leaders rebuffed her.[9] They were irate over President Chen's statements before the election about a new constitution and his comments after the election to the *Washington Post*. They opposed U.S. arms sales to Taiwan. They said the Patriot missiles and submarines in the most recent arms package sold to Taiwan by the United States were designed to negate China's best military options against Taiwan: a missile attack and a naval blockade. Chinese leaders were also angry at this time that President Bush announced U.S. support for Taiwan's joining the World Health Organization, as this was seen as a stamp of approval for Taiwan's sovereignty.[10]

Chinese military brass apparently perceived that they could intimidate the United States. China had recently put two Russian-made Sovremenny-class destroyers, the *Fuzhou* and the *Hangzhou*, into operation. They were called "aircraft-carrier killers" and reportedly would prevent U.S. carriers from getting too close to Taiwan. China had also just sent a new locally built submarine to sea, apparently without the United States' being aware of it until it appeared on a Chinese Web site. It was timed perfectly for maximum impact.[11] Taiwan's new weapons were not in operation. And the United States was preoccupied in the Middle East and its military stretched way too thin, so Chinese military leaders calculated.

But the Bush administration did not blink; rather it accepted the challenge and decided to do some intimidating itself. Actually, U.S. operations were planned well in advanced and coincided almost exactly with the Chinese operations; it seemed that the United States had anticipated the Chinese war games. The U.S. exercise, called Summer Pulse, was reportedly designed to increase American preparedness for any global crisis. Seven aircraft carrier groups participated along with fifty ships, six hundred aircraft, and 150,000 troops. It was reported to be the largest naval exercise the United States ever held.[12] Though the "training" was done in different parts of the world, the timing and other aspects of the move signaled that it was aimed at China. Military experts revealed it was held in response to tension in the Taiwan Strait. One military strategist said it was "gunboat diplomacy" and was intended to warn China "not to step over the line" regarding Taiwan.[13]

Adding to U.S.-China tensions, Congress passed a resolution reaffirming America's promise to supply Taiwan with arms, saying it was concerned about China's deployment of missiles aimed at Taiwan. Officials in China criticized the U.S. legislative body for interference. *People's Daily* subsequently carried an editorial saying that the U.S. actions "exposed a wild ambition for world domination."[14]

—∿∿—

In December 2004 Taiwan had another election: a legislative contest. As in the spring, the campaign and the election's aftermath generated the high level of tension between the United States and China—with Taiwan acting as provocateur.

The campaign reflected deep feelings of bitterness that followed the March election. Pan-blue continued to charge that "Chen had stolen the election . . . that the shooting was fake . . ." "It was choreographed in advance," one adamant supporter said. Pan-blue spokespersons cited the fact that a large number of voters, meaning the military and the police, had been disenfranchised by President Chen, who ordered them to remain at their posts. They would have voted for Lien and Soong. They mentioned pan-green's campaign machine immediately taking advantage of the shooting by trying to implicate pan-blue and China. Pan-blue stopped its campaign out of respect, thinking the president and vice president were seriously injured; pan-green went on campaigning.

After holding large protest rallies, some of which turned violent, pan-blue challenged the validity of the election. They called for a recount of votes. They asked for judicial intervention. Lien and Soong proclaimed that Chen's victory was tainted and that his presidency was not legitimate. They called him a crook and a fraud. They decried the ethnic bigotry spawned by the "Chen dictatorship." They said Chen and his government were corrupt and had hijacked the election process, that "democracy had devolved."

President Chen called Lien and Soong sore losers. He expected the public to agree with him more the longer they carried on the protest. Some Chen spokespersons said that pan-blue had caused such chaos that Taiwan was in a state of anarchy, and that was one of the situations China had said on numerous occasions was justification for its invading the island. "This is exactly what pan-blue wanted," they asserted. "The pan-blue traitors would help China's military when it arrived."

In mid-April, pan-blue officials issued a statement describing the shooting as "a day that will live in infamy." They offered additional reasons to doubt pan-green's account of the event. They concluded that only because of the "phony shooting" did Chen and Lu get enough votes to win.[15] Pan-blue, with its majority in the legislature and unified because of the election defeat, passed a bill creating a "Truth Commission" to, it said, "ascertain the facts." President Chen, noting that it had investigative powers that belonged to the executive branch, called it unconstitutional. He allowed it to be formed, but then stonewalled.

At this juncture, Henry Lee, a noted forensic expert (who had given evidence in the O. J. Simpson trial), issued a delayed report on the shooting. Lee said that the president and vice president had actually been shot. But he suggested it was not a genuine assassination attempt, in view of the small-caliber bullets used and where they hit. He added that the crime scene had not been preserved, making it difficult to say much more. Lee's report did not by any means end the controversy. In fact, it made the shooting appear more mysterious.

While pan-blue's protest was annoying to many potential voters and the Nationalist Party appeared to be splitting over the question of whether Lien should resign as chairman and if so who should replace him, pan-green seemed to face equally serious problems. Thus it was difficult to predict who would win the coming legislative election. Observers noted that "some agencies" of the U.S. government were irate with Chen and didn't care if they influenced the election in pan-blue's favor. This patently was the case with the Department of State and seemed to have spread into the White House. Then came evidence this view was true, or so believed many people in Taiwan.

In September, without any warning, the FBI arrested former Deputy Assistant Secretary of State for East Asia, Donald Keyser, in a restaurant just outside Washington. The bureau hinted it was a "spy case." What Keyser had done (taking unauthorized trips to Taiwan and providing "talking points" documents to Taiwan officials), however, seemed trivial. Some said he was being used to "send a signal to President Chen."

On the heels of the Keyser "incident," Secretary of State Colin Powell, while on a trip to China, told members of the press that Taiwan "is not independent."

He even asserted that Taiwan does not enjoy sovereignty. "That is our firm policy," Powell declared. Leaders in Taiwan, as expected, were upset. Foreign Minister Mark Chen called it a "breach of trust." Powell's statements flabbergasted almost everyone in Taiwan. Some opined that "the U.S. is about to betray us." Powell later said that U.S. policy had not changed, obliquely saying that he had misspoken. But most observers thought that this experienced diplomat would not make such an egregious error; rather he said it deliberately to tell the Chen administration to keep its independence rhetoric to itself and not try to provoke China to its political advantage in the election campaign.

Further complicating formulating an election strategy, especially for pan-green, the United States was holding a presidential election in November. Some in the Chen administration were angry with President Bush over the "pressure" he had put on Taipei and his "proactive negative statements" about President Chen provoking China. Some pan-green labeled the Bush administration "conservative, just like pan-blue." On taxes, welfare, and a number of issues they were right. Pan-green had an affinity for John Kerry. But Kerry's worldview was something else. Senator Kerry liked Europe. His outlook was Eurocentric. He didn't seem to like or care about Asia. He certainly did not talk of Asia's growing importance to the United States, as Bush and Republicans did. Most of all, Kerry said that the United States "should not spill its soldiers' blood to protect Taiwan." One might conclude, and pan-green leaders did, that a Kerry administration would not adhere to the security guarantees in the TRA and would not come to Taiwan's rescue if China should lay siege to the island. In that event Taiwan would have to surrender or China's PLA would lay waste to the island. Taiwan would not only not be independent, it would not survive in its present form. So President Chen kept quiet about the U.S. presidential election.

He did talk about independence, but carefully. He used the usual barbs to criticize the opposition: past oppression, current obstructionism, and corruption. Premier Yu promised to wipe out vote buying and block the KMT from selling its media holdings to foreigners. Chen also played the ethnic card. He called on "his people" to vote for the DPP. He vilified China to stir up local nationalistic sentiments.

Pan-blue used its usual pitch: it would make the economy grow, maintain law and order and social stability, end ethnic bigotry, and avoid war with China.

The juggernaut in the campaign was the issue of Taiwan's buying the US$18.2 billion package of weapons allocated by the Bush administration in 2001. The cabinet had approved the purchase at the time, but then the matter had gotten bogged down in the legislature. Pan-blue sought to use it as leverage against Chen. They wanted to embarrass him to gain political advantage. And they did.

The United States was not happy about the delays. Taiwan was not doing its job. But the United States did not blame pan-blue. Washington was too angry with Chen. Pushing the purchase got Chen into hot water with members of his party and many supporters. The DPP had long opposed large defense spending.

That money should go to social welfare, many DPP supporters thought. So Chen didn't want to be too out front on the issue. But pan-blue forced him to. Some said sarcastically, "Chen says he wants independence; but he isn't willing to fight for it." Some called him "incredibly naive." Some said he was a "born coward."

Chen hoped to marginalize and defuse the issue. But he couldn't. He could not control the media in Taiwan. In August it was reported that U.S. defense strategists working together with their Taiwan counterparts did a computer simulation of a Chinese invasion. The conclusion: Taiwan could hold out for only six hours, not the few weeks it had been assumed before.[16] Several newspapers wrote, some of them headline stories, about Taiwan's nuclear weapons program. Was Taiwan working on an atomic bomb again? Some speculated that was the case. The alleged nuclear weapons project was portrayed as logical and necessary in view of China's missile buildup and Taiwan's doing little to counter it.

Seemingly confirming these reports, top-level officials in Taiwan had been debating the matter of Taiwan acquiring deterrence to cope with China's growing missile threats. In September Premier Yu spoke of evoking a "balance of terror" policy. "If you attack Kaohsiung...I will counterattack Shanghai," he said.[17] There were even discussions about bombing China's Three Gorges Dam.[18] Some described this as apocalyptic.

On top of all of this, less than a month before the voters were to cast their ballots, the press reported that during a flight to the Pescadores, President Chen's plane (which he was on) was diverted because Chinese fighter planes got too close.[19] Did China intend to shoot down the plane and kill Chen? Nobody knew, or at least nobody said.

Going into the stretch, President Chen and his party appeared frantic to find new issues that would resonate with voters. Chen looked for ways to provoke China. But he was hemmed in. "Damn the United States," said one of his advisers. The president called for Taiwan's textbooks to be revised. When Japan did this, Beijing had gone ballistic. In one of his statements Chen called Sun Yat-sen (the revered father of Nationalist China) a "foreigner" (meaning he was Chinese, not Taiwanese). This was indeed provocative.

Chen again called for a referendum. He also said he wanted to replace the "Chinese constitution" with a Taiwanese one. When Chen did this, the United States promptly warned him, through Richard Boucher, a Department of State spokesperson, that the United States was opposed to any referendum that would change Taiwan's status. He referred to President Chen's 2000 inauguration speech promises. Boucher said, "We take...that pledge very seriously."

—ᴍᴍ—

When the returns were in, pan-blue proclaimed victory. Pan-green admitted defeat. President Chen accepted blame and said he would give up his position as head of the party. Premier Yu offered his resignation. Lien Chan said that the people had spoken and that the pan-blue victory was "a victory for the Republic of China." James Soong said the victory meant the people were not supportive of Taiwan's independence. It was not a big win for pan-blue, but it reversed the tide of pan-green victories since 2000. Pan-blue would continue to control the legislature. Pan-green would be unable to pass legislation without pan-blue's cooperation.

The DPP had not done as well as expected or as well as its leaders had promised. President Chen wanted to control the legislature; he would not. Increasingly citizens were self-identifying as Taiwanese, not Chinese; so why would pan-green lose? Some attributed pan-green's defeat to a poor election strategy. Its leaders indeed focused on Taiwan's national identity too much and forgot about key bread-and-butter issues. Some said China was restrained and didn't do anything to anger voters and that this helped pan-blue. In addition, pan-blue, it was said, "stole" pan-green supporters by opposing the arms bill and suggesting the money better be spent on welfare and education.

Some said the United States influenced the election against Chen. Washington certainly didn't help pan-green, as it had in previous elections. It seems it helped pan-blue. Its criticisms of President Chen for provoking tensions were quick and frequent and sometimes bitter. Chen couldn't use the independence issue effectively enough to help his party and his bloc. Department of State officials said they were determined not to let Chen set the agenda on U.S.-China policy. More salient still, they were not going to let him start a crisis between the United States and China. America was too involved in the Middle East. More candid officials said that China "mattered"; Taiwan didn't, and they were not going to let "that little fart" (meaning Chen) start trouble just to help himself politically. Just before the voting, though the news didn't get to Taiwan until after the election, Richard Armitage, Assistant Secretary of State and one of the big foreign policy making players in Washington, said Taiwan was a "landmine" in U.S.-China relations. This reflected the fairly common view espoused by the Department of State that Taiwan "wasn't worth it." The United States should dump Taiwan, some said. Was this the view of the White House? Sometimes, or so it seemed. Where would this lead?

After the election there was the perception in Washington that Chen was now more dangerous than ever. Some said he might behave like "an injured beast." Certainly he was upset with the setback and wanted to do something. Perhaps that explains the rumor that was reported in the Taiwan papers a few days later, that during a high level foreign policy meeting in the White House President Bush said Chen was a "troublesome son-of-a-bitch."

But if Chen was troublesome, so was Beijing. Chinese leaders didn't take the election setback for pan-green as a victory and bask in the sun and enjoy it. China apparently viewed it as something to exploit and intended to strike a blow. Indeed, Beijing's reaction was not one of hopefulness; rather it was aggressive in tone. Not only that, but actions were going to follow; China's legislature was preparing to pass a law forbidding Taiwan's independence to lock this in as policy. This would take away flexibility for present or future leaders.

But the United States beat China to the punch. In mid-February 2005, the U.S.-Japan Security Consultative Committee, the organization that oversees the defense agreement that governs military relations between the United States and Japan, met. The consensus of the meeting: Taiwan was a "mutual security concern." For the United States, this was obvious, but for Japan to say this was a major policy change.

Japan had reason. For fifteen years, Japan had worried about China's military buildup. And during that time Tokyo's apprehension increased as China passed huge defense budgets every year and put more weapons and weapons systems into operation. Some Japanese media critics said Japan was "helping China" do this. Tokyo was still giving China large amounts of financial assistance and loans. It wasn't going to China's military directly, but it allowed China to divert its own money to the military, so it was almost the same thing. Commentators were saying that Tokyo was providing the money for China to "hang" Japan. Japan was also tired of China's complaining about Japan's revising its school textbooks to "cover up," according to China, Japan's World War II atrocities and objecting to Japan's prime minister visiting Yasakuni Shrine in Tokyo—the burial site of Japan's war dead.

Japanese felt China was interfering in Japan's domestic affairs. What if Japan complained about China's distorting the events of World War II? (The Communists took credit for defeating Japan and gave none to the Nationalists and little to the United States.) And what of China saying its human rights abuses were its domestic concern and none of anyone else's business?

Just before Japan made the decision to formally state that Taiwan was a matter of Japan's security concern, North Korea had unashamedly announced that it had nuclear weapons. Tokyo might say, if it needed an out, that its decision was prompted by a security concern pursuant to North Korea's shocking statement. Alternatively, Japan might have been thinking that it believed intelligence reports to the effect that China had assisted North Korea to go nuclear. Indeed, China in the past had taken the position that the more nuclear powers there were the better to offset America's "nuclear monopoly."

Linking Taiwan directly to the issue of the "China threat," some weeks earlier the Japanese military had discovered a Chinese submarine in Japanese waters. This was taken by Japan as an "act of belligerence." Some said China was testing Japan's readiness. Taiwan's intelligence had reportedly given Japan a heads-up about the submarine. President Chen even said so publicly.[20]

The United States, of course, pushed Japan into making this security policy statement. But Japan was willing or saw it had no choice. Earlier, when Secretary of State Colin Powell told Japan that it needed to get rid of Article 9 (the "peace provision" that in the Japanese constitution that restricted Japan's rights to re-build its military and act as a "normal country" in the military realm) if it wanted U.S. support to become a permanent member of the U.N. Security Council, which China opposed.

The director of the Central Intelligence Agency, Porter Goss, had recently said on record that China's military build-up was "tilting the balance" in the Taiwan Strait.[21] Secretary of Defense Donald Rumsfeld expressed deep concern about the expanding strength of the Chinese Navy. Congress heard their statements. Security pundits said that the United States was preoccupied with Iraq and did not at all want a crisis in the Taiwan Strait. Washington sought to keep Taiwan under control. In the meantime, to deal with China it needed to balance China's military expansion with allies.

Beijing reacted to Japan's decision with obvious anger. The Foreign Ministry said that any joint statement about Taiwan "interferes in China's internal affairs and hurts China's sovereignty." Spokespersons condemned "irresponsible remarks" about China's military buildup. Chinese leaders stated that the United States and Japan had defined Taiwan as a regional issue and that their statement changed the U.S. security relationship with Japan from defending Japan to a "regional pact." And China would not stand for that.

This may explain what it did just days later. The Chinese government had been contemplating a law to ban Taiwan from declaring independence, making it mandatory that China take military action if it did. The law was called "the Anti-Secession Law." When the law was suggested earlier, Taiwan expressed strong opposition to it. In fact, an opinion poll indicated eighty-three percent of the population opposed it.[22] In early March, DPP leaders called it a "war-mandating law" and criticized it with considerable verve. Premier Frank Hsieh suggested immediately deleting the term "Republic of China" from the Taiwanese constitution in order to break formal and legal ties with China.[23]

The United States had also criticized the proposed law. But Beijing was undaunted. Hurriedly, on March 14, China's legislature, the National People's Congress, met and by a vote of 2,896 to 0 passed the law. It went into effect the same day. It declared that "if secessionist forces move to declare independence or the possibilities for peaceful reunification become exhausted" China will "employ non-peaceful means and other necessary measures to protect its territorial integrity." After he signed the law, President Hu advised the military to prepare for a possible war.[24]

In reaction President Chen called on citizens to join a rally to oppose the legislation and express Taiwan's anger. Several hundred thousand people came. Some burned Chinese flags in front of television cameras and defaced images of China. The crowd sang American protest songs.[25] Defense Minister Lee Jye called for more military spending. Tensions ran high.

Secretary of State Condoleezza Rice criticized China's action. Congress called hearings. Numerous senators and representatives lambasted the law.

What were China's motives? With the European Union debating whether to end the arms embargo against China that was put in place after the Tiananmen massacre, it seemed Beijing didn't care what Europe thought or did. Chinese leaders seemed to want to get back at Japan for putting Taiwan within its area of "security interest." Damn Europe's reaction. Damn Taiwan's response. And damn what America might do. China's military may have demanded the law and civilian leaders, including Hu Jintao, could only cave in lest they lose the support of the generals.

In addition, China had long hated it when U.S. officials cited the "U.S. law passed by Congress" (the TRA), saying they were constrained by it. Now Chinese leaders could say they lacked flexibility in dealing with the Taiwan issue. Said one observer, "China now has its TRA." Chinese leaders would indeed be boxed in. No leader could now be moderate on Taiwan. As a consequence war looked much more likely, maybe inevitable.

Just a few days later, Taiwan responded. Said one observer, "Taiwan upped the ante." The Ministry of National Defense announced the successful test of its Hsiung Feng (Brave Wind) II-E cruise missile. The missile was capable of hitting targets a thousand kilometers away. That included Shanghai, China's largest city, and other major metropolitan areas in Southeast China. A military spokesperson said the missile would go into mass production soon.[26] Not to be upstaged, China conducted its own missile test. It fired a Ju Lang-2, a submarine launched ballistic missile that could put nuclear bombs on cities all over the United States from subs hidden in the vast Pacific Ocean.[27] This put the United States in grave danger.

In July, Major General Zhu Chenghu, Dean of China's National Defense University's Strategic Studies Institute, caused a major flap when he declared that China "would attack more than one hundred American cities with nuclear weapons if the United States interferes in a war between China and Taiwan." American officials protested, but Chinese Communist Party leaders refused to refute the statement, leading observers to say this was really China's thinking. The U.S. House of Representatives forthwith passed a motion calling on the Chinese government to repudiate Zhu's comments, fire him, renounce the use of force against Taiwan. China did not respond to any of the demands.[28]

Barely seven months later the U.S. Department of Defense published its Quadrennial Defense Review and cited China as the "country with the greatest potential to challenge the United States militarily." It also mentioned China's "steady . . . secretive military buildup in the pace and scope . . . which . . . already puts regional military balances at risk." The report recommended the production of weapons aimed at the "China Threat": units to fight unconventional foes, attack submarines and other high tech weapons.[29]

PART V

CONCLUSIONS

13

The Taiwan Strait Is a Flash Point

T he previous pages of this book have painted a pessimistic picture, suggesting that future conflicts, including more serious ones, between the United States and the People's Republic of China over Taiwan are likely. There is, of course, another argument: that there will be no coming conflict, no serious one at least, and that the problems that have evoked several crises between the United States and China over Taiwan to date either will fade or can be resolved. In other words, there will be no war.

In fact, many policy makers, as well as a large number of academic pundits, espouse the view that the United States and China will avoid any serious conflict that could result in war in the future. The thrust of the argument is this: because the United States and the People's Republic of China have strong mutual interests—strategic, political, and especially commercial—they will work out their differences.

A review of the arguments pro and con; domestic variables in the United States, China, and Taiwan that influence the triangular relationship; and the nature and structure of the international system, any of which may encourage or discourage a conflagration, is in order.

—ɷ—

The most frequently heard argument against Washington-Beijing hostility leading to another, more serious military conflict is that trade has so linked the United States and China, and China and Taiwan into mutually dependent relationships that none of the three countries would dare consider policies that truly risk war. Investments and other commercial ties are equally weighty and will likewise, it is said, propel the United States and China, and China and Taiwan, toward more mutual understanding and closer, friendlier relations.

More specifically the argument, seeing Beijing as the most likely aggressor, is that China launched a series of reforms after Deng Xiaoping came to power in 1978 and with those reforms there grew a realization within the Chinese leadership that China should, through trade, take advantage of the international division of labor to make the nation prosper (other approaches having obviously failed). The United States was critical to this plan's success. America, the world's largest market, soon became an important buyer of China's exports and hence a vital trading partner. In fact, from exports to the United States of just over US$300 million in 1978, China's economic ties with America boomed such that by 1992 Beijing sent nearly US$26 billion of products or services to the American marketplace. During this period the proportion of China's foreign sales going to the United States rose from only a few percent to 30 percent, making the United States the world's top consumer of Chinese-made products.

It thus became the generally accepted wisdom that, with its economic growth being export driven and the United States the biggest consumer, Beijing would be foolish to pick a fight with the United States. Adding to the force of this argument, social and political stability, even the regime's survival, hinged on sustaining this situation. In fact, it was said with great frequency that the paramount goal of the new Chinese leadership was to keep Washington-Beijing relations on track and avoiding any conflict that might upset the relationship.[1] Chinese leaders, in fact, said this openly and often.

Meanwhile, the United States became addicted to its growing trade with China. By 1998, China had become the sixth largest buyer of U.S. products. Profit margins were high. The health of many big companies in the United States, in fact, became dependent on the rapidly expanding China market. Big business in the United States became so enthralled with China—America's fastest-growing foreign market—that it came to constitute a pro-Beijing China lobby, one that exerted enormous political clout in the United States. Labor in some ways also gained. Exports to China by the end of the 1990s guaranteed the jobs of 300,000 American workers many of them union members.[2]

U.S. investments in China also played a role in building better U.S.-China relations. China used American capital to build factories to export and improve the infrastructure to get its products to ports. Both facilitated its export boom. By 1998 there were over 26,000 U.S-funded projects in China, worth US$45 billion.[3] Both individual and corporate investments generated impressive profits, thus building commitments by U.S. individuals and companies to continuing good relations with China.

The same things happened between China and Taiwan. Before 1987 when indirect trade was established, commercial relations across the Taiwan Strait were insignificant. Trade grew to US$1.7 billion that year and continued to skyrocket after that, reaching US$5 billion in 1990, US$11 billion in 1993 and US$20 billion in 1995. By the end of the decade, cross-strait trade exceeded US$30 billion annually. As a result, cross-strait relations changed in a critical way: Taiwan and

China became major trading partners; in fact in the mid-1990s China became Taiwan's second largest export market.[4]

Taiwan's investments in China grew almost proportionally. From 1991 to 1995, according to Taiwan sources, investors made more than eleven thousand applications, worth more than US$56 billion, to invest in China. According to Beijing sources, Taiwan investment projects in China numbered nearly thirty-two thousand and were worth more than US$114 billion.[5] After Hong Kong, Taiwan became China's largest "foreign" investor, edging out the United States, Japan, and Europe. When Hong Kong reverted to China in 1997, Taiwan became number one. U.S.-Taiwan trade and investment ties, which began much earlier, continued to expand, as did the commercial "stake" each had in the other.

Thus not only was there a case for mutual or symbiotic economic self-interest linking the three, making hostility among them undesirable if not unthinkable, but history had a lesson to share: countries that are deeply connected by trade and other commercial interests do not go to war. They instead resolve their problems by negotiations. As students of international politics often point out, France and Germany have long been hostile neighbors. Now that they are locked together in an economic community and commercial relations between them are extensive, war between them is not likely enough to consider seriously. The truism that people and nations doing business with each other don't fight has many supporters. Simplifying the argument, one writer put it this way: "No two nations that both have McDonald's stores have ever gone to war." (China and Taiwan, and, of course, the United States all had lots of McDonald's hamburger franchises: 578 in China and Taiwan at this time.)[6]

The argument that commercial relations keep the peace is further strengthened by the fact that in the case of China's relations with both the United States and Taiwan, economic ties were fostered to a large degree by the development of a free market economy in China. Free market capitalism has been, both traditionally and in the present era, the wellspring of democracy. And it is widely known that democracies, like nations that trade, do not go to war. The grist for this argument is so plentiful that many accept it as being self-evident.

As already noted, since 1978 China has steadily adopted a free market economic system. By the 1990s, China's private sector was as large or larger proportionally than most Western capitalist democracies. Democracy thus seemed inevitable. As a matter of fact, if one looks beyond its reported human rights condition and compares fundamental freedoms and civil rights under the present regime with those of China under Mao (rather than with Taiwan or Western democracies), China has changed dramatically for the better. Chinese citizens no longer experience Chinese Communist Party and government efforts to totally control their lives as in Mao's day. They can travel, move their residences, and set up businesses. They can talk more candidly. Compared to the past, freedom abounds in China.

Meanwhile, the decentralization of the economy under Deng's rule has resulted in a manifestly more open and free local governments throughout China. This has also advanced the cause of civil liberties and democracy.[7] In fact, if one looks at local politics in China rather than national politics, one sees other important changes. Elections at the local level in many parts of China are competitive. This is where democracy started in Taiwan. It then seeped up. It will likely do this in China as well over the next two or three decades.

China in other ways shows that it is democratizing. It is establishing a meaningful legal system and the rule of law. The press is freer. The use of the Internet, a good sign in terms of predicting the growth of basic freedoms, some say, is expanding rapidly.[8] Many observers of China believe that links with the outside world, especially with the West, will ensure that these democratic trends continue. Contacts with the West have already created extensive bonds of friendship and mutual understanding.

Regarding China's foreign contacts, some of the specifics are telling. China sends more foreign students to the United States than any nation in the world. Chinese students have done well, and most have returned to China. Tens of thousands, in fact, have gone back, many to assume important positions in government, business, and elsewhere. They have taken American culture and democratic ideals with them. They have facilitated various other forms of interchange, not to mention encouraging more students to go to U.S. universities.

There are similarly broad cultural ties between the United States and China. Nearly all large and medium-sized cities, and even many small cities, in the United States have sister cities in China. There are China friendship groups all over the United States. Military exchanges, which were canceled after the Tiananmen massacre, have been put back on track. Many of China's top-ranking military officers have been to the United States. Most have enjoyed the trip and the "American experience" (as many of them call it). And they have established cordial ties with counterpart American military officers, who have gone to China in significant numbers. This certainly makes conflict by miscalculation between the militaries of each country less likely, and means it can more easily be de-escalated or contained if it does occur. It will no doubt also dampen anti-American sentiment in the military in China over the long run.

Perhaps most important, China has many new leaders that are foreign educated and understand and like the United States. This was the case of Taiwan a couple of decades ago, and Taiwan, many say, is a bellwether that forecasts China's future. The first generation of leaders (Mao and Chiang) didn't speak a foreign language, didn't spend much time outside of China, and didn't know much about the West. And they hated each other. Deng Xiaoping and Chiang Ching-kuo were different. They were "great reformers," and neither carried so much baggage from the past. Lee Teng-hui and Jiang Zemin noticeably cared even less about past feuds and were even more international and more unabashed democratizers than their predecessors. The new generation of leaders in both China and Taiwan are reportedly even more enlightened and democratic in their outlooks. In fact, these words have been used to describe both Taiwan's President Chen Shui-bian and China's President Hu Jintao.

Another reason China is unlikely to be aggressive, it is said, is that China is a country that does not have a martial tradition. Historically, soldiers were not revered in China. Further evidence against the "China danger" thesis is the fact that historically China was never a naval power and only infrequently invaded other lands (but rather was often invaded itself). Currently China, it is noted, does not have a military that can project power. It has no aircraft carriers. It does not have troops stationed beyond its borders and possesses no foreign bases.[9] Thus, China, in terms of its basic nature, is not an aggressor nation.

One more argument against a U.S.-China conflict is that the United States is too far ahead of China in terms of military power for China to challenge America for the next twenty years at least. The United States currently has ten to twenty times as many nuclear weapons and delivery systems as China. China's military is weak in many other areas as well. It would hence be insane for China to pick a fight with the United States over anything, including Taiwan, for at least a generation. Chinese leaders have, in fact, said this.[10]

By the time China catches up with the United States, as the argument against China's being a threat to the United States goes, it will be a democracy so permeated by American culture it will have no inclination to act aggressively toward the United States, Taiwan, or anyone else. On the other side of the coin, there is the argument that the United States will not engage in a land war because of the lessons learned in Vietnam. Asia is a "quagmire."

Then there is the impact the media (which, almost as a requirement of the profession, magnifies any situation where there is loss of life, especially that of Americans). The U.S. antiwar media has played up the danger of a U.S.-China conflict and will in the future, thus helping prevent it. Supplementing this argument is the fact that American families are now small and cannot stand to lose a son (or daughter). Certainly America is different from what it was fifty years ago. Add to these arguments the view held by many in America that Taiwan is too small, too insignificant, and too far away for the United States to shed blood over. And, as China acquires more nuclear weapons and delivery systems that can explode them over America's cities, a nuclear balance of terror will evolve. This prevented war between the United States and the Soviet Union during the Cold War; it will prevail in future U.S.-China relations.

Finally, there is diplomacy. Diplomatic talks can resolve U.S.-China disagreements. The two sides talk; in fact, they very effectively resolved their problems as U.S.-China relations evolved from extreme hostility during the early phase of the Cold War to a friendly relationship during the 1970s and 1980s. This will no doubt continue.

—ɯ—

There are, of course, fallacies in these arguments as well as counterarguments.

Trade no doubt lessens the probability of conflict between nations. So do other commercial ties, usually. But there are no guarantees. Moreover, examples

abound of conflicts and wars between countries that had very extensive economic ties at the time. The United States and Japan were very much engaged in
commercial relations when Japanese forces bombed Pearl Harbor. U.S.-German
trade before World War II was large. Many other cases can be cited. More to the
point, concerning both U.S.-China and China-Taiwan relations, one might argue
that economic involvements have made their relations worse. Considerable
evidence suggests this. Economic ties increased very markedly, at what most say
were unprecedented rates, between both the United States and China and China
and Taiwan in the 1980s, the 1990s and after, at the same time that political and
strategic relations (and relations overall) deteriorated. Thus, when talking about
two prongs of the Washington-Taipei-Beijing triangle, economic links and dependency seem to have made the relationships worse, not better.

Indeed, there may be a genuine negative connection. U.S.-China relations
have been plagued by serious problems coinciding with the growth in trade. Most
apparent is a huge trade imbalance (or deficit for the United States of US$162
billion in 2004 and over US$200 billion in 2005). In fact, Americans focus on
this more than the value of trade itself.[11] Clearly the deficit has sparked new and
quite virulent protectionist sentiments and anti-China feelings in America.

The champions of protectionism (and isolationism)—unions, environmental
groups, and what some call the big government/welfare constituency—have all
been active, and at times well organized, in bashing China. All three constitute
major voting blocs, and all have good relations with the media. These groups
have to a large extent kept the Democratic Party hostile toward China since the
Tiananmen massacre, aided, of course, by human rights groups (which incidentally see trade as a weapon to use against China). Religious groups on the
political right have had a similar though weaker influence on the Republican
Party. Various of the groups just cited portray U.S. trade with China as being
comprised of items that the United States doesn't need and can purchase (and,
as a matter of fact, should) from other less-developed countries that have better
human rights records. They point out that goods exported from China are frequently products that are produced in prisons by individuals that are incarcer-
ated for their political beliefs, or "prisoners of conscience." The benefactors of the
trade relationship, they argue, are the evil Chinese government and American big
business—large companies that are the enemies of organized labor, the environment, and the poor because they take jobs and tax monies abroad to build factories
that pollute without restraint and use their profits to buy American politicians.
The losers are U.S. workers, who lose big.[12]

The political left in the United States used to be China's friend, but is so no
longer. In recent years anger in the United States over American companies'
moving factories to China and outsourcing jobs there as well as China's buying
U.S. companies and holding the United States hostage by purchasing large
quantities of treasury bills has noticeably made U.S.-China relations worse. In
China, hard-liners contend that trade and foreign investments have created a

new relationship of imperialism and exploitation. Foreigners in residence do not stand in line, live in luxury with Chinese servants, and profit from China's cheap labor. And this is not to mention their causing large discrepancies in incomes and wealth in China (begetting a rich and privileged class that spawns corruption, Westernization, and decadence). Hard-liners in China argue that more extensive commercial relations with the United States have paralleled a growth in crime (especially drug use), juvenile delinquency, prostitution, and other social ills. Leftist hard-liners conclude that China has become literally infected with American "spiritual pollution." They also assert China has become beholden to the United States and that dependency has led to foreign, that is American, control over China. (Why else would America support economic ties with China?) This will lead later to economic decline. They warn that it will in the long run make China a weaker not stronger nation.[13]

Many Chinese leaders, in fact, say China can adjust to cutting commercial ties with the United States, and should rather than succumbing to economic control by Washington.[14] Reformist pro–free trade leaders in China are constantly under the gun. Hence, both in America and in China there are strong forces that disbelieve and openly refute the arguments about the "so-called benefits" of trade and other commercial relations between the two countries.

There have also been frequently heard warnings in Taiwan that too much trade with and huge investments in China are not good. Taiwan leaders, notably Lee Teng-hui and Vice President Annette Lu, but many others as well, have charged that it is dangerous for Taiwan to send more than 10 percent of its exports to China, since Beijing could sever the relationship at any time. Lee, in fact, when he was president, advocated that Taiwan "go south" in its economic relations, to Southeast Asia, to avoid more extensive ties with China. President Chen Shui-bian changed that policy, but in mid-2001 advocated (though inconsistently) a policy of keeping Taiwan's companies at home, due to fear of a loss of Taiwan's industrial base.

Clearly, many political leaders and voters in Taiwan, see a contradiction between growing economic ties with China and Taiwan's independence. Many advocate promoting economic links with the United States and Japan while limiting commercial relations with China. They call the commercial relationship with China dangerous and believe China is trying to hook Taiwan through commercial links.

It is also questionable whether free market capitalism has produced much democracy in China. On the contrary, it may have produced something quite different. Capitalism does not necessarily produce democracy. There are a number of well-known cases where free market capitalism devolved into fascism and militarism, as in pre–World War II Japan, Germany, and Italy. Many observers of Chinese politics say this is what has happened in China. They cite the Tiananmen massacre, religious persecution, and the fact that China executes more people yearly than all other countries in the world combined. They label China's political system "fascist." Obviously China is not yet a democratic nation.

Even though the evidence about China's political system is still confusing, there are many people in the United States, Taiwan and elsewhere who believe China's government is despotic, and this is a description of China frequently seen and heard in the Western media.

Many of the factors that appear to have fostered democracy in China need reassessment. In terms of its political impact in China, sending students and establishing cultural and other ties with the United States may have been grossly exaggerated. Furthermore, the Taiwan experience is hardly a valid analogy. China's population is over 1.3 billion—compared to Taiwan's twenty-three million. This is a sixty-fold difference. Students who have returned to China from the United States, therefore, have had much less impact than students who returned to Taiwan twenty or thirty years ago. The situations, in other words, are non-comparable. One might say that one-sixtieth of the influence returning students had in Taiwan is not much. In addition, at the onset of Taiwan's democratization America had a military presence in Taiwan and gave Taiwan large amounts of military and economic aid. The United States has not and is not giving China aid. And, relatively, trade and investment with and in Taiwan, when it experienced positive political change, were manyfold larger than U.S.-China trade and investment today.

There are likewise perceptible differences between the students who went to American from Taiwan as compared to those from China. Many of the students from Taiwan were from intellectual families; many were ordinary people or people aspiring to accomplish something in life. Almost all admired America or had a strong proclivity to like the United States. Most students from China have been sons and daughters of top leaders of the Chinese Communist Party and other politically connected people and were thoroughly screened before they were allowed to go to America. They are obviously a different breed, which probably explains why the latter have not accepted American values, including democracy, as did the students from Taiwan. In addition, students from China have gone to America to study during a time of intense anti-American nationalism in China (the opposite situation from Taiwan). They thus returned home with much less positive views of the United States.

Numerous Chinese students, after going back to China, criticized the United States. Some have taken part in or have become leaders promoting the nationalistic, hate-America fever that has overcome the country in recent years. For example, the popular 1993 television series "A Beijinger in New York" (which Chinese students who had been in the United States helped make) promoted the theme that China does not need the United States. One of the main characters at one point in the program yells, "F— them! They were still monkeys up in the trees while we were already human beings. Look at how hairy they are; they are not as evolved as us." In another case, Qian Ning (son of the former Minister of Foreign Affairs Qian Qichen) authored a book entitled *Studying in America*, in which he says proudly, "Life abroad fosters patriotism." Similarly, the 1997 bestseller *The Plot to Demonize China*, a diatribe against the

United States, was written in part by a student who not only studied in the United States but stayed on to teach at a major American university, while incidentally maintaining close ties with Jiang Zemin and other top Chinese leaders.[15] Thus, one could argue that the experience of Chinese students from China in the United States not only is different from the students from Taiwan but is in considerable measure a negative one. The same may be said of cultural and other exchanges. The impact on China of sister-city relations and so can not be seen as very profound, given China's size and the fact that the sister-city program has coincided with growing anti-American nationalism in China.

The fact that China may be becoming a democracy and Taiwan is already one may not be good evidence the two will not go to war. Recent well-regarded empirical studies indicate that nations in the process of democratizing are more likely than others (including nondemocratic countries) to start a conflict. According to one study, the opening up of the selection process of the chief executive (which some say is vital to democratization) doubles the likelihood of war.[16] This seems to have special application to Taiwan. The opposition DPP formed, grew, and won elections coinciding with Taiwan's democratization. DPP leaders have deliberately incited Beijing (calling for an independent Taiwan, burning Chinese flags before television cameras, asserting that Taiwanese are not Chinese, and more). President Lee's visit to the United States, which was intended to be provocative, had popular support in Taiwan. The people of Taiwan voted for Lee in 1996 and Chen in 2000, and "did so democratically and to spite China." Chen Shui-bian has regularly incensed leaders in China with calls for an independent Taiwan, which he connects to the island democratizing. Democracy, Chen contends, means Taiwan has the right to choose its future, and that may mean secession. In response, Chinese leaders mock Taiwan's democracy. They say it is a plot to weaken China and keep its split. They disagree completely with President Chen. And they hate him.

The argument that China's prosperity will make it want peace also needs to be seen in the context of China's increasing military spending: China has been able to build up its military in ways that seriously threaten Taiwan (and U.S. military forces in the region) because of its economic success and the money that has provided. In short, prosperity has made China more aggressive, not less.

The argument that China's military is far behind the United States and will take two decades at least to catch up is in some important respects both false and irrelevant. It certainly doesn't give proper weight to China's sudden advances in military capabilities since the Tiananmen massacre. China has made startling advances in military prowess. Probably more important is that most people in the United States, especially the public, the media, and Congress, don't believe China is a military weakling. Thus China's growing military capabilities creates hostility in U.S.-China relations, whether significant or not. The fact that the United States has something in the vicinity of twentyfold as many nuclear weapons as China doesn't change the fact that China possesses more than a few nuclear bombs and can explode some of them over American cities. This gives

Chinese leaders (especially those in the military) some measure of confidence in dealing with the United States. China's generals indeed have threatened to nuke U.S. cities more than once and notwithstanding America's military superiority. In addition, the fact that China will improve its nuclear weapons and its overall military capabilities vis-à-vis the United States seems axiomatic. Beijing has the money and is spending it. Moreover, the process has been facilitated to a degree perhaps unprecedented in history by purchasing weapons from Russia and by its stealing technology from the United States, which, it is worth noting, makes it less acceptable than it would be otherwise to Americans.

To say that China cannot catch up also provokes the Chinese government, in the context of its intense nationalism, to do more. Some Chinese leaders have said that arguing that China cannot (or should not) catch up is "a racist notion held by white America." The belief that China needs a long time (or even any time) to reach parity with the United States anyway is probably self-deluding. The United States and China fought a vicious war in Korea when China had no nuclear weapons. At that time, Washington doubted China would fight the United States because of America's nuclear superiority, but China did. Beijing, it should also be remembered, fought the United States indirectly in Vietnam and won, when its military prowess relative to the United States was significantly less than it is today.

That Beijing is preparing for "asymmetrical warfare" and has directed its military planning toward U.S. weaknesses or "holes" in its capabilities seems to make the nuclear and high-tech advantages belonging to the United States less important, perhaps not important at all. American strategists have expressed worry about this. Many feel that U.S. forces are too heavily reliant on state-of-the art weapons and may be very vulnerable to lesser enemies. China's leaders have said the same thing.[17]

Finally, it should be observed that China's current military objective is not to catch up to the United States in nuclear weapons. China says with considerable clarity that it does not need to do this. Its current strategy is to gain military dominance in East Asia, aiming particularly at the Taiwan Strait and the South China Sea. This does not require parity with the United States military. If China can achieve a position of being able to seriously put U.S. forces in East Asia at risk, it will, in the minds of many strategists both in China and the United States, control the world's most dynamic region, and eventually the world itself. To do this, Beijing must make U.S. military personnel and American allies feel vulnerable to China's improved and increasingly numerous short-range missiles, according to its calculations. It needs to demonstrate that it is the ascending power and the United States is declining or is in a steady state. So far, China is succeeding.

That China is not by nature an aggressor but a peace-loving nation is belied by the fact that China historically was ruled by a despotic government that exhibited most of the traits of the bloodthirsty authoritarian systems elsewhere. Believing China was different is patently not justified by the facts. For the record,

China had nearly three times as many men under arms as did Rome during the Roman Empire at a time when it had a population of about the same size.[18] China historically was located in what is now "north China." Chinese forces killed, assimilated (to a large degree by force), or expelled most of the population of south China. Thais and Vietnamese once resided in what is now China. China subjugated numerous peoples and would-be nations on its borders. China's territory is ten-fold what it was when China started to keep records. It is double what it was in the Ming Dynasty five hundred years ago. China, according to one count, has grown by four thousand square miles annually in the modern era.[19] In 1950, China invaded Tibet, exterminated a large number of Tibetans, and populated the area with Chinese. Subsequently Beijing forced Chinese into all of its other border regions that were populated by minorities. China fought wars with India, the Soviet Union, and Vietnam in the 1960s and 1970s. It has taken territory claimed by Vietnam and the Philippines in the South China Sea only recently.

On the other side of the equation, though not heard with great frequency in recent years, the view that the United States is not an aggressive nation or lacks the will to fight a nation like China seems nothing short of blind faith. This notion is certainly discredited when one looks at the facts, notably America's Asian wars. In just one night in March 1945, U.S. forces, bombing Japan, killed more than eighty-three thousand unarmed Japanese civilians. In the last five months of World War II in the Pacific, American bombing raids slaughtered more defenseless nonmilitary Japanese people than the combined number of U.S. combat deaths in all of its foreign wars in its entire history. America, it hardly needs to be mentioned, is the only country ever to use nuclear bombs. In Korea, U.S. soldiers killed nearly a million North Korean civilians, thirty times the number of U.S. soldiers lost. The United States accounted for another three hundred thousand civilian deaths during the Vietnam War, and in the Gulf War from one hundred thousand to a quarter of a million Iraqi soldiers who didn't even see the American planes that wiped them out en masse.[20]

Have times changed? It is difficult to imagine the United States not reacting to almost any serious incident of Chinese aggression in Asia. The United States is an Asia power in the minds of most Americans. Its trade across the Pacific is more than double its trade with Western Europe. It has sizeable investments in East Asia. It has binding treaties with Japan, South Korea, and a law (the TRA) that mandates that it keep a sufficient level of American forces in the Far East to ensure the United States keeps its commitments to Taiwan. In any event, while the United States has been known to let its guard down it has not often run from an attacker or aggressive power; that is not the American tradition.

It is said that the United States, because of its experience in the Vietnam War, will not engage in a land war in Asia, especially with China. The fact is that it doesn't have to, and any conflict that Taiwan might ignite would not be that kind of war. The U.S. plan in a future Taiwan Strait engagement is to destroy the Chinese air force and navy and if further actions are needed destroy Chinese military capabilities at home and perhaps cities in the process. In short, the U.S. military would not fight a Vietnam-style war against China.

That Taiwan is small and not worth fighting for is likewise not a convincing argument. U.S. trade with and investment in Taiwan are substantial. More importantly, Taiwan constitutes a vital strategic and intelligence asset for the United States. Even more critical is the belief (no doubt true) that letting China have Taiwan, regardless of the circumstances or conditions, would fatally undermine Washington's credibility, its global military strategy, and America's dominant power role in the region.

In any event, it seems a contradiction to argue that China is way behind the United States in military terms yet say the United States is too afraid of China to defend Taiwan.

—ɯ—

Domestic politics, including internal political trends, in the United States, China, and Taiwan similarly cast doubt on the notion that the Taiwan issue can be easily defused or that conflict between the United States and China can be prevented.

In the case of the United States, throughout these pages mention has been made of the different views of China/Taiwan policy espoused by the executive and legislative branches of the government. Congress supports Taiwan; the executive branch (notably the Department of State) supports China. Moreover, the polarization in views has become increasingly acute in recent years. There is a host of reasons for this.

Congress has long believed its input into the process of formulating foreign policy represents America's plural society, its openness, and its democracy. The White House and the Department of State espouse a quite different viewpoint— that the executive branch should be supreme in the area of foreign policy making and that negotiations should often be conducted in secret. In the struggle between the two branches of government, Congress has been winning. Congressional influence in making foreign policy has expanded for numerous reasons: the impact of technology, especially the Internet; the proliferation of public opinion polls; and Congress's quick response to lobbying groups interested in changing U.S. foreign policy.[21] The end of the Cold War and global trends, especially democratization, have also favored Congress having a greater role in foreign policy making. During the Clinton administration, inattention to external affairs and the low level of competence among its foreign policy makers caused Congress to assume more authority in foreign policy.[22] Contentious issues suggest the struggle between the two branches of government will persist and may even get worse. Differences between Capitol Hill and the White House on human rights, spying, foreign campaign contributions, arms sales, and nuclear proliferation suggest fundamental feuds over policy issues that connect to conflicts over turf.

U.S. China/Taiwan policy has been one of the most divisive issues between Congress and the White House. Since passing the TRA in 1979, Congress has unabashedly favored Taiwan over China.[23] In ensuing years the TRA (which contradicted the Normalization Agreement) made it difficult for the executive branch to maintain good relations with China and deal with and protect Taiwan as the TRA mandated. Congress contradicted what to Beijing was the most important tenet of U.S. China policy: one China. Making the situation worse, after 1989, Congress and the U.S. media became almost permanent critics of China. They no longer viewed Taiwan as a pariah; China assumed that role. The 1996 crisis amplified America's hostility toward China. The negative view of China in America is currently underscored by the perception that China is destroying the U.S. economy by its unfair commercial practices and that China is an aggressive power since its military spending is expanding (and very fast) at a time when others in the region are not.

Just as making China policy in the United States is vexed by institutional differences, U.S. policy making in China experiences similar problems. Factionalism in the Communist Party in China has long been apparent. It is arguably characteristic of one-party systems. In the past it revolved around disparate ideological views defined largely in terms of economic policy, especially growth strategies. Factional struggles centered on the degree of central planning of the economy and the importance of ideology versus professionalism (called the "red versus expert" controversy). Foreign policy was seldom a defining issue, but recently it has become *the* issue in China's internal political struggles.[24] The right faction wants better relations with the United States, at least temporarily. This, they say, is the path to a rich and strong China. The left rues the fact China has become divided between rich and poor and that crime and corruption have become rampant and are threatening social stability, and it exploits these problems. Its adherents condemn "spiritual pollution" and say America is peddling this to weaken China. They use Chinese nationalism to their advantage.

The shift from a dominant leader, Mao, to less dominant and possibly more democratic ones, Deng Xiaoping and his successors, to a large extent set the stage for this situation.[25] In addition, Deng was in a hurry and was impetuous in putting his reform policies into operation. He thus created opposition. In 1983, when the left made a resurgence, Deng had to retreat. He moved to the left, backtracked on the reforms, and repudiated close ties with the United States. He was forced to oversee the purging of his closest associates. This happened again in 1989 and to a large degree explains the Tiananmen massacre. Deng's Achilles heel was the Taiwan issue. It was certainly his main weakness in his struggle with the political left and at times the military brass.

As the rift between China's reformists on the one hand and leftist and military leaders on the other grew, the latter came to see conflict with or over Taiwan as beneficial to them, and inevitable. If Deng wanted to make China great and powerful again, he had to "protect its territory," meaning recovering its lost lands. Most Chinese leaders believe Taiwan was and is a part of China. As a matter of record, it is hardly an exaggeration to say that no Chinese leader, even Deng, could say differently or act differently and survive.

Jiang Zemin was even less adroit than Deng at playing down the Taiwan issue. Being more a populist and needing more than other leaders to exploit nationalist sentiments, Jiang was also more vulnerable. Hu Jintao, who faces very divisive domestic problems, is even less able to ignore (or make concessions on) Taiwan.[26] Meanwhile nationalism in China injected a large measure of irrationality into Chinese decision making. It turned the Taiwan matter into an emotion-laden one and into a nonnegotiable issue between China and the United States.[27] Will this change?

Three situations or trends seem to ensure that the Taiwan issue will not fade. Rather it will become an even more sensitive and explosive issue in years to come.

First, while Deng's economic reforms (continued by his successors) were successful and enjoyed mass support, they also created problems. They were built on policies of decentralizing the economy and free market principles. Political decision-making authority moved accordingly. This weakened the central government's control at a time when greater authority was needed to keep the lid on. Concern grew about China breaking up. As this happened nationalism was needed even more. Chinese leaders accepted the dangerous baggage attached to nationalist sentiments. And they did little about (and at times encouraged) anti-Americanism. Taiwan remaining independent was seen as a danger as its status would encourage separatist movements in Tibet, Xinjiang Province, and elsewhere. A separate Taiwan, in other words, was, according to a Maoist cliché, the "spark that would start a prairie fire."

Second, in the milieu of fervent and hard to control nationalism and powerful centrifugal social and political forces, the military became the guarantor of China's unity and its territorial integrity, which were increasingly seen as synonymous. The military is also tough on Taiwan. Military leaders loathe talk of a separate Taiwan and hate those of Taiwan's leaders who advocate it or say that democracy justifies it. The military's budget and its political clout are improved by its hard line on Taiwan and officers say that taking a moderate position on Taiwan is a "career breaker." It seems this situation is unlikely to change.

Third, Jiang Zemin was a weaker leader than Deng. In addition, Jiang had no reputation as a military leader. As a consequence, he had to make more concessions to the military to get the generals' support. Making this situation worse, Jiang tried to negotiate with Taiwan and failed. His credibility and reputation were badly hurt as a result, making concessions almost out of the question.

Hu Jintao inherited this unhappy situation. Hu's strategy has been to cite America's one-China policy and hope Washington will keep the Chen administration in line. But given the domestic situation in the United States and the constraints imposed by Congress and the Taiwan Relations Act this will work marginally at best. Likely it will fail.

Experts on Chinese politics say there are other equally serious problems. China is unstable. In view of the fact it has undergone such far-reaching economic and social change in recent years this is quite understandable. More specifically, China has moved from radical communism under Mao to what some call "market Leninism" or "capitalist dictatorship." As noted earlier some say it is evolving toward fascism. Economically, politically, and socially, one thing seems certain: China is in a state of flux. Economically, China, once one of the most egalitarian countries in the world, is now one of the least. Currently in China 0.1 percent of the population holds one-third of the nation's private savings. According to a recent book published in China called *Pitfalls of China's Modernization*, sixty percent of Chinese citizens believe that those people who have gained wealth in recent years have done so illegally.[28] Greed and jealously that this wealth produced, according to observers of China, are out of control.

In recent years there have been regular reports of worker and peasant riots. Some have been called "revolts" and even "revolutions." In 1998, nearly a thousand strikes and group protests were officially reported. In 1999, the number increased. Later one writer estimated the number of protest demonstrations throughout the country was more than a hundred thousand.[29] In 2005, the government reported (no doubt underreporting as usual) eighty-seven thousand public order disturbances.[30] Millions of people are "employed" in China's decaying and notoriously inefficient state enterprises. Most of China's banks, by Western standards, are bankrupt. A "floating population" of vagrants numbers as high as three hundred million; rampant corruption and other problems plague China's leaders. By almost any reckoning China faces serious internal political dilemmas.[31]

No wonder the government is nervous about political instability. Recent crackdowns on religious and martial arts groups (such as Falun Gong), suppressing dissidents, increasing the use of capital punishment, are all symptomatic. Nationalism is the glue that holds China together. Rapid economic growth is the sole source of the ruling Chinese Communist Party's credibility. In this atmosphere, if Taiwan tries to formally secede and America protects it, China may well act irrationally.

—◊◊◊—

Last but not least, Washington and Beijing espouse very different, basically opposing, views on international politics. They disagree seriously on the nature of the international system's recent changes in its structure and rules. And as China has gotten stronger the disagreement has gotten more serious. It is hardly an exaggeration to say their worldviews will ultimately collide.

In 1991 there occurred a monumentally important, epoch-making event for American foreign policy decision makers and the public alike. American intellectuals subsequently made popular the term "the end of history" to describe it. That event was the collapse of the Soviet Union. In the view of Americans (and most of the world, though patently not China), this happened because communism failed. Put another way, capitalism/democracy proved the superior system. As a result of the United States "vanquishing" the Soviet Union and communism (they were seen as one and the same by America), the post–World

War II era of bipolarity ended. The resulting international system was a unipolar one. As leader of the victorious bloc, now the only bloc, the United States was accorded a special, hegemonic role in the new system. The United States was at once the dominant military, economic, political, and cultural leader of the world. Few countries (if any) have ever enjoyed such an advantaged position. America was truly the "king of the mountain."

China's global role, in the minds of Americans (the public and most decision makers alike), dramatically diminished. China was one of the defeated nations of the former communist bloc. In addition, the ascendancy of military and leftist hard-liners after the Tiananmen massacre caused U.S. policy makers to think China had regressed to Maoist totalitarian and isolationism. Indeed China had. This further convinced Americans that China would not play an important role on the stage of international affairs. In the minds of most people in America, China did not deserve a place at the table given the brutal regime in Beijing that had committed the mass murder of students demonstrating for democratic reforms in Tiananmen Square.

Connected to this view, America perceived that democracy was the wave of the future and the essence of the "new world order." America had a "responsibility" to spread democracy, which gave the United States a mandate to remake the world. Nondemocratic countries would have to change. Those that resisted would not be respected players in the international system. This included China.

After George W. Bush became president in 2001, the Neocons soon dominated foreign policy making. They perceived U.S. dominance (especially in military power) ordained America with a commanding role in world affairs even more than previous regimes. They argued that the United States had a mission to preserve international order; regional and global institutions, even allies, would often be of little help in doing this. They adamantly called for the United States to democratize the world.[32] Their views and policies further exacerbated the differences between America and China.

After September 11, 2001, America's will to dominate increased exponentially. China, it was thought, would have to fall in line and join the U.S.-led war on terrorism. The fact China did (and forthwith) was further proof the United States was the world's preeminent power and China was not a contender. China was, and would continue to be, a follower.

Notwithstanding China's decision to support the United States in the war against terrorism, Chinese leaders did not concur with America's interpretation of world events or its view of international politics or the international system. Beijing's policy makers viewed international politics from a radical realist or realpolitik perspective, a Hobbesian view of the world. Nations are sovereign and they covet this. They do not want to follow a global leader.

China's bitterness about its treatment at the hands of Western imperialism in the past and its current aggressive nationalism constituted the wellspring of this view.[33] China's rise confirmed it. Chinese leaders thus rejected unipolarity. They and intellectuals in China that followed the Chinese Communist Party line, labeled the "so-called unipolar system" a "hegemonic system." They bitterly condemned it. Hegemony, or a hegemonic system, in Chinese parlance, was one wherein superpower bullying would undermine sovereignty and the nation-state system. The basic rights of nations would be sullied. It would be an autocratic, oppressive, unequal, and patently a bad system. Chinese leaders said the international system was, or should be (they said both) a multipolar one led by several great powers but comprised also of lesser powers. The great or large powers were the United States, Russia, the European Union, Japan, and (last but certainly not least) China.[34] If Chinese leaders seemed at times to acquiesce to America's dominance, it was not sincere and in the minds of Chinese leaders was only temporary. There was something else on the minds of Chinese leaders.

They attributed the Soviet Union's collapse to poor leadership. Its demise was certainly not, to Chinese leaders, a product of communism's failings. Chinese policy makers cited "evil, counterrevolutionary forces" in the Soviet Union as the reason. They spoke of Moscow betraying communism and unwisely listening to the advice of Western academics. In other words, the West's plot to destroy the Soviet Union had succeeded and China had to beware.

To Chinese officials, China became more important as a result of the fall of the Soviet Union, not less. China, some of its leaders promptly announced, was now the undisputed leader of the anti-U.S. bloc. Comporting with this view, Chinese decision makers' statements and actions showed anger and paranoia. In early 1990, Deng Xiaoping proclaimed that "international hostile forces" (meaning the United States) have now focused on China and will stir up trouble and bring difficulties and pressures on China. But there was planning and calculation in China's world view, not just emotion.

Leaders in Beijing, of course, recognized that China needed the United States. China's continued economic development depended on good (or at least working) Sino-American relations. Therefore, China could not attempt to overthrow the American dominated unipolar system immediately. But they could later.

China perceived that the United States faced disabling domestic weaknesses. Many Chinese leaders thought the United States lacked the will to be a world hegemon. Hence China could promote a different kind of international system (namely multipolarity) and in the long run (evidently not so far away) defeat the United States, after which China would be the world's dominant power. Indeed, there was evidence to support the Chinese claim that America didn't have what it took to create and sustain a U.S.-dominated unipolar system.

The debate in the United States about the new world order was at first shrouded in confusion. Then strong opposition to a dominant U.S. role in the world developed. President George H. W. Bush never defined what he meant by "the new world order." Nor did his administration design a grand strategy for the post–Cold War era. That was left to the next president. But the Clinton administration, instead of assuming the United States should rule, tried to act in the name of a universal system or world government. The United Nations and other global institutions were to be strengthened and upgraded. This, however, did not work, and Clinton had to reverse course and settle for a U.S.-led system. In the meantime, opportunities were irretrievably lost and support for America's global leadership waned and opposition to it grew.

Meanwhile America's declining interest in world affairs, as reflected by Clinton's domestic policy focus, the cutting of the military's and the intelligence community's budgets along with foreign aid, and statements made by U.S. leaders (which became seen as a U.S. withdrawal or isolationist policy as expressed in the "Tarnoff Doctrine"), all evoked doubt whether the United States would continue to be a global leader.[35] The view that the world was dividing along cultural lines became fashionable in academe and in various quarters of government involved in formulating foreign policy.[36] The need for aligning with Europe based on the "West versus the rest" notion also became popular. Its supporters said that the United States had to bring part of the world into its fold and then work on the rest.

Washington thus placed an unusual emphasis on Europe, keeping and even expanding NATO (given there were serious potential conflicts and threats elsewhere). Critics, including China, said this was racism and proved Washington's unwillingness to cope with the responsibilities of the United States being a global hegemon. Beijing's conclusion: Washington was not qualified to lead the world. Beijing also observed that many economists spoke of a tripolar world of economic blocs that challenged, even undermined, Washington's hegemonic global role.[37]

The Neocons refurbished the view that America's global leadership was needed and justified. Their views became widely accepted after September 11, 2001. Beijing joined the United States in the war on terrorism. But Chinese leaders did not accept America's worldview. In fact, China continued to oppose it—especially in its deeds. China's military budget increases and its aggressive actions outside its borders did not abate. In fact, they more and more seriously challenged America's hegemonic policies. For example, China contributed to nuclear proliferation, gave military aid to rogue states, spied on the United States (more than any other country), threatened the global financial order, and so on. All of this was intended to weaken America's global influence. At times China's leaders foreswore such actions, but they did not desist.

Currently Chinese scholars and writers side with Western scholars who condemn America's "pretenses to empire" and criticize the Neocons. They even speak of the demise of the "fifth empire": after the Third Reich of Nazism, the "fourth" (the Soviet Union), and now America.[38] Beijing has said that China plans to be the dominant power in East Asia, as it was historically. Will it stop there? From there China may go on to dominate the world.[39]

The first major obstacle to eliminate in China's scheme to expand its Asian and then global influence is Taiwan. So China puts more and more missiles close to the Taiwan Strait to intimidate the island's leaders and populace and U.S. troops in the area that may protect Taiwan. As one writer put it, Taiwan is part of China via Beijing's historical view of its Mandate of Heaven. But China's mandate is not only about Taiwan; it never was.

—\m—

In summation, Washington and Beijing parted ways in 1989. That year was eventful. Three events (clear signals the Soviet Union was in a state of collapse, the Tiananmen Square massacre, and a historic democratic election in Taiwan) changed the course of history. All pushed U.S.-China relations into a downward spiral. Subsequently, a series of "incidences" occurred between the United States and China. This culminated in the missile crisis of 1996. That event was a point of no return; relations between the two did not return to normal. The situation surrounding the crisis was described this way: there was a serious conflict between the world's only superpower (a nation that feels it won the Cold War and is now the leader of the world that bears moral responsibility for making the world a democratic one) and the biggest country in the world by population and the planet's fast rising power, a nation infected by virulent nationalism, and one that challenges America's global perspective and its dominance in international politics.

Making the situation more dangerous, there was, and is, the nonnegotiable issue of Taiwan dividing them. China says Taiwan is its land and it will not allow Taiwan to opt for independence. The United States, by law, has to defend Taiwan, and no doubt will. Adding to the "danger equation," Taiwan has become a democracy—making most of its population and a majority in the United States and the rest of the world feel that it deserves to decide its own future. In Taiwan, a growing majority of the populace favors independence to unification. This is a recipe for trouble.

The domestic situations in both countries and the nature of international politics meanwhile ensured that China and the United States will remain mutually antagonistic. In 2000, a new leadership came to power in Taiwan before its time. Resorting to populism and needing to rally its supporters, it found provoking China by calling openly for succession politically expedient. Thus, the Taiwan Strait, the most explosive place in the world, saw tension between Taiwan and China and the United States and China increase.

The future looks, if anything, worse. There will be more confrontations and it is very possible one of them will escalate out of control.

Notes

CHAPTER 1

1. For details on the missile crisis, see John W. Garver, *Face Off: China, the United States and Taiwan's Democratization* (Seattle: University of Washington Press, 1997), chapter 1, and Ralph N. Clough, *Cooperation or Conflict in the Taiwan Strait* (Lanham, MD: Rowman and Littlefield, 1999), pp. 5–7.

2. The Pescadores may or may not have been a significant site: some observers opined that the Pescadores would be the stepping-stone for a military assault on Taiwan (it had served this role in the past).

3. See Suisheng Zhao, "Taiwan: From Peaceful Offensive to Coercive Strategy," in Yong Deng and Fei-ling Wang, ed., *In the Eyes of the Dragon: China Views the World* (Lanham, MD: Rowman and Littlefield, 1999), p. 214.

4. "Reunification on One-China Basis," *Beijing Review*, February 19–25, 1996, p. 5.

5. "Qian on World and Regional Issues," *Beijing Review*, March 25–31, 1996, p. 7.

6. Garver, *Face-Off*, pp. 96–97.

7. *Wen Hui Pao*, March 21, 1996, p. A2, cited in Bruce Gilley, *Tiger on the Brink: Jiang Zemin and China's New Rulers* (Berkeley: University of California Press, 1998), p. 156.

8. See Patrick Tyler, *A Great Wall: Six Presidents and China* (New York: Century Foundation, 1999), p. 10 and the rest of chapter 2.

9. Ibid.

10. A former U.S. ambassador to China made this observation. See James R. Lilley and Chuck Downs, "Introduction: Crisis in the Taiwan Strait," in James R. Lilley and Chuck Downs, ed., *Crisis in the Taiwan Strait* (Washington, DC: National Defense University Press, 1997).

11. James Mann, *About Face: A History of America's Curious Relationship with China, from Nixon to Clinton* (New York: Alfred A. Knopf, 1999), p. 337.

12. Mann, *About Face*, p. 337.

13. Tyler, *A Great Wall*, p. 7.

14. Bill Gertz, *Betrayal: How the Clinton Administration Undermined American Security* (Washington, DC: Regnery Publishing, 1999), p. 82.

15. See Tyler, *A Great Wall*, p. 22.

16. See Martin L. Lasater, *The Taiwan Conundrum in U.S. China Policy* (Boulder, CO: Westview Press, 1999), p. 248.

17. Reuters report from Taipei, February 17, 1996, cited in Lasater, *The Taiwan Conundrum*, p. 258.

18. Edward Timperlake and William C. Triplett II, *Red Dragon Rising: Communist China's Military Threat to America* (Washington, DC: Regnery Publishing, 1999), p. 156.

19. The hearing was recorded by the Federal Document Clearing House, Inc., and was found on the Internet (Lexis-Nexis) dated March 14, 1996.

20. Garver, *Face Off*, p. 99.

21. See David Albright and Corey Gay, "Nuclear Nightmare Averted," *Bulletin of Atomic Scientists*, January/February 1998, pp. 54–60.

22. The Nuclear Non-Proliferation Treaty of 1968 contains such a provision.

23. Mann, *About Face*, p. 337.

24. See Garver, *Face Off*, chapter 13, for further details on Asia's reaction to the U.S. show of force.

25. Phillip C. Saunders, "China's America Watchers: Changing Attitudes towards the United States," *China Quarterly*, March 2000, p. 56.

26. Sankei Shimbun, April 28, 1996, cited in Foreign Broadcasting Information Service, April 28, 1996.

27. Cited in Shu Yuan Hsieh, "Nuclear-Weapon-Free Zone in the Taiwan Strait," in Paul H. Tai, ed., *United States, China and Taiwan: Bridges for the New Millennium* (Carbondale, IL: Public Policy Institute, Southern Illinois University, 1999), p. 172.

28. *China Daily*, March 19, 1997, p. 4.

29. *Newsweek*, May 23, 1999.

CHAPTER 2

1. See *The Truth about the Beijing Turmoil* (Beijing: Beijing Publishing Company, 1989). The editorial board of *The Truth about the Beijing Turmoil* edited this book.

2. "Tiananmen: What Did Happen?" *Asiaweek*, December 22–29, 1989, pp. 30–33.

3. A Chinese official said this to the author, who was known to him from several books and reports on human rights in China.

4. A Chinese official made this statement to the author. According to one observer, there were prodemocracy rallies in 123 other cities at this time. See Richard Baum, *Burying Mao* (Princeton: Princeton University Press, 1994), p. 276.

5. See Edward Timperlake and William C. Triplett II, *Red Dragon Rising: Communist China's Military Threat to America* (Washington, DC: Regnery Publishing, 1999), chapter 2.

6. There are numerous books and articles about the Tiananmen massacre.

7. The government later published a glossy book containing some of the grisly pictures of soldiers that had been mutilated, castrated, burned, and so on. See *The Truth About the Beijing Turmoil*.

8. Nicholas D. Kristof and Sheryl WuDunn, *China Wakes: The Struggle for the Soul of a Rising Power* (New York: Times Books, 1994).

9. See Roberta Cohen, *People's Republic of China: The Human Rights Exception* (Baltimore: University/Maryland School of Law, 1988).

10. Ibid.

11. David M. Lampton, *Same Bed Different Dreams: Managing U.S.-China Relations, 1989–2000* (Berkeley: University of California Press, 2001), p. 265.

12. See *United States and China Relations at a Crossroads* (Lanham, MD: University Press of America, 1995). This is a report by the Atlantic Council of the United States and the National Committee of U.S.-China Relations.

13. Bruce Gilley, *Tiger on the Brink* (Berkeley: University of California Press, 1998), p. 151.

14. See, for example, Yu Quanyu, "China Leads the U.S. in Human Rights," *Beijing Review*, October 3–9, 1994, cited in John F. Copper and Ta-ling Lee, *Coping with a Bad Global Image: Human Rights in the Peoples' Republic of China, 1993–94* (Lanham, MD: University Press of America, 1997), pp. 269–70.

15. I am reminded of several discussions I had with residents of Taiwan after Mao died and Hua Guofeng assumed power. Some major newspapers in the United States had speculated, based on facial resemblances and a known connection Hua had with Hunan Province (where Mao was born and had lived when he was young and for some time even past his youth), that Hua might be Mao's illegitimate son. Several people told me that this was "crazy" based on the fact that they could tell where Hua grew up from his accent. They told me not only the province (one not near Hunan), but also the district of that province. Information later disclosed by Beijing confirmed that they were right.

16. I heard this frequently from both citizens and officials in Taiwan at this time.

CHAPTER 3

1. Seymour Hersh, *The Price of Power*, cited in Mann, *About Face*, p. 44.

2. Ralph N. Clough, *Island China* (Cambridge: Harvard University Press, 1978), pp. 26–27.

3. Tyler, *A Great Wall*, p. 170.

4. A Chinese official told the author this shortly after the Tiananmen massacre.

5. Tyler, *A Great Wall*, p. 269.

6. Tyler, *A Great Wall*, p. 299.

7. For details, see Dennis Van Vranken Hickey, *United States-Taiwan Security Ties: From Cold War to beyond Containment* (Westport, CT: Praeger, 1994), pp. 77–90.

8. Mann, *About Face,* 265–266.

9. For details see Ralph N. Clough, *Reaching Across the Taiwan Strait: People to People Diplomacy* (Boulder, CO: Westview Press, 1993), p. 183.

10. "Qian Warns Washington over Retaliation Moves," *South China Morning Post*, September 24, 1992, p. 10.

11. Alexander Nicoll and Mark Nicholson, "China to Boycott Arms Talks," *Financial Times*, September 16, 1992, p. 6.

12. See June Teufel Dreyer, "China's Military Strategy toward Taiwan," *The American Asian Review* (1999), pp. 5–6.

13. Lu Ning, *The Dynamics of Foreign Policy Decision Making in China* (Boulder, CO: Westview Press, 2000), p. 171.

14. Some say that France was not really dealt with harshly by China, even though Beijing clearly treated it differently from the United States. The reason France did not get castigated or cut out of trade deals for its actions is that French officials paid large bribes to some important people in Beijing.

15. See Ming Zhang and Ronald N. Montaperto, *A Triad of Another Kind: The United States, China and Japan* (New York: St. Martin's Press, 1999), p. 19.

CHAPTER 4

1. Mann, *About Face*, p. 326.

2. See Clough, *Cooperation or Conflict in the Taiwan Strait*, p. 2.

3. For a vivid account, see Tyler, *A Great Wall*, pp. 271–273. Christopher also gives his own view of the incident; see Warren Christopher, *Chances of a Lifetime* (New York: Scribner Publisher, 2001), p. 92.

4. See Andrew J. Nathan and Robert S. Ross, *The Great Wall and the Empty Fortress: China's Search for Security* (New York: W. W. Norton, 1997), pp. 130–31.

5. See "Lee's U.S. Entry Visa Protested," *Beijing Review*, June 12–18, 1995, p. 7.

6. See Steven Strasser et al., "This Is Not the Right Way to Treat Others," *Newsweek*, October 23, 1995, p. 12. Christopher, on the other hand, said he advised Clinton to give Lee the visa, as did National Security Advisor Anthony Lake and Secretary of Defense William Perry, fearing that "Congress would work some mischief to the Taiwan Relations Act if we did not." See Christopher, *Chances of a Lifetime*, p. 243.

7. "China Issues Strong Protest to U.S.," *Beijing Review*, June 12–18, 1995, p. 18.

8. *Straits Times*, October 1, 1995, cited in Lijun Sheng, *China's Dilemma: The Taiwan Issue* (Singapore: Institute of Southeast Asian Studies, 2003), p. 66.

9. Li Jiaquan, "Lee's U.S. Visit Defies Agreement," *Beijing Review*, June 26–July 2, 1996, p. 19.

10. See Sheng, *China's Dilemma*, p. 26.

11. See Julian Baum, "Up and Running," *Far Eastern Economic Review*, September 7, 1995, p. 14.

12. Ren Xin, "Speech Exposes Lee's Real Aim," *Beijing Review*, July 3–9, 1995, p. 27.

13. See Suisheng Zhao, "Changing Leadership Perceptions: The Adoption of a Coercive Strategy," in Suisheng Zhao, *Across the Taiwan Strait: Mainland China, Taiwan, and the 1995–1996 Crisis* (London: Routledge, 1999), p. 110.

14. For details, see Zhao, "Changing Leadership Perceptions," p. 110.

15. Sheng, *China's Dilemma*, p. 27.

16. Philip C. Saunders, "China's America Watchers: Changing Attitudes towards the United States," *China Quarterly*, March 2000, p. 55.

17. Garver, *Face Off*, p. 74.

18. Ibid.

19. See David Shambaugh, "Taiwan's Security: Maintaining Deterrence amid Political Accountability," *China Quarterly*, December 1996, p. 1304.

20. See "China Military Exercise Planned for before Election," *China News*, November 26, 1995, p. 1.

21. Lampton, *Same Bed Different Dreams*, p. 52.

22. See *China Post*, February 28, 1996, cited in Clough, *Cooperation or Conflict*, p. 3.

23. Mann, *About Face*, p. 334.

24. Ibid.

25. James Kynge, "Taiwan to Study Need for Nuclear Weapons," Reuters, July 28, 1995.

26. Patrick E. Tyler, "Tough Stance toward China Pays Off for Taiwan Leader," *New York Times*, August 29, 1995, p. A8.

27. Sheng, *China's Dilemma*, pp. 24–25.

28. For details, see John F. Copper, *Taiwan's Mid-1990s Elections: Taking the Final Steps to Democracy* (Westport, CT: Praeger, 1998), chapter 3.

CHAPTER 5

1. This was being reportedly widely in the United States, notably by liberal publications.

2. For details on China's posteconomic size and influence and how this translated into its international influence, see John F. Copper, *China's Global Role* (Stanford: Hoover Institution Press, 1980).

3. See William Overholt, *The Rise of China: How Economic Reform is Creating a New Superpower* (New York: W. W. Norton, 1993).

4. See Sterling Seagrave, *The Lord of the Rim: The Invisible Empire of the Overseas Chinese* (New York: Putnam, 1995).

5. "War of the Worlds," *Economist* (Global Economy section), October 1, 1994, p. 4.

6. Jim Rohwer, *Asia Rising: Why America Will Prosper as Asia's Economies Boom* (New York: Simon and Schuster, 1995), p. 117. A number of other writers were saying such things. Even the World Bank was very optimistic about China's economic prospects. See, for example, *The East Asia Miracle* (London: Oxford University Press, 1993).

7. Kristof and WuDunn, *China Wakes*, p. 14.

8. John Naisbett, *Megatrends Asia: Eight Asian Megatrends That Are Reshaping Our World* (New York: Touchstone Books, 1997).

9. Two writers who adamantly argued against a China threat described China as the "largest and economically the most dynamic newly emerging power in the history of the world." See Nathan and Ross, *The Great Wall and the Empty Fortress*, p. xi. Two others, who are generally seen as friends of China and who sought to promote better U.S. relations with Beijing, write that "No nation in history has undergone as total a transformation as has China during the quarter century from 1972 to 1997." See Orville Schell and David Shambaugh (eds.), *The China Reader* (New York: Vintage, 1999), p. xvii.

10. Daniel Burstein and Arne deKeijzer, *Big Dragon China's Future: What It Means for Business, the Economy and the Global Order* (New York: Simon and Schuster, 1998).

11. See Maria Hsia Chang, *The Labors of Sisyphus: The Economic Development of Communist China* (New Brunswick: Transaction Publishers, 1998), chapter 8, for a discussion of Chinese nationalism and many of the points made below.

12. See Bruce Gilley, "Digging into the Future," *Far Eastern Economic Review*, July 20, 2000, pp. 74–77.

13. Mel Gurtov and Byong-Moo Hwang, *China's Security: The New Roles of the Military* (Boulder, CO: Lynne Rienner, 1998), pp. 70–73.

14. Richard Bernstein and Ross H. Monro, *The Coming Conflict with China* (New York: Alfred A. Knopf, 1997), p. 44.

15. Ibid., p. 45.

16. Ibid., pp. 22–23.

17. Ibid., pp. 27–28.

18. Gurtov and Hwang, *China's Security*, p. 73.

19. Ross H. Monro, "Taiwan: What China Really Wants," *National Review*, October 11, 1999, p. 47.

20. Ibid., p. 48.

21. Ibid., p. 48. The author cites the magazine *The Navy*.

22. Ibid., p. 48.

23. Chang, *The Labors of Sisyphus*, p. 210.

24. Saunders, "China's America Watchers: Changing Attitudes towards the United States," p. 45.

25. Cited in Bernstein and Monro, *The Coming Conflict with China*, p. 49.

26. Barbara Opal-Rome, "PLA Pursues Acupuncture Warfare," *Defense News*, March 1, 1999, p. 4.

27. Chong-pin Lin, "Info Warfare Latecomer," *Defense News*, April 12, 1999, p. 23.

28. See John Pomfret, "China Ponders New Rules of 'Unrestricted War,'" *Washington Post*, August 8, 1999, p. 1.

29. For details, see John W. Garver, "More from the 'Say No Club,'" (review essay), *The China Journal*, January 2001, pp. 151–58.

30. Based on Gallup Polls cited in Steven W. Mosher, *China Misperceived: American Illusions and Chinese Reality* (New York: New Republic, 1990), p. 210.

31. Ibid.

32. The commentator in question is Meg Greenfield of the Washington Post. This is cited in Mosher, *China Misperceived*, p. 208.

33. The former was Leo Orleans; the latter William Hinton. See Mosher, *China Misperceived*, pp. 208–210.

34. Alvin Toffler and Heidi Toffler, *War and Anti-War: Survival at the Dawn of the 21st Century* (Boston: Little, Brown and Co., 1993).

35. Mann, *About Face*, p. 333.

36. Ibid.

37. George Will, "China's Turn," *Washington Post*, April 17, 1997, p. 10.

38. Robert Ross, "Why Our Hardliners Are Wrong," *The National Interest*, fall 1997, pp. 42–52.

39. See Susan V. Lawrence, "Brave New World," *Far Eastern Economic Review*, June 17, 1999, p. 13.

40. Ibid.

41. Lorien Holland, "Selective Targeting," *Far Eastern Economic Review*, June 17, 1999, p. 14.

42. See Daniel Klaidman and Mark Hosenball, "The Chinese Puzzle," *Newsweek*, June 7, 1999, pp. 44–47, and Adam Cohen, "When Companies Leak," *Time*, June 7, 1999, p. 44.

43. See Vernon Loeb and Walter Pincus, "Planted Document Sows Seeds of Doubt; Spy Experts Wonder What China Hoped to Reap," *Washington Post*, May 28, 1999 (from www.lexis-nexis.com).

CHAPTER 6

1. See John F. Copper, *Taiwan's Mid-1990s Elections: Taking the Final Steps to Democracy* (Westport, CT: Praeger, 1998), chapter 4.

2. Actually Beijing's actions probably made a 5 percent difference in favor of Lee.

3. For details, see Christopher Hughes, *Taiwan and Chinese Nationalism: National Identity and Status in International Society* (London: Routledge, 1997), and Alan W. Wachman, *Taiwan: National Identity and Democratization* (Armonk, NY: M. E. Sharpe, 1994).

4. For details, see John F. Copper, *Taiwan: Nation-State or Province?* (Boulder, CO: Westview Press, 1999).

5. "We Must Defend Ourselves," *Newsweek*, May 20, 1996, pp. 38–39.

6. "Taiwan's President Challenges China on Eve of Inauguration," Cable News Network (posted on Web site on May 17, 1996, www.cnn.com).

7. See "Quarterly Chronicle and Documentation," *China Quarterly*, June 1996, p. 693.

8. "Policy on Taiwan Hard and Fast," *Beijing Review*, April 1–7, 1996, p. 4.

9. Garver, *About Face*, p. 153.

10. Ibid., p. 156.

11. Ibid.

12. "News Briefing by Chinese Foreign Ministry," *Beijing Review*, April 1–7, 1996, p. 9.

13. Garver, *About Face*, p. 156.

14. See Patrick Tyler, "Taiwan's Leader Wins Its Election and a Mandate," *New York Times*, March 24, 1996, Section 1, p. 1.

15. *Times-Picayune*, March 24, 1996 (found at www.lexis-nexis.com).

16. *St. Louis Post-Dispatch*, March 24, 1996 (found at www.lexis-nexis.com).

17. Lasater, *The Taiwan Conundrum*, p. 270.

18. Tyler, "Taiwan's Leader Wins."

19. *New York Times*, March 24, 1996, Section 1, p. 14.

20. *Wall Street Journal*, March 25, 27 and 29, 1996 (found at www.lexis-nexis.com).

21. Both stories were written by James Cox. See *USA Today*, March 25, 1996, p. 4A and 6A.

22. Keith B. Richburg, "China Fails to Sway Election in Taiwan' President Lee Wins Big Despite Threats," *Washington Post*, March 24, 1996, p. A1.

23. Nick Rufford, "Taiwan Defines Peking Fury as 'Traitor' Lee Wins Poll," *Sunday Times*, March 24, 1996 (found at www.lexis-nexis.com).

24. "China Must Talk to Lee," *Financial Times*, March 25, 1996 (found at www.lexis-nexis.com).

25. "Martial Make-Believe; The Chinese Need to Live with Reality," *Guardian*, March 25, 1996, p. 10 (found at www.lexis-nexis.com).

26. Choo Li Meng, "Impressive Voter Turnout of 76% in Historic Election," *Straits Times*, March 24, 1996, p. 13.

27. Christine Loh, "Taiwan Shows Mainland the Way," *South China Morning Post*, March 25, 1996, p. 20 (found at www.lexis-nexis.com).

CHAPTER 7

1. Orville Schell, "Communicating with China," in Paul H Tai (ed.), *United States, China and Taiwan: Bridges for a New Millennium* (Carbondale, IL: Southern Illinois University Press, 1999), p. 153.

2. Ni Feng, "Recent Developments in Sino-American Relations," *Beijing Review*, June 29–July 5, 1998, pp. 7–9.

3. Li Haibo, "Harmony Benefits Both Sides," *Beijing Review*, June 29–July 5, 1998, p. 4.

4. Ni Feng, "Recent Developments in Sino-American Relations," *Beijing Review*, June 29–July 5, 1998, p. 9.

5. Li Jinhui, "China and the U.S.: Seek a Real Strategic Partnership," *Beijing Review*, June 29–July 5, 1998, p. 11.

6. "China, US Vow Further Cooperation," *Beijing Review*, July 13–19, 1998, p. 4.

7. Ming Wan, "Human Rights and Democracy," in Deng and Wang, ed., *In the Eyes of the Dragon*, p. 108.

8. "Fruits of Clinton's Visit," *Beijing Review*, July 20–26, 1998, p. 15.

9. See Robert A. Manning, "A PRC-style Monroe Doctrine?" *China Post*, August 20, 1998, p. 2 (originally published in the *Los Angeles Times*).

10. Bruce W. Nelan, "Did the Summit Matter?" *Time*, July 13, 1998, p. 40.

11. Nancy Bernkopf Tucker, "Dangerous Liaisons: China, Taiwan, Hong Kong, and the United States at the Turn of the Century," in Tyrene White (ed.), *China Briefing 2000: The Continuing Transformation* (Armonk, NY: M. E. Sharpe, 2000), p. 244.

12. Jay Branegan, "China Photo-op Diplomacy," *Time*, July 6, 1998, p. 66.

13. Bruce W. Nelan, "Did the Summit Matter?" *Time*, July 13, 1998, p. 40

14. Ibid., p. 41.

15. See Jay Chen and Deborah Kuo, "Congressman Urges Clinton to Clarify Policy on Taiwan," *China Post,* July 6, 1998, p. 3.

16. See Stephanie Low, "Gov't: U.S. Should Not Discuss Taiwan with PRC," *China Post*, July 1, 1998, p. 1.

17. See for example, Bernard T. K. Joei, "U.S. Must Not Become a 'Troublemaker,'" *China Post* (international edition), July 3, 1998, p. 2.

18. See Jaw-ling Joanne Chang, "Lessons from the Taiwan Relations Act," *Orbis*, winter 2000, p. 68.

19. Jeffrey Parker, "Taiwan Has Changed, Not U.S. PRC Policy," *China Post*, July 6, 1998, p. 4.

20. Sofia Wu, "Nearly 40% Back an Independent Taiwan: DPP Poll," *China Post*, July 24, 1998, p. 3. The same poll reflected that only 1.1 percent of Taiwan's population favored quick reunification.

21. Stephanie Low, "Lee Thanks U.S. for Keeping Promise," *China Post*, July 3, 1998, p. 1.

CHAPTER 8

1. See John F. Copper, *China Diplomacy: The Washington-Taipei-Beijing Triangle* (Boulder, CO: Westview Press, 1992), pp. 44–45.

2. For details, see Patrick Tyler, "The (Ab)normalization of U.S.-Chinese Relations," *Foreign Affairs*, September/October 1999.

3. Nat Bellocchi, "U.S. Policy Toward a Changing Taiwan," in *The Legacy of the Taiwan Relations Act: A Compendium of Authoritative 20th Anniversary Assessments* (Taipei Government Information Office, 1999), p. 2.

4. For details, see June Teufel Dreyer, "China's Attitude toward the Taiwan Relations Act," in Fred Steiner and Chu-lien Yan (eds.), *The TRA at Twenty: The Legacy of the Taiwan Relations Act* (Taipei: Government Information Office, 1999), pp. 92–133.

5. Copper, *China Diplomacy*, pp. 75–78.

6. Ibid.

7. See Robert G. Sutter, *Chinese Foreign Policy Development after Mao* (New York: Praeger, 1986), p. 99.

8. See Copper, *China Diplomacy*, pp. 70–71, for further details.

9. Ibid., pp. 46–56.

10. See ibid., pp. 88–95, for details.

11. Ibid., p. 88.

12. Ibid., p. 90.

13. Actually, two human rights organizations were established at this time. One was concerned with human rights both in China and Taiwan; the other, launched by opposition politicians, focused mainly on Taiwan.

14. See annual editions of *The Republic of China: A Reference Book,* published by the Government Information Office in Taipei.

15. Officials in Taiwan made the statements to me.

16. Martin L. Lasater, *The Changing of the Guard: President Clinton and the Security of Taiwan* (Boulder, CO: Westview Press, 1995), pp. 139–41.

17. Ibid., pp. 142–43.

18. Ibid., pp. 145–49.

19. Ibid., pp. 149–52.

20. "Nations Condemn Chinese Missile Tests," CNN, March 8, 1996 (on the Internet at www.cnn.com).

21. "U.S. Navy Ships to Sail Near Taiwan," CNN, March 10, 1996 (on the Internet at www.cnn.com).

22. "Crisis in the Taiwan Strait: Implications for U.S. Foreign Policy," hearing before the Subcommittee on Asia and the Pacific, Committee on International Relations, House of Representatives held on March 14, 1996 (Washington, DC: U.S. Government Printing Office 1996), p. 6.

23. N. K. Han, "CNA on U.S. Official's Congressional Testimony on China," China News Agency, April 24, 1997 (from Foreign Broadcast Information Service on the Internet at www.lexis-nexis.com).

24. This working is found in House Resolution H2342 of March 19, 1996, and Senate Resolution S2622 of March 21, 1996. A joint resolution came from these two resolutions. For the complete text, see the Congressional Record or, on the Internet, www.policy.com (under Taiwan policy).

25. Ibid.

26. "Gingrich's Freedom to Disagree Eludes Ministry Spokesman," *The Nikkei Weekly*, April 14, 1997, p. 6.

27. Seth Faison, "Gingrich: U.S. Would Come to Aid of Taiwan," *Palm Beach Post*, March 31, 1997, p. lA.

28. Jim Abrams, "U.S.-Taiwan Security Act Criticized," Associated Press, October 26, 1999 (on the Internet at www.lexis-nexis.com).

29. "White House Opposes Bill Aimed to Boost Taiwan Security," Agence France-Presse, September 16, 1999 (on the Internet at www.lexis-nexis.com).

30. "China Opposes US Bill to Strengthen Military Ties with Taiwan," Agence France-Presse, October 28, 1999 (on the Internet at www.lexis-nexis.com).

CHAPTER 9

1. Paul Bracken, *Fire in the East: The Rise of Asian Military Power and the Second Nuclear Age* (New York: Harper Collins Publishers, 1999), p. 56.

2. Ibid., p. 47.

3. "Arms Deal Reportedly Approved," *Proliferation Issues*, March 22, 1993, p. 53.

4. "U.S. Reported to Back Taiwan Missile Project," *Washington Times*, March 3, 1993, p. A2.

5. "Source: Military Interested in Joining TMD," *China Times*, October 23, 1995, p. 1, cited in Foreign Broadcast Information Service, October 23, 1994.

6. "Taiwan: Military Defends Decision to Deploy Patriot Missiles," AFP (Hong Kong), May 30, 1996, cited in Foreign Broadcast Information Service, May 30, 1996.

7. Bear Lee, "Defense Minister Says TMD to Cost Taiwan $9.23 billion," Central News Agency, March 24, 1999, cited in Foreign Broadcast Information Service, March 24, 1999.

8. "Poll Supports Taiwanese Missile Defense," *Janes Defense Weekly*, March 24, 1999, p. 14.

9. "Taiwan Will Not Fire First in Any Clash with China: Defense Minister," Agence France-Presse, July 2, 2000.

10. Taifa Yu, "Taiwanese Democracy under Threat: Impact and Limit of Chinese Military Coercion," *Pacific Affairs*, Spring 1997, pp. 7–36.

11. Kwan Weng Kin, "China 'Massing Troops, Planes in Fujian,'" *Straits Times*, January 25, 1996, p. 23.

12. Bill Gertz, "Chinese Exercise Targets Taiwan, US Troops," *Washington Times*, January 26, 1999, p. 1.

13. Cited in Bill Gertz, *Betrayal: How the Clinton Administration Undermined American Security* (Washington, DC: Regnery Publishing, 1999), pp. 102–103.

14. Bill Gertz, "China Deploys New Missiles, Increasing Threat to Taiwan," *Washington Times* (weekly edition), November 29–December 5, 1999, p. 1.

15. Gao Junmin and Lu Dehong, "A Dangerous Move," *People's Liberation Army Daily*, January 24, 1999, p. 4, cited in Foreign Broadcast Information Service, January 24, 1999.

16. Chen Yali, "TMD Issue Detrimental to Sino-US Relations," *China Daily* (on the Internet at www.lexis-nexis.com), January 27, 1999.

17. Cited in *Defense News*, February 1, 1999, p. 22 (on the Internet at www.lexis-nexis.com).

18. See Milton Ezrati, *Kawari* (Reading, MA: Perseus Books, 1999), p. 237.

19. See Chester Dawson, "Blueprint for Controversy," *Far Eastern Economic Review*, July 13, 2000, pp. 19–20.

20. Ibid.

21. Ibid.

22. See Michael J. Green, "The Forgotten Player," *National Interest*, Summer 2000, p. 45.

23. See Lampton, *Same Bed Different Dreams*, p. 107. The difference was 64.3 percent for Japanese and 59.9 percent for Americans.

24. Ching Cheong, *Will Taiwan Break Away? The Rise of Taiwanese Nationalism* (Singapore: World Scientific, 2000), p. 251.

25. Ching, Will Taiwan Break Away?" p. 257.

26. According to a poll conducted in late 1998, 57 percent of Americans thought the development of China as a world power was a threat to the United States—higher than the threat of military power in the Soviet Union (34 percent), Islamic fundamentalism (38 percent), or global warming (45 percent). In March 2000, respondents said that Chinese nuclear weapons were a threat to the United States by a margin of 81 percent to 16 percent. See the Gallup Organization (at www.lexis-nexis.com).

27. David Albright and Corey Gay, "Nuclear Nightmare Averted," *Bulletin of Atomic Scientists*, January–February 1998, p. 57.

28. "Prospects for Further Proliferation of Nuclear Weapons," Memorandum from Director of Central Intelligence, September 4, 1974, cited in ibid.

29. Ibid., p. 59.

30. Ibid., p. 54.

31. David Tanks, "Theater Missile Defense in East Asia," in *Theater Missile Defense and U.S. Foreign Policy Interests in Asia* (Washington, DC: Woodrow Wilson Center, 2000), p. 12.

32. See Brian Hsu, "Lien Says Taiwan Needs New Long-Range Missile," *Taipei Times*, December 9, 1999 (on the Internet at www.taipeitimes.com).

CHAPTER 10

1. Edgar Snow, *Red Star Over China* (New York: Random House, 1938), pp. 88–89.

2. See Jane Rickards and Anne Meijdam, "Lee's Parting Shot," *Asiaweek*, July 23, 1999, p. 18–19. The authors say that the shift in policy had been contemplated for more than a year.

3. This argument was made by a number of high officials in Taipei after the fact. See especially Mainland Affairs Council Chairman Chi Su's statement on July 12. This and other statements were published in *Taipei Speaks Up: Special State-to-State Relationship* (Taipei: Mainland Affair Council, 1999).

4. Foreign Minister Jason Hu said that Beijing had offered South Africa US$850 million for this purpose. See Thomas J. Bellows, "Taiwan and Mainland China: Diplomatic Competition and Conflict," *The American Asian Review*, Winter 1999, p. 9.

5. Sheng, *China's Dilemma*, p .215.

6. Lampton, *Same Bed Different Dreams*, p. 65.

7. Ching, *Will Taiwan Break Away?*, p. 174.

8. Sheng, *China's Dilemma*, p. 216.

9. See Li Shin, "Communist China Criticizes and Curses the 'Special State-to-State Relationship," *Exchange*, October 1999, p. 31.

10. "Fiery Face-Off" (editorial), *Asiaweek*, July 30, 1999, p. 14.

11. "Taiwan, An Inseparable Part of China," *Beijing Review*, July 26, 1999, p. 7.

12. "Is it Possible That Li Denghui Can Realize His 'Taiwan Independence' Dream Through the 'Military Consolidation Plan,'" *Liberation Daily*, July 21, 1999 (from Foreign Broadcast Information Service—China, July 21, 1999).

13. Linda Griffin, "PRC Mulling War Games: HK Paper," *China Post*, July 14, 1999, p. 4.

14. See John Pomfret, "China on Taiwan, What Comes Next?" *Washington Post*, July 18, 1999.

15. Both are quoted in Julian Baum and Shawn W. Crispin, "Upping the Ante," *Far Eastern Economic Review*, July 22, 1999.

16. "Political Bureau Studies New Strategy Against Taiwan," *Cheng Ming* (Hong Kong), August 1, 1999, pp. 9–11 (from Foreign Broadcast Information Service—China, August 1, 1999).

17. See John Pomfret, "China, Taiwan Battle with Artful Threats," *Washington Post*, July 16, 1999.

18. Julian Baum, "Mind Games," *Far Eastern Economic Review*, August 12, 1999, p. 22.

19. Reported in *Kissing's Record of World Events*, August 1999.

20. See Stratfor Special Report entitled "Taiwan Seeks to Redefine Cross-Strait Tension by Drawing Chinese Fire," August 5, 1999 (on the Internet at www.lexis-nexis.com).

21. Reported in *Global Times* and cited in *Keesing's Record of World Events*, August 1999, p. 12104.

22. Jane Perlez, "China and U.S. Are Reported to Trade Threats on Taiwan," *New York Times*, August 13, 1999 (from the Internet at www.lexis-nexis.com).

23. See Michael Laris and Steven Mufson, "China Mulls Use of Force Off Taiwan, Experts Say," *Washington Post*, August 13, 1999 (from the Internet at www.lexis-nexis.com).

24. "One China Is an Indisputable Fact," *Beijing Review*, August 30, 1999, pp. 8–10.

25. "China Issues Stern Warning to Taiwan," Reuters, September 1, 1999 (from the Internet at www.lexis-nexis.com).

26. See David Lague, "Bellicose Perry Beats the Drums of War," *Sydney Morning Herald*, September 15, 1999 (from the Internet at www.lexis-nexis.com).

27. "PLA Landing Exercises Successful," *Beijing Review*, September 27, 1999, p. 5.

28. Cited in Todd Crowell, "A Tense Wait for Answers," *Asiaweek*, July 30, 1999, pp. 16–18.

29. "'All We Need Is Confidence,' Lee Tells Nation," *China Post*, July 15, 1999, p. 1.

30. Koo Chen-fu, "Establishing Peaceful and Stable Relations Across the Taiwan Straits," *Exchange*, August 1999, pp. 24–28.

31. "Newsmakers," *Asiaweek*, August 6, 1999, p. 10.

32. Ching, *Will Taiwan Break Away?* p. 144.

33. Christopher Bodeen, "Taiwan Blames China for Instability," Associated Press, August 21, 1999 (from the Internet at www.lexis-nexis.com).

34. "Taiwan Refuses to Rescind Statehood Claim Despite China Pressure," Agence France-Presse, September 15, 1999 (from the Internet at www.lexis-nexis.com).

35. Frank Chang, "Survey Respondents Stand behind ROC's Parity Principle," *Free China Journal*, September 10, 1999, p. 2.

36. Maniak Mehta, "Taiwan's View of Reality Raises Hackles in Beijing," *Free China Journal*, September 23, 1999, p. 7.

37. Lee Teng-hui, "Understand Taiwan: Bridging the Perception Gap," *Foreign Affairs*, November/December 1999, pp. 9–14.

38. Ching, *Will Taiwan Break Away?* p. 164.

39. Crowell, "A Tense Wait for Answers," *Asiaweek*, July 30, 1999, pp. 16–18.

40. Ibid., p. 17.

41. "U.S. Delegation to Visit Taiwan, Discuss 'Statehood' Claim," Agence France Presse, August 23, 1999 (from the Internet at www.lexis-nexis.com).

42. Cited in the *Washington Times*, July 30, 1999.

43. Julian Baum, "Mind Games," *Far Eastern Economic Review*, August 12, 1999, p. 22.

44. "Taiwanese President's Comment Inspires GOP to Renew Attack on Clinton's 'One China' Policy," *CQ Weekly*, July 24, 1999, p. 1813.

45. See Walt Barron, "Gilman: Reject Beijing's Idea of 'One China,'" *CQ Weekly*, September 11, 1999, p. 2127.

46. Agence France Presse, August 15, 1999 (from the Internet at www.lexis-nexis .com).

47. See, for example, David Shambaugh, "The Taiwan Tinderbox," *Time*, July 26, 1999.

48. "China's Nervous Rulers," *Washington Post*, July 21, 1999.

49. "Taiwan Threats," *Washington Post*, July 14, 1999, p. A22.

50. Jane Perlez, "U.S. Asking Taiwan to Explain Its Policy after Uproar," *New York Times*, July 13, 1999, p. A3.

51. Editorial, *New Republic*, August 16, 1999 (from the Internet at www.lexis-nexis.com).

52. "Hush, Hush Taiwan," *Christian Science Monitor*, September 9, 1999 (from the Internet at www.lexis-nexis.com).

53. See NewsBank Info Web, Los Angeles Times, July 13, 1999, and August 6, 1999 (on the Internet at www.newsbank.com).

54. Greg May, "Mending U.S.-Taiwan Relations after State-to-State," *Taiwan International Review*, November 1999, pp. 44–47.

CHAPTER 11

1. For details on the 2000 election, see John F. Copper, *Taiwan's 2000 Presidential and Vice Presidential Election: Consolidating Democracy and Creating a New Era of Politics* (Baltimore: University of Maryland School of Law, 2000).

2. Ibid., p. 43.

3. For background on the candidates, see John F. Copper, *Historical Dictionary of Taiwan (Republic of China)* (Lanham, MD: Scarecrow Press, 2000).

4. Soong was born on the mainland but went to Taiwan when he was seven. Clearly he called Taiwan home.

5. In Taiwan, one's "ethnic" categorization comes from one's father. It also comes from the language (or dialect) one speaks. Lien speaks Taiwanese.

6. Hsu Hsin-liang, a former DPP leader, ran as independent. Li Ao, one of Taiwan's foremost intellectual critics, ran as the candidate of the New Party though he did not have, or accept at this time, party membership.

7. "Killer Quakes Claims over 1,700," *China Post* (international edition), September 22, 1999, p. 1.

8. Desmond Cheung, "Cross-Straits Tremors," *Topics*, November 1999, pp. 47–48.

9. Neither Lee nor Soong has stated clearly why they became enemies. Many said it had to do with Lee's mainland policy. Others said it was a conflict between two strong personalities. One author said they had a serious disagreement when Soong suggested that Taiwan join with the People's Republic of China against Japan during a dispute over the Diaoyutai Islands (Senkaku Islands in Japanese). See Ching, *Will Taiwan Break Away?*, p. 63.

10. It was true that Lee and others had observed that Chiang Ching-kuo was very honest and didn't leave much to support his family when he died. Lee Teng-hui stated that the money in question was not so allocated. The suit against Soong was dropped months later, signaling that the case was not valid, though some also said that this was done in the spirit of reconciling with Soong after the KMT lost the election.

11. For an account of the above statements, see George Gedda, "Chinese Stand on Taiwan Worries U.S.," Associated Press, February 20, 2000, and Steven Mufson and Helen Dewar, "Pentagon Issues Warning to China," *Washington Post*, February 23, 2000 (on the Internet at www.lexis-nexis.com).

12. Ching, *Will Taiwan Break Away?* p. 73.

13. Ibid.

14. Ibid.

15. Ibid., p. 68.

16. Lee Teng-hui, in a book published in the spring of 2001, stated that Lien had been the one who attacked Soong.

17. See Sheng, *China's Dilemma*, p. 92 for details.

18. For details, see Larry M. Wortzel and Stephen J. Yates, "What the Election in Taiwan Should Mean to Washington and Beijing," *Executive Memorandum* (The Heritage Foundation), March 31, 2000, p. 2.

19. "Taiwan Stands Up," *Economist*, March 25, 2000, p. 24.

20. "House Votes to Applaud Taiwan on Elections," *China Post* (international edition), March 30, 2000, p. 1.

21. For details on the above press comments, see Copper, *Taiwan's 2000 Presidential and Vice Presidential Election*, pp. 49–50.

22. See Nayan Chanda and Susan V. Lawrence, "Final Deadline," *Far Eastern Economic Review*, May 18, 2000, p. 16.

23. See Ching, *Will Taiwan Break Away?* p. 32.

24. See Bruce Gilley and Julian Baum, "Crude Tactics," *Far Eastern Economic Review*, June 29, 2001, p. 25.

CHAPTER 12

1. For details on the election, see John F. Copper, *Taiwan's 2004 Presidential and Vice Presidential Election: Democracy's Consolidation or Devolution?* (Baltimore: University of Maryland School of Law, 2004).

2. For details, see John F. Copper, "Taiwan in Gridlock: Thoughts on the Chen Shui-bian Administration's First Eighteen Months," in John F. Copper (ed.), *Taiwan in Troubled Times: Essays on the Chen Shui-bian Presidency* (Singapore: World Scientific, 2002), pp. 19–51.

3. For details, see John F. Copper, *Taiwan's 2001 Legislative, Magistrates and Mayors Election* (Singapore: World Scientific/Singapore University Press, 2002).

4. Copper, *Taiwan's 2004 Presidential and Vice Presidential Election*, pp. 50–54.

5. I was at the Government Information Office in Taipei with a dozen foreign reporters when the news was announced. All remarked something to this effect.

6. "Taiwan's President Chen Shui-bian," *Washington Post*, March 29, 2004 (online at www.washingtonpost.com).

7. "PRC Begins Week-Long War Games," Reuters, July 17, 2004 (online at taiwans ecurity.org/Reu/2004/Reuters-170704.htm). The deadline for Taiwan's recovery was put at 2020.

8. Ibid.

9. George Friedman and Bill Adams, "The China Crisis," *The Geopolitical Intelligence Report*, July 20, 2004 (on the Internet at www.blackwaterusa.com).

10. Ibid.

11. Ibid.

12. John Glionna, "China, U.S. Each Hold Major War Exercises," *Los Angeles Times*, July 20, 2004 (online at taiwansecurity.org/News/2004/LAT-200704.htm).

13. Ibid.

14. Cited in Ibid.

15. Lawrence Chung, "U.S. 'May Be Using Spy Scandal as a Warning'; Washington Could Be Playing Up Incident as a Way of Telling Taiwan's Chen to Go Easy on Separatist Remarks, Say Analysts," *Straits Times*, September 23, 2004 (on the Internet at lexis-nexis.com).

16. "Taiwan Could Fend Off China Attack for 2 Weeks-Paper," Reuters, August 12, 2004 (on the Internet at taiwansecurity.org).

17. Ko Shu-ling, "Taiwan Premier Heralds 'Balance of Terror,'" *Taipei Times*, September 26, 2004 (on the Internet at www.taipeitimes.com).

18. See "The Dragon Next Door," *Economist*, January 15, 2005, p. 7.

19. "Taiwan President Diverts over Chinese Jets," Associated Press, November 10, 2004 (on the Internet at taiwansecurity.org/AP/2004/AP-101104.htm).

20. "Taiwan Offers Intelligence about Chinese Sub Intrusion into Japan," Central News Agency, November 19, 2004 (on the Internet at lexis-nexis.com).

21. "China Military Buildup Threatens U.S. Forces: CIA chief," Agence France-Presse, February 17, 2005 (on the Internet at lexis-nexis.com).

22. "83% of People Oppose Anti-Secession Law," *China Post*, December 25, 2004 (on the Internet at www.chinapost.com).

23. "Taiwan Ruling Party Leaders Attach China's 'War Mandating' Law," BBC, March 8, 2005 (on the Internet at www.lexis-nexis.com).

24. Ross Peake, "US could invoke ANZUS over Taiwan," *Canberra Times*, March 15, 2005 (on the Internet at www.lexis-nexis.com).

25. Mark Magnier, "Anti-China Protestors Inundate Taipei," *Los Angeles Times*, March 27, 2005 (on the Internet at www.lexis-nexis.com).

26. Rich Chang, "Missile Test Successful, Report Said," *Taipei Times*, June 6, 2005 (online at taiptimes.com).

27. "Beijing Tests New Missile," *Straits Times*, June 27, 2005, p. 9.

28. See Wang Zheng, "US Congress Calls for Sacking of Chinese General, *Epoch Times*, July 25, 2005 (at www.theepochtimes.com/news/5-7-05/30545.html).

29. "Pentagon Report Singles Out China as Potential Military Rival," AFP, Feb. 4, 2006.

CHAPTER 13

1. Witness business lobbying for WTO, for example.

2. For details, see John T. Dori and Richard D. Fisher Jr., *U.S. and Asia Statistical Handbook, 1998–1999* (Washington, DC: The Heritage Foundation, 1998), pp. 8–9.

3. See Nicholas R. Lardy, *China in the World Economy* (Washington, DC: Institute for International Economics, 1994), p. 34; "Chronicle and Documentation," *China Quarterly*, September 1999, p. 792.

4. See "Taiwan Brief," *Topics*, March 2000, p. 8, for details.

5. See Suisheng Zhao, "Economic Interdependence and Political Divergence: A Background Analysis of the Taiwan Strait Crisis," in Suisheng Zhao (ed.), *Across the Taiwan Strait: Mainland China, Taiwan and the 1995–1996 Crisis* (London: Routledge, 1999), p. 24.

6. See Thomas L. Friedman, "This is a Test," *New York Times*, March 21, 2000, p. A23.

7. See Henry S. Rowen, "The Short Road to Democracy," in Owen Harries (ed.), *China in the National Interest* (New Brunswick: Transaction Publishers, 2003), pp. 127–37.

8. Internet usage doubled in China in 2003 and 2004.

9. One might note, however, that China has stationed troops in areas in the South China Sea that are disputed territory. It is also said to have a base in Myanmar.

10. This has been noted in virtually all of the anti-American, nationalistic publications coming out of China in the last decade. Deng himself said this frequently.

11. Ted C. Fishman, *China, Inc.: How the Rise of the Next Superpower Challenges America and the World* (New York: Scribner, 2005), p. 13.

12. From 2000 to 2003, the number of manufacturing jobs lost in the U.S. exceeded the total jobs lost. During that time long-term unemployment for those losing manufacturing jobs increased 260 percent. Erskine Bowles, running for Congress from North Carolina, China's illegal exports to the U.S. accounted for the closing of three hundred textile plants. See Fishman, *China, Inc.*, pp. 178–179.

13. This view can be found stated very strongly in a book entitled *Crossed Swords* (*Jiaofeng*) published in China a few years ago. See Joseph Fewsmith, "Historical Echoes and Chinese Politics: Can China Leave the Twentieth Century Behind?" in Tyrene White (ed.), *China Briefing 2000: The Continuing Transformation* (Armonk, NY: M. E. Sharpe, 2000), p. 35.

14. Chinese leaders stated this repeatedly after the Tiananmen Square massacre. It was heard frequently in following months.

15. See Peter Hays Gries, "A 'China Threat'? Power and Passion in Chinese 'Face Nationalism,'" *World Affairs*, Fall 1999, pp. 63–75.

16. See James C. Hsiung, "Shadow Boxing or Real Movement? Cross-Strait Relations in 1998," in Chong Chou Lau and Geng Xiao, *China Review* (Hong Kong: Hong Kong University Press, 1999), pp. 95–96. In later pages the author applies the argument to Taiwan.

17. See James Lilley and Carl Ford, "China's Military: A Second Opinion," in Harries (ed.), *China in the National Interest*, pp. 266–274.

18. See Steven W. Mosher, *Hegemon: China's Plan to Dominate Asia and the World* (San Francisco: Encounter Books, 2000).

19. John Derbyshire, "Why We Ought to Fear China and Its Plan of Dominance," *Washington Times* (weekly), August 28–September 3, 2000, p. 28.

20. See Walter Russell Mead, "The Jacksonian Tradition and American Foreign Policy," *The National Interest*, Winter 1999/2000, p. 5.

21. James M. Lindsay, "The New Apathy: How an Uninterested Public Is Reshaping Foreign Policy," *Foreign Affairs*, September/October 2000, pp. 2–8.

22. See Sebastian Mallaby, "The Bullied Pulpit: A Weak Chief Executive Makes Worse Foreign Policy," *Foreign Affairs*, January/February 2000, pp. 2–8.

23. See Ted Galen Carpenter, "Confusion and Stereotypes: U.S. Policy toward the PRC at the Dawn of the 21st Century," in Ted Galen Carpenter and James A. Dorn (eds.), *China's Future: Constructive Partner or Emerging Threat* (Washington, DC: The Cato Institute, 2000), p. 63.

24. See Joseph Fewsmith, *Dilemmas of Reform in China: Political Conflict and Economic Debate* (Armonk, NY: M. E. Sharpe, 1994) for background.

25. See Lampton, *Same Bed Different Dreams*, p. 288.

26. Some scholars say Hu is the leader of a populist faction that is in contention with an "elite faction." Thus he has to play to nationalist sentiment. See Cheng Li, "The New Bipartisanship within the Chinese Communist Party," *Orbis*, Summer 2005, pp. 387–400.

27. Some say that because Chinese leaders needed an outlet for the nationalist fervor they promoted anti-Japanese demonstrations and policies; others say, under pressure from the left and the military, they simply couldn't care that they likely created an enemy. See Richard Lowry, "Time for the Sun to Rise," *National Review*, July 4, 2005, pp. 29–31.

28. See Li Cheng, "China in 1999: Seeking Common Ground at a Time of Tension and Conflict," *Asian Survey*, January 2000, p. 121.

29. Ibid., p. 123. Author cites Information Center for Chinese Democracy and Human Rights in Hong Kong. Also see "Rural Alert," *Asiaweek*, September 22, 2000, p. 22.

30. Joseph Kahn, "Pace and Scope of Protest in China Accelerated in '05," *New York Times*, January 20, 2006.

31. Fishman, *China, Inc.*, p. 7, suggests China's uncounted workforce ranges from ninety to three hundred million.

32. For an excellent assessment of the Neocons in power, see James Mann, *Rise of the Vulcans: A History of Bush's War Cabinet* (New York: Penguin, 2004).

33. For details, see Harish Kapur (ed.), *As China Sees the World* (New York: St. Martin's Press, 1987).

34. See Suisheng Zhao, "Beijing's Perception of the International System and Foreign Policy Adjustment after the Tiananmen Incident," in Suisheng Zhao (ed.), *Chinese Foreign Policy: Pragmatism and Strategic Behavior* (Armonk, NY: M. E. Sharpe, 2004), pp. 141–42.

35. In 1993, Undersecretary of State for Political Affairs Peter Tarnoff, made a speech declaring that the United States did not have the resources or the will to be the leader of the international community. Many observers saw this as the launching a U.S. isolationist policy. Tarnoff said specifically: "We don't have the leverage, we don't have the influence, we don't have the inclination to use force."

36. See Samuel P. Huntington, "The Clash of Civilizations," *Foreign Affairs*, Summer 1993. This article became one of the most widely ever read among the foreign policy elite and had a considerable impact on decision makers as well.

37. See Lester Thurow, *Head to Head: The Coming Economic Battle Among Japan, Europe, and America* (New York: William Morrow and Company, 1992).

38. Peter Hays Gries, "China Eyes the Hegemon," *Orbis*, Summer 2005, pp. 404–5.

39. See Russell Ong, *China's Security Interests in the Post-Cold War Era* (London: Curzon Press, 2002), chapter 8 and especially p. 159.

Index

ABOUT THE AUTHOR

JOHN F. COPPER is Professor of International Studies at Rhodes College in Memphis, Tennessee. He is the author of more than twenty books and has testified before the Senate Foreign Relations and House Foreign Affairs Committees.